THE WINE IS BITTER

THE UNITED STATES AND LATIN AMERICA

Milton S. Eisenhower

THE WINE IS BITTER

THE UNITED STATES AND LATIN AMERICA

DOUBLEDAY AND COMPANY, INC., GARDEN CITY, NEW YORK, 1963

LIBRARY OF CONGRESS CATALOG CARD NUMBER 63–12959
COPYRIGHT © 1963 BY THE JOHNS HOPKINS UNIVERSITY
ALL RIGHTS RESERVED
PRINTED IN THE UNITED STATES OF AMERICA

TO L. R. EAKIN

Whose daughter, my wife, so loved Latin Americans that she earned affectionate abrazos.

Contents

Preface

There is absolutely no doubt in my mind that revolution is inevitable in Latin America. The people are angry. They are shackled to the past with bonds of ignorance, injustice, and poverty. And they no longer accept as universal or inevitable the oppressive prevailing order which has filled their lives with toil, want, and pain. The terrible realization has dawned upon them that the futility of their lives and of their parents' lives need not have been, that it is the bitter fruit of an evil system of injustice. And so they are filled with a fury and a determination to change the future.

How will they change it? The enlightened among them—the good leaders, most intellectuals—call for a peaceful revolution, a series of sweeping reforms to topple the oligarchists, the corrupt, the dictators. But there are loud and insistent voices demanding violent revolution. The Communists and their fellow travelers feed the fury of the underprivileged with half-truths and false promises. They nourish a lust for revenge and a cynical conviction that only blood will wash away injustice.

The choice between these two courses is awesome. Cuba has succumbed to the lust for blood and violence. The remainder of the hemisphere teeters precariously on the verge of revolution—peaceful or violent.

For eight years I traveled and studied in seventeen of the twenty Latin-American countries. When I began, the voice of revolution was muted; the pleas of the privileged and the underprivileged alike were for massive economic assistance similar to that which we had extended to Europe under the Marshall Plan. Then suddenly the mood changed and the quiet rumble of discontent became a strident drumbeat. Decades of sullen frustration suddenly crystallized into a wedge of anger which split Latin America asunder.

Architects of our Latin American foreign policy were jolted into a perplexing dilemma. They quickly realized that orthodox methods of helping our southern neighbors achieve a better life were not sufficient—indeed, orthodoxy seemed to be abetting the growing anger and discontent. They recognized that swift social change had to be part of economic growth. But the problem was to stimulate social change without violating the sacred hemispheric policy of nonintervention in the internal affairs of other nations.

Out of many months of tortuous conferences, intramural and extramural, came the concept of collective intervention. Legal authority for this was embodied in Public Law 86-735, enacted by our Congress early in September 1960; in the Act of Bogotá, promulgated by representatives of twenty American republics a few days later, and in the Charter of Punta del Este, formulated in August 1961. The Alliance for Progress, involving all the nations of the hemisphere except Cuba, was launched.

This was the answer to the Communist demand for violent revolution. But it was not a negative response of the peoples of the United States and Latin America to the threat of Castro Communism. In fact, it was conceived before Castro seized power in Cuba and was well advanced while he was still a hero in the months following his triumphant march into Havana on January 1, 1959. Faced with the breakdown of orthodox methods, the enlightened leaders of the hemisphere had forged the concept of the Alliance for Progress as a positive effort to solve one of the oldest problems of mankind—justice and well-being for all.

Optimistically, one may assert that the Act of Bogotá, the Charter of Punta del Este, and the Alliance for Progress constitute a modern Magna Carta of the Americas: land for the landless, tax systems that are fair and honestly administered, self-help projects to provide low-cost housing and better health facilities, concerted attacks on illiteracy, determined efforts to reduce economic instability that has long plagued the Latin-American countries, and democratic institutions that protect freedom and the human spirit.

Pessimistically, many contend that this noble effort is doomed to failure because it is too late and because the oligarchists and Communists alike will not permit it to succeed, albeit for different reasons.

The United States has a crucial role in this drama. Our aid can be decisive in helping Latin Americans build better institutions, increase income, and purge injustice from their society. We must be swift and generous.

No one could spend a great deal of time with Latin Americans—political leaders, intellectuals, laborers, farmers, Indians, mestizos, whites, rich, poor, and dispossessed—as I have done without developing a genuine and abiding affection for them. They are the most engaging persons I have met in a lifetime of travel to most parts of the world. They are not, as too many believe, concerned mainly with the siesta and the serenade. They are a hard-working people who cherish individualism and human dignity. I state my feeling of friendship at the outset, for in this book I am critical of many of the policies, practices, and attitudes prevalent in the hemisphere, and I am anxious that this candor should not obscure my true feelings for the people and their capabilities.

Knowing Latin Americans as I do, I believe that they will choose peaceful revolution, and that they will, in most of the republics, win the future without civil wars. I do not say this glibly, for I realize that the slightest spark could touch off flaming conflicts in a dozen different places in the hemisphere. I am aware of the harsh resistance that any effort for change will meet. I know the awesome dimensions of the problem that confronts the moderate Latin-American leader and the perils which he must negotiate to survive and triumph. But these things notwithstanding, I have a faith in the peoples of Latin America and their cause. They have demonstrated a monumental patience in the face of abuse, and now that they are so close to a just and peaceful future, I think and pray that they will work for it rather than kill for it.

A small portion of the material in this book has been published previously in *Life* and other magazines, in official government reports, and in numerous pamphlets and addresses. For permission to use such of this material as is copyrighted, I am grateful, but it is so widely diffused herein that I cannot give credit in each instance. I am indebted to hundreds of governmental, educational, industrial, labor, and agricultural leaders in this country and throughout Latin America, including most of the presidents and cabinet members of the Latin republics, for the information and friendly help they have so generously given me. To mention them would be to risk omissions; this might not be an offense to them, but it would be to me.

In the actual writing of this book I am deeply obliged to Ron Wolk, editor of the *Johns Hopkins Magazine*, for his editorial assistance; to Ambassador John C. Drier (formerly our Ambassador to the Organization of American States and now Director of the Latin-American program of the Johns Hopkins School of Advanced International Studies), for reading the manuscript and making substantive suggestions; and to Freeman Wright who, as a doctoral candidate in political science at Johns Hopkins, found time to help me with research.

MILTON S. EISENHOWER

THE WINE IS BITTER

THE UNITED STATES AND LATIN AMERICA

Book I

1 The long shadow of the past must not be allowed to darken forever the future. The American nations are beginning a grand alliance for progress. Success is not certain, but it is imperative.

THE FINANCE MINISTER AND I HAD BEEN CHATTING AMI-cably for several hours in his air-cooled office one humid afternoon in the summer of 1958. The sumptuous furnishings were in vivid contrast to the poverty which marked his country.

"It is imperative," he was saying, "that the United States lend us a great deal of money at low interest rates. We must have it at once to begin building the schools, houses, and hospitals we so desperately need."

I knew how much his people needed these things, but I had heard and responded to almost identical statements from other high officials in Latin America, and I was vaguely irritated. "You know as well as I do that foreign capital for social improvement projects is almost impossible to get," I replied. "International and United States lending institutions prefer to grant credit for projects which will increase production and thus provide the income that makes possible many types of development, including social institutions."

"Of course, I know that," he answered, "and I also know that my people need schools and hospitals and decent low-cost housing."

An idea had been nagging at me and I decided to test it: "I'll tell you what," I said, "you establish a national corporation similar to our Federal Housing Authority and provide the capital for labor and other local costs, and I shall do my best to persuade private or public lending agencies in the United States to supply the dollar capital for the purchase of materials to be imported for the project."

He was genuinely astounded as I suspected he would be.

"You must know, Milton," he protested, "that we have no local savings. We are having a difficult time getting enough tax revenue to meet normal operating costs. If these social improvements are to be made, they must be completely financed by foreign capital."

I chuckled and shook my head. The finance minister and I were friends of long standing, and we could speak with candor. As a graduate of two distinguished American universities, he understood our proclivity for forthrightness as well as our language. So I said: "It happens, my friend, that your personal income is about four times greater than mine. Yet I pay in taxes to my government twenty times as much as you pay to yours." I raised my hand to ward off his protest. "If your govenment will institute a level of taxation comparable to ours, you will get at least some of the local capital you need. You have some very wealthy families who are investing their money in the United States and Europe, and these surplus funds are essential to your own development. And if you do this, I can tell you that the people of the United States would be much more eager to help you than they are now. After all, my government must raise public funds to help you by taxing the American people—and you won't even tax yourselves to a comparable point of sacrifice."

He had settled back as I talked, and his smile was a blend of comprehension, tolerance, and sadness.

"My dear Milton," he said softly, "if we tried to collect the income, sales, capital gains, and other taxes that you have in the United States, we would have a revolution. And this time, the revolution would be led by the very people on whom the maintenance of freedom and democracy in this country depends."

This small part of one conversation summarizes in an amazingly revealing way much that I had come to understand about Latin America and United States-Latin American relations. Stripped of all qualifications, the key fact is this: Social and economic progress in Latin America is dependent upon a change in the attitude expressed by the finance minister that afternoon and upon ensuing far-reaching social reforms. This will determine whether our efforts to help Latin America in the coming decade contribute to rising levels of well-being for all people in the nations south of the Rio Grande, or instead bolster prevailing inequities and injustices; whether they improve hemispheric cooperation within a framework of freedom and human liberty, or intensify anti-Americanism and foster Castro Communism.

It took me several years to face this cardinal fact realistically.

My special interest in hemispheric relations began in 1946 when, as vice-chairman of the United States delegation to an international UNESCO conference, I spent six weeks in Mexico. Brief excursions to historic spots close to Mexico City, sandwiched between arduous conference sessions, whetted my appetite to know more about the Mexican people, their history, customs, and attitudes. Friendly members of the Mexican delegation learned of my interest and doors were miraculously opened to me. I visited with President Miguel Alemán Valdés, with educational, labor, and business leaders, with bellboys, and with taxi drivers. I became fascinated with the cultural diversity of the country and grew fond of the people—though I was dismayed by the ultra-nationalism and anti-Americanism I encountered among some.

When I returned home, I sought to gain a deeper understanding of Mexico and, later, of Latin America as a whole. I wanted to satisfy myself about a good many things: Why were illiteracy, poverty, and ill health so prevalent in the Latin republics? Why were we charged with dollar imperialism and with holding Latin American nations in a colonial status? Had we not tried to be helpful with private and public loans and with technical assistance? In view of the fact that we voluntarily gave up imperialistic pursuits in Central America and in the Caribbean—an unparalleled act—why did the suspicion persist that we would, if it suited our convenience, violate the sovereignty of our southern neighbors? Were the nations of the hemisphere truly vital to one another and, if so, could we do more to strengthen relationships? Had not President Franklin Roosevelt found the full answer to this problem when he proclaimed the Good Neighbor policy?

I discovered that our literature on Latin America was at that time remarkably inadequate. Today, a plethora of books, pamphlets, and articles pour from the presses of our country, but in 1946 I had considerable difficulty in locating relevant material. There was, of course, the sterile textbook ("Latin America is an area of spectacular geographic contrasts"), the properly factual encyclopedia ("The term 'Latin America' is not entirely adequate in its implication of the nature of this complex area"), the helpful, sunny guidebook ("Among North Americans, the best-known Latin-American nation is Mexico, a favorite tourist attraction and a compatible neighbor for many years"). But there was very little about the postwar situation. I wanted to know how Latin America had fared during the war, what peace would do to its trade, to what degree it had industrialized, the living conditions of the people, its political problems, the trends which were shaping its future. I was curious about the monolithic "Party of the

Institutionalized Revolution" which had gained power in Mexico, about Guatemala's Juan José Arévalo and his unusual support by middle and upper lower classes, about the nineteenth-century-style dictator, Tiburcio Carías Andino, who ruled Honduras, about the threatened failure of democracy in Costa Rica, about what was said to be a model democratic regime in Uruguay.

With effort, I gradually learned enough to convince me that inter-American relations were marred by pervasive, serious, and persistent misunderstandings. Many of the enduring misconceptions had to do with the very problems which seemingly required solving. Obviously a firm partnership among the American nations, as envisaged by the Good Neighbor policy, could not be constructed on sands of prejudice and suspicion— the inevitable and bitter results of ignorance and misunderstanding.

I began concentrating not on the conditions within a single country (save as these might shed light on larger problems) but on those hemispheric facts and circumstances which might have the greatest relevance to foreign policy. I hold no brief for this approach, but I had to start somewhere, and I confess that this assignment for myself has been so time-consuming over the years that I have never substantially deviated from it. I am conscious of the fact that a great many scholars, diplomats, and businessmen know much more about Brazil or Chile or Ecuador than I do. Indeed, other than Mexico (to which I have traveled many times, occasionally for extended periods), I have never found it possible to linger long in a given country. In these travels, and in reading and learning from others, I have tried to distill out the cogent historic, economic, social, cultural, and psychological facts which might help me judge the validity of our evolving policy toward Latin America.

This general and personal concern, leisurely pursued and designed solely to satisfy my own curiosity, was suddenly transformed into a high degree of official responsibility.

When Dwight David Eisenhower was elected to the presidency, he earnestly hoped to visit all American republics in the early months of his Administration. He was convinced that a dependable hemispheric partnership was essential to our future in freedom. Unfortunately, however, crises in general East-West relations and constant specific threats to nations on the periphery of the Soviet hegemony prevented such visits. So the President asked me if I would undertake for him and Secretary Dulles a series of study-good-will trips that would provide, hopefully, a fresh perspective

—a basis for a sweeping review of prevailing policies and programs. Of course I assented.

A few days later, on April 12, 1953, speaking in the stately Pan American Union building in Washington, D.C. to high officials of the twenty Latin-American republics, the President announced that he would send me as his Personal Representative and Special Ambassador on a fact-finding trip to seek ways to strengthen relations between the United States and their countries. At this point in his address, to his astonishment and mine, conference members spontaneously rose to their feet and gave him an ovation.

I was listening by radio; as the applause mounted, phrases I had read flashed through my mind: "Yankee, go home," "Dollar imperialism," "Dictator lovers." Why then should this modest gesture by the President of the United States, in sending his brother as his representative to their countries, evoke such a heartening response?

On a moment's reflection I felt I knew the answer. Frustrations, sometimes bitter disappointments that may lead to harsh words, are bound to occur in any family, including a family of nations. But in a family, the first flush of anger passes and differences are resolved by a sympathetic desire to understand each family member's viewpoint—a desire based on a deep feeling for family ties and welfare. Surely there are similar feelings between the nations of Latin America and the United States, and in the normal course of events we might well expect our difficulties to be ironed out in an atmosphere of understanding and concern for one another's well-being.

But today, the abnormal has become the normal; in moments of stress between our nations, before reason and understanding have had a chance to resolve critical issues, propagandists move swiftly to magnify misunderstandings. With insidious skill they ascribe sinister motives to the United States; they persuade Latin Americans that we will sacrifice their welfare to our own; they convince even the best informed (as a young intellectual demonstrated to me in Costa Rica one day) that "the United States depresses the economies of Latin America to enrich itself." In an atmosphere of suspicion, doubt, and fear, the big lie flourishes like an evil weed and stifles understanding. And the development of understanding, among individuals or groups or nations, takes time—a frustratingly long time. In this age of explosive change and impatient demands, action is often insisted upon and sometimes taken before mutual understanding has been achieved.

This impediment to partnership, caused by serious (though sometimes ludicrous) misunderstandings was, I'm sure, in the minds of Latin-

American officials that afternoon as President Eisenhower spoke to them. So their spontaneous response indicated approval of a new effort to overcome the intellectual barrier to better relations. It was also an expression of friendly family interest in a new United States leader who was well known to them (even though his specific views on Latin America were not) and who, in one of his first public addresses, was demonstrating his devotion to hemispheric solidarity.

Thus I began eight years of special governmental assignments which would reach their climax in several radical changes in United States policy —the final and most far-reaching one only five months before President Eisenhower left office. This crucial policy change laid both the national and inter-American foundations for President Kennedy's Alliance for Progress proposal and its quick acceptance by most Latin-American republics at Punta del Este, Uruguay, in August 1961.

I plunged into intensive briefing sessions, despite the inconvenience of frequent travel from my university, Penn State, which is located, a sage former president once explained, in the exact geographic center of the state, equally inaccessible to all parts.

I became impressed with the knowledge, viewpoints, and wisdom of such men as John Foster Dulles; John Moors Cabot, Assistant Secretary of State for Inter-American Affairs; Thomas C. Mann, later to be Assistant Secretary of State for Economic Affairs; Samuel W. Anderson, Assistant Secretary of Commerce for International Affairs; Andrew N. Overby, Assistant Secretary of the Treasury; Samuel C. Waugh, later President and Chairman of the Board of the Export-Import Bank; Eugene R. Black, President of the International Bank for Rehabilitation and Development, and, several years later, R. R. Rubottom, Jr., Assistant Secretary of State for Inter-American Affairs at the time the foundation for the Alliance for Progress was constructed. The notion that most of our foreign affairs are handled by inept individuals of the ugly American legend is a shocking misconception; it has become a shibboleth used by the uninformed to express contempt for what they do not understand.

It is only human, I think, for individuals to cling too long to traditional attitudes and beliefs, and government officials, being human, sometimes attempt to fit yesterday's policies to today's problems. They are perhaps more noticeable in their weakness than most of us, because they perform in the unmerciful spotlight of public scrutiny. But there are few men who can boast that their original attitudes and convictions have kept pace with the swiftly evolving world around them—even a liberal member of the Supreme Court is likely to be a conservative before he retires.

Official positions, nevertheless, are not taken fortuitously or lightly; usually each policy view is historically based and finely reasoned. But if a policy is to remain valid in the face of bewilderingly rapid social change, it must be frequently, even continuously, reviewed. And if necessary it must be altered to meet new conditions and circumstances. The principal virtue, therefore, in having me, an educator with no permanent governmental responsibility, serve as Personal Representative of the President of the United States in taking a new look at our relations with Latin America was that my activities would require the help of federal officials responsible for Latin-American affairs and would thus cause them to seek new perspectives, too.

Being the brother of the President had considerable advantage so far as my work abroad was concerned, for Latin Americans have deep feelings of family loyalty and pride. At all times they extended to me the same courtesies they would have to the President, had he been among them. But in Washington, D.C. my unique status had its disadvantages. I'm sure that some officials, possibly doubting my qualifications for the job, feared that I would use this family relationship to bypass them and to get my ideas and recommendations to the President. But I was quite conscious of the difficulties I could cause by going directly to the Chief Executive with new-found wisdom. I recalled how cabinet tempers had flared when President Franklin Roosevelt's Personal Representative Harry Hopkins constantly advised him on important issues without clearing through appropriate agency heads.

I therefore adopted a practice in July 1953, with my first fact-finding mission to the ten republics of South America, and adhered to it in all my subsequent studies. I took with me the Assistant Secretaries of State, Treasury, and Commerce whose official duties encompassed the Latin-American area. Occasionally the President of the Export-Import Bank joined our group. An aide of the Assistant Secretary of State for Inter-American Affairs, W. Tapley Bennett, Jr.,—an engaging, sensitive, tireless worker—became my personal assistant. In each host country, the United States ambassador attended all meetings and participated in all discussions. Thus, in addition to automatically achieving a fresh view of existing policies and programs by responsible federal officials, this practice also provided reasonable assurance that an interloper would not bypass the President's regular advisers upon completion of each set of studies. I made it clear that after each trip all members of the mission would be consulted as I prepared reports for the Secretary of State and the President. Indeed, a report was not submitted until it had been formally approved by all relevant members of the Cabinet.

On the whole I am glad that I followed this practice; but because I adhered to it so slavishly and would not make an exception, I missed an opportunity to spare the United States some serious difficulties—as I shall explain in another chapter.

Several years after the first studies in the ten republics of South America were completed and our official report and recommendations had been approved as United States policy, President Eisenhower joined the chiefs of state of the other American republics in a meeting in Panama, commemorating the first inter-American conference (convened by Simón Bolívar). He was recovering from an ileitis operation, so I was present to substitute in sessions which he felt he could not attend. Under a broiling sun—in a meeting that dragged interminably—the President spoke to his colleagues for only ten minutes. He proposed that each name a personal representative and that these twenty-one representatives determine how the Organization of American States might be strengthened, particularly in the economic and social areas. The objective was, he explained, to have the OAS become as vital a force in social and economic affairs as it had proved to be in political affairs. The proposal was unanimously approved, possibly with the undue expectation that the United States would greatly increase its assistance to Latin America.

The committee thus formed met in Washington, D.C. shortly thereafter. As the representative of the President of the host country, I became chairman of the group and was involved for the next nine months in lengthy plenary and sub-committee sessions in Washington. In the academic year of 1956–57, I fear I neglected my duties at The Johns Hopkins University, which I had joined as President immediately after the trip to Panama. Our meetings resulted in a unanimous report to the twenty-one Presidents, but the unanimity was achieved only by postponing, at my insistence, final positions on two proposals which were vigorously supported by the other representatives. Ironically, I was sympathetic with the views of the other representatives, but long-established United States foreign policy dictated that officially I oppose the creation of an Inter-American Bank and new authority to finance social as contrasted with economic projects. I was convinced that we ought to change these policies, but my arguments with State and Treasury Department officials late at night after the formal conference sessions were at least temporarily in vain. Hence, in formal conference I was obligated to defend traditional policy. This was an unhappy but not a new experience; I had learned from twenty years in the federal service that one may, in inner councils, differ vehemently with a standing or proposed policy, but once a decision is made by the authorized official one must uphold it or resign. Departure from such practice would cause chaos.

Despite our official stand, I listened sympathetically as Pedro Beltrán, an eminent scholar and leading citizen of Peru, pleaded with us to break with the orthodoxy of private and public banking and make massive quantities of credit available for social projects. But despite his enlightened point of view, Pedro Beltrán did not link his request for social development loans with a demand for social reform by the Latin-American nations themselves; his emphasis was exclusively on external assistance. Had we accepted his advice and added to it the missing ingredient of internal reform, we would now be safer from the threat of Castro Communism in the Western Hemisphere. And Latin-American-United States relations would be a good deal better. But most important, the misery of countless people might have been lightened.

It was more than a year later, in the summer of 1958, that the United States put aside long-held orthodox views to participate in the establishment of an Inter-American Bank. Douglas Dillon, then Under Secretary of State for Economic Affairs, was becoming increasingly interested in Latin-American matters, R. R. Rubottom, Jr., a new and wise Assistant Secretary for Inter-American Affairs was on hand, and the times obviously demanded a new approach. Then in 1960, we again broke tradition and took the initiative in obtaining organic authority to make loans for social development.

In 1958, I submitted a second major report to the President. I had made study trips to the five republics of Central America and to Panama and had made several intensive and analytical investigations in Mexico as a sort of pilot research project applicable to the hemisphere. The report, parts of which I shall discuss in some detail later, was approved as official policy, just as the 1953 report had been.

This work in Latin America had been interesting and gratifying, but the greatest personal satisfaction came early in 1960, when I accompanied President Eisenhower on a spectacular trip to Brazil, Argentina, Chile, and Uruguay. The trip was truly a triumph of friendship. It demonstrated once more that the differences in this hemisphere are indeed those of a family, with no lessening of the deeper love for family ties. In thirty-two addresses, the President eloquently expressed his hope that the needs of all Latin Americans could be met in a social system that protects freedom and human dignity. He let the people know that their welfare is our concern and that we would work to develop new and pioneering programs for progress. A critical reading of those addresses, of his special message to Congress in August 1960 (conceived on the trip), and of several talks made later by President Kennedy, will convince even an ardent political partisan that the Alliance for Progress proposal made by President Kennedy in 1961 did not envision a major shift in policy; on the contrary, it was the next logical step in our constantly evolving programs.

Fortunately, American foreign policy is seldom altered in any material degree by changes of administration. Promises made by one administration must not be repudiated by another; the actions begun by one President must not be halted capriciously by his successor. Such behavior would cause confusion and perhaps serious trouble. Indeed, our integrity would be brought into question.

Foreign policy is not unlike a river, sometimes smooth and moving imperceptibly, sometimes turbulent and rapidly surging forward. Man can build dikes or dams, harness the river's energy, and use it to serve or destroy. But he cannot stop the river from flowing. Well-conceived foreign policy must have continuity; it certainly must adjust to changing conditions, but it must also move ever onward.

We are at a point in history where we must give substantial assistance to Latin America, just as we drew resources from Europe to speed our own progress during the Industrial Revolution. Americans know this. Regardless of political party, we want to be a helpful partner in the Western Hemisphere enterprise. We want the advantages of education, good health, prosperity, and freedom for *all* Latin Americans. Opinions may differ on the methods for reaching these goals, but the goals remain the same regardless of the administration in power.

The Alliance for Progress can usher in a new era of glorious hemispheric partnership. It is the next logical step in progressive programs ardently fostered by Presidents Roosevelt and Eisenhower. On the other hand, the Alliance for Progress could fail—or could backfire. But if this happens, the fault is not likely to be with the United States—a fact which offers little consolation.

It is imperative for us to realize that the success or failure of the Alliance for Progress is not wholly for us to determine. If the intelligent leaders of the other American republics do not move swiftly to correct historic injustices and inequities and to bring about a social revolution by peaceful means, Castro-type revolutions may rock and wreck country after country south of the border. The hemisphere is truly on the verge of violent upheaval, and bloody revolutions will almost certainly lead to military or Communist dictatorships. This is the challenge to the Americas; though no single country can unilaterally assure the success of the Alliance, we can all do everything in our power to make it work. There is no satisfactory alternative.

2　We can talk of people as statistics, producers, consumers, masses, and resources, but we can never make them anything but people. The solutions to our problems are primarily human solutions.

However we describe Latin America, whatever symbols or statistics we use, however concerned we are with economic theories, military policies, or political complications, we must always remember that we are talking about people. If this new adventure in progress fails, it will be because people failed. The obstacles to fruitful hemispheric cooperation—whether economic, intellectual, or political in nature—are fundamentally human problems. And solutions—if they are ever to be found—must be human solutions.

More than two hundred million people occupy the eight million square miles south of the Rio Grande. This is 8 per cent of the world's population on 19 per cent of the world's inhabited lands. Forty years from now nearly six hundred million people will live there—more than twice as many as will inhabit North America.

What is the lot of these people today? What will it be tomorrow?

It is difficult, perhaps wrong, to generalize about the peoples of twenty quite different republics. Thus, for example, Cubans are completely enslaved while Uruguayans enjoy what many deem to be exemplary democratic institutions; the population of several countries is predominantly white while other populations are racial mixtures. Hence, accuracy in analysis logically requires considerable detail about each republic. But this is not practical in a broad review of the evolving relationships of the United States with all of the countries of Latin America.

Certainly by our standards, present conditions in most Latin-American countries are intolerably bad; by any standards they are unjust and oppressive. As they now spawn misery and discontent, so do they breed violence. The majority of Latin Americans cannot read or write; illiteracy ranges from 13 per cent in one country to 70 per cent in several, and to more than 80 per cent in one. Education is a rare privilege. Nearly two-thirds of all Latin Americans till the soil, but few own the land. Land ownership and income distribution are disproportionately unbalanced to an almost unprecedented extent in favor of the privileged classes. The masses of agricultural workers are trapped in a feudalistic system which makes serfs of them. Although the political power of the land barons (in one country, for example, 5 per cent of the people own 90 per cent of the land) has decreased from the absolute level of the past century, it remains potent enough to prevent all but the most glacial social and economic reforms. The unwillingness of rich landowners and other privileged groups to permit tax reforms and even honest tax collections seriously cripples the ability of governments to foster social and economic development. The English concept of *noblesse oblige* has not substantially influenced Latin America's upper classes, save in a few countries. There had been no Latin-American Magna Charta.

The people in most countries have not been able by democratic procedures to win reform or to use governmental power and facilities to achieve what they think is desirable. Total production is minimal, housing is deplorably bad, and health facilities are woefully inadequate. The income of workers is incredibly low, ranging from seventy-five dollars a year in Bolivia to three hundred dollars a year in the best areas of several countries, including Argentina, Brazil, and Mexico. In some areas, rural folk still remove their hats and stare at their feet in the presence of their employers.

Victimized by this system, Latin-American agricultural workers usually live in huts of mud or wattle. In payment for their toil, they are permitted to grow their own food on a tiny segment of the employer's land, but their inadequate diet leaves them hungry, undernourished, and easy prey to disease. Few of them ever venture beyond the sight of their villages, and those who flee to the cities are likely to find themselves crowded into slums. They are living anachronisms, subsisting in seventeenth-century conditions and yearning for the opportunities of the twentieth century. They are becoming dissatisfied, angry, and dangerously restive.

The roots of the current situation may be traced directly to the attitudes of the early Spanish who came to the New World. The *conquistadores* and their followers sought personal enrichment so that they could return to Spain and live like gentlemen. They felt no need to band together to solve common problems and to build a permanent civilization.

Most of the early Spanish in the period of the conquest did not bring their families. Indian women replaced absent wives. Thus, the mestizo was born. Large segments of the Indian populations—with their ignorance, poverty, and strange customs—were brought into Spanish colonial life. Unfortunately for the sake of an integrated society, however, many of the Indians remained isolated on the less desirable land of the hillsides and mountain plateaus where they exist today in separate cultural milieus.

At first, most of the Indians were treated cruelly and impersonally. The *conquistadores* viewed them as hindrances to, or sources of, personal enrichment; only a few felt otherwise. Whether the Indians were mistreated or slaughtered, bribed or pampered depended on the attitudes of the *conquistadores*.

A more permanent society began in Spanish America with the coming of holders of land grants, mine owners, and priests, and the tradesmen, merchants, and few professionals who came to serve them. The landowners and mine operators were soon faced with a serious manpower problem: It was beneath the station of a Spanish nobleman (hidalgo) to work with his hands. Similarly, Spanish soldiers, if they stayed in the New World, often became landowners and were not apt to work. Other immigrants from Spain, who were not noblemen, often assumed the same aristocratic attitude toward manual labor. This made the Indian the principal source of productive energy, so the settlers divided the supply among themselves in accordance with the *repartimiento* system. But this system was judged cruel and lacking in human dignity by the Spanish Crown and the Roman Catholic Church, which saw the Indians as rational beings capable of conversion to Catholicism. Temporarily at least, they forced the abandonment of *repartimiento* slavery, and the adoption of the *encomienda* system, under which a local representative of the Crown assigned an appropriate number of Indians to each settler. For their labor, the Indians were to receive physical protection, minimal biological requirements, and spiritual education. Even then, there were those who protested the injustice. The Dominican Friar Bartolome de las Casas ("Apostle of the Indians") spent fifty-five years fighting for their rights. Though frustrated by powerful vested interest, betrayed by his colleagues, and oppressed by the authorities, he struggled in vain to improve the lot of the Indians.

The *encomienda* system was ignored when the Crown and the Church lost their influence over the landowners. Not until the end of the eighteenth century, a few years before the Wars of Independence, did a Spanish king feel strong enough to force the landowners to return to the unpopular *encomienda* system.

Meanwhile, Spanish mineowners had adopted an equally harsh practice in obtaining workers. Indians in mining areas were forced to leave their homes periodically and work in the mines under abominable conditions for scant if any wages. The Crown and the Church, though disapproving, felt powerless to stop the practice.

Thus, severe social stratification and injustice began at once and continued throughout the colonial period.

No serious threat of revolt developed among the Indians, for their material well-being had been bad before the white men arrived. Contrary to romantic descriptions of early Indian societies, and aside from certain splendid achievements of the Toltecs, Aztecs, Incas, and Mayas, most American Indians had been as destitute and as sternly ruled by their own leaders.

In general, Indians remained an inferior mass whose function was to provide cheap labor for the privileged classes. They stoically endured their maltreatment until the Tupac Amaru II uprising in Peru in 1780 when they first bore arms in large numbers against their masters. The rebellion was unsuccessful.

It was more than a hundred years later—in the twentieth century—that widespread movements for the meaningful inclusion of Indians in society began. This ideal, *indioismo*, received political embodiment in the Mexican revolution, the Peruvian *Aprista* movement, and, later, in the Bolivian National Revolutionary Movement. It is a movement which draws strong support from Latin-American intellectuals, and it has also become a persistent theme of Communist propaganda in the largely Indian nations of Mexico, Guatemala, Ecuador, Peru, and Bolivia.

Not far above the Indians on the rigidly stratified colonial social scale were the mestizos, who filled the role of petty officials, such as overseers on plantations. Above the mestizos were the *criollos*, white persons born in the New World. Most of the landowners, businessmen, and professionals were *criollos*. At the apex of this sternly controlled society were the *peninsulares*, residents of Spanish America who were born in and would probably return to Spain. Crown and Church officials, who represented the cream of society, were invariably *peninsulares*, much to the chagrin of the *criollos*.

The struggle between the Crown and the Church, on the one hand, and the feudal nobility, on the other, had been transferred to the New World from the Iberian Peninsula. This contest for power, which had its roots in the Roman, Visigothic, and Moorish background of Spain, was not the only Spanish contribution to Latin America. The Spanish also brought with them certain attitudes which have persisted through many generations. One is a deeper concern for self than for society. This is not selfishness of a penurious variety, for Spanish Americans are traditionally generous. Rather, it is an abiding respect for the will, personality, and dignity of oneself. If this admirable trait were matched by an allegiance to and concern for the community of persons, it could lead to a rapid improvement of the general welfare. In most countries this has not occurred.

Another attitude shared by the Spanish and Latin Americans is an inclination to place higher value on intellectual creativity in the humanities than on the practical ability to build and make things work. Social mores have caused many intelligent Latin Americans to become poets, writers, artists, and philosophers, not engineers or inventors. There can be no doubt that such attitudes and value judgments have thrown social and economic progress out of balance. They also indicate why Latin Americans believe that we are too concerned with materialism, pragmatism, and the technological rather than spiritual aspects of life. Latin Americans yearn for prosperity, but they want social well-being first; they want to be free to make their own life with their own concept of human dignity. "*Nuestro vino es agrio, pero es nuestro vino,*" said the Cuban revolutionary leader José Martí: "Our wine is bitter, but it is ours."

Major elements of the economic structure of Spain, developed in the Middle Ages, were also transferred to Spanish America. It was Spain's economic policy toward the New World that proved to be the chief cause of colonial revolt.

The Crown received its "royal fifth" from the mines. Colonial merchants were forced to buy manufactured goods from Spain; raw materials were shipped to the mother country and returned in processed form. Despite Spanish mercantilism, considerable wealth was created in the colonies and the demand for goods often exceeded the supply. Resentment against the Spanish monopoly grew stronger. Economic exploitation and deprivation became central in the *criollo* Spanish antipathy toward Spain and led to the war of independence.

Only the *criollos* won justice in the wars of independence. Long denied choice of administrative positions in their own land, they had also seen their modicum of local self-rule extinguished by a parallel royal administration. When news of local revolts against the Crown spread across Spanish America in 1810, the *criollos* were more than willing to participate. The wars, which continued for fourteen years, were supported by the mestizos and the Indians, for they assumed that any change would be an improvement. It was a false assumption. The *criollos* won independence from Spain, gained power, took land from the Church, and intimidated the Church hierarchy. Then the *criollos* were free to employ even stricter labor systems.

The *latifundios* (large landholdings), with their semi-slave labor, survived the wars intact. Essentially self-contained, they remained aloof from other streams and forces in the newly independent countries.

Only in the early phase of the Mexican war of independence did the struggle assume the nature of a social revolution. Two country priests, Father Hidalgo and Father Morelos, led revolts that demanded land for the peasants and other social reforms. The Mexican *criollos*, however, preferred a more conservative type of revolution and successfully achieved it when Agustín de Iturbide led Mexico to independence. Social reform was postponed—for almost a century.

After the wars of independence, Latin America was virtually in anarchy. Region was often pitted against region, landowner against landowner. Eventually strong dictators emerged to unify their nations. Called *caudillos*, they were usually dynamic men who aroused the hopes of the people for a better life, but they were easily dissuaded by the conservative aristocracy from embarking on social change.

A new struggle developed. In the nineteenth century, *mestizos* grew in social prestige and economic power and were, in some countries, able to form new parties which challenged the conservative aristocrats. Unhappily, the *mestizos* had lost any feeling for their Indian ancestors, and political struggles with the conservatives were fought over such issues as clericalism and federalism, not social reform. Politics became characterized by rigged elections, or by subversion of the popular will by strong armies formed by the privileged "to maintain internal security."

These conditions did not go completely unchallenged. Two forceful leaders in Argentina—Juan Bautista Alberdi and Domingo Faustino Sarmiento—successfully led forces in 1852 that overthrew the landowners' dictator, Juan Manuel de Rosas; thereafter, during the latter half of the nineteenth century, considerable economic progress was made by the republic. In Chile, the privileged classes developed a spirit of *noblesse oblige* strong enough to allow some social reform and economic development, including the extensive public works projects of the Balmaceda regime in the 1880s. The new spirit was not potent enough, however, to cause Chilean landowners to break up portions of their holdings, and thus Chile, otherwise progressive, remains shackled by a feudalistic land control.

Argentina and Chile were, and still are, nations without large Indian populations. Indian nations have had to wait until the twentieth century for social progress.

And most still wait.

Mexico is the only Indian nation that has made significant progress, with benefits reaching all classes of the population. At the turn of the twentieth century, Mexico was under the iron-fisted rule of Porfirio Díaz, whose concern for development centered in the enrichment of himself and a few cronies. He sought large quantities of foreign capital and encouraged the establishment of even larger *latifundios*. To attract capital and conservative support, Díaz bargained away domestic control over natural resources and sold most of the land owned by Indian communities to foreign investors and *latifundistas*. In 1910, when Mexico's revolution began, a fourth of her land was held by foreigners; that owned by Mexicans was held by less than 3 per cent of the population. Indians could not find land. A few privileged were prosperous. The plight of Indian peons and mestizos was desperate. Mexico of the early 1900s was called "The mother of foreigners and the stepmother of Mexicans."

Interestingly, the revolution was sparked by a constitutional issue. Francisco Indalecio Madero, its first leader, attacked Díaz because electoral privileges had been denied the Mexican people and because the Díaz clique had become old and sluggish in its thinking. But the kindly Madero, who has since been canonized in the liturgy of the Mexican revolution, was soon betrayed and succeeded by General Victoriano Huerta—a ruthless tyrant who was overthrown mainly because of Woodrow Wilson's refusal to recognize him and persistent efforts to undermine him. Wilson, with the objective of discrediting Huerta, seized upon a trifling incident to order the United States Navy to attack and capture Veracruz. Huerta was forced to flee the country. (Despite the good thus done, Mexico became, and remains, a leading critic of intervention. "Our wine is bitter, but it is ours.")

Huerta's successor, General Venustiano Carranza, was not progressive, but to consolidate his control he included in the constitution of 1917 provisions insisted upon by such reformers as Emiliano Zapata and Luis Cabrera: He accepted, for example, a far-reaching land reform policy and a progressive labor code which embodied the best provisions of the codes of several Western nations.

Following Carranza, presidents talked much of revolutionary ideals, but income and landownership disparities in Mexico were not adjusted significantly until early in 1934 under the administration of Lázero Cárdenas, who was to become a harsh critic of the United States, an extreme leftist, and a collaborator of Latin-American Communists. Cárdenas broke up *latifundios* and transferred the land to Indians and others who obtained it either on an individual basis or as community holdings. American and British oil company holdings were expropriated, a step which reduced production but boosted Mexican spirit.

Thereafter the revolution embarked on a more moderate, but not a less effective course. Emphasis turned to industrialization, electrification, increased and more diversified agricultural production, education, more equitable taxation, honesty in government, and a wide diffusion of the benefits of production. Presidents Alemán, Ruíz Cortines, and Lopez Mateos deserve great credit for the progress Mexico has made in recent years. Though Mexico today is still a land of marked contrasts between the wealthy and the poor, a substantial middle class is growing rapidly. Mexico has its extreme leftists, Cárdenas among them, who call for more rapid change through state control, but the vast majority is convinced that the road being traveled is the right one, and the atmosphere of urgency and danger that marks more backward nations is no longer present.

Mexican progress stands in sharp contrast to the slowness with which the Indian republics of Ecuador, Guatemala, Peru, and Bolivia have moved. In these four countries all indicators of economic progress and social justice remain low. Illiteracy ranges from 47 per cent in Ecuador to 71 per cent in Guatemala. Average per capita annual income is $200 in Ecuador, $170 in Guatemala, $155 in Peru, and only $75 in Bolivia; yet each of these nations has its coterie of wealthy families that have long ruled the country. Taxes bear heavily on the poor, and such taxes as are levied on the rich are often evaded. Direct taxes account for only about 20 per cent of the public revenues; 80 per cent is derived from sales and excise taxes, customs, and other sources which bear regressively upon the whole population. In contrast, in the United States about 81 per cent of federal revenues is obtained by direct taxation.

In Bolivia a reform movement is in its early stages. President Paz Estenssoro, in the early years of his first administration, nationalized the tin mines which have long dominated the economy and the politics of the country, and instituted a modest program of land reform. Seventy per cent of the population was illiterate in 1952 when the reform movement began. The feudalistic landholding system was one of the worst of the hemisphere. Indians on these lands received no compensation. Only 5 per cent of them spoke Spanish. The effort in reform, not yet showing much success, has been to give the Indians land and education.

In Ecuador, 300 *latifundios* comprise 65 per cent of all the land in use, while 14,000 small holdings constitute only 3 per cent of the land farmed. In a typical Indian village in the Andes of Peru, only one Indian out of 325 can read and write. Four million Indians live in the Andean highlands and interior jungles, much as they did when the Incas and Spanish viceroys ruled Peru.

Progress in the mestizo nations of El Salvador, Nicaragua, Honduras, Colombia, and Panama has been dangerously slow. Average annual income is about $200 a person, save in Panama where tourist and canal expenditures make it considerably higher. In El Salvador nearly 58 per cent of the people are illiterate, agricultural and other workers receive about fifty cents a day in wages, a handful of wealthy plantation owners pay a minimal amount of taxes, and the wealthy send surplus funds abroad for investment. In the fall of 1960, a military junta took over the government and sought to institute land reform. A second junta took control in 1961. It found that of the republic's 2,500,000 people only about 9000 were on the income tax rolls, and a great many of these evaded actual payments. Landowners protested vigorously when the junta proposed the inclusion on the tax rolls of 50,000 persons earning more than $200 a month, and they threatened to bring a third and more conservative junta to power. In Nicaragua, the Somoza and a few other families have incomes approaching those of the wealthy families in the United States. (It is often said that the income of the Somoza family is higher than that of all others in the nation.) The situation in Honduras is comparable to that of Nicaragua, though there are fewer rich families. In Colombia, where the liberal and conservative parties have temporarily halted civil strife that has long retarded national progress, direct taxes account for nearly 42 per cent of the public revenues, and during the Lleras Camargo administration an honest effort was made to administer tax programs fairly and efficiently.

The Dominican Republic, Haiti, and Paraguay, all caught for years by dictatorships, have achieved little in the way of social justice. Annual income varies from $75 in Haiti to $125 in Paraguay. Direct taxes account for only 8 per cent of public revenues in Haiti; data are not available for the other two countries. The Dominican Republic has finally rid itself of the Trujillo family, but its future course is now uncertain.

Argentina, Costa Rica, Chile, and Uruguay, nations with predominantly white populations, have met their responsibilities of promoting the general welfare with varying success. The per capita annual income of $495 in Chile, $410 in Costa Rica, and $380 in Argentina is exceeded only by that of Venezuela, while Uruguay's average income is only about $200 a year.

Chile has reduced illiteracy to less than 20 per cent of the population, its tax system is above average in progressiveness, and its social security programs are generous. Nearly 50 per cent more of its budget is devoted to social security than in the United States budget. But Chile is backward in the area of land reform, with 75 per cent of arable land held by only 5 per cent of landed proprietors.

Costa Rica pridefully points to the fact that it has more teachers than soldiers. Actually, it has no army—only a national guard (police) equipped with small weapons. The literacy rate of 80 per cent indicates the general concern for education. More than any other Latin nation, Costa Rica is characterized by small landowners. While net income is not high on these small farms, basic human needs are moderately well met.

Argentina has the highest literacy rate in Latin America—about 87 per cent. Income distribution is more conducive to democratic progress than in many other countries, a diversified economy is being vigorously promoted, and the tax system is more equitable than it was in previous years. The recent resurgence of supporters of Juan Perón and the toppling of President Frondizi have created a new instability in this potentially great nation.

Uruguay is usually considered to be the most democratic and socially-progressive country of the Latin republics. Literacy is almost as high as that in Argentina. Education is energetically supported at all levels, public health programs are extensive, and the tax system is reasonably equitable. Russell Fitzgibbon, in his book *Uruguay: Portrait of a Democracy*, points out that in the early 1950s more than eighty pieces of social legislation were enacted. Unfortunately, total annual income is low.

Venezuela, a country victimized by dictatorships until recently, is now introducing a wide range of social reforms under the leadership of President Romulo Betancourt. High income from oil and iron ore boost the average per capita income to $1050, the highest in Latin America. Direct taxes account for nearly 32 per cent of public revenues.

Only the Cuban situation, which is discussed in Chapter 13, and Brazil remain for comment.

Brazil has distinguishing attributes, mainly its Portuguese background, large Negro population, and separate pattern of settlement. The Portuguese of the early sixteenth century were a cosmopolitan, seafaring people. With early links to Negro Africa and a large Jewish population, they were less prone than the Spaniards to establish rigid stratifications. This reduced the sense of superiority which the white race might otherwise have felt, but it did not overcome the low status of the Negroes and Indians.

While the total society was structured less sternly than that of Spanish America, some rigidities developed.

The patriarchal, slave-holding culture that grew around the Brazilian equivalent of the *latifundio*, the *fazenda*, yielded political and social results not too different from those in Spanish countries. The *fazendas* have remained empires within an empire; they are outposts of regionalism which have been capable of resisting changes threatened by the central government.

Like other Latin American elite, many Brazilian landowners have preferred safe foreign investments to the risks involved in developing domestic enterprises. The rich potential resources of Brazil remain largely untapped, except for promising and rapid growth in the south of the nation.

Though the indicators of social justice—literacy rate, average wage, and distribution of land and wealth—show Brazil to be somewhat more advanced than many of the nations with Spanish backgrounds, Brazil drags and stumbles under the force of the controlling class, which has prevented the national government from instituting a tax system which would provide the nation with revenues necessary to finance programs of social development and reform.

Northeast Brazil is a tinderbox that could ignite into fiery rebellion at any minute. There, seven states form an area larger than Venezuela and twice as large as the combined area of the five republics in Central America. More than 75 per cent of the people in northeast Brazil work the land—as crudely as their ancient ancestors did. Nearly one-half of the land is owned by 2 per cent of the people, and even where smaller plots exist, the holders often do not have clear title and must pay rent to the rich landowners.

The people of northeast Brazil are among the poorest in the hemisphere, earning less than $100 per capita annually. Only 20 per cent of the people are literate and only 5 per cent over ten years of age have completed elementary school. The average life expectancy in the state of Paraíba is thirty-one years.

Under the leadership of Francisco Juliao, "Peasant Leagues" have formed to champion the cause of the peasant. The Leagues propose to solve the problems of the area quickly and directly, proclaiming "reform or revolution!" As his mentors, Juliao seems to have chosen Marx, Mao, and Castro.

Aware of the danger in northeast Brazil, the government has established a special department, SUDENE, to reduce pressures through long-needed improvements. Among its plans are the migration of one million peasants to areas better suited for small-scale farming, the development of light industry, and the improvement of agrarian techniques. Even though actual land reform is yet to come, SUDENE's long-range programs are impressive and they have won the support of the Alliance for Progress.

So far Juliao and his Peasant Leagues have been willing to await governmental action, but violence flares from time to time anyway. The acting president of the League in Paraíba and his predecessor have both been shot, and on one ranch, where one thousand families work the land for one absentee owner, a group of tenants attacked and killed their hated manager with their hoes. There is no guarantee that such incidents will not touch off an armed uprising that could result in a repeat of the Cuban revolution.

3   Where there is little meaning in life, there is little respect for death.

NEITHER DEMOCRACY NOR PROSPERITY CAN BE BUILT ON a foundation of ignorance, but in Latin America education is generally a luxury for the rich. Members of the elite classes are well educated, many of them graduates of universities in Europe and the United States. Members of the scanty middle class are literate, and some of them have attained higher levels of education. But the lower classes, including the Indians, are generally illiterate. The low level of education in Latin America is both a cause and effect of the stratified culture which restrains progress.

Efforts to expand and improve educational opportunities have been uneven. Thus, less than 16 per cent of Nicaraguan children between five and nineteen years of age are in public or private schools, but more than half of such children are in the schools of Costa Rica, Panama, and Argentina.

Low national income is usually cited as the major reason for the dearth of educational facilities and opportunities, when, in fact, the lack of elementary knowledge and management skills is a *cause* of low national income. It is noteworthy that widespread (if primitive) educational facilities were developed in the United States when the nation and most of its people were very poor. In a few Latin American nations it has been shown that a governmental program, seriously and expertly undertaken, even with minimal financial support, can improve conditions. Dazzling proof was provided by two Mexican educational leaders, José Vasconcelos and Jáime Torres Bodet.

Vasconcelos, the first Secretary of Public Education in 1921, initiated an ambitious program: He and his successors constructed a large number of rural schools to provide the hitherto neglected Indians with basic education. Emphasis was placed on technical and practical training. Strenuous efforts were made to recruit and train teachers and, in two decades, illiteracy was reduced from 70 to 50 per cent of the people.

Expenditures by the national and municipal governments for public education were pitifully small, but generous in the context of Mexico's poverty. True, they were tragically inadequate to overcome the obstacles erected by the enormous number of villages requiring schools, poor transportation over rugged terrain, the multilingual problem and, most important, the rapidly expanding population. The significant thing is that a valiant attack on a fundamental problem was begun.

In 1944, Secretary of Education Jáime Torres Bodet dramatically called for each literate Mexican to teach at least one illiterate countryman to read and write. This appeal dramatically symbolized the situation for the people. It worked for a time and is now being stepped up.

After serving as Minister of Foreign Affairs of Mexico, Torres Bodet, a cultured, highly educated man, became Director General of the United Nations Educational, Scientific, and Cultural Organization. When he returned to Mexico, he again became Secretary of Education. In 1960, he persuaded the administration of President Lopez Mateos to devote an unprecedented proportion of the national budget to education, making it the biggest single item, with twice as much as is allocated to the military. The primary concern of the Department of Education remains the knotty problem of improving rural education. Rural schools are still inadequate numerically, and 80 per cent of them contain but three grades. The best teachers tend to go to the cities, attracted by higher salaries and better living conditions. The passionate idealism of the post-revolution period caused inspired volunteers to teach in remote spots, but this zeal has vanished. Torres Bodet is trying to overcome difficulties such as these and to equalize the level of teaching quality by standardizing salaries.

The Mexican Government has begun to supply free textbooks in large quantities. This relieves impoverished Indians and mestizo farmers and workers of what for them has been a serious financial burden.

Mexico's recent economic progress has been reflected in a steady improvement in the educational system. Better and more educated persons are helping Mexico to advance economically. The progress is reciprocal.

However, the high birth rate in Mexico—3.3 per cent a year, one of the highest in the world—is threatening the adequacy of the planned facilities. There are not enough teachers for a strong secondary school system. Cultural isolation and resistance by the Indians to the educational endeavors are discouraging. But, all things considered, one may be cautiously optimistic about the future of Mexican mass education.

In Argentina, Chile, Costa Rica, and Uruguay, the situation is roughly comparable to Mexico's. Panama has achieved more in relation to her resources than any other country. Elsewhere the picture is darker.

Primary schools are insufficient in number and woefully inadequate, good teachers are scarce, and the population increase is awesome. Too few of the remote areas have schools, and where they do exist pupils tend to drop out early, often at the end of one year. Economic hardship, cultural differences, and the inability of parents and students to see the benefit of education combine to reduce school attendance.

Enough students complete the six-year primary schools, however, to render the number of secondary schools deficient. Few secondary schools exist in rural communities. Bright farm and village youngsters who want to further their education must somehow find money to subsist in the cities. Seldom can their parents provide the funds. A few self-reliant and ambitious students may be able to acquire education from books read at home, but too often a frustrated desire for education culminates either in burning discontent or helpless resignation.

Most of the six-year secondary schools are designed to prepare students for general college work or for professional specialization. Entrance into institutions of higher learning follows completion of courses in these schools, which are similar to the European *lycées*.

The need for vocational secondary schools is pressing. Those which exist lack modern equipment. Chemistry laboratories may lack running water, shops may have no electricity, future mechanics may practice with a few discarded antique automobiles.

Public and private preparatory schools share about equally in training students for college. The numerous private schools are mostly clerically supported and are often oriented toward the wealthy. Both types of school are frequently charged by university officials with failing to alter their programs to meet modern requirements. For the first time, many universities are beginning to emphasize scientific and technical education; leaders of these institutions are prone to criticize preparatory schools in which the emphasis is on the traditional classical type of education.

The training of teachers for primary and secondary schools is entrusted to teacher institutes similar to the older normal schools in the United States. Students usually enter these institutes after secondary schooling, but some enroll immediately after completing primary school. Many Latin

American governments have given the creation of teacher institutes high priority—so much so that sometimes the institutes do not have the desired number of students, for incentives to enter the teaching profession are meager.

The United States has tried to be helpful in improving primary and secondary education in Latin America. On a visit to Bolivia, I saw personnel of the International Cooperation Administration (now called AID) working directly with the rural population in building and operating schools suitable to the environment; and in the past nine years, AID has spent about three and a half million dollars on the Bolivian program. In Paraguay I was escorted by the Foreign Minister to the first vocational school and to the first agricultural school of the country—both established and managed with our assistance. In Ecuador, Honduras, and Nicaragua I visited every classroom in the American schools and had to make a brief talk to each class! In general, the United States has helped establish, manage, and improve schools as demonstration projects in most of the Latin-American republics.

Perhaps the most touching experience I had in the years of travel among our southern neighbors occurred in Ecuador. I very much wanted to meet a man I considered to be a leading statesman of the hemisphere—former President Galo Plaza Lasso. Our ambassador thought this would be difficult, for the President at that time, José María Velasco Ibarra, evidently felt insecure in his position and he did not want any public attention given to the former President, who had been Ecuador's most popular, liberal, and enlightened leader. My disappointment was brief, for I learned that Galo Plaza Lasso was chairman of the board of the American school, which I could legitimately visit. By planned coincidence, he was there. Our two-hour conversation was as pleasant and revealing as I had anticipated, but what impressed me most was the affection which the students, ranging from six to about eleven years of age, obviously had for him. As I prepared to leave, he bade me good-bye in the privacy of his tiny office. The students followed me into the street. Some hugged me. Others gave me wild flowers. One presented me with a small elephant he had carved (and which I still have). They obviously had a warm regard for the United States, which gave the school each year a few thousand dollars for its meager budget.

Latin America's one hundred universities are very different from the two thousand institutions of higher learning in the United States.

In this country, boards of trustees strive to keep the institutions aloof from partisan politics, protect them from interference by governmental and other political leaders, entrust management of the educational program to the faculties, and guarantee academic freedom.

In Latin America, universities usually are confederations of separate faculties joined only through their participation in certain university councils. Most faculty members serve only part time, deriving most of their income from outside professional activities. (Notable exceptions in this regard are the University of Costa Rica, where a third of its faculty of 150 teaches on a full-time basis; the University of Mexico, and the University of the Andes in Colombia.)

The universities, lacking continuous faculty control, are student-oriented. The student voice in control is often decisive. Arturo Morales-Carrion, an official of the State Department, says the students possess "a passion for freedom—academic freedom, freedom from restraint, freedom from government intervention—a passion so extreme that it tends to make some universities a state within a state, an island of defiance where authority is dangerously near the vanishing point." Because student groups are an active force in partisan politics, politicians often retaliate by taking control of the universities.

When I visited San Marcos University in Lima, Peru, in 1953, I learned that it had been closed a few months before by the President of the republic who was dissatisfied with the teachings of the several faculties. Each faculty of the university was reactivated only when the President was satisfied that his objections had been met. This was not an uncommon occurrence. In the United States we would consider a political penetration of higher education to be a disaster. But in Latin America, where the struggle is to overcome historic social stratifications, discord and controversy, fomented by students, faculties, and political leaders, may be an essential intermediate step to an improved total environment.

For many years, faculty members and students have freely criticized their governments and existing social conditions. Today, in democratic countries, they suffer little retribution; indeed, in most such countries the universities have a high degree of autonomy. But in countries still controlled by dictators, the historic interference by political leaders prevails. Thus, the University of Havana is completely subjugated, deprived of all freedom.

Most Latin American university students today lean to the left. Emotionally, they attack the United States as a symbol of alleged exploitation. Frustrated by their nation's lack of progress in combating poverty—and usually not because of ideological convictions—a small percentage has af-

filiated loosely with the local Communist Party. The violent student demonstrations against the liberally democratic policies of President Betancourt
of Venezuela in the autumn of 1960 illustrate the more radical student
attitude. In contrast, however, were the work of the Catholic Action student party against a Communist attempt to take over Guatemala and the
opposition of socially progressive Catholic student groups to Juan Perón
in Argentina. The common denominator is not always a lack of modera-
tion, as is commonly supposed; often it is a genuine concern for their
people.

It is not uncommon for young men to concentrate on maintaining
themselves as university students for other than academic reasons. The
motive may be a liking for prestige, or a desire to exercise some control
over university affairs, or to have an effective base for political activities.
In many countries, any person who pays the modest university fee is carried on the rolls as a student; clever Communists regularly pay the fees
and seldom attend classes.

A few years ago I met a delegation of "university student leaders" in
Guatemala. Their thesis so slavishly adhered to Communist dogma that
I checked on them with the rector of the university, a friend; not one of
my conferees attended classes but all were listed as students.

Traditionally, Latin American universities have concentrated on law, the
humanities, and medicine, and their students have been limited largely to
the financial, social, and military elite. Hence, scientists, engineers, economists, and others necessary to spearhead economic development have
been at a premium.

Recently, however, Latin American educators, realizing that education
is essential to economic and social development, have called for a system
that includes emphasis on sequences in the sciences, technologies, economics, business administration, accounting, veterinary science, agriculture, and other practical fields. They have also sought to attain higher
academic standards, more full-time teachers, more students from the mid-
dle- and low-income groups, a disassociation of student politics from university policy, and freedom from church and state influences. As a consequence of the new emphasis on the "practical" phases of education, most
universities have become overcrowded. Shortages of laboratory equipment,
modern textbooks, and highly trained teachers have become imposing
handicaps. Inflation has made it nearly impossible for them to buy books
and equipment from the United States, or to finance doctoral or post-
doctoral education in the United States for highly promising students.

An encouraging development occurred in Bogotá, Colombia, in 1949.

Most Latin American universities are financed by governments, churches, or both. Lacking the traditions of academic freedom established early in the United States by independent universities, the nature of financial support of institutions of higher learning in Latin America tends to slow down movements to attain complete autonomy. The University of the Andes in Bogotá was created as "a non-denominational autonomous . . . entity which . . . is pledged to the highest standards in education, to the dissemination of culture and to the research into, and the publication of works of scientific, cultural or artistic merit." It is strictly private. It has far more students enrolled in its School of Engineering than in its Liberal Arts College. After two years of courses the university arranges for its better engineering students to carry out some of their studies in the United States. The university also encourages classroom participation of students and informal student-faculty relationships—a break from the austere relationship inherited from European institutions.

Other institutions of this type are likely to develop elsewhere in Latin America. They, as well as older institutions, will place increasing emphasis on rigorous studies in mathematics, physical and biological sciences, and technologies—without sacrificing the older classical subjects. As this occurs, students are likely to concern themselves more with serious intellectual growth and less with politics and student control of the universities—mainly because formal education will have meaning, will be preparing them for constructive work. University leaders do not anticipate or desire that student concern for social justice should diminish; the hope is that the university graduates will be of increased practical usefulness to the nation while working during their lifetimes for peaceful change through democratic processes.

Changes in the programs and practices of Latin-American institutions of higher learning will not suffice. A vastly more extensive system is needed. In moments of despair it is said that there is an impervious circle around Latin-American higher education: There cannot be more universities until a heightened economy can finance them, but the economy will not advance until more highly trained people are available for this purpose.

The circle must be broken. I have seen this done in several cities, notably in Rio de Janeiro, Mexico City, and Caracas.

I was particularly impressed by what I saw in Caracas, for it was my first experience of the kind. The construction of a wholly new university city was almost completed when I visited there in 1953 as my associates and I started our first mission to Latin America. We stood on the roof of the library building, and the rector of the university pointed out various features of the campus with a pride and enthusiasm usually identified by Latins with "braggart *Yanquis*." The dictator, Marcos Pérez Jiménez, had dipped into his treasury, fattened by the influx of dollars from oil and iron ore, and set aside $134,000,000 for the creation of a model home for the Central University of Venezuela.

I confess I felt a tinge of envy.

What American educator—aware of the seemingly uncorrectable inefficiencies that develop in a university which has taken a hundred years to build, or discouraged by the growth of slums around his institution—would not like to buy open land and construct all the essential buildings in harmony with a master plan—the basic sciences, social sciences, and humanities in the center, as the hub of a wheel; the professional schools emanating out, as the spokes, and student and faculty housing on the periphery?

But economic, social, and cultural development in the United States, as in all advanced nations of the world, has been a slow and gradual process. Even with current prosperity, few colleges or universities in the United States could find the resources to erect entirely new plants, with all facilities for thousands of students.

Pérez Jiménez, motivated by a desire to enhance his nation's prestige and to build a living monument to himself—though possibly he had been persuaded also that highly trained men were needed for the economic development of Venezuela—had appropriated (with a dictator's ease) the funds to build a city devoted to higher education.

My mind flashed to responsibilities at Penn State. For some months I had been working to obtain about ten million dollars for buildings made imperative by a burgeoning growth in population and an insistently growing demand for college admission, and as yet I did not know whether the funds would be forthcoming from the General State Authority. So, in the panorama below me, I viewed the mass of well-designed and solidly-built structures—none of them as yet occupied—with one eye jaundiced and the other filled with admiration.

While $134,000,000 for a new university city in a relatively poor nation seemed to me to be extravagant, nonetheless I inwardly applauded. For I knew that after only an hour's plane ride from the thriving city of Caracas I would soon see wild, untouched jungle. I would pass through the villages and by the farms of hundreds of thousands of people who could not read or write, and who were suffering from diseases and malnutrition, thus lacking the strength for sustained production. I would see babies and youngsters

33

everywhere, representing a population growth as great as the increase in total national production.

Surely then, the new home for the Central University of Venezuela, provided that it symbolized a determination to foster education at all levels—from the elementary grades to the highest levels of post-doctoral study—signified the beginning of a new era in Venezuela. With increased education, perhaps even an entrenched dictator could eventually be overthrown. Indeed, when I was talking to Colonel Pérez Jiménez the next day I could scarcely refrain from repeating Wendell Willkie's daring comment to Stalin, who had been boasting of the growth of education in the Soviet Union: "Aren't you afraid you will work yourself out of a job?"

I doubt that the Central University of Venezuela was in its new home long enough to claim a correlation of its inheritance of a new plant with the overthrow of Pérez Jiménez almost five years later. But I hope that the future will show a correlation between new democratic leaders, in nation after nation, and a spectacular expansion in the number, quality, and size of their colleges and universities.

Public and private agencies in the United States provide considerable help to higher education in Latin America. The United States pays a substantial share of the cost of the 500 fellowships granted annually by the Organization of American States. The Ford, Rockefeller, Carnegie, and other foundations provide numerous fellowships and scholarships. The International Cooperation Administration in 1960 had contracts with nearly twenty Latin-American countries; under these contracts, 120 United States technicians were in Latin-American universities helping with programs in public administration, agriculture, science (including atomic science), health, housing, industry, and labor; nearly 1600 Latin-American teachers and advanced students were sent to United States universities for training. The State Department, in the 1950s, sent more than 700 United States students to various Latin-American universities and brought nearly 3000 Latin-American students to this country for university study or teaching.

Private and public assistance from the United States, plus their own governmental grants and family assistance, have enabled about 12,500 Latin-American students to study each year in colleges, universities, hospitals, and industrial laboratories of the United States. In relation to the 3,750,000 United States students enrolled in our own colleges and universities, this number is small, but as a means of lifting the level of Latin-American education and enterprise the effort is significant.

From the moment they are born, Latin-American babies face a strong prospect of death. One in ten dies before it is a year old. Fifteen per cent of all deaths occur in the one to five age group.

This high mortality rate is due largely to diarrheal diseases. Typhoid fever and malaria also have wrought havoc among children, as they did among all age groups. But these are controllable diseases, and public health programs are making notable headway in containing them.

Latin-American physicians are often undertrained and nearly always overburdened, especially in rural areas. In the United States, the average number of patients per doctor is about eight hundred. In some Latin-American countries the average is six thousand.

Even in comparatively advanced Chile, farmers in the southern region have one doctor for every five thousand persons, but in Santiago there is one for every nine hundred.

Although many diseases require hospitalization, hospital beds are luxuries for the ill. About four times as many people use each hospital bed as in the United States and, as always, facilities are most limited in rural areas.

Unsanitary and inadequate water supplies are leading contributors to disease. The Pan American Sanitary Bureau estimates that as high as a 60 per cent reduction in deadly diarrheal disease could result from potable water supplies. A leading authority on Latin-American sanitation problems, Dr. Abel Woman, discovered that in many rural areas 100 per cent of the population was without a piped supply either in homes or nearby courtyards.

Low nutritional levels make Latin Americans more susceptible to diseases. For every child that dies of malnutrition in the United States more than three hundred die of the same deficiency in some Latin-American nations. In Bolivia the average daily caloric intake per person is about eleven hundred. Only in Argentina and Uruguay is the caloric intake as high as twenty-five hundred, compared to thirty-two hundred in the United States. Within a meager diet, the protein, mineral, and vitamin levels are low, as they are also, indeed, in the high-starch, high-caloric diets. Diseases of metabolic deficiency and anemia are significant killers. Body cells are not built up to sufficient strength to resist the omnipresent diseases and epidemics.

Again the awesomely increasing birth rate compounds the difficulties. Even radically improved health programs, capable of meeting today's needs, will be insufficient in a decade. Ironically, success of health programs will serve to raise the population and strain facilities further. This raises the delicate and emotionally charged question of birth control, a knotty problem in most underdeveloped countries. Since the answer to a rapid population increase cannot in an enlightened nation be neglect of health, and since the most optimistic estimates of increasing productivity is 2.5 per cent a year, it seems inevitable that the Latin-American countries will have to face up to the need for a type of education which might more humanely hold down total population growth. In June 1962, Chile led the way in this regard by becoming the first Latin-American republic to establish an official governmental committee to study the country's high birth rates and to prepare a nationwide program to bring them under control. And in the same month, seven Latin-American nations sent delegates to a twelve-day seminar in New York to study measures to control the spiraling birth rate.

The United States has given effective assistance on health problems in nearly all the Latin-American republics. In the Andean countries the horrible disease of yaws has been essentially eliminated by the use of penicillin. Malaria has been greatly reduced in all countries, eliminated in a few. Smallpox has been brought under control.

We have helped to construct sixteen health centers and have introduced mobile health clinics which are highly useful in rural areas. We have also contributed to the construction of milk pasteurization plants and to programs designed to improve nutrition.

In Brazil in 1953 I learned what a modicum of expert assistance, given in the right spirit, can truly do. The story was told proudly by a Brazilian doctor who had received graduate training in the United States. Nine years before, he explained, public health programs were almost unknown in his vast land. Nelson Rockefeller had visited the country and had agreed to help finance a *Servicio de Saude Publica*. The United States provided most of the technical personnel, who would be withdrawn as local persons were trained. We also put up ten dollars for each dollar provided by the Brazilian Government. By the time of my visit, all but one of our experts was gone, and he remained only as an adviser. Brazil was providing 90 per cent of the funds of a greatly increased budget for the purpose. The *servicio* was operating fifteen regional programs, three hundred health units, and twenty hospitals. It had either designed or supervised construction of hundreds of safe-water systems and had trained more than eleven thousand Brazilians for public health work. Malaria had been eliminated in large areas of the country, and great progress had been made in the treating of other diseases. More than eight million Brazilians had been served by the *servicio*. In the summer of 1960, a team of experts from The

36

Johns Hopkins University was asked to evaluate the public health program of Brazil. Two decades earlier it would have been found to be primitive, almost non-existent; in 1960, it received praise from the distinguished doctors of Johns Hopkins.

Housing conditions in Latin America are not likely to be endured peacefully much longer. Slums on the outskirts of such beautiful and modern cities as Lima, Santiago, Caracas, Rio de Janeiro, and Mexico City are among the world's worst. Attracted by the city's glittering promise, poor farmers, agricultural workers, and villagers migrate in great numbers to urban areas. When they cannot find jobs to finance rents within acceptable residential areas they are forced to pitch ramshackle huts in the muck and filth of the peripheral slums.

In the hearts of the cities, housing conditions are often substandard. One- or two-room dwellings are shared by several families; they are often without piped water, bathrooms, and other essentials basic to home life in North America. In Panama City, I was told by high officials, nine persons are cramped in each room. Homes in rural towns and Indian villages match those of the city slums.

A man who has a decent house has something worth conserving. He is apt to be more moderate in his pursuit of other goals, more likely to favor democratic change rather than violent upheaval. This is commonplace and has not been heeded in the past by many Latin-American leaders.

The United States has paid a substantial share of the cost of maintaining the OAS Center in Bogotá, which trains young architects from all Latin-American countries in the techniques and economies of low-cost housing projects. In Nicaragua, we provided funds to finance an experimental self-help housing project. As I shall explain later, the development of low-cost, self-help housing on a massive scale became a major element of the Act of Bogotá and the Charter of Punta del Este, both initiated by the United States.

Latin Americans are the first to deplore the fact that their people generally are not as productive as they should be—that every republic is deficient in the use of its human resources. In contrast, the average productivity of the individual citizen of the United States is the highest on earth; 7 per cent of the world's people live in the United States and produce 50 per cent of the world's goods.

Yet, in one sense at least, the initial advantage was with Latin America. A significant number of Europeans lived in Spanish and Portuguese

America a century before extensive colonization developed in North America. Moreover, the Spanish found important Indian civilizations, some of which were moderately well advanced in cultural and scientific areas. No North American Indian tribe could match the irrigation system, political organization, and masonry of the Incas; the arts, roads, social cohesion, and skills in mathematics and astronomy of the Mayans; the trade and commerce of the Aztecs.

The quality of the early Spanish conquerors and settlers was no less than that of the early English, Dutch, and French in North America. Both groups were composed of hardy individuals and both had their educated men.

But crucial factors favored North America.

The colonists who settled here came to stay. Motivated by a desire to escape political and religious tyrannies, they dared to bring their families with them. Few intended to get rich and return to Europe. Homes were built. Fields were cultivated. Primitive schools were established. The colonists faced their problems with the foreknowledge that what they did and what they built would have to be lived with and would affect the welfare of their descendants.

When waves of immigrants, many of them illiterate, began to come to the colonies, the conviction grew that education must have high priority. If freedom was to be meaningful, if the people were to be self-governing and creative, and if a dynamic new nation was to be built, many of the people would have to have the benefit of education.

By the close of the eighteenth century, Jeffersonian democracy had begun to elevate rule by the common people to an exalted role and, logically enough, a nationwide movement for mass education, featuring church-state separation and public and private support, was initiated. Jefferson preached an enlightened gospel: As he saw the growth of cities and the beginnings of industrialization and specialization, he contended that freedom could be maintained and enhanced only so long as there was an ever-rising level of education and understanding among all the people. He wrote the charter of the University of Virginia with such wisdom that it can serve today as a model for institutions of higher learning in the United States.

The Jeffersonian spark was fanned into flame by the equalitarianism that characterized the economic, political, and social aspects of Jacksonian democracy. By the time the United States underwent its Industrial Revolution in the nineteenth century, it was able to draw from a pool of educated, healthy, and farseeing men for its supply of workers, technicians, and managers. Science and technology spread to agriculture. When new social injustices appeared as a by-product of industrialization and urbanization, the reforms of the Theodore Roosevelt, Woodrow Wilson, and Franklin Roosevelt eras came about in short order. Many may feel, as I do, that some of these reforms went too far—to the point of endangering individual initiative and fiscal integrity of government—but there can be no doubt that the development of social justice in the United States has made it immune to the militant dogma which today threatens the nations of Latin America.

Any analysis of the achievements of the United States and its advantage over Latin America must obviously consider many factors: rich resources, an enormous free-trade area, a population of hybrid vigor, universal education moving ever toward higher levels, a philosophy which sanctifies the human spirit and fosters incentives for individual and group achievement, and a competitive enterprise system which is largely self-regulative, daring, and imbued with an inexorable momentum.

It is not one of these factors, but a blend of them all, that accounts for the growth and power of our country. I believe it is quite correct to say, however, that education is the base of the pyramid. Only an educated population can exercise the basic social power wisely, create and manage the vast productive enterprise, and create and sustain the enriching cultural phases of society. Further, education has been the wellspring of a continuing social revolution in the United States. It is important to note that social revolution began in this country with the first appearance of the colonists, proceeded with enormous force for many years, entered a period of calm for a time, and now, again, has been moving rapidly for another sixty years.

Latin America awaits its social revolution.

I have dwelt on this description of our progress only to suggest that attitudes, ideas, and motivation are as important in a country's development as are its natural resources. Some of the ingredients which have made for progress in the United States exist in all the nations of Latin America, and all of the ingredients exist to some extent in a few. But the influences which in the United States brought evolutionary change over a long period of years have been dammed up in most Latin-American countries. Reservoirs are now full. Dams threaten to collapse. In this situation, Communist propagandists need no weapon other than the prevailing order. In their viciously fought war of words, they distort the truth, ascribe sinister motives to the warmest-hearted, and promise what a Communist system can never deliver. But their most effective weapon remains what history has bequeathed to (or, more accurately, imposed upon) the people.

The time has passed when we can take refuge behind boundaries or comfort in the distance which separates us from other men. The day is gone when we can ignore injustice because it does not touch us, when we can close our ears and eyes to pain and misery which laps futilely against the walls of our own well-being and wealth. The indisputable prophecy of the past, the compelling revelation of the present, and the inevitable certainty of the future is interdependence.

4

In a shrinking world, we must enlarge our selfhood, extend our allegiances to the higher concept of mankind. As technology has condensed space and time, so has it linked our destinies and reduced the alternatives. Men will live or die together.

I WAS A FRESHMAN IN HIGH SCHOOL BEFORE FIRST VENturing forth into the great, wide world: I traveled one hundred and fifty miles down the Union Pacific tracks from Abilene to Kansas City.

At that time, I would have found it unbelievable that I would one day travel to nearly every region of the earth—and even more incredible that I would do so with greater physical comfort and less fear of the unknown than I experienced on that first trip to Kansas City.

Abilene, where I spent my youth early in this century, was a happy, self-contained community. My brothers, our friends, and all of our families lived full, unrestrained, self-sufficient lives. Virtually isolated, we were undisturbed by an intrusion from other parts of the nation or the world. Our thoughts were circumscribed, uncomplicated by events that took place beyond the range of our vision.

Our self-containment was also economic and social. A livelihood depended on our own efficiency, and on the bounty of the surrounding farmers which was determined largely by the weather. My father, who migrated to Kansas in the 1870s after a family sojourn of nearly a hundred and fifty years in Pennsylvania, used to say that when he was a boy on the prairies the most important economic problem was to trade eggs for sugar and salt.

Social life was also simple. The decades of epic poetry that had characterized the struggles of the Cavaliers and the Puritans had been followed by a good many years of pedestrian prose. The warriors for freedom, the crusaders for righteousness, and the fighting visionaries belonged to another age and no longer set the tone for Kansas. A complacency had settled with summer gentleness upon the land and the people. Children played with their neighbors in a backyard world limited only by their imagination, and their parents visited on front porches, rocking quietly in Sears, Roebuck chairs. Pleasures were homemade, unpurchased—and all the more appreciated because of that. We knew little about faraway peoples or lands and had little cause to think about them. When in the stereopticon we saw colored pictures of alien places, such as Ireland, or England, or India, we were impressed mainly by their strangeness, their differences.

Then, almost without warning, Abilene woke suddenly to the realization that shattering changes were upon the land. They were neither expected nor understood, but farmers were soon aware that despite perfect weather, hard work, and good crops, they could be hurt by a devaluation of currency in Britain or a sharp increase in tariffs in Italy. Soon, the nation called the men of Abilene to arms, not seemingly because of anything the folks of Abilene had done, but because of an explosion in the Balkans, and later because of infamy in the Pacific and in Europe. Gradually, my home town of Abilene—once a world in itself—shrank until it was an almost invisible dot on a global map.

We came to understand that man had so shaped the affairs of the world that no community could live any longer by itself. This nation's growing industrial complex demanded imports from some sixty other countries (thirty-eight separate imports go into the manufacture of an automobile), and those nations needed the dollars we paid them to buy the wheat so abundantly grown on the vast land surrounding Abilene. America had become a giant in the world, and with its wealth and strength came inevitably the burdens of world leadership, accompanied by perplexing and often frustrating responsibilities. Through our stereopticons we had glimpsed unknowingly a part of our future, for Abilene and all other American towns were forced into closer bonds of interest with faraway peoples and nations. To assure a degree of harmony in sharing a shrinking planet, the nation entered into social, cultural, and political arrangements, and then into a system of mutual security for the very preservation of lives and a democratic way of life.

The Abilene—and the Kansas—experience called for rapid changes in outlook and even in human allegiances. The first white men to enter the Kansas territory were wilderness men: hunters, trappers, explorers, completely self-reliant and solitary, with no permanent allegiance to anyone. Then came the Puritans and Cavaliers, and these necessarily felt an intense allegiance to their groups. Each man came to identify himself with his town, but (and this is important) he did so without sacrificing any of his allegiance to his family or his own inner being. He simply expanded his selfhood, his area of self-identification, considerably beyond those of the wilderness man. Soon settlements were closely bound together by highways and railroads, by laws and customs, under the aegis of state governments, and state pride was born—a still larger selfhood, a still larger area of self-identification—but again without sacrifice of allegiance to self and family and community.

For a time, the tendency toward an enlarged self-identification, toward a wider, more inclusive, and more effective allegiance became temporarily blocked. This was the period of ultra-statism and isolationism when people talked about the Bible Belt and George Washington's wisdom in admonishing us to avoid foreign entanglements. This was a time when "furriners" were a threat. But as the time passed, there came an objective understanding of, and personal identification with, all significant national problems, and still later with international affairs. This, too, was achieved without the loss of cherished allegiances to groups and institutions closer to home. People began to realize that it was possible to be interested in the world without diminishing their concern for the United States.

My own experiences, though happily of shorter duration, parallel and so illustrate those of my town and state. My own first allegiance was, of course, to my family, which was remarkably close-knit and self-sufficient. Like others, we raised nearly all of our own food, repaired our own shelter, and made our own amusements. There was no felt need to identify myself, in earliest childhood, with a special area beyond my home and family.

When I went to school I experienced the first broadening of personal allegiance. It was, surprisingly, painless. I happily identified myself with the Abilene community. Still, I had no cause to identify myself or my community, in any vital or knowledgeable way, with state, national, or world movements. When we heard about a war in a distant region of the earth, I felt only such emotions as were aroused by a good Western pulp story.

Then, when I became a college student, fifty miles from home, and drilled in the Army Training Corps in the closing months of World War I, my area of self-identification was abruptly enlarged. I began to feel the weight of the problems of Kansas and, to some degree, those of the United States. I began to see that my earlier attitudes had been narrowly limited, that the world was both larger and more complicated than I had imagined.

Indeed, this world seemed, in some of its aspects, actually terrifying when, upon my graduation, I was suddenly plunged into its problems.

When I received my bachelor's degree, the faculty offered me an instructorship, and I accepted eagerly. In the meantime, at the urging of a friend, I had also applied for a position in the United States foreign service. I had not started on my academic duties when a telegram arrived from the Secretary of State, a man named Charles Evans Hughes, offering me a post in the consulate at Edinburgh, Scotland.

I was in a dilemma. I went in to see the president of the college, Dr. William M. Jardine, one of the most affectionate, amiable men and at the same time most satisfying friends I ever had. In a few brief sentences, I explained my predicament.

He leaned back in his chair and said, "You're fired. There is no place in this institution for you during the next two years." Then he grinned. "After that, if you want to return to academic work, I guarantee a place for you on the faculty. Now go away and make up your mind!"

Today, thoroughly immersed as I am in the venerable traditions and intricate methods of faculty control of college and university education, I am amused by the highhanded way in which my dismissal was handled and the promise of a future academic appointment given.

At the moment of my dismissal—the kindest favor ever bestowed upon me—began a concern for international affairs which has continued throughout my lifetime.

First in Scotland, then in Washington, D.C., still later in Europe, the Middle East, and Africa, and finally in nearly all the republics of Latin America, I was required to identify myself personally with problems far outside any area of allegiance I had known before. In the beginning I was, quite naturally, bewildered by the novelty and complexity of these problems, and even more especially by attitudes I encountered abroad. I recall how inadequate and even insecure I felt when on the first assignment in Great Britain I found resentment of the United States because we expected repayment of the loans we had made to that country during World War I.

With a wisdom that was wholly accidental (for it was only a statement made in argument) I suggested to my British acquaintances that if they would cancel the debt which the British Government owed to its own people, we of the United States might be more amenable to canceling what Britain owed us.

Indignantly they scoffed at my ignorance. An internal debt was clearly distinguishable from an external one. Why should the citizens of Britain cancel the bonds they held? The government owed them money, didn't it? But an external debt was quite a different matter. Payment of it would cause imbalances in international exchange, and in any case hadn't Britain fought the war for us while we belatedly made up our minds to come in for the common protection of freedom?

My sense of direction at this point was far from being developed, and my confusion was monumental. But gradually I came to understand that each nation, like each family, thinks first of its own welfare. What it advocates for the community of nations, it may be unwilling to adopt as a principle in internal affairs. Foreign relations of all nations are developed within this concept of self-interest. One hopes that self-interest will achieve a high level of enlightenment, for the crucial problem, obviously, is to have national interest and the interest of the community of nations coincide, or to have the goals of the international community so shared and so persuasive as to induce all nations to subordinate those selfish internal purposes which are not in accord with the general good. In other words, our task is to develop, at least among the free nations and eventually among all nations, a true allegiance to the common destiny of mankind, without in any way diminishing—indeed, by strengthening—allegiance to nation, state, community, and family.

This concept finds at least verbal expression, if not genuine commitment, in such phrases as "the Atlantic Community," "the American family of nations," "the West," and "Western civilization."

We are, it seems to me, in a transitional period in history in which we are groping for the means of making effective supra-national allegiances, for we know that only through effective economic, social, and military cooperation can we hope to achieve our own national destiny. But efforts to make this larger allegiance firm and dependable often break down as national interests prevail. In this regard, I think it must be conceded that the record of the United States, while not unblemished, is equal and in many respects superior to that of any other country. Perhaps this is partly due to our exacting interdependence with many other nations and to the responsibility of world leadership which has been placed upon us; but surely it is also an indication of a maturing outlook.

The phrase "the American family of nations" has special significance for us. The United States is in a very real sense the heart of the inter-American system, not only because of our great strength, but also because we are convinced that our own welfare and that of the other American republics are inextricably bound together.

Having spent a good many years trying to help improve relations among the nations of the Western Hemisphere, I suspect I will be charged with bias when I contend that good relations in this area are truly imperative to our future—*more important, in fact, than our relations with any other area of the world.*

This conviction is not new. It is not, I think, a vested position, resulting simply from a special responsibility spread through time. I had come to this conclusion long before President Eisenhower asked me, in 1953, to undertake the series of assignments in Latin America as his Personal Representative. I was persuaded then, as I am now, that stable, satisfactory relations between the United States and the nations of Latin America are crucial as we seek to build a cooperative peace characterized by freedom and rising levels of well-being.

There is abundant evidence of hemispheric interdependence.

The trade of the United States with the Latin-American republics was about $3.5 billion in each direction in 1953, and today it totals about $4 billion.

As a market for our industrial and commercial exports, Latin America is as important to us as all of Europe, and more important than Asia, Africa, and Oceania combined. Our sales to Latin America encompass the entire range of our national production. And Latin-American republics import more from the United States than from Europe or the other continents.

Reciprocally, the United States is of key importance to every Latin-American country, both as a market for their products and as a source of essential imports.

The copper, tin, zinc, iron ore, manganese, and other minerals we obtain from Latin America are vital constituent parts of the machinery we in turn ship there. The dollars we spend on coffee, sugar, tropical fruits, and wool, as well as metals, finance their purchase of transportation and industrial equipment and many consumer goods. The industrial and military items produced by the United States to defend the free world require a continuing supply of a great variety of strategic materials from Latin America.

This trade on the whole is mutually advantageous, though my friends in Latin America dispute this. Their disagreement stems from one of the most serious problems in inter-American affairs—the shifting relationship of what are called free market and administered prices. This has been a severe handicap to Latin-American economies, and although I understand

and sympathize, I must point out (and discuss more fully later) that the United States cannot be held to blame.

United States private and public loans and investments in Latin America exceed $11 billion.

More than 30 per cent of all United States *private*, long-term foreign investment is in Latin America. It totaled about $6 billion in 1953 when I began my official studies, and it amounts to more than $9 billion today; this is larger than the amount United States enterprisers have invested in any other part of the world, save Canada. Such investment of private capital is important not only to the United States as an earning asset, but also to Latin America as a stimulant to productivity and economic progress. It contributes to the development of individual countries in practically all fields of endeavor, from electric power and heavy industry to the manufacture of finished goods and their distribution to consumers.

Contrary to the outrageous and continuous criticisms of Communists and ultra-nationalists in Latin America (that the United States is exploiting the country and the peasant, that we are in league with the rich landowners and dictators to oppress the people), United States private capital has helped conquer the wilderness, expand employment, raise wages, construct hospitals and schools, and raise the living standards of at least some of the Latin-American people. As I shall point out later, the historic record is spotted but the modern record is good. Unfortunately, the historic record lingers in memory, and the contribution of American private capital is not always understood or appreciated; often its incursions into Latin-American life are used spuriously to "prove" our "enmity" to the people.

Aside from some worthless bonds sold to America by Argentina and several other Latin-American countries during the 1920s and expropriation of American property in Mexico, Bolivia, and Cuba, United States private investment in Latin America has earned a satisfactory return. In some countries, the retained earnings average higher than they do in the United States, and the amounts brought back to the United States for distribution to stockholders give individual investors about the same return on their money as do investments in the United States.

The record of *public* loans to Latin-American countries is even better than that of private credits and investments. Public credits extended to our southern neighbors have exceeded $4 billion, half of which has been repaid. With the exception of Cuba, our sister republics have established a persuasive record in using this capital wisely, and in repaying the loans with interest and on time. The loans have enabled Latin-American nations to build highways, airports, and piers; to irrigate lands and open new areas to cultivation; to combat inflation and to improve and expand mining and industrial enterprises.

Military relations between Latin-American countries and the United States are closely related to economic interdependence, to the role being played by the United States in defense of the free world, and to the strategic location of our countries with respect to one another.

The military strength of Latin-American nations is relatively small, designed mainly to preserve internal order—though sometimes also for the sake of national prestige. It would be fallacious and dangerous, however, to assume that the military weakness of the Latin-American nations indicates that they are not significant in the system of collective security which the free world has tried so desperately to build.

In the event of war—assuming that hydrogen bombs would not bring about mutual annihilation in a few hours or days—some of the essential resources of the world would undoubtedly fall into the hands of the enemy. The resources of Latin America would then be of enhanced importance. A Latin America under the control of or allied with our enemy could deny these resources to us and open broad lines of attack against us. And Fidel Castro has demonstrated with devastating clarity that "it can happen here"!

We have been generally preoccupied with the Soviet Union, her satellites, and the nations along the periphery of the Communist powers. We have concentrated a good deal of our economic aid and nearly all of our military assistance in Europe, the Middle East, southeast Asia, and the remainder of the Far East—in nations whose military forces are deemed to be essential in halting the forceful spread of Communism. But we should not believe, as too many unfortunately do, that the republics of Latin America are, in a military sense, the backyard of our world.

When Communism threatened to engulf Guatemala in 1954 the American people became uneasy. For the first time we began to fear that the *backyard* could suddenly become a path for Communist invasion and a haven for Communist subversion. We breathed in relief when forces favoring democracy restored Guatemala to its normal place in the American family of nations, and we proceeded to forget the truth that had begun forcing its way into our consciousness.

The victory of the egocentric, brutish Castro over the despicable dictator Batista, the subsequent partnership of Castro with Khrushchev, Khrushchev's blatant threat to rain missiles on the United States should it invade Cuba, the establishment of Cuba as a focal point of propaganda and subversion for Castro Communism, and the presence of Soviet missile bases in Cuba—these ominous events belatedly caused us to realize with distressing abruptness that Latin America is not and never has been, militarily, a "backyard" in the modern world struggle.

A friendly Latin America, on the other hand, can do more than provide strategic materials; it can help guard the lines of communication and shipment, including the Panama Canal. It can provide logistics bases for our armed forces. It can, as several countries did in World Wars I and II and in the Korean War, supply forces trained in the use of standardized weapons.

Yet to me, the greatest military importance of Latin America, in the coalition of the free world, is not in what it is or has, but in what it might be—for itself and for the cause of freedom and humanity. Whether this great potentiality will ever be realized depends upon many things. Surely we can find in it added incentive to encourage the nations of Latin America to accept far-reaching social reforms, to foster universal education, and to undergo periods of austerity as an essential starting point in solid and accelerated economic growth.

The military, financial, and economic interdependence of the American republics is matched by their political and cultural interrelationships. Despite recurring difficulties, most of the nations of this hemisphere have been dependable political partners.

The United States supported the Latin-American nations in their struggle for freedom hesitantly and weakly, to be sure, but with considerable good effect. The doctrine enunciated in 1823 by President Monroe was designed to protect the newly won independence of nations of this hemisphere and to permit the community as a whole to grow to maturity free from domination by any transoceanic power.

Working together, the nations of this hemisphere have frequently developed political principles and techniques of international collaboration which later have been adopted by other parts of the world. Thus, the present global student exchange and technical cooperation programs were initiated by action of the United States and other American republics before World War II. The NATO Treaty of 1949 was foreshadowed by the Act of Chapultepec of 1945 and the Treaty of Rio de Janeiro of 1947. The inter-American system, the most influential regional grouping in the world, preceded the United Nations.

The American republics, significantly, developed the principle of the sovereign equality of nations. Indeed, it may be proudly said that the American republics have been building a system under which all nations, great and small, poor and rich, educated and illiterate, may live together in peace, and in a desire to help one another. (The bases of this cooperation are set forth in the charter of the Organization of American States.)

The record of the American nations in settling disputes by peaceful means has been unique, and this hemisphere has therefore generally been spared the destruction and bloodshed which have so often occurred in other parts of the world.

Latin-American nations and the United States have worked and voted together in the United Nations and other international organizations on most political issues.

Abiding political relationships between the United States and the Latin-American nations are of supreme importance to every citizen of the hemisphere. If we, with our long record of cooperation, should falter in our relationships, what hope can there be for cooperative progress toward peace in a larger world where the record has been far less encouraging?

Unfortunately, discernible cracks in the inter-American structure have appeared.

The people of the United States have been shocked by the failure of the Latin-American masses to view Castroism in the same way we do; by the crude disregard of the constitution and free elections in Argentina which resulted in the imprisonment of President Frondizi; by the attacks upon us in Panama; by the partial disaffection of Brazil, the largest country in Latin America, into which we have poured generous amounts of aid. This generation of Americans does not feel responsible for the unwise acts of earlier leaders and is eager to begin anew with a bold and imaginative alliance. Yet, much recent literature in Latin America has repeatedly recalled some of the less happy events of history as if they had occurred today. We admit United States intervention in the internal affairs of Latin-American countries and many instances of downright imperialism—but these things are done with, and we would like to forget them and attend to the business at hand: building a dependable and mutually beneficial partnership.

Recent incidents, attitudes, and disaffections merit calm analysis. They should not prejudice us prematurely, or blind us to the larger fact of inescapable interdependence.

Nations of great cultural diversity must cooperate in the struggle for peace within freedom, justice, and higher living standards, no matter what provocations may arise. This is surely a difficult and trying task; it is by no means insurmountable. We have the problems of cultural diversity in the United States. Labor struggles with management; Catholics oppose federal aid to public schools exclusively; sections of the South cling to traditions and a way of life that are distasteful to most of the North; liberals and conservatives struggle for supremacy in local, state, and federal governments; even people of Irish and German descent have been known to come to blows in Pennsylvania. But in diversity we have found unity. There are sufficient common beliefs, allegiances, and aspirations among the disparate groups in the United States to make democratic cooperation lasting and effective.

Certainly cooperation is more difficult to achieve among nations with great cultural diversity. This is the root of the East-West struggle: The Communist nations of the East, with their rejection of God and adherence to a militant, imperialistic, dialectical materialism are in violent opposition to the nations of the West with their deeply felt adherence to the cardinal principles of the Judaeo-Christian philosophy.

At least the diversity in the Western hemisphere (though notable) is within the philosophic framework of Western civilization—a civilization which seeks to establish and maintain institutions and processes that will attain supreme human values and rules of conduct proclaimed by its religious concepts.

Until recently, the culture of Latin America was oriented toward Europe. The leaders of these nations came in great numbers from Spain and Portugal. Many came from England, Italy, and Ireland. For generations, those who could afford to do so sent their children to Europe to be educated.

During the past thirty-five years, this has changed remarkably. Today, nearly 85 per cent of the students of Latin America who go abroad for study come to the United States. Nearly eight thousand students from Venezuela alone are now in preparatory schools, colleges, and universities of the United States. And thousands more would come if they could afford it. Their tourist travel is predominantly to the United States. Large numbers of United States citizens live in Latin America and each year hundreds of thousands more enjoy the rewarding experiences of travel in Latin America. Bi-national institutes and courses in schools are making English the second language of Latin America.

In short, there is an enriching cross-fertilization between our predominantly Anglo-Saxon culture and the Latin culture (often blended with strong and proud Indian influences) of the other American republics.

The true significance of cultural exchange and interinfluence is this: Abiding cooperation must begin with common goals. In a broad sense, at least, we have these common goals. However, unless there is more than a superficial knowledge of and sympathy for one another's cultures, problems, and hopes, economic, political, and military cooperation will crumble under the strain of crises. And the one thing I can say with certainty is that Latin-American nations will face in coming years crises enough to try even the most tempered relationships.

Despite acknowledged interdependence and common goals, neither the United States nor Latin America has succeeded in eliminating the ignorance and the persistent, sometimes almost malicious, misunderstandings which prevent us from solving perplexing problems. Both sides must realize that genuine understanding and fruitful cooperation do not spring up spontaneously; they flow only from hard, determined effort. Both sides need to dig deeply into the facts and circumstances which cause problems to dangle and irritate, to elude any solution. Each government must understand and sympathize with the other's problems, methods, purposes, actions, and failures to act. And each must know whether good or bad faith is involved.

Since in most of the American republics the basic social power resides in the people, regardless of their degree of democracy (in only a few are the people ignored), it is obviously imperative that the people as well as the governments understand. Foreign policy today is rarely formed by small cliques. It is influenced by agricultural, labor, industrial, educational, and civic organizations—all of whom, whether informed or ignorant, find myriad ways to influence national governments and international councils.

I must emphasize that those responsible for improving relations among nations must focus much of their effort on mutual understanding. They must use existing methods and find new ones to clear away the underbrush of ignorance which chokes off any lasting political, cultural, economic, and military cooperation.

Nations, like people, have dignity and pride; friendship between large and small nations can only grow out of respect—respect for each other's rights, interests, goals, and sensibilities. In inter-American affairs, we may subscribe to this requisite of mutual respect; we may observe closely the requisite of sovereign equality of states which demands that problems be solved by negotiation rather than coercion; we may sincerely strive to observe the requisite that all American nations adhere to mutual goals of peace, freedom, independence, and prosperity. We may (and I believe we do) meet all these essential requirements for cooperation among American nations and still fail, unless we also bring about a far better understanding among governments and peoples than now exists.

On one trip to the southernmost countries of Latin America, I spent an hour with an intelligent Uruguayan. He was an ardent Christian, anti-Communist, and ultra-nationalist. He also was familiar, at least superficially, with history, and he said to me earnestly and with some passion: "You of the United States are to blame for the rise of Castroism in Cuba and its acceptance by many others in this hemisphere. You seized the island from Spain and opened it to your robber barons who plundered most of its basic resources. You forced the Cuban workers to produce a single crop so that, in turn, they could get industrial products only from you. You allied yourself with the Cuban leaders who crushed the common people under their boots."

I was stunned by the bluntness and bitterness of his speech. This young man, perhaps twenty-four years old, comes from a prominent family wealthy enough to permit him to get a university education. He belongs to a left-wing but not Communist youth organization which meets regularly to discuss national and international problems. He is articulate, personable and, in a political sense, magnetic. I suspect he is destined to be one of the future political leaders of his country. If his lack of understanding is as great as his statement seemed to reveal, if his feelings are as deep as he displayed, what must be the attitudes of the masses of Latin America who have had far less opportunity than he to read, listen, analyze, and discuss the basic issues that will shape our common future? And, perhaps more importantly, where but to disaster can such misunderstanding lead?

5 We cannot afford the luxury of ignorance; it costs too much.

IN THE 1960 PRESIDENTIAL CAMPAIGN, BOTH CANDIDATES made assertions about the dangerous situation in Cuba which did nothing to enlighten the people of the United States and caused considerable puzzlement in Latin America. I was disappointed. It has always seemed to me that a nationwide presidential campaign should be a mammoth exercise in adult education. Each candidate should adhere scrupulously to the truth as he sees it and give his honest judgments on major issues.

During the television debate on October 21, 1960, Senator Kennedy referred to testimony given before a Senate Committee by Ambassadors Arthur Gardner and Earl E. T. Smith, both of whom had been in Cuba during the Batista regime and were known to be friendly to Batista. Smith, who had followed Gardner in the post, was replaced by a career officer when Castro came to power. Said candidate Kennedy: "[they] warned of Castro, [and] the Marxist influence around Castro . . . both of them have testified that, in spite of their warnings to the American Government, nothing was done." A few moments later, he said scornfully: "Most of the equipment and arms and resources for Castro came from the United States, flown out of Florida and other parts of the United States to Castro in the mountains."

These statements could only be interpreted to mean that our government knew, when Gardner and Smith were ambassadors in Cuba, that Castro was a Communist and that therefore we should have opposed his revolutionary seizure of power; we should have supported Batista against Castro.

54

Nothing could so have guaranteed a permanent loss for the United States in Latin America, as I shall amplify later. The senator must have known this. He had made speeches on the floor of the Senate, prior to Castro's regime, denouncing Batista as one of the most hated dictators in hemispheric history. But at the time of the campaign, Batista was no longer an issue. Castro was. So misstatements of fact and attitude seemed to promise at least a temporary political advantage—*domestically*.

Vice President Nixon, in replying, had a strategic opportunity to tell the correct story: Our abhorrence of all dictators; our imposition of strict neutrality toward the forces in Cuba nine months before its climactic conclusion; our patient efforts to woo Castro to democratic procedures, including free elections; our unprecedented tolerance in suffering insults in the vain hope that Castro would in time accept the fundamental concepts which govern relations among the American republics.

Nixon did not do this. Instead, he, too, directed his gibes only at Castro. He told of efforts, when it had become clear that Castro was determined to go the route of imperialistic Communism, to isolate Cuba and to obtain a censure of Castro by our sister republics. He also spoke of the massive aid which the Eisenhower administration had poured into Latin America. But he, like Kennedy, missed the mark widely.

Many people in the United States do not as yet understand the full implications of the Cuban affair. The television debate compounded their confusion. In Latin America, the effects of the debate were dismal, indeed. Latin Americans found in them confirmation of their belief that we preferred Batista because he had protected our property rights, and we hated Castro solely because of his alliance with Soviet Russia.

If understanding is the basis of respect, and respect is the basis of cooperation, our esteemed presidential candidates provided prime examples of how not to strengthen our multilateral society. Because of misunderstanding generated by irresponsibility and ignorance, the foundations of our inter-American alliance are precariously weak. Surely the fault is with Latin America as well as the United States. But our shortcoming is more pronounced and reprehensible, for it is due primarily to ignorance. Theirs is chiefly due to misinterpretation.

I became highly sensitive during the early months of World War II to the urgent need for international understanding as a prerequisite to achieving national purposes. President Roosevelt asked me to make a governmental study which shortly thereafter led to his issuing an Executive Order establishing the Office of War Information, now the United States Information Agency. Roosevelt appointed Elmer Davis Director and me Associate Director of the Office of War Information.

In the overseas branch of OWI, our aim was threefold: (1) to keep our allies accurately informed of United States purposes and actions so that cooperation would not falter when differences of opinion arose; (2) to persuade neutrals to remain neutral or to join the allied cause; and (3) to confound the enemy by making the German and Japanese peoples aware of Allied victories which their governments tried to keep from them and by trying to persuade them of the justice of the Allied cause.

To tailor our information precisely to the several target areas, we needed to know the prevailing attitudes of the peoples and governments toward the United States, and we set out to learn them.

I shall never forget the rude shock when our research staff brought in its findings. While views about us varied country by country, and especially by the Allied, neutral, and enemy categories, there was a stereotype that permeated them all: The Americans are all rich, nightclubbish, gangsterish, addicted to licentious pleasures, prejudiced, and incurably frivolous in their outlook upon the world.

Why should there be such absurd misconceptions? The research staff had an answer: The most powerful and universal interpreter of the United States in all foreign nations was the motion picture. Attitudes created by Hollywood were fortified by other "evidence."

I recalled working as a young vice consul in Edinburgh. The Scots, too, had developed a stereotype of us that was based on motion-picture characters and themes. This view was then substantiated, they felt, by the indisputable evidence provided by the two hundred thousand Americans who visited Edinburgh each year. Fully 90 per cent of them, unobtrusive and well-mannered, went unnoticed. But perhaps ten per cent, loud and uninhibited, confirmed the Hollywood caricature. An American was frivolous, uncultured, and rich, always drove a sleek black car, and wore a dinner suit with a bow tie too carefully knotted. Books offered additional support for their stereotype. Sinclair Lewis' *Babbitt* achieved wide circulation in Scotland, as it did in Western Europe, generally.

Our misconceptions of others are often as ridiculous as theirs are of us. Thus, our stereotypes of the Latin American are definite and erroneous: He is lazy, darkly handsome, and capricious. He insists upon a siesta no matter what, and he prefers a palace revolution to an election. His philosophy is revealed in one word—*mañana*. To us, Latin Americans are happy natives with ruffled sleeves and broad-brimmed hats, dancing and strumming guitars.

The intellectual problems we struggled with during the war to correct misunderstandings were miniatures compared to those of today. Russian propaganda, incessant and global (in more than forty languages), depends for its effectiveness on the constant repetition of the big lie, on giving its own evil meanings to good words and ideas. The only antidote to lies is truth. But truth to be most effective must precede the lie; then the lie will not be believed. In the absence of truth, lies spread rapidly, like leaves in a gale.

Before we consider the intellectual shortcomings of others—and particularly their response to world propaganda in the cold war—we should first look anxiously and objectively at our own.

How many Americans, I wonder, would be so ill-informed as to inquire, as a man did of me as I was preparing to depart on a fact-finding trip: "What is the capital of Latin America, anyhow?" I find it unbelievable but true that although we want in an emotional way to be thought of as good neighbors, we know pitifully little about them. Hence, we are often guilty of wishful thinking, or of fruitless non-thinking, and of ill-conceived positive action which does not reflect informed, critical reasoning.

The average citizen of the United States knows more about Europe and the Soviet bloc, and possibly more about the Middle East, than he does about Latin America. Former President Alberto Lleras Camargo of Colombia points out that "North Americans are inclined to judge all of Latin America in a lump . . . Every report of an act of violence or arbitrariness is thought of as applying to the entire area. The stable and democratic countries, or the periods of stability and democracy in a single country, do not receive enough notice to counteract this impression."

The area is generally neglected by our elementary and secondary schools, and only a few colleges and universities have study sequences which penetrate deeply into Latin-American history, political economy, political science, diplomacy, and culture. In the public schools, students learn of Latin America only as it appears in American history courses. Geography, as taught traditionally, did little more than list principal products, capital cities, major rivers, and mountain ranges. Students learning Spanish gently brush the edges of Latin-American culture. But, to my knowledge, our high school students have no elective course in Latin-American history which compares with those in American or European history. Institutions of higher learning are only slightly better. I know of a major university which offered a program in Latin-American studies but had to abandon it: only one student enrolled.

During most of the century, the mass media of the United States only occasionally carried news reports from the twenty republics, and these usually covered highly dramatized events which were lifted out of the context of national life. Such events, violent political upheaval, for example, fitted neatly into our preconceptions. They were doubly misleading. They told us nothing of heroic efforts in some countries to overcome illiteracy, of persistent attempts to solve public health problems, of the economic struggles of the millions of people whose income might be little more than a hundred dollars a year, of the efforts of liberal and enlightened groups to fight Communism while seeking to persuade powerful leaders to enact social reform before violence erupts. Nor did they tell us of the strong tide-flow toward democratic institutions in some countries or of actions which we sometimes took that were needlessly harmful to them.

Dean Edward W. Barrett and Professor Penn T. Kimball of the Graduate School of Journalism at Columbia University, in a background paper prepared for an American Assembly meeting in 1959, pointed out that "With a few notable exceptions, newspapers . . . give minute space to the other Americas. Whether this be cause or effect, the level of interest in and knowledge of Latin Americans among even educated United States citizens appears shockingly low." Evidently reporters and broadcasters do not believe that their clients are interested in Latin America. Barrett and Kimball noted that the failure to provide news "perpetuates the ignorance of the reader, and this ignorance leads to the lack of interest."

No news is good news, some say, but from Latin America we have played good news as no news.

For a time, when Communism threatened Guatemala, our mass media sent special reporters and commentators to Central America, and inflow of information to us increased in volume and quality. Soon, however, as leaders friendly to the United States took control of the government, an indifferent silence ensued. This silence was again rudely shattered when Castro took over in Cuba and formed an open alliance with Russia. The flow of news from the south increased, too, when Brazil, traditional friend of the United States, hesitated in making a decision as to neutralism or a modified alliance with the United States or a possible coalition with the Soviet Union. It picked up with the trouble in the Dominican Republic and then again with the toppling of Frondizi in Argentina.

Recently, the Board of Governors of the new Inter-American Bank met in Buenos Aires and listened for three days to eloquent speeches by Latin

Americans in behalf of the Alliance for Progress. But in our newspapers, this chorus of praise was nearly obscured by reports of two speeches critical of the Alliance.

In Mexico City, according to reputable United States correspondents who were there, an American television camera crew *hired* Mexican students to stage an anti-*Yanqui* demonstration when the announced Castro Communist demonstration failed to materialize.

In 1958, when I was in Panama, our press carried major stories of students "picketing the United States Embassy." But all the students had done was to post some signs saying: "The Canal is ours," "Give us half the revenue," and so on. On that same trip through Central America, I was accompanied by a contingent of United States reporters who were waiting to see a repeat of the violent demonstrations two months before against Vice President Nixon. When nothing happened, the reporters filed dozens of stories about the "excess security guards."

Although I keep reminding myself of the necessity to sell newspapers, I cannot help feeling angry and disgruntled with the United States press.

With only sporadic attention to critical developments in Latin America, the mass media have been little better than our schools in contributing to that human comprehension which would help translate into effective action the emotional friendship we hold for the people of Latin America.

Even now, as newspapers, magazines, and television carry more news and more interpretive features about Latin America, the information tends to spread in a vacuum, for most of us do not have the knowledge of Latin-American history, culture, and problems to assess events correctly. Hence, the news tends to shatter our composure, to change our characteristic and shallow emotional desire for friendship into temporary hostility. In short, we are either angry when we think of Latin America these days, or we don't think of it at all. This is surely true when we, believing as we do in our own national integrity, learn that Latin Americans do not always accept without reservations our assurances of good intentions.

The educated among them know our history as well as their own. They are aware of the condescending attitude of the United States toward them for a hundred years and of our numerous interventions and acts of imperialism. They find it difficult to trust us completely, to overlook the possibility of new offenses.

It is galling to us to have to persuade them, by word and deed, again and again, that the historic change in our policy which occurred formally at Montevideo in 1933 (when Secretary of State Cordell Hull gave formal expression to the Good Neighbor policy) now gives positive assurance that we will not again violate their sovereignty, that we are committed to the policy of free choice for all peoples, and that we will cooperate with them fairly and continuously in workable programs designed to contribute to their welfare and uphold their national dignity.

Our assurances do indeed come into question when we take action that injures both the dignity and the economy of Latin America. We took just such action in the late 1950s.

The trouble began in Congress with certain legislation that, as it developed, hurt the economies of Mexico, Nicaragua, Peru, and other nations. Back in 1933, the United States, in an attempt to establish fair prices for domestically grown cotton, gradually induced our farmers to reduce cotton plantings by 7,300,000 acres. This, among other things, caused our exports to decline. Other countries, including Mexico, Nicaragua, and Peru, responded naturally to the world market situation and increased their cotton plantings by 7,000,000 acres. Mexican cotton production rose from 500,000 bales in 1933 to 2,000,000 in 1958. Mexico built gins, highways, and other facilities to handle this enlarged undertaking. Cotton became the main earner of foreign exchange.

Then, a quarter of a century after our cotton program was initiated, the Congress decided it was time for us to regain our historic share of the world cotton market. Without consulting the Secretary of State—thus giving our diplomats no chance to meet with leaders of Mexico and other nations—the Congress directed the Secretary of Agriculture to subsidize the export of American cotton to whatever extent was required for us to be competitive. The subsidy began at five cents a pound and was later increased. All of this the Congress accomplished most cleverly—by inserting a legislative rider in an indispensable appropriation act which the President was compelled to approve.

Latin American reaction to this move—which immediately disrupted the economies of Mexico and other countries—was quick, deep, and bitter. Leaders there did not criticize the United States for wanting to regain or retain a fair share of the world cotton market. This they could understand. What they could not comprehend, and the point to which their sharpest criticism was directed, was the failure of a friendly nation to consult them in advance on methods to ease the impact of a sudden change in American policy. They also spoke vehemently of our observing and defending one policy for twenty-five years and then, without warning, adopting another.

President Eisenhower, then Under Secretary of State Christian A. Herter, R. R. Rubottom Jr., Assistant Secretary of State for Inter-American Affairs, Thomas C. Mann, Assistant Secretary for Economic Affairs, and other officials moved quickly to repair damaged relationships as best they could. After frequent and prolonged consultations, and at the initiative of the United States, an inter-American consultative council on cotton was set up. Members of the council represented the American nations whose production and sale of cotton had importance to their economies; its purpose was to maintain mutual information on production, marketing, and prices, and possible changes in intentions and plans of the participants. The mere assurance that we would not again take such action without consultation did a little to ease the shock.

From conversations with legislative leaders, I am convinced that the Congress had no intention of injuring Mexico and other Latin countries. But ignorance must be classed as a cardinal sin in almost all human endeavors, and certainly in those affecting international relations.

Unfortunately, a second incident during the same period did nothing to help the situation. During World War II, marginal lead and zinc mines were opened in the United States to meet war demand. They remained in production after the war ended. Eventually, world surpluses of these metals forced prices down. Producers, including Canada, Mexico, and Peru, became quite concerned and urged the development of an international marketing agreement, based on the principles of the international wheat agreement, which they hoped would at least temporarily help stabilize world prices.

The issue became a serious political one in the United States. Demands for congressional action to impose higher tariffs on lead and zinc became almost irresistible. Although congressmen from the states affected by this one problem could not muster enough votes among themselves to enact legislation, coalitions are quick to develop in Congress. Groups threatened (or fearful of being threatened) by imports willingly support the minority, in anticipation of similar cooperation when they might themselves need help.

To forestall a special tariff action by Congress, President Eisenhower instituted a quota system, which temporarily reduced our importations of the metals whose prices were declining.

While shortly thereafter prices of lead and zinc became fairly stable, our unilateral action on quotas was a discordant note in inter-American harmony. Fortunately, representatives of the injured countries recognized the pressure-group politics; they also knew that the President chose the lesser of two evils.

Again, the Congress was thinking exclusively of the welfare of one segment of our private enterprise. More distressing, perhaps, was that Congress gave no indication that it was even aware of the consequences in the hemisphere if higher tariffs were levied on lead and zinc. The President knew. For eight years he promoted liberal trade policies in the belief that stability and liberality in the rules of trade are in our own best interest as well as in the interest of friendly nations. Of the scores of appeals for restrictive measures brought before him, he reluctantly took action unfavorable to others on only four commodities. It was an unparalleled record—but across-the-board records offer slight comfort to nations hurt by one quota.

These examples suggest how domestic actions, sometimes taken with little thought of Latin-American relations, can seriously deter larger purposes. They also demonstrate an alarming ignorance or apathy among legislative representatives. The people of this country fail to realize this. Nor do they seem to comprehend that restrictions on trade and subsidization of exports do not benefit the general economy of the United States. Yet this was the aim of the offending measures.

What actually occurred in both of these situations was the transfer of an economic disadvantage from concentrated groups to widely diffused groups. How? Look at the effect of these actions on our trade with Mexico alone.

In rounded averages, we sell to Mexico each year about $900 million in goods and services and buy about $550 million in return. The disparity in these transactions is usually covered by a Mexican net gain in tourist expenditures; some 550,000 Americans visit Mexico annually and spend from $500 million to $600 million. Fewer Mexican visitors to the United States spend less and the discrepancy in international exchange of goods and services is about balanced. In some years, when the balance is not so tidily achieved, a flow of additional investment capital from the United States to Mexico helps maintain fairly constant dollar reserves in Mexican banks.

A substantial decline in Mexico's dollar earnings, due to her failure to sell cotton, lead, and zinc in normal quantities, results almost automatically in a reduction of Mexican purchases of American manufactured products. She buys fewer motor cars, building materials, heavy equipment, and consumer goods of all kinds. Our actions on cotton, lead, and zinc were quickly followed by Mexican tariff increases, by Executive action, on hundreds of manufactured items normally imported from the United States.

The total consequence, then, was this: Domestically we transferred an economic disadvantage from the producers of cotton, lead, and zinc, to a great multitude of industries, but the loss to any of these other industries was too slight to bring these groups marching to Washington to demand corrective action in *their* behalf. Internationally, we lost. The economies of several friendly nations were injured; tempers rose and led to retaliatory measures; our good faith in adhering to policies that recognize mutuality of interest was again brought into question.

We should gain maturity of judgment from such events as these, for in a changing world our Congress will often be faced with demands to protect a minority at the expense of the national welfare. In each case persuasive arguments will be developed. Rather than to shuffle economic difficulty from one segment of society to another at the expense of the nation and our allies, it would be preferable and cheaper in the long run to finance an adjustment within the disadvantaged domestic group. We would have been wiser to let the high-cost domestic producers of zinc and lead close their mines, and then, through financial aid and training, help owners and workers find outlets in economically justifiable enterprises. Since I first suggested this in an article published in the *Country Gentleman* in 1942, I cannot be accused of grasping for a principle that is merely protective of inter-American affairs.

As demonstrated by the 1960 presidential campaign debates mentioned at the beginning of this chapter, misunderstandings about Latin America are sometimes fomented by political candidates who are willing to mar our national reputation abroad for an assumed temporary domestic advantage.

In the campaign of 1956, Adlai Stevenson declared that I had assumed responsibility for United States relations with Latin America, that I had, on a visit to Argentina in 1953, offered vast sums of money to dictator Juan Perón, and that the Administration had in fact put money into Argentina. "A principal result," he said, "seems to have been to allow Perón to take money out of Argentina—for himself."

Mr. Stevenson must have known his statements were incorrect. Yet, even when Secretary of State Dulles issued a coldly factual statement to the effect that my conversations with Perón had not touched upon the question of loans, that the Administration had not lent and had no intention of lending money to the Perón Government (the previous Democratic administration had lent Argentina many millions of dollars), the charge was repeated to a nationwide television audience. Perhaps the candidate won some votes; he may have embarrassed some Republicans; and he succeeded in raising my blood pressure a few points. But the real damage done by his misrepresentation of fact was in Latin America. There his remarks were carried prominently in the press at the very time that the

United States was being accused of cherishing freedom and democracy for itself while supporting dictators in Latin America.

It is true that the Eisenhower administration, for military reasons and on the basis of procedures developed to the point of final action by the Truman administration, had decorated the dictator of Venezuela and the quasi-dictator of Peru. That most of the nations of Latin America had done the same, and with much more pomp, did not excuse the bad judgment of the United States. I did not know about these two incidents until months later. Then I learned that the State Department had been unhappy about the decorations, but the military view, that this was necessary diplomatically, had prevailed. These two mistakes made Stevenson's Perón story all the more credible at a time when the dictator was most detested throughout the hemisphere.

Had it not been serious, I could have been amused. President Eisenhower, Foster Dulles, and I had been uncertain for several weeks over whether I should go to Argentina on that first ten-nation study-goodwill visit. The arguments against going were obvious. But there were arguments in favor of such a visit. In 1953, Perón was doing all that he could to organize a so-called "third force," aimed against the United States, and primed throughout the hemisphere by labor attachés in the Argentine embassies. We wanted to analyze both the methods and the effectiveness of this anti-United States campaign, and it seemed desirable to try developing information at the source of the trouble. But more important, shortly before my trip began, Perón had issued an order which prohibited the circulation of American newspapers and magazines in Argentina, and had given notice to the United Press, Associated Press, and International News Service that they would not be permitted to send dispatches from the country. American newspapermen would have to leave.

Secretary Dulles called in the Washington heads of the three press associations and outlined the dilemma we faced in deciding whether I should visit Argentina on this first mission. The unanimous advice, vigorously stated, was that I should stop in Buenos Aires at least for a short time. So the schedule was devised in such a way that I would be in Argentina on a Saturday and a Sunday—Perón normally spent weekends at his country estate.

To say that I was amazed at the reception Perón staged is a gross understatement. Red carpets, colorful bands, military honor guards, and other diplomatic courtesies were everywhere. United States Ambassador Albert F. Nufer whispered as we drove from the airport to Perón's office for an initial discussion: "Perón has decided that his third force is a failure. He's been looking for an excuse to reverse his policy and is seizing upon your visit as that excuse."

Perón greeted me enthusiastically in his office, spoke only of general matters, insisted that he must take me to a prize fight and a football (to Americans, soccer) game, and that I must have luncheon with him on Sunday at his country home.

He did not mention my veto, just before my arrival, of his outrageous suggestion that I should lay a wreath on the grave of Evita Perón. I insisted on laying a wreath—a diplomatic imperative—at the grave of the liberator, José de San Martín. Perón complimented me for my sensitivity in doing such a gracious thing, and then insisted upon calling for me personally at the United States Embassy to escort me to the football game and to a boxing match.

Diplomatic niceties so crammed those two days that I was fearful there would be no opportunity to carry out the two purposes of the brief visit. Fortunately, my companions, Jack Cabot, Sam Anderson, Andy Overby, and Tap Bennett were not required to attend the sporting events and were able to dig out a good deal of background information about the third force activities. But only I could bring up the question of restoring rights to American press associations, newspapers, and magazines.

On Sunday, an hour before I was to leave for the airport, I paid a formal farewell call on Perón. There was no time to back in: "I can't understand why you have ordered restrictions on American press representatives," I said bluntly, "I hope you will reconsider your decision."

Perón is an expansive and ebullient man, always perched on the edge of great belly laughs. He was surprised but kept smiling. "Your press people have been vilifying me with malicious propaganda," he replied. "And I have reason to believe that these attacks on me are instigated by the United States Government."

I had anticipated this. As I delivered a brief speech on how a free press operates—something obviously unknown to him—I took from my pocket a new editorial from the New York *Times* which heatedly criticized an action taken by President Eisenhower. Laying it before him, I said: "A free press has the right and the obligation to speak out, to criticize when necessary, to express its own views. But it does not speak for the government; official United States policy is expressed only by federal officials."

A dawn of understanding—or something—flashed on his face. As we stood up, he said solemnly: "Freedom will be restored to your news agencies, newspapers, and magazines within forty-eight hours."

Then I took a risk. That Perón ignored the thinly veiled offense seemed to confirm that my visit was being used as an excuse for a major change in policy. I said to the dictator: "I trust you do not object to my notifying the American press representatives before I leave of the assurance you have just given me." It was barely a question. We stood looking at each other for a few seconds. Then his smile broadened, he shrugged, and spread his hands in assent.

At a one-minute stop at the embassy, as we speeded toward the airport, I asked an attaché to telephone the reporters and tell them that at the airport I would give them information of interest.

They were in a side room when I arrived. I explained that the restrictions imposed two months earlier, in May, would be lifted within forty-eight hours. In my naïveté, I expected perhaps a few words of appreciation, or possibly of astonishment. What I heard can only be described as "grunts."

As I started down the normal diplomatic line to say the traditional farewells to Argentine officials and our own embassy personnel, the Foreign Minister of Argentina put his hand on my arm and asked me to wait for a few moments. He did not say why.

Screaming sirens were heard. Motorcycles and a string of black limousines pulled up at the airport entrance. Perón stepped out—coming to see me off personally, a gesture reserved for chiefs of state and often not even observed then. He was carrying a large photograph album. He came up and showed me that it contained pictures of my two-day activities in Buenos Aires. He pointed proudly to the last picture—it was my farewell visit to his office only thirty minutes before.

Perón grinned, "The only problem I could not solve was to have a picture in this book of your plane taking off from our airport, but I'll send it to you in Asunción tomorrow."

He did, by special air courier.

That was the totality of my brief visit on a single weekend in Argentina. The truth was well known to our embassy staff, to State Department and White House personnel, and to all American correspondents in Argentina. Any statements that I had discussed and offered loans to Perón or that the Administration had granted him credits could only be pure fabrication for political purposes—a misrepresentation that contributed to misunderstanding and confusion both in the United States and in all of the countries of Latin America.

Misconceptions about Latin America are created not only by politicians and mass media representatives, but also by business leaders. Sometimes the comments and charges of industrialists are made in good faith but without essential knowledge. Sometimes men with selfish interests knowingly make false statements which poison the American mind and enrage the Latin Americans.

When President Victor Paz Estenssoro, in his first term as Chief Executive of Bolivia, nationalized the tin mines and started a modest program of land reform, many American business leaders promptly called him a Communist. Their statements were widely published. Their view was upheld, in strong language, by the previous mine owners who lived sumptuously abroad.

The Paz Estenssoro Government most assuredly instituted reforms. The President and his associates may have been inexperienced, sometimes critical of us, and more inclined to socialism than Americans generally prefer. But they were not Communists, though his Minister of Labor was an extremist of Marxist leanings and many believe he belonged to the local Communist Party.

In Bolivia I listened for hours to explanations of the Bolivian tin mine expropriation in conversations with President Paz Estenssoro, his Foreign Minister, and his able ambassador in Washington. I recall distinctly spending most of one day at a small military school down a mountain. (Unaccustomed to high altitudes, I thought I would collapse when I arrived high in the Bolivian mountains. But President Paz Estenssoro thoughtfully had arranged to have an oxygen tank in the car and in my living quarters— and a physician gave me injections of some fluid twice daily. Our trip down the mountain to the military school was for my benefit.) The Bolivians charged that the mines were inefficient but profitable to the owners. They insisted that the government received little in taxes from the mines, that net earnings were exported to France, the United States, and other countries for investment, that the mine owners had deliberately fought the development of agriculture so that there would always be a surplus labor supply for the mines, that the cost of importing food kept the country impoverished and threatened starvation of hundreds of thousands of individuals when the price of tin dropped below world norms. Further, they claimed that the owners would be paid a fair sum for the nationalized mines, but that the owners stubbornly refused to negotiate to this end.

I also talked at length with some of the Bolivian and American owners, the latter being only minority stockholders. They contended that they had paid large sums annually in taxes to the Bolivian Government, that nationalization was politically motivated and unjustified, and that the offer of compensation was specious, for it assumed that payments could be made from mine earnings which would never materialize under political management.

Although I have read numerous pamphlets and other documents on this problem, I confess I have never been able to learn precisely where the full truth lies. I am, however, convinced of two things: Neither the first nor the second Paz Estenssoro administration has been "Communist," and officials were honestly convinced that expropriation with compensation was in the long-time interest of the nation. Unfortunately, mine efficiency and revenues *have* declined under public management, just as the previous owners predicted.

Certainly the land reform movement was not "Communist." A high percentage of the Bolivian population is Indian. They till the land for a few landowners, their only income being the vegetables grown on small plots of land assigned to them. Feudalism is far closer to Communism than the system of owner-operated farms installed by the Paz Estenssoro Government. Why we should call land reform under such circumstances Communism is beyond me.

One more point in behalf of the Bolivian leaders: Rapid peaceful social change is the only way to avert violent revolution in Bolivia; physical strife would be the surest way of giving the Communists control.

It is harmful in our own country and devastatingly hurtful throughout Latin America for us carelessly or maliciously to label as "Communist" any internal efforts to achieve changes for the benefit of the masses of the people. There are enough actual efforts, covert and overt, of Communist penetration into Latin-American labor, government, and education to tax our ingenuity. We should not make the mistake of issuing wholesale, unintelligent charges that muddy our thinking, provide a verbal smoke screen for the Communists, and cast before the world an image of us as irresponsible sophists. Indeed, I am convinced that a cardinal reason many Latin Americans do not take as seriously as they should the current world struggle for the minds and hearts of men is that they see it primarily as a power conflict, and they see our anti-Communist efforts mainly as an insistence upon sustaining the prevailing order. Precision in our thinking and public statements would help. We should not confuse each move in Latin America toward socialization with Marxism, land reform with Communism, or even anti-yankeeism with pro-sovietism.

United States businessmen also cause trouble when they advocate an approach to foreign economic development that is exclusively that of private enterprise. Obviously, their assumption is that the system of competitive enterprise as we know it here also exists in Latin America. Since in many of the Latin-American countries private enterprise fails to display a social conscience, does not spread its benefits widely (indeed, often tends to widen the great chasm between social classes), and is in a sense at the heart of the issue which causes the people to demand social change, our uninformed and generalized statements cut rather than heal.

I am persuaded that if private enterprise in Latin America had the attributes that ours has, it would win mass acceptance. Certainly I believe profoundly that economic freedom is inseparable from political and social freedom, and that a socially conscious private enterprise system is the most productive system yet devised by man. It is most harmonious with the spirit of democracy for it decentralizes decisions, encourages individual responsibility, and promotes personal growth. As Justice Holmes said, every man is capable of greatness.

But as things stand at present, most Latin Americans would rather socialize poverty than perpetuate the inequities of their country's own private enterprise. We must recognize the vast differences between enlightened capitalism and capitalized feudalism, between a system that merits militant labor support and one that leads to labor discontent and often bitter opposition, between a practical economic democracy and an entrenched economic plutocracy.

Words, as others have said, are weapons in the struggle for men's minds and allegiances. We should therefore be careful to use words and express ideas in phrases that, translated in Latin America, reflect our true meaning. Our obvious intention is to say that the system we ourselves enjoy would, if accepted in Latin America, make for a higher rate of growth than socialized enterprises. I am deeply convinced this is true. But Latin Americans must be shown first that our economic system *could* be developed in their countries (over the opposition of the oligarchists) and that it will in fact be superior because it distributes its benefits more fairly than they have ever known.

Even this book helps, in a sense, to perpetuate a serious misunderstanding. I am concerned primarily with those conditions and circumstances which are essentially hemispheric in scope and thus have the greatest bearing on American policies. Hence I must make constant references to inter-American relations, Pan Americanism, American republics, and Latin America. These phrases imply a cultural, political, and social unity which does not exist. Of course there are many common denominators in hemispheric affairs. There are also vast differences. In some respects each republic of Latin America is as different from the others as it is from the United States. We are sufficiently sophisticated with respect to Atlantic affairs that we do not assume our problems with Great Britain are the same as they are with Belgium or West Germany. An equal sophistication —one that we can achieve only after we destroy the caricature—in understanding the American republics would be enormously helpful. In fact, the ignorance and apathy which have so far twisted our efforts to build a meaningful relationship with our southern neighbors become more and more dangerous.

6

To understand, it is not enough to have facts, to listen, to think—one must want to understand.

Misconceptions are most effectively destroyed by replacing them with new and inspiring concepts.

THE ELEVATOR OPERATOR, TAXI DRIVER, OR HOTEL CLERK you meet in Latin America will probably speak acceptable English. If a blank expression on the face of a taxi driver encourages the traveler to try his faulty but conscientious Spanish to the extent of "A *la escuela, por favor*," the reply will be, "Okay, okay . . . I take you to the school."

In conversations with government officials, penetrating questions will arise about a bill introduced in our Congress—a bill that will never achieve the dignity of committee hearings. If it bears on trade relations, credit policy, or some other aspect of inter-American concern, they will have considered it in detail. When the visitor must confess that he never heard of the bill, there will be exclamations of surprise and disbelief. One must explain that thousands of bills are introduced in the United States Senate and House of Representatives that never receive and probably do not merit serious consideration.

Young intellectuals sprinkle their conversations with meaningful phrases from American presidential papers, the Congressional Record, and American philosophic writings. And they do so with a fluency and logic that are alarming and sometimes mortifying.

In short, the leaders and literate peoples of Latin America know a good deal more about us than we know about them.

Perhaps this is so because their dependence upon us is so pervasive that they have to scan our history, to read literature that reveals the American character and attitudes, to foster bi-national institutes which are rapidly making English their second language, to follow closely our major political struggles, and to keep watch for bills in our Congress which might affect them.

But knowledge is not enough. True understanding is the imperative.

As I traveled I found that certain misunderstandings have a monotonous uniformity. At first, I felt that, after hours of discussion with a particular group, much misinformation had been dissipated, that we had approached a common denominator of facts, ideas, and outlook, and that we had made some progress. But as time went on, I came to feel that the human mind, like a rubber band, can be stretched considerably only to snap back to its original position when released. As I revisited groups which I thought had accepted some of my explanations, I often ran into the same criticisms based on the same misunderstandings. Perhaps this proves the need for constant repetition of facts and ideas and for new ways to express and underscore them.

Everywhere I've gone in Latin America I have heard the assertion that the United States considers other areas of the world to be more important. This conviction seems to be based on several things—one historically true, the others erroneous.

It must be admitted that beginning with the Monroe Doctrine—a "big brother" policy, despite its good intentions—the United States maintained a patronizing attitude toward Latin America. Thirty years ago we realized our error and established a policy of mutual respect and non-intervention. But the past does not die easily—especially since Latin Americans generally believe there is new evidence of United States condescension and neglect.

Latin Americans have, for example, watched with amazement our spending of billions of dollars in Europe, the Middle East, and the Far East under the European Recovery and Mutual Security programs. Deeply disturbed by our failure to give them a significant role in these programs and to meet fully their demands for public loans, they contend that here is proof that we consider other areas more important to our welfare.

This reasoning overlooks fact: While the productive resources of Europe were being destroyed by war, the nations of Latin America enjoyed an unprecedented boom in their trade with us. In general, it has remained at the war level, or has increased. The situation in Europe after the war is not comparable to the present situation in Latin America; we make a mistake when we speak of initiating a "Marshall Plan for Latin America."

Our assistance to Europe—to overcome devastation caused by a war in which we were a partner—restored that area as a buying market and a source of supply. Naturally, we benefited, but so did Latin America; indeed, half of Latin America's prewar trade was with Europe, and failure to restore this market would have had devastating consequences in their economies.

Furthermore, our massive expenditures to help nations defend themselves against an aggressive and imperialistic world Communism have benefited Latin America as well as all other nations which cherish freedom.

Another difference is relevant. The Marshall Plan expenditures in Europe, concentrated in a relatively few years, had a built-in guarantee of success, for the task was merely to reconstruct what had been destroyed. The necessary economic, social, and cultural mechanisms, under experienced leadership, already existed to assure successful operation once the factories, schools, hospitals, highways, railroads, and so on were restored. In Latin America, the problem is far greater and quite different. The people must lift the level of their entire culture. Education, agriculture, and industry must be diversified and expanded; feudal ideas must be discarded and replaced by a system of competitive enterprise that yields social justice; and above all, leadership in every phase of human activity must be developed.

Latin Americans discount the differences between postwar Europe and their own plight; they feel that the $4 billion in public credit we have extended to them in the past twenty years (with $2 billion of this outstanding) and the $9 billion of private credit (now yielding great benefits in many countries) are mere pittances compared to what we have done for others. This, they say, proves that few Americans share my belief that no area of the world is as important to our future as Latin America.

Our mammoth world expenditures have created a second misunderstanding. Most Latin Americans, including the educated and sophisticated, seem to believe that our wealth is unlimited. They regard our failure to meet all their requests for credit as sheer perversity. They have no comprehension either of the sacrifices the American people make to meet the burdens of world leadership or of the possible limitations of our robust economy.

I shall never forget how surprised the urbane Minister of Finance of one Latin American country was when I pointed out that our income taxes range as high as 91 per cent and our corporation taxes are 52 per cent. He did not realize that we are one of the few nations in the world with a capital gains tax and that when one dies, the government may take a large portion of his estate.

Federal, state, and local taxes now amount to more than a fourth of our national income. Despite these high taxes, our federal budget is often out of balance by billions of dollars, thus causing harmful inflation. For some years, because of foreign aid, military expenditures abroad, a flow of investment capital out of the United States, and a reduced favorable balance in trade, we have found ourselves embarrassed and endangered by a growing foreign short-term debt. It exceeds our entire supply of gold. This situation, if it ever got out of control, could plunge the United States, and therefore the free world, into a catastrophic crisis.

Once, in Chile, I explained these facts to a mature intellectual. He was not impressed. It is difficult for a man wearing shoes to plead financial problems to a man walking barefoot. He referred to a document he had received from the United Nations written by Paul Hoffman: In the decade of the fifties, he read, the per capita income of the United States increased $530 to $2000; in other industrial countries it had increased more than $350 to a total of $800; in the underdeveloped countries it had increased less than one dollar a year to a total of $100. The average annual per capita income in Latin America ranged from $80 annually in Bolivia to $500 in Venezuela. (His figures were wrong, but his point was clear.)

The intellectual added: "Any policy of small ideas, small efforts, small concessions, and small-scale aid will merely accentuate the great imbalances and run counter to the increasingly persistent aspirations of the world's dispossessed, thereby preparing for the triumph of revolution." He later placed his argument in a letter to the United States ambassador in Chile.

I pointed out to him that even if the people of the United States were willing to be taxed still more—and if this produced more public revenue (which is doubtful, for higher taxes might lower production)—it would be difficult for us to spend more abroad in the face of the international imbalance that was already causing misgivings in the financial circles of the world. I reiterated that financial illness in the United States could create an epidemic of panic throughout the free world. The need was not so much for more money, in my judgment, but for a wiser use of it in Latin America to speed social reform.

He was even less taken with these arguments.

Perhaps the most prevalent misunderstanding, one charged with deep emotion and invariably brought up, is that we fix prices to the detriment of Latin America. Everywhere, I have heard, in one form or another, the charge that "We must sell to you at prices you are willing to pay, and we must buy from you at prices you dictate." More curtly: "You depress our economy to enrich yourself."

Though they are wrong, there are grounds for their bitterness. A high proportion of Latin-American exports to the United States are agricultural and mineral products, prices of which are subject to wide fluctuations in the world markets. When coffee reached a dollar a pound some years ago, fifteen nations in Latin America began to enjoy unprecedented prosperity. Then a frugal America began brewing more cups of coffee from each pound, substituting milk or tea for coffee, and otherwise showing buyer resistance.

Tempers rose in Latin America. Later, because of overproduction, world prices of coffee dropped to forty cents a pound. Was it serious? Each time coffee dropped a cent a pound, the annual income of Colombia, for example, declined $8 million. The economic distress that resulted caused much pain. That we were their largest purchasers, that the United States Government had taken no official action either when prices rose or fell, that many other countries maintain tariffs on coffee whereas we do not— these facts did not shake their conviction. We had maliciously forced down the price of coffee.

Compounding the bitterness and adding to their suspicions is the fact that Latin America buys from us manufactured goods—everything from large dredges and electric trains to business machines and consumer goods —whose prices are less flexible. These prices, too, are generally determined in the competitive markets of the world. Nevertheless, their trend is upward. Of course, there have been temporary variations in the relationship of raw commodity and administered prices, but once the war and postwar reconstruction demand was satisfied, raw commodities tended to decline and manufactured goods to rise in price.

A high percentage of manufacturing costs is wages. These are relatively inflexible and steadily on the increase. Of course, this is a disadvantage for Latin America as customers. But the crucial point to be recognized is that the view in Latin America that we fix prices to our own satisfaction is untrue.

Communists watch changing price relationships carefully. Every incident involving disadvantage to our neighbors becomes the subject of global, regional, and local propaganda. On several occasions, the Soviet Union has directly caused price declines in Latin America and then cleverly and with typical Communist maliciousness blamed the United States. The world price of tin ore in the immediate postwar period dropped from $1.12 to 82 cents a pound. In Bolivia, this caused widespread suffering and some starvation. To help, the United States stockpiled a good deal of tin ore, shipped surplus foods to the country, extended loans for highway and other projects to create jobs. Suffering continued. Bolivia was then producing only half of the food its people consumed. Dollar and sterling earnings were needed to buy food for most of the people. Their average income was considerably less than a hundred dollars a year. Any drop in foreign exchange earnings meant actual starvation for those already suffering malnutrition.

Russia gradually accumulated a surplus of tin ore. When American stockpiling and a world marketing agreement promised to ease the problem, Russia dumped the surplus on the world market, again breaking the price of ore. Soviet radio stations, Communist leaders in key spots such as Mexico City and La Paz, as well as Communist cells throughout the hemisphere, unleashed violent propaganda against the United States, callously charging that again the imperialist robber barons of the United States were crushing the economy of the poor in order to enrich themselves. Because this propaganda coincided with a general belief that we fixed world prices, it was believed—despite obvious evidence to the contrary. Russia normally exports only seventeen hundred tons of tin ore a year. In the latter part of 1958 she suddenly began exporting eighteen thousand tons a year.

Still another misunderstanding—this one both political and economic—was poignantly placed before me in the American Embassy in San José, Costa Rica, one quiet Sunday afternoon. A group of university students had come to talk. Their spokesman had studied in the United States. His English was impeccable.

"I admire the United States for its internal policies and progress," he said. "Your democracy, which spreads its benefits to every element of your society, seems to me to approach, at least to be struggling toward, perfection. But you are illogical, for you seem unconcerned about the fact that competitive private enterprise in our countries usually benefits only a few, leaving the masses in desperate poverty. And you support Latin-American dictators and others who want above everything else to maintain the prevailing order. How can you favor a socially-conscious private enterprise system and a great free democracy for yourself, but give support to dictators and private entrepreneurs in Latin America who stubbornly refuse to work for the benefit of *all* the people?"

"You are raising two quite different matters," I replied, "and both are widely misunderstood in Latin America."

I tackled the dictatorship charge first, for my visit was taking place only two months after Vice President Nixon's trip on which he was confronted with the same argument in every country.

"Since 1933," I explained, "the United States has lived by a policy of non-intervention in the affairs of other nations. This is especially true with regard to Latin America. You would like to have it both ways. You want us to pledge non-intervention, yet you expect us to pass moral or political judgments on the degree of democracy in our sister republics. The expression of such judgments would, in themselves, be a form of intervention." My young friends were listening with interest, it appeared, and I continued: "In the mid-1940s we saw a ray of hope for escaping this dilemma. The Foreign Minister of Uruguay proposed that the American republics encourage the growth of democracy in Latin America by collectively taking action against governments which flagrantly violated human rights and basic democratic principles. This could allow us to deal with dictators. The United States supported this proposal for collective intervention. You—the Latin American nations—overwhelmingly defeated it."

I argued that the policy of non-intervention, if correctly interpreted, is right. I pointed out that interventions by us prior to 1933 helped strong men of dictatorial tendencies to firm up their powerful holds internally. And I contended that the proof is in the pudding: Depending upon where one draws the line between dictatorship and democracy in the complex structures of Latin-American governments, there were from ten to fifteen dictators in Latin America when we adopted the policy of non-intervention; there were about ten when President Eisenhower took office; there were only three or four as we chatted that pleasant Sunday afternoon in 1958. There could surely be no doubt that we did not choose to support dictators; we were and always had been committed to freedom and independence for all peoples; we fervently hoped that all countries in the hemisphere would cast out dictators and embrace democracy.

It could be argued, I conceded, that the United States should withdraw recognition from all dictatorial regimes, including Russia, her satellites, Spain, Yugoslavia, Egypt, and a host of others. In the Wilsonian period, recognition had implied moral approval. But since the early 1920s—the early Jeffersonian policy was re-established by Charles Evans Hughes—recognition had merely represented a judgment that the government in power could maintain internal order and would meet its international commitments. A few Latin-American nations took exception to our policy, but most nations, including most Latin-American republics, had a policy identical to ours.

Once recognition was extended, we were obliged to cooperate with the government and the people. Our methods and programs were virtually the same for dictatorial regimes as for democratic. We had granted aid, for example, to such disparate nations as Poland, Yugoslavia, Spain, and

Uruguay. Surely it could be seen that this did not indicate approval or disapproval of the type of government in power.

I admitted to the young scholars that we had made mistakes; we should not have decorated Odría of Peru and Pérez Jiménez of Venezuela, no matter what the military arguments might have been at the time. In our dealings with dictators throughout the world—whether Communist, Nazi, or any other type—we should be scrupulously formal and correct. With democratic leaders, we can be as warm and informal as local customs permit. Vice President Nixon had suggested a distant handshake for dictators, an enthusiastic *abrazo* for democratic leaders. I thought this a good idea.

(I recalled the talk with these students two years later, when the American nations collectively, at San José, Costa Rica, recommended breaking relations with the Trujillo regime. The United States was the first to give substance to the recommendation. I should have enjoyed gloating a bit before my skeptical young friends.)

I directed one more comment to the student leader's accusation that we support dictators. Our basic policy, I pointed out, so eloquently expressed by many United States Presidents, is free choice of peoples. Hence, while we would oppose the coercive imposition of any form of government by external forces, we are compelled to accept the results of any development representing the will of the people of the country or resulting from purely internal power struggles. We deplore dictatorship in any form. Indeed, even the most democratic government in Latin America has some dictatorial tendencies and authority. Uruguay, generally thought to be the democratic model, sometimes acted autocratically. When I was in that country in 1953, the Council—the Uruguayan substitute, as in Switzerland, for a President—had seized an American packing plant, with no constitutional amendment, no authorizing act by the national assembly. This seemed to me to prove the existence of some degree of dictatorial authority.

The second charge made by the student leader that pleasant afternoon— that we do nothing about the fact that in some countries the rewards of private competitive enterprise reach too few people—has a double implication. Again, under a strict policy of non-intervention, I said, we could do nothing directly about the matter. The question obviously was how much influence we could use in encouraging proper social reform without openly being charged with violation of the fundamental non-intervention policy. This was a delicate matter which had been bothering me deeply for more than a year—since the meeting of the twenty-one presidential representatives in 1957. I had reached the tentative conclusion that here was an area in which the Latin-American republics had to act in concert. The dilemma for us, I argued, was the futility, on the one hand, of our extending further financial aid without social reform in the recipient country, and the incongruity on the other, of granting aid with offensive strings attached. If the nations did not act on this matter together, clearly we could not go on construing non-intervention to mean aloofness, either actual or apparent, from all internal matters of policy and structure.

The Costa Rican students applauded this defense of the policy of free choice of peoples and non-intervention, but they said that our assistance programs for the past fifteen years had made the rich richer and the poor poorer. It appeared to them that we had been unconcerned about this—a statement I had heard repeatedly from labor leaders, market women, members of university clubs, and many others.

Here there is surely a serious misunderstanding. Our technical cooperation programs, initiated by Nelson Rockefeller in 1942 and now costing many millions of dollars a year, are helping to improve agriculture, health, education, other social services, transportation, and certain industrial enterprises. The intent has always been to benefit all the people. A loan of $54 million for the construction of a highway from Cochabamba to Santa Cruz in Bolivia, for example, may at first put money into relatively few hands, but the purpose is to open up the country to general economic development, and more especially to make feasible a vast agricultural enterprise in the lower country of Santa Cruz, thus conferring benefits eventually on all. The same is true of nearly every project under what we now call the "Point IV" Program. Merely because the ultimate effects of this aid are not at once apparent does not mean that they are for the few.

The misunderstanding has another dimension. Private foreign investment in Latin-American countries is much larger than public investment. Most will acknowledge that the United States private enterprises in their countries pay higher wages than local industries, that they willingly pay all taxes imposed on them (which many domestic industries and citizens do not), that they often build highways, schools, and hospitals in the communities where they operate. Nevertheless, people equate these private United States enterprises with their own, and domestic industries may not, because of national policies, benefit labor or the people generally to the extent that ours do—to the extent they should. The Costa Rican students illogically insisted that somehow our enterprisers should subtly influence changes in their laws, customs, and institutions. If this were done, we would surely be charged with intervention and "dollar imperialism."

The most startling and discouraging misunderstandings in Latin America about us are prevalent among the poor, the distressed, and the downtrodden. These are people with little freedom. They own no property. They are illiterate, and their allegiance is limited to their immediate families and villages. To make misery bearable, they apparently need a common enemy, and they choose, strangely, the only one which has tried—ineptly at times, perhaps—to help. Soviet and Castro agents move among these people insidiously and spread lies: The imperialistic, war-mongering United States helps the generals to keep the rich in power; the capitalists want to keep you in slavery so they can steal your minerals and metals to keep their greedy industrial machines running; you will not get justice even if you beg—you must take it, fight for it.

Our counterpropaganda has not usually impressed them for two reasons. In the first place, while we may explain patiently and in simple terms the nature of the help we provide, they see no change in their own situations; the Communists have only to sympathize with the destitute to be accepted, while we must try to show that our technical assistance loans and other aid will lead to a better life—which they doubt. Second, and more important, the lot of the common man will not be changed in Latin America except through major changes in policies and programs of their own countries; anything we do can only be supplementary. If, in counterpropaganda, we were to speak candidly and point to the real source of the trouble, we would be evicted from every Latin-American country for the most blatant type of intervention. Bluntly, I must say that Communist propaganda identifies the United States with the obvious ills of the people, but counterpropaganda cannot shift the blame to the right people.

No society is free of contradictions. Not surprisingly, one can find them in abundance in attitudes expressed in Latin America. Thus, ultra-nationalists insist that all United States capital coming to their countries is imperialistic, and then criticize us for sending more to other areas of the world than we send to them. Intellectuals charge the United States with evading its moral responsibility in failing to induce social reform and yet they charge intervention when the Export-Import Bank or the World Bank lay down quite reasonable conditions in loan agreements. We are charged with levying exorbitant interest rates for public loans, but their own normal interest rates vary from two to three times as high as we require for our public loans. The masses plead for a new social order, one which, in the words of a Chilean, "would be closer to Lincoln's immortal definition, 'government of the people, by the people, for the people,'" and in the same argument they condemn us for attacking the Castro dictatorship. It is widely asserted that "greed continues to be the prime mover in economics, sacred selfishness the highest order for governments and the dominant social classes, and practical materialism the entire moral philosophy guiding Western conduct" (obviously including the conduct of the United States). But in the same breath, it is asserted that "from the standpoint of Christian moral theology the United States is obliged to share its prosperity and wealth" (which was accumulated under the criticized "practical materialism").

We are a nation of contradictions and inconsistencies, too, and we should not be too smug in underscoring those of others. My purpose is not to excuse our failings. My purpose is not to contend that contradictions are unique to Latin America, but that they reflect deep-seated misunderstandings which must be cleared away in any total effort to improve hemispheric relations and to help the American republics advance economically in freedom.

Just as our own politicians sometimes deliberately make damaging misstatements for selfish personal reasons, so too do political leaders in Latin America. There is, however, usually this difference: False charges here are designed to confound a domestic political opponent and to misrepresent him to our voters who have only the friendliest intentions toward most of the nations of Latin America. In Latin America, however (as in the rest of the world), it seems sometimes the fashion is to make the United States the whipping boy in political campaigns to appeal to existing prejudices.

In Panama, where poverty is rampant, the people look upon the Canal Zone, and especially the Canal Company, as a possible economic resource, a savior. This may not be realistic, but it is understandable. There is a great difference, however, between this naïveté and the actions of a Panamanian presidential candidate who knew better, who had served in a position that enabled him to possess all the facts, yet who sought to inflame the people by saying: "The United States has made more than a hundred million dollars out of the Canal, but we whose resource is involved have not received one cent." Such irresponsibility can only cause one to despair, for as I shall show later, the United States has not made a profit from the Canal operation in its fifty years of operation, while Panama has received substantial economic benefits.

Certainly even the most visionary knows that freeing human minds of prejudice and ignorance, and developing clear, objective, creative reasoning with respect to international problems will take a great deal of time. Language and other cultural barriers, while not insurmountable, are formidable. Furthermore, there is not always the same incentive to solve problems, and in many cases, even among thoughtful, well-educated men, there exist a basic philosophic difference. Anyone who devotes considerable time to international affairs is likely at times to become discouraged. I do. International situations seem to become ever more complex, seem to defy the simple, clear-cut solutions that appeal to the young. We are involved with peoples who are strangers to us, who resent our wealth but demand our aid, who rely on our friendship but make a scapegoat of us. We may find consolation in saying that these people are wrong, in declaring that they misunderstand us, and in insisting that they need us more than we need them, so let them make an equal effort to build a meaningful relationship. But this is a shallow and dangerous salve for a wounded pride. The millions of Latin Americans who grow restive with each passing day are unaware of and unconcerned with the subtleties of argument, with the political nuances. They want a better life. They are increasingly determined to get it. The obstacles in their way—whether we or their own leaders are responsible for them—must be removed as swiftly and peaceably as possible by reasonable people on both sides. For hunger has no conscience and desperation no reason, and revolution is born of both.

7 There is a dangerous myth abroad in this land that an ordinary citizen can do nothing to influence the destiny of his country and the world. I have not decided whether this is a rationalization or an epitaph.

A FEW MILES FROM PUCALLPA, PERU, AT THE HEADWA-
ters of the Amazon, a German doctor operates a small hospital. His name is Theodor Binder. He settled in Lima more than ten years ago to work in the Medical School of the university and among the Indians in the wretchedly poor district of the city. Dr. Binder became a Peruvian citizen and became as fluent in several Indian dialects as he is in German, English, and Spanish. Six years ago, he moved to Pucallpa and established his rather primitive hospital; it has one of the most amazing outpatient clinics in the world.

Indians travel hundreds of miles to see Dr. Binder. They trust him. He is connected with no government agency. His modest support is private—some from private agencies in the United States. The Indians camp near his clinic for months, getting treatment, learning hygienic practices, developing skills as nurses. United States doctors who have visited him testify that his work is remarkably successful. But the crucial point in my evaluation of Dr. Binder is economic and social, not medical. Because they trust him, the Indians confide in him; they tell him about their poverty—as if it weren't painfully obvious. They complain to him about being dispossessed by landowners from their huts and the tiny pieces of land they have farmed. They say that help will not come from the Peruvian Government. The United States, they are convinced, is imperialistic and selfish, committed to support the men in power. The Indians tell Dr. Binder that revolution—violent revolution—is the only answer, and they assure him that Fidel Castro's agents will help them to win as he helped the poor to win in Cuba.

Dr. Binder lives simply, as do his few assistants. Patiently, as he dresses a wound or splints a fracture, he tells the Indians in their own language about the Communists. He tells them that this totalitarian society, like all others, sucks the essence from liberty and leaves it a shell. He tells them that Communism admittedly destroys truth, individualism, altruism. Dr. Binder describes how the conspiracy works, how it disguises itself and infiltrates the host like a virus to capture the vital function of the host. He does not preach, but his quiet talk peels the skin of deceit and distortion from the Cuban revolution and reveals the cruelties and the injustices which Castro's agents neglected to mention. Dr. Binder has a way of helping people to understand the basic ideas and motivation of the United States, of seeing its unparalleled generosity to others. He does not "whitewash" the United States or excuse its blunders. He concentrates on fundamentals.

Men—young and old—who come to Dr. Binder's clinic in a mood to fight, leave determined to work. They learn that they cannot seize freedom and prosperity; they must build it.

Enough Dr. Binders in enough places could make a colossal dent in the barrier of misunderstanding that separates us from Latin America.

It is easier to analyze problems than it is to solve them—especially in so complicated an area as human understanding.

Reasonable people know that ignorance and misinformation can create tensions or disputes. They may agree that corrective action should be bold, heroic, and unprecedented. But some measures which should be undertaken to eliminate ignorance and misconceptions may seem pollyannaish or melodramatic. These may be condemned without serious thought.

When my associates and I, on our first study excursion in 1953, agreed that the fundamental problem in inter-American relations is intellectual, we felt that corrective action would mainly be an intensification and improvement of traditional activities: student and teacher exchanges, an increased flow of truthful news and good interpretive reporting, efforts to surmount language barriers, and systematic discussions in locally organized foreign policy or philosophic associations which were lightly scattered throughout the Americas.

By 1957, as the twenty-one personal representatives of the American Presidents proceeded with their work, I concluded that orthodox methods of communication and information, valuable as they are, were not sufficient to assure the intellectual and moral foundation of abiding hemispheric action. By then the tremendous, ugly power of ignorance and mistaken notions had been impressed upon me. That power was increasing, largely through the activities of Marxist and other left-wing cells. So I urged my fellow representatives to recommend the creation of new mechanisms, under the aegis of the Organization of American States, whose salient purpose would be to build "closer ties between the various countries through mutual knowledge of their individual cultural, economic, and social characteristics in the American community. Attainment of this far-reaching purpose requires coordination that will channel the joint efforts and strengthen the action of the American republics in the undertaking. . . . a matter of vital importance to be assured of the understanding, support, and participation of the public."

I insisted that the public relations activities of the OAS should be strengthened, local offices of the organization should be established in all member countries, private participation in the affairs of OAS should be promoted, and the various governments should—and this is the important point—"set up National Commissions for the Organization of American States."

After prolonged discussion, this recommendation was adopted. When the report in cold type was later considered by the chiefs of state, the recommendation no doubt appeared to be meaningless. Nothing happened.

By now, I had generated a crusading zeal for the proposal, a zeal which, on reflection, I realize is attributable in part to my work with William Benton who, as Assistant Secretary of State in 1946, induced me to become the first Permanent Chairman of the United States National Commission for UNESCO. The United States National Commission had a hundred members, some selected at large by the Secretary of State and sixty nominated by national organizations whose regular educational, discussional, and informational programs reached forty or fifty million United States citizens with great regularity. In addition to the National Commission activities, I had accepted membership on the UNESCO Executive Board in Paris, and had attended four international conferences of the organization. While in my opinion UNESCO has proved to be ineffectual in building the structures of permanent peace in the minds and hearts of men, as it was designed to do, there could be no question that the United States National Commission for UNESCO had initiated domestically a potent nationwide educational program in international affairs.

Here, it seemed to me, was one way to overcome some misconceptions in the Western Hemisphere. It could be more successful than the National Commission for UNESCO, for among the nations involved there was no

Iron Curtain, motivation would be high, and the dimensions of the task, while large, were not as forbidding as the global task of UNESCO.

For a time, despite my missionary campaigning among all who would listen, the idea seemed destined for limbo. Yet I persevered—obnoxiously so at times. In a report to President Eisenhower, published in December 1958, I urged the United States to take the lead in persuading OAS to give the highest priority to the development of an intellectual climate in the Americas which would stimulate effective cooperation. First on my list of specifics was that the Organization should prevail upon each American republic to establish a national commission of distinguished citizens who would voluntarily assume as their major extramural responsibility the promotion within each country of the type of broad understanding so obviously required. Commission members should include, I suggested, educators, editors, writers, leaders of business, agriculture, and labor, public officials, and prominent citizens representing social and cultural institutions. In the larger countries, I hoped that a hundred distinguished individuals noted for their objectivity would be willing to serve on each national commission. In the smaller countries, twenty or more would be enough. There was no rush to adopt my suggestions.

Then a flicker of hope appeared. The wife of the Secretary-General of the Pan American Union sponsored a series of educational meetings which were designed to bring solid information about inter-American affairs to the wives of United States diplomats, Supreme Court justices, senators, representatives, and officials in the Executive establishment. I was asked to inaugurate the series.

Vice President Nixon presided. The room was filled to capacity mostly with ladies, but with Secretary-General Dr. José A. Mora and others of the Pan American Union staff present. I built a talk around the opportunity which the OAS had to take leadership in developing instruments for the building of intellectual solidarity in the Americas. Evidently, I persuaded Dr. Mora and some others. Not long after, the Council of the Organization of American States officially endorsed the recommendation as it had originally appeared in the report of the committee of twenty-one presidential representatives.

There the matter stood for nearly two years, waiting for a few countries to implement it with enough pomp and success to persuade others to follow. Then there developed a movement to set up national commissions for the Alliance for Progress under the auspices of the Organization of American States. Ecuador was the first to implement the recommendation.

A national commission as a single instrument cannot quickly erase misunderstanding, as words from a blackboard. But it can be the focal point of immense significance. It can, first, help its membership achieve a balanced understanding among themselves. Then it can spread its influence. Most of the members—representing, in our country, for example, the League of Women Voters, The American Legion, the Chamber of Commerce, the AFL-CIO, the American Farm Bureau Federation, the General Federation of Women's Clubs, and so on—could, through their house organs, locally sponsored discussion groups, and lectures, gradually accomplish what has never been successfully achieved in the field of foreign affairs—an informed electorate, the key to an up-to-date, virile, successful foreign policy. I think it is likely that local commissions, modeled on the national organization, would spring up in communities throughout the United States, and possibly in neighboring countries, as some fifty did in the rural state of Kansas in support of the educational efforts of the United States National Commission for UNESCO.

A national commission, comprised of eminent, objective, dedicated individuals could soon attain dignity, influence, and trust. In addition to bringing truth to bear in the types of enduring misconceptions mentioned, the members of a national commission could quickly counteract malicious rumors and subversive propaganda.

In the Latin-American countries it would be imperative that commission members be people who are widely trusted. If they came only from prominent families, for example, they would be suspect, probably considered to be propaganda agents of the United States. In each country there are labor and farm leaders, educators and businessmen, priests and cultural leaders who have or could develop general acceptance. Each commission should become a focal point of accurate facts and ideas, and the motivating force in a nationwide program of adult education designed to achieve understanding of inter-American affairs among all classes.

I have pointed out that sometimes individuals in the Americas encourage misunderstandings for what may seem to be temporary political advantage; this is especially true in some Latin-American countries. A prime responsibility of national commissions should be to persuade prominent politicians that this is self-defeating. Political leaders must, in fact, be leaders: Each has a profound responsibility for keeping his people accurately informed with respect to those great problems and issues that determine relationships among nations.

We have normally depended upon the mass media to keep the people informed. In a free society there are strong arguments for this. We accept the view, to be sure, that public officials should tell the people about our own governmental actions, and the reasons therefor. But we have not felt that governments should accept responsibility for spreading objective truth about other nations—about their policies, problems, attitudes, acts, and failures to act. Reluctantly, I have concluded that the American governments themselves should assume considerable responsibility for keeping their citizens adequately informed with respect to crucially important inter-American problems. The Organization of American States should, in my opinion, urge this upon member governments. Thus if Panamanian-United States difficulties seem to be building to a climax, as I am sure they will again, the Foreign Offices in the two countries should see to it that *both the United States and Panamanian views in all their details* are made available to the mass media, to the national commissions, and to other organizations that will help promote an understanding of the problems involved.

The OAS should also initiate and supervise a greatly expanded system of scholarships and fellowships; of a massive exchange of students, teachers, and others among all the republics. It was my good fortune to have the Committee of Presidential Representatives support me in recommending that the OAS be given authority to administer five hundred scholarships as a supplement to those granted unilaterally by several governments, principally by the United States and private organizations within the United States. This is a good start—but only a start.

These few OAS activities would not be decisive, but they would be helpful. The major responsibility for encouraging genuine understanding in hemispheric affairs rests with each government and many private agencies within each country.

A deficiency, serious enough to single out, is, again, in the field of the mass media. Leading newspapers, magazines, radio and television networks, and press associations of the United States maintain foreign correspondents throughout the world, but unfortunately the ablest of these are usually assigned to Western and Eastern Europe. Better and more correspondents are needed in Latin America.

Several years ago an eminent New York newspaperman, who for years worked in Latin America, pointed a finger of professional dismay at the "hotfooted transients" who represent some segments of the United States press in Latin America. This brand of reporter specializes in the one-night stand, stopping in a capital city only long enough to pick up a bit of palace-guard gossip. He does not have the time to develop the knowledge and perspective so essential to accurate, well-balanced, meaningful news stories and interpretive articles. We obviously need fewer transients and more correspondents who are steeped in the total culture of a country.

In the United States, with newspapers daily reaching sixty million readers, and radio and television reaching more, our media must decide that Latin America is as newsworthy as any other region. Events in Cuba, Brazil, Chile, and Panama have brought encouraging results in this regard, but not for the right reasons.

Newspapers in Latin America have reached a circulation of over fifteen million. Since their foreign news comes primarily via the United States press associations, their coverage of us is better than ours is of them.

Latin-American newspapers have many more dispatches from the United States than they do from their neighboring countries. I am inclined to think this has some influence in encouraging the all-too-prevalent attitude that hemispheric affairs are not, in actuality, those of a family of nations, but are, instead, the problems of each of twenty nations with the United States. A few years ago, I read an anecdote in the International Press Institute *Bulletin* which made the point sharply: At a luncheon in Washington, a Chilean publisher charged that the United States correspondents dispatched only sensational news and ignored the basic economic and social problems of the continent. A New York *Times* correspondent, who had spent several years in Latin America and probably agreed with the charge, quietly asked the publisher: "And how much news does your newspaper in Chile publish about the basic economic and social conditions in Ecuador?"

Because of lamentable illiteracy in many Latin-American republics, radio and, increasingly, television are becoming more important in international communications than the newspapers. Moreover, not an Iron Curtain, but a Lace Curtain exists in some of the countries—mild, but provoking and sometimes harmful censorship. By all legitimate means, every trace of censorship should be eliminated. Every free nation should uphold the philosophy that if human beings everywhere are exposed to all ideas, good and bad, and all possible facts and reports, both true and false, lies will die of their own poison, truth will prevail, the mass judgment will be valid, democratic processes will be strengthened, and international cooperation will be facilitated.

The Inter-American Press Association has tried to mitigate the situation, with moderate success. In some countries leaders seek to subjugate the press. They close down newspapers, tighten up censorship, ram through legislation, and intimidate. International covenants which guarantee freedom of expression are sometimes violated; no agreement is better than the good faith of its signatories.

The press is completely at the mercy of the government in Cuba (as it was until recently in the Dominican Republic). Unfortunately subtle malpractices also exist in some other Latin-American countries, including several that have reached a reasonable degree of democratic practice. While the Inter-American Press Association should continue to do all it can to win complete press freedom, I think that government representatives, especially in OAS sessions, should tackle this problem and try to reach a prompt solution. National commissions, if established, could also be helpful. Ideas, facts, and interpretations must flow freely between all the Americas, be disseminated, and heard and read by the people.

It is not, of course, the primary responsibility of press associations to promote understanding and hemispheric cooperation; their job is to report news. That is one cogent reason for having a United States Information Agency. Press associations' deficiencies on southbound news are partially overcome by the substantial press, magazine, radio, and other dispatches provided by USIA. The agency does not, however, supplement news brought to the United States by the mass media; it is legally forbidden to do so. Either the State Department Information Office or USIA should have the authority and the funds to do this, for we need information that is left out of commercial wire-service coverage.

In Latin-American countries, several activities have accomplished a good deal, and some hold great promise: bi-national institutes, American libraries, and American schools.

One of the most touching experiences I have had in my travels occurred late one night in Asunción, Paraguay. I had been to eight other countries on this trip, and Paraguay was my next-to-last stop. The Latin-American press had run many columns on the visit. On my second day in Paraguay, somewhat tired and a bit homesick, I unexpectedly visited the bi-national institute where twelve hundred persons, ranging in age from ten to forty, were studying English. Some classes were for beginners; others were for more advanced students who were exploring American history and literature. I spoke to five classes, partly in Spanish and partly in English; then to my astonishment the students poured from their classrooms and surrounded me. They gathered around in the courtyard, shaking my hand and shouting sincere and enthusiastic expressions of friendship. Maybe it was fatigue, or homesickness, or perhaps it was the almost tangible aura of goodwill which filled the courtyard—in any case, I was deeply moved.

I have visited such schools in Mexico, Chile, Colombia, Brazil, and elsewhere. In São Paulo, seven thousand students were regularly attending classes. The cost to the United States for these institutes is negligible. Modest fees paid by the students provide a high degree of self-support. The program should be expanded, and for once we should emulate Latin America—we should establish bi-national institutes and encourage thousands of our citizens to learn to speak Spanish or Portuguese accurately and fluently. The National Education Act should be amended to provide modest assistance to this end, particularly in the developmental stage of the undertaking. We of the United States are lackadaisical linguists, partly because of our distance from other language zones, and partly, I suspect, because we have not previously felt the need to learn. Now the need is clear.

Flying over Colombia in a private plane, I sat in the co-pilot's seat and chatted with the pilot, a handsome and robust Colombian.

"You speak very good English," I said to him.

He smiled and explained that it hadn't always been so. He had spent some time in the United States when the only English he knew was "ham and eggs." He would go into a restaurant, try to read the menu, then give up in despair and say, "ham and eggs." Finally he got tired of eating breakfast three times a day, so he studied his English dictionary and ventured into a New York restaurant.

After scanning the menu, he looked up at a big, surly waiter and said, "Biffsteck."

The waiter frowned ominously and growled: *"What?"*

Whereupon my pilot friend replied meekly: "Ham and eggs."

American libraries in Latin America are small, but they are ardently used. In one library in Tegucigalpa, Honduras I learned that each available book was borrowed on an average of five times a year, and readers begged for a wider choice. A good library is a silent but effective cultural outpost; if books are selected wisely, the library can contribute mightily to understanding. It cannot, of course, reach illiterates directly, but each informed person can be a center of knowledge and inspiration, and thus books, magazines, and libraries may have a widening influence. We should increase the modest annual investment we now make in libraries in the Latin-American countries.

More than seventy-five thousand students, mostly Latin Americans but also children of our diplomatic corps and of American businessmen, are enrolled in schools supported partly by the United States Government. These schools adhere to our methods and standards of education, develop an intelligent loyalty to our country, and to inter-American solidarity, and receive the prideful applause of the communities in which they are located. In Ecuador, the school is the most creative instrument for international friendship and democracy in that country. Our total contribution to these schools in Latin America is about $150,000 a year. We can afford more than this—especially for so promising an investment.

More labor leaders in Latin America should be brought to this country for extensive visits so that they may understand fully how a good private enterprise system works and see the responsible place that free workers occupy in our society; every possible encouragement should be given to the newly established American Institute for Free Labor Development, whose function is made clear by its name.

The informational and cultural activities of USIA should be expanded. The private foundations of the United States which now provide many scholarships and fellowships for foreign students should be more generous in their allocations to Latin Americans. United States business firms with major undertakings in Latin America should provide their representatives regularly with succinct information on United States policies and attitudes and encourage these representatives, most of whom are completely at home in the use of Spanish or Portuguese, to be better interpreters of our attitudes and actions. More Americans should defer their visits to Europe occasionally and travel to Mexico City, San José, Lima, Santiago, Montevideo, Rio, and Caracas. (This is no hardship. The attractive side of Latin America is glorious.) Activities of United States medical groups which occasionally send teams of experts to Latin America to demonstrate new scientific equipment and techniques should be supported generously. In the United States, more local foreign-policy groups should be organized and they, as well as long-established ones, like those in Dallas, Los Angeles, and Cleveland, should devote a generous share of their programs to United States-Latin American relations. Many colleges should establish solid majors in Latin-American studies; more graduate schools should develop regional studies and research in this area, and our secondary schools should offer an elective course in the history of inter-American relations. (The war with Mexico alone is a fascinating case history—if not all luster for the United States.) We should encourage more of our colleges and universities to establish close cooperative relations with comparable institutions in Latin America (this practice has long been common between our universities and those of the Middle East and Far East). Developments in Latin America are encouraging; thus, there are now more than sixty cooperative projects between United States and Latin-American universities in fifteen countries.

The private effort in Mexico of prominent Mexican and United States businessmen to develop mutual understanding should be duplicated in other Latin-American countries. In Mexico City, a score of leading Mexican and United States bankers and industrialists meet regularly, primarily for self-education that may lead to better economic cooperation between their two countries. They also sponsor a Mexican version of our 4-H Clubs; serve as hosts to prominent United States visitors, not as a social exercise but as a means of promoting deeper understanding of the Mexican culture, and carry on other projects, all designed to build a firmer Mexican-United States friendship.

Most of the activities I have mentioned come up for discussion whenever knowledgeable persons of goodwill get together. Yet inter-American relations continue to deteriorate, and increasing misunderstanding, fanned by evil propagandists, is a direct cause. What is needed in each country is a point of dedicated interest and stimulation. A national commission in each country could become not only a vital educational force in its own right, but could encourage others to carry forward the types of desirable activities I have mentioned.

This chapter opens with Dr. Theodor Binder and his work with body-and-soul-sick peasants. There are thousands of Pucallpas and millions of weary peons, but very few Dr. Binders. Good men like the doctor are never available in huge numbers but I suggest that there could be Dr. Binders everywhere in Latin America. By reassigning priorities in activities now financed—particularly private activities, for the Dr. Binders should not be public employees—there would need be no great increase in cost. A national commission in each country, of the type I have suggested, could facilitate the spread of this type of educational and health services. The dividends would be monumental.

A highly encouraging development occurred at Punta del Este, Uruguay, in August 1961 at the special meeting of the Inter-American Economic and Social Council. The ministers, who had met to work out the details of a new ten-year program of economic development, as envisaged in the Act of Bogotá, recognized that the attainment of economic goals demanded the understanding and active cooperation of all the peoples of

93

the Americas. "It is essential," the ministers declared, "that public opinion be fully informed of the causes that have brought about this movement, of the goals it seeks, and of its successive achievements."

The ministers solemnly appealed to news agencies, publicity media, radio and television companies, and foundations, to intensify efforts to "put an end to present ignorance of conditions prevailing in the countries of the Americas and their peoples." They emphasized the need for conferences, seminars, and round tables to study the main economic and social problems of the hemisphere and their possible solutions.

"We must," the ministers said, "summon public opinion of the Hemisphere, and especially of trade unions, labor organizations, and student associations, in order that they may become informed of the social implications of the Alliance for Progress and participate actively in the dissemination of information on its objectives and in the discussions and implementation of its programs."

Broadening their appeal beyond the economic objectives of the conference, the ministers pleaded for a spread, among the peoples of the Americas, of "knowledge of each other and of all problems besetting the American nations." To this end, they called for the creation of new information media for cultural and educational purposes in those regions of the Americas where they do not exist and the strengthening of such agencies in areas where they are deficient. They asked the Organization of American States to convoke, as soon as possible, an inter-American conference on Information Media, for the purpose of "promoting the most appropriate action for informing public opinion on these development plans and to mobilize it [public opinion] in their favor."

This is the first time ministerial representatives of the American republics have plainly and emphatically said that a vast inter-American cooperative effort can succeed only if ignorance is replaced with understanding. The approval which the committee of twenty-one presidential representatives gave my proposal for national commissions more than four years previously was, I fear, a courteous gesture to me. At Punta del Este the ministers were deadly serious. Not the least of my satisfaction is this: If the recommendations which I have been making about the means of achieving mutual understanding and respect are idealistic, at least I am now joined—only Guevara of Cuba dissenting—in my blissful state by eminent statesmen from all the Americas.

Book II

Latin America's economic problem is staggering in scope and complexity. It is almost as hard to come to grips with as the nebulous and elusive problem of misunderstanding. The aspect of it which most seriously jeopardizes our relations with Latin America is the relationship of the prices of the primary commodities which Latin America exports to the prices of manufactured goods which she buys. Here is a frustrating combination of the intellectual and economic problem, for Latin-Americans have long been convinced that we arbitrarily and capriciously fix prices to their detriment.

Even if we could convince them otherwise, the economic problem would remain to plague us. Latin America is still in the agricultural age, with nearly two-thirds of its people working the soil. But agricultural production is hampered by ignorance of modern farming methods, by a feudalistic land ownership system, and by a lack of diversification. To free itself from the soil, Latin Americans worship at the shrine of the dynamo. They believe that industrialization is the key to prosperity. There is much truth in this, but they frequently do not plan carefully, and they lack the trained people and the money to keep their industries growing and producing efficiently. More money will solve the problem, they insist. But additional aid is not in itself sufficient. There must be economic stability, development plans, and valid priorities.

Our efforts to help have been, until recently, the orthodox ones: Diversify agriculture and make it more efficient; develop a diversified industry; extend massive amounts of credit for development projects which will produce jobs and income. The four chapters which follow deal with this traditional approach to Latin America's economic problem. But they also reveal a growing awareness on our part that the orthodox approach, while essential, is inadequate. Indeed, we have seen to our dismay that orthodox aid by itself could actually lead to a hatred of the United States, rather than to appreciation and abiding cooperation. The traditional approach, we concluded, cannot succeed as long as Latin America tries to build on a foundation of social injustice.

8   Logic has never been a successful substitute for food.

NOTHING MAKES LATIN AMERICANS MORE RESENTFUL,
more hostile, more distrustful of the United States than the suspicion—
indeed, the conviction—that we capriciously and maliciously fix prices to
their detriment. Of all the serious misunderstandings which hamper cooperation in this hemisphere, none is more persistent, more pervasive in
scope than this certainty that the United States plays fast and loose with
the world market.

The anger and bitterness underlying this charge boiled over in 1957–58
during a recession in the United States. Prices of manufactured goods
(which we sell and Latin America buys) continued to climb, while prices
of raw commodities (which Latin America sells and we buy) declined.
Latin-American economies suffered. Consider a hypothetical case: A small
Latin-American country exports its coffee crop to the United States for,
say, $100 million. This $100 million allows it to purchase that much manufactured goods from the United States. When the price of coffee suddenly
drops, as it might well do, this Latin-American country earns only $70
million for its coffee exports to the United States. To make matters worse,
the prices of manufactured items in this country rise by 10 per cent. Hence,
the Latin-American country is pinched on both ends. Its coffee sales will
only buy about 63 per cent of what it bought the year before. Few Latin-
American countries are prosperous enough to absorb this kind of loss, and
the resulting hardship is blamed on the United States.

In El Salvador, where coffee exports earn nearly 80 per cent of the foreign exchange, I once conferred at length with several hundred coffee producers in an earnest effort to convince them that the United States Gov-

ernment had not driven down the price of coffee from the high point it had reached several years previously. Neither, I claimed, were private buyers, roasters, or distributors to blame.

At first, the producers doubted my explanation that coffee prices are determined in the competitive markets of the world. They pointed out that during World War II and immediately afterwards, we had put price controls on products purchased from Latin America. At that time, we had bought heavily from Latin America but, because of shortages of goods and shipping, had not been able to send them equivalent amounts of manufactured products. As a result, Latin America had accumulated large exchange reserves. After the war, when restrictions were removed and Latin America was able to spend its reserves, prices of United States goods had skyrocketed. Hence, they had been doubly injured—first by controls which limited their earnings and later by higher prices for our products when reserves could be used. This was indisputable proof, the coffee producers insisted, that we had fixed prices to our own advantage.

Their point was well taken, but I explained that wartime restraints were by no means representative. Citizens of the United States had also been hurt by price controls, rationing, and the ensuing higher prices when goods became available. This was simply one of the sacrifices all of us had to make in producing for and fighting a war—a war which protected the freedom of Latin America as it did ours.

They remained unimpressed, so I shifted the discussion to the area of their special interest: coffee. Coffee prices had been erratic; they had reached a dollar a pound a few years before and were then hovering around forty cents. This conditioned all their reasoning.

I pointed out that a decline in coffee prices did not really benefit the United States because the nations hurt were compelled to buy less from us. We had everything to gain, as they did, from reasonable stability in price relationships: Then they could avoid economic calamity and political and social instability, and our manufacturers could plan production and export schedules on more predictable bases. Therefore, even if the United States Government had authority to control prices—which it patently did not—we would have had no incentive to do what they thought we had done. We recognized that a sharp drop in coffee prices was distressing to coffee-producing countries—especially when most of the nations' foreign exchange was obtained from this single commodity.

With some members of the coffee producers' association convinced of my sincerity on this point—though they may have thought me naïve in economic matters—I ventured to offer suggestions on the difficulties of supporting prices artificially.

I pointed out that I had had a good deal of experience with the effort of our government to stabilize prices and incomes of American farmers. I had been a career officer in the U. S. Department of Agriculture in the 1920s and 1930s when prices of agricultural commodities in the United States—especially such export commodities as wheat and cotton—had fallen sharply. The relationship of farm to non-farm prices which had prevailed in the fifty-year non-war period to 1914, a period deemed reasonably normal, had been rudely disturbed beginning in 1920, to agriculture's disadvantage.

President Herbert Hoover had tried to ameliorate the difficulty by adopting the ever-normal granary concept of ancient Egypt: The government would buy up surpluses in time of plenty and then release them to the markets in the lean years. The difficulty had been that surpluses continued to mount, the general economic depression had deepened, and wheat, cotton, and other farm prices had continued to slide downward with toboggan speed. President Hoover's effort had cost the United States $345 million, and it had accomplished little. Nonetheless, it had been a serious attempt to tackle a perplexing and threatening problem and it had led inexorably to the next step, taken by Franklin D. Roosevelt when he became Chief Executive in 1933.

(President Roosevelt was deeply respected in Latin America. So the coffee producers showed more interest now.)

By then, the market price of wheat had dropped to twenty-five cents a bushel, of cotton to five cents a pound. Farmers had stood watch with shotguns to prevent mortgage companies from foreclosing on their farms. We had been close to insurrection in the United States.

The government had developed a series of programs designed, first, to bring supply into balance with effective demand, and second, to maintain a fair relationship between the prices of the commodities farmers sold and the prices of things they bought. The government took acreage out of production and paid farmers not to use it; farmers were assured of at least a minimum return on their products; the government purchased surpluses and stored them.

After a quarter of a century with these programs, an objective observer would concede that they had at best enjoyed only moderate success. Every effort to reduce acreage devoted to surplus crops and fibers had been accompanied by increased farm efficiency, so that total production had not declined. It increased. We had resorted to vast governmental purchases, as the Farm Board had done under President Hoover, and then we had employed export subsidies and gifts in an attempt to move these surpluses into world markets at propitious times.

During World War II, our problem was temporarily solved. World production of food and fiber had declined drastically, and an unlimited demand quickly took over. Farm prices had risen to 117 per cent of parity (the objective of farm legislation was a 100 per cent parity in the relationship of raw commodity and administered prices). There had followed four or five golden years for the United States farmer. Debts had been paid off and bonds had been purchased and stuffed into safety deposit boxes without being counted. A farm millennium had been reached.

The Congress, evidently wishing to claim some of the credit for the happy state of farm constituents (there was surely no other reason for what was done), had amended the Farm Acts to guarantee 100 per cent parity for specified agricultural commodities, the previous guarantees having been lower. Since prices, just prior to the war, had hovered at levels which yielded 75 to 80 per cent of parity, it seemed harmless and politically advantageous, when they skyrocketed to 117 per cent of parity during the war years, to assure absolute parity.

Congressmen had argued that if farmers were to be induced to expand production to meet war needs, they would have to be promised by federal laws that they would not suffer during postwar years when demands would inevitably decline. This was a specious argument, for farmers would have expanded production anyway, as they always had, simply in response to favorable prices.

The wartime amendments to the Farm Acts had spelled tragedy in the postwar years, for under the full-parity guarantee, farmers had become indifferent to the need of reducing production, even though upon the cessation of hostilities foreign demand for our farm products had declined sharply.

We had stored more and more surplus commodities at prices above those of the open market; at the same time we had begun to spend a billion dollars a year to move surpluses to needy countries. It was not easy to give away anything, and especially agricultural commodities which were grown with varying degrees of efficiency in every area of the globe. For commodities, either given away or sold at discount prices, were likely to come into direct competition with similar ones sold by other countries. Indeed, the charge had often been made that the United States flagrantly had interfered with normal trade channels and prices.

And then, bringing it home to the coffee producers, I added that even in Latin America, which ought to be sympathetic with our efforts to stabilize raw commodity prices for our farmers, we had encountered opposition to our program of surplus disposal. An official of one Latin-American country had wagged his finger in my face when we shipped surplus rice to Peru, saying that we had maliciously deprived his country of a normal sales outlet. (Later, in 1960, when we sought to ship almost unlimited farm surpluses to Chile during the aftermath of its disastrous earthquake, two Latin-American nations objected because one nominally sold wheat, the other cotton, to Chile.)

The annual cost of United States efforts to stabilize domestic prices of agricultural commodities, I explained, had ranged from five to seven billion dollars; this included payments to farmers, storage charges (two million dollars a day), losses in selling to foreign buyers at prices less than the government had paid when the commodities were taken into storage, and costs incident to gifts. I tried to persuade the members of the coffee producers' association that the United States' experience needed to be considered with mature care, as they and others sought a method of stabilizing coffee and other commodity prices. Several facts had become clear in our experience:

First, price-fixing may help temporarily to stabilize income, but it cannot guarantee parity prices, the objective in all such schemes.

Second, artificially supported prices encourage producers to continue with high output, even increase it; hence such plans are self-defeating unless other heroic efforts are made. Before greater difficulties develop, it is essential to bring supply and demand into harmony, and the question is whether political leaders will be courageous enough to take the right actions.

Third, in the United States we were dealing through a single political authority with maximum opportunity to influence production, purchasing, marketing, and prices, and yet at enormous cost we could point only to limited success. It seemed likely, therefore, that a similar effort on an international scale—with many producing nations involved and with no supra-national political authority to manage controls and assure compliance with the rules agreed upon—would be a much more formidable one. The cost might be prohibitive.

The fifteen coffee-producing nations in Latin America and the six in Africa might look critically and long at our experience, I urged. I did not want to see our mistakes copied throughout the hemisphere.

My long conversation with the coffee producers had perhaps done some good. They were, I'm sure, convinced that the United States had not maliciously fixed coffee prices to the detriment of their countries. They conceded that the problem was highly complex, but they were certain that a determined stabilization effort had to be made.

The people of the United States have to look at this problem critically too, but with sympathy, for the raw-commodity nations are now seeking precisely what our own farmers demanded in the twenties and thirties, and still insist upon today: a stabilized, parity relationship between the prices of commodities on the open market and the prices of industrial goods. We cannot be so hypocritical as to approve a stabilization program for ourselves, and then oppose a similar one *in principle* in our dealings with them. Our only basis for opposition would be that a permanent international effort might be impracticable.

Happily, the State Department, reversing long-standing policy, took the initiative at about this time in establishing commodity study groups to explore all possibilities. Our officials realized how serious this whole problem was in Latin America. Rampant and serious misunderstandings might be overcome if all facts were assembled, analyzed, and published. And here was the cornerstone of the structure of United States-Latin American economic relations; we could no longer ignore the problem or meet it with a negative attitude.

Since coffee is produced by fifteen Latin-American and six African countries, and since coffee prices at that time were unsatisfactory, the first study group was set up to tackle the world coffee problem.

Under the chairmanship of Thomas Mann, United States Assistant Secretary of State for Economic Affairs, representatives of the countries which produce coffee began to bring together and analyze pertinent facts about coffee production, marketing, and prices. For the first time there was achieved unanimous agreement on basic facts: The people of the United States buy more than 65 per cent of the coffee exported from Latin America, and consume more coffee per person than those of any other nation in the world, including the producing nations themselves. There was obviously no mechanism in the United States, private or public, which for long could control prices of the coffee sold to the people of the United States; the competitive situation among grinders, roasters, wholesalers, and retailers makes this impossible. It made no sense, therefore, and was misleading to the citizens of the producing nations, to blame the United States for the economic troubles in the coffee-producing business. One approach clearly must be that of trying to sell more coffee to countries that could afford to buy it. Germany, the study group found, had two taxes on coffee, an import tax and the equivalent of a sales tax. Elimination of these taxes would probably cause Germans to buy two million more bags of coffee each year. The United States could hardly be blamed for West German taxes on coffee and for the unwillingness of the German people to drink more at the prices they had to pay.

The study group dug deeper. Surpluses in the producing countries were already proving to be costly and difficult, yet production was outpacing consumer demand. Production was going up 5 per cent a year, consumption only 2 per cent. Though coffee prices were already harmfully low, greater disaster seemed imminent. Also, the situation was uneven. Some countries had, over a ten-year period, increased production greatly, others very little or not at all. Therefore, if any attempt were made to have a joint effort toward reducing production, a base period of production would have to be agreed upon.

Brazil, the largest producer, faced the greatest problem. Her surplus production had grown until it amounted annually to 40 per cent of the crop. She had on hand enough coffee to satisfy her customers for a year and a half. A large share of Brazil's budget was going to stabilize prices of coffee to her farmers. Still more acres were being devoted to coffee, and better varieties were making it possible for farmers to produce more on each acre.

The six producing nations in Africa presented a worrisome problem, too. Relative newcomers to the world coffee market, they already supplied the United States with 10 per cent of its coffee imports. This was galling to Latin-American producers who supplied 90 per cent, for, they charged, had it not been for United States aid to Europe during the Marshall Plan period, Europe could not have financed the expansion of coffee production in Africa.

With the study group continuing to function, emergency action was taken. The producing nations of Latin America agreed to a marketing plan as a temporary expedient, under which Brazil would withhold as much as 40 per cent of its production from the world market, others a lesser amount, and the smallest producer only 5 per cent. Total marketings would roughly equal demand. This action halted the decline in coffee prices at about forty cents a pound, but by now the studies had progressed far enough to convince the producers that this in itself would not be enough.

First, they feared "bootlegging." A single nation with large supplies in storage could ship more than its quota and wreck the stabilization scheme.

To prevent this, the United States was requested to cooperate by restricting coffee imports to assigned quotas. Since the request seemed reasonable to me, I suggested that the authorizing legislation be considered. But even this would only be partially effective; to be completely so, all importing nations would have to follow suit in policing the quota system.

Second, the producing nations realized that more efficient production was necessary to lower costs, and this would require research and educational extension services. High-cost coffee acres ought to be shifted to the production of grain crops—especially those which were being imported. Better-quality plants would have to be developed through plant breeding. Costly soil erosion in some areas would have to be controlled.

Third, and most important, new markets would have to be found.

The marketing agreement initially instituted as a result of the work of this study group was subsequently amended to include several of the African nations. It has done some good in terms of temporary price stabilization, but the greatest contribution of the study group has been in having key leaders of the coffee industry for the first time come face to face with the facts. They now agree that there is no single solution to the problem, that the United States has not fixed prices, and that we are willing to work with them in defining clearly the multiple actions which would best assure good results.

The value of developing accurate information was so obvious that commodity study groups were also set up for cotton, wool, cocoa, lead, and zinc. These six study groups began compiling and disseminating a great deal of information which helped to dispel emotional misconceptions harmful to the United States.

On September 28, 1962, an agreement was entered into by twenty-three member states of the United Nations which may herald a new era of economic cooperation and to some extent alleviate Latin America's difficulties caused by price fluctuations. After weeks of debate and dissension, twenty-three coffee-producing and -consuming nations signed an international stabilization agreement and other countries indicated they would soon follow suit. This marketing agreement is expected to yield a fair return to coffee growers without appreciably increasing the cost of coffee to consumers. To avoid a price war which could send the price of coffee plummeting, the producing nations will adhere to export quotas which, of course, will involve considerable stockpiling in some countries. Importing nations will do their part by reducing or holding down import and sales taxes on coffee and by adhering to the quota system. In addition, there will gradually be established a fund which may be used to help the producing nations diversify their agriculture and thus become less dependent on coffee.

Exports of primary products (agricultural commodities, ores, timber) from Latin America account for 90 per cent of their outgoing foreign trade, and for 15 to 20 per cent of the gross national product in many countries. The incomes received from primary products are of decisive influence in the economies of Latin America. Most people do not realize that prices for these commodities sometimes fluctuate as much as 25 to 50 per cent between years. Imports will therefore vary greatly, depending on the previous year's experience with exports. Between 1952 and 1962 the combined price index of commodities sold by Latin America went down in every year but one. This has been especially true of coffee, wheat, corn, tin, cotton, sisal, lead, nitrates, wool, zinc, and sugar. However, a gradual increase in the volume of exports to all parts of the world, including the United States, which takes about 50 per cent of the total output, has increased income from exports by about 20 per cent.

While industrial nations have continued to make substantial gains in production, they have not proportionately increased their purchases of minerals from Latin America. The more efficient use and re-use of metals and the development of substitutes, such as plastics, has enabled manufacturers to hold down their purchases. Thus, raw material-exporting nations have watched industrial nations increase production by 150 per cent when they have increased their sales by only 25 per cent.

The argument of laissez-faire economists that the price mechanism will cause supply to adjust to demand has been proved erroneous with respect to primary-product production—especially agricultural production. If prices decline, growers tend to increase production in order to sell more units and thus not suffer a drop in gross income. In mining, production costs, including depreciation, interest, and other overhead charges, remain high regardless of the world market situation. Thus in the face of a fall in demand, mine owners, too, are likely to increase production in an effort to sell more units.

Numerous efforts of producing nations to bring some degree of economic stability internally, in the face of wide world market fluctuations, have met with indifferent success. In the early 1950s, Chile held copper off the world market, hoping for higher prices, but as the stockpile grew, the retrogressive influence on world prices increased, for purchasers knew that eventually this surplus would have to be sold; moreover, stockpiling encouraged the production of substitutes for copper, especially aluminum. The large supply of coffee in Brazil became a constant threat to the market. In general, these internal schemes are a combination of the Hoover ever-normal granary plan, and the programs of the Commodity Credit Corporation of the United States. The experiments have been as costly, relatively, to Latin America as ours have been to us, and the Latin-American countries have been less able to meet financing requirements. The Latin-American countries have also resorted to changes in export taxes as a means of minimizing the fluctuations in prices paid to producers. They have sometimes manipulated exchange rates applicable to the conversion of foreign earnings into hard currencies. But these manipulations have been a burden to national budgets, and of questionable value to producers.

The attitude of the United States on price stabilization has gradually changed. In all administrations prior to 1933, the view was that a free market situation was fair to producers and consumers alike, and provided the only workable system of keeping supply in balance with demand. The reasoning was that control mechanisms were automatic, decisions were vastly decentralized as they should be, and governmental intervention would not only be wrong in principle, but would be doomed to failure.

The Roosevelt administration departed from this view with respect to wool, sugar, and wheat—not because of our concern for the nations from which we purchased primary commodities. The United States does not produce enough sugar and wool to satisfy consumer requirements. Internal political pressures led to the development of stabilization programs for these two commodities, chiefly to get satisfactory returns on domestic production, though foreign producers also benefited, especially Cuba.

Wheat was a different problem: Several countries, including the United States and Canada in this hemisphere, were large surplus producers. Competitive selling or dumping was deemed to be beneficial to none. Hence a wheat marketing agreement was developed and approved by numerous producing and purchasing countries. The wheat plan is similar in principle to what the Latin-American nations have long requested for their primary products.

Many of the commodities which have most worried Latin America are not produced in the United States, such as coffee, bananas, and tin; some, such as copper, lead, and zinc, are produced in the United States, but are also imported. The Roosevelt and Truman administrations adhered to the free market philosophy with regard to such commodities. But the Eisenhower administration, recognizing that Latin America's problem was becoming more and more acute, took a different view.

In earlier years, a decrease in income from exports might cause the Latin Americans to buy fewer consumer goods. Now, as industrialization in Latin America increased, a drop in dollar income could retard essential economic growth. It could cause, as in Brazil, a cutback in oil imports and thus force a rationing of productive energy; factories might have to close for a few days each week, causing unemployment and hardship. And, as always in the victims' eyes, the United States eagle becomes the vulture. With interdependence an inescapable fact, and stability in trade relations more than ever a necessity, neither the United States nor Latin America gained from these situations.

Unfortunately at this time, Congress insisted upon subsidizing cotton exports, and the President felt impelled to institute quotas to regulate the importation of lead, zinc, and oil, as I have explained in a previous chapter.

The recriminations which became rampant led to the United States' initiating the commodity study groups, first under the leadership of this country and later of the United Nations. In 1959, the Senate Subcommittee on Inter-American Affairs, of the Foreign Relations Committee, directed its research staff to make an exhaustive analysis of this problem. The researchers assembled an impressive array of historic data and summarized the arguments for and against commodity agreements.

On the affirmative side, they pointed out that "acting singly, nations can do little to mitigate commodity problems in circumstances where collective action offers some hope." Even the stanchest advocates of free markets must agree that swift and substantial changes in commodity prices are often useless, they said. Since individual governments were attacking the problem, it seemed reasonable that they should pool their efforts to achieve greater precision, consistency, and mutual reinforcement in their respective measures. Furthermore, international agreements did not of themselves create the conditions most often objected to by opponents—interference with free market forces. *National* schemes *did* but international action might well lead to more rational results.

On the negative side, the Senate's researchers pointed out that commodity agreements postponed the inevitable economic adjustments needed in the production of primary commodities; they might lull participating countries into the delusion that they can escape the necessity of cutting back production or taking other essential measures to remedy the difficulty. Commodity agreements protect high-cost producers and eliminate incentives to promote efficiency; thus, they are unfair to consumers. Experiences with agreements such as those for wheat, wool, coffee, and sugar, showed that it was difficult to negotiate a satisfactory agreement; compromises between producer and consumer interests might result in an agreement which was wide of the mark and worse than no agreement at all. And, the researchers warned, an agreement usually involved international control over national economic policies, thus impinging on sovereignty—a warning which at first must have frightened our friends in Latin America as much as it did members of the United States Senate.

But after weighing all the evidence, the research scholars for the Senate subcommittee concluded: "The question is a pragmatic one. *If it appears that cooperative international action can help us to solve a persistent problem, then such action should at least be sought—especially in cases where other lines of attack on the problem have failed.*"

Nonpartisan concern for the problem began to grow. Former Governor Adlai Stevenson and former Senator William Benton, upon returning from a study trip to numerous Latin-American countries, reached the conclusion that the United States would have to depart from some of its older concepts and work actively with Latin America for a permanent solution to the problems of price relationships.

"We must lend a more sympathetic ear to the Latin American desire for commodity price stabilization," wrote Senator Benton. "We must make clear that we are eager to cooperate in finding ways to reduce the hardships of erratic fluctuation. We should examine suggested solutions, commodity by commodity. And we must make up our minds that we are willing to enter into international agreements that will help stabilize markets, even though this seemingly contravenes our basic doctrine of free market prices."

Meanwhile, this question was being discussed in detail by President Eisenhower's Advisory Committee on Inter-American Affairs. Under Secretary of State Douglas Dillon and Assistant Secretary Rubottom were giving special consideration to the problem in these sessions. The committee came to the conclusion that our changing attitude which had been evident for several years would have to be accelerated. We would have to cooperate in reasonable efforts to stabilize price relationships. In September 1960, at Bogotá, Under Secretary Dillon concurred on behalf of the United States in an inter-American resolution that "urgent attention be given to the search for effective and practical ways, appropriate to each commodity, to deal with the problem of the instability of exchange earnings of countries heavily dependent upon the exportation of primary products."

Later, Douglas Dillion, as Secretary of the Treasury in the Kennedy administration, again gave expression to the new United States attitude. He joined the representatives of the Latin-American nations in the Punta del Este conference in Uruguay in declaring that "the economic development of Latin America requires an expansion of its trade, an increase in income received from exports, *and a lessening of cyclical or seasonal fluctuations in the incomes of those countries that still depend heavily on the export of raw materials.*"

At the same conference, Secretary Dillion entered into other significant agreements that bear upon this problem:

"Importing member countries should reduce and eliminate . . . all restrictions and discriminatory practices affecting consumption and importation of primary products." (The United States restricts the importation of commodities, such as wool, meat, sugar, and certain minerals which compete with United States-grown products. We do not have tariffs on commodities not domestically produced, such as tin, coffee, bauxite, and bananas.)

He also agreed to a Charter declaration which called for the "highest possible degree of processing in the country of origin." Latin America obviously wishes to prepare coffee in final form for consumption, for example, rather than shipping the beans to the United States and other countries for processing. One difficulty is that the United States consumers prefer various blends, and this requires the importation of varieties of coffee from different countries prior to processing. The Latin-American countries also wish to convert bauxite to alumina prior to shipment, and to process other agricultural commodities and minerals in their countries, thus increasing their income and often reducing their shipping costs.

The Charter of Punta del Este called upon the Secretary-General of the Organization of American States to bring together a group of experts, appointed by the Latin-American governments, to determine how to raise funds to be used in market stabilization programs; to suggest how an international fund for the stabilization of export receipts might best be established, and to prepare a draft plan for "compensatory financing."

The expectation of the countries represented at the Punta del Este conference—including the United States, but excluding Cuba, which did not sign the Charter—is that producer and consumer countries will actively participate in stabilization programs for the primary products of our southern neighbors.

The United States attitude, then, gradually changing over the years, is now substantially in harmony with that long expressed by Latin-American republics. New commitments have been made. We are on the verge of new continental experiments to stabilize prices of primary products. Some agreements may work. Others may fail—disastrously. Problems after failure may be more difficult than those now confronting us. But it is vitally important that Latin Americans know that we want to cooperate in any feasible way to help them win economic justice in the disposal of their export commodities. No longer will we veto their suggestions with obsolete shibboleths.

Said the researchers for the Senate Subcommittee on Inter-American Affairs: "We should free ourselves from the traditional position that international attempts to influence commodity trade, prices, and production are somehow reprehensible."

In recognition of mutuality of interest, as well as for sheer humanitarian reasons, we must maintain a cooperative attitude. It is imperative, of course, that stabilization efforts be fairly successful. Our relations with Latin America will improve immeasurably when the people—left-wing, right-wing, middle-of-the-road—realize that we do not, as they fear, crush the economies of Latin America in order to enrich ourselves, and that we do not maliciously fix prices of the things they sell to us and buy from us. But our indignant cries of innocence, however justified, will accomplish nothing; we must act. We must cooperate wherever possible with Latin Americans as they seek reasonable methods of price stabilization. We must stop letting the interests of small segments of our economy outweigh the interests of the nation and of our allies. It is not enough to have analyzed the problem; we must help solve it.

9   In the arid climate of greed and ignorance, where the land takes more from a man than it gives, the seed of revolution grows best.

THE FARMER ROSE FROM HIS KNEES AS I WALKED THROUGH the dusty field toward him. He wiped his hands across the seat of his ragged trousers and watched me approach, squinting into the sun. I thought he was smiling, but as I came closer, I saw that he was not, that squinting had pulled his cheek muscles and stretched his mouth into a completely humorless grin. He straightened from the crouch that years of bending over the earth had made his natural posture—a painful effort but pride required it.

He had little to be proud of. The yellow earth from which he scratched a meager living belonged to a wealthy landowner, a feudal baron in the twentieth century. The hut beyond him was nothing more than a rickety-looking framework covered with mud and bits of vegetation. In and about the hut, at least seven or eight children, most of them tiny, dirty, and nearly naked, played in the dust. A narrow, angular woman squatted before the door with wooden dish and pestle.

Standing before this poor peon, I could feel his sour anger and sorrow. I don't really think his resentment was directed at me in particular; rather it was part of him, like the bent back and the dust. Yet in his sullen gaze I lost whatever urge I'd had to speak with him. And I was suddenly very conscious of the difference between us, of my fine clothes and good health.

Though I had only recently visited Latin America for the first time, I had seen enough to dull the shock of such absolute poverty and hopelessness. But never before had I felt the full force of it as I did that sweltering afternoon in the dust. I exchanged greetings with him clumsily, shook his hand, waved to his family, and walked back to the car on the road.

We drove for a few minutes in silence, as if my companions sensed how deeply I'd been moved. Then one of my Latin-American hosts turned to me and said gently: "In this brief moment, you have met many of my countrymen."

Of course, I knew the statistics: Most of the Latin-American countries are heavily dependent on agriculture and from a half to two-thirds of all the workers are engaged in farm production. I also knew that the vast majority of these people were virtual slaves to a wealthy and privileged few who owned the land. But these statistics had been so remote, so sterile and academic, until that dusty meeting with a mestizo peon.

In most of Latin America, primitive methods of farming still prevail in discouraging abundance. In every country one sees patches of hybrid corn, fertilized land, and improved cultivation methods, surrounded by vast areas burdened with traditional practices. It is not at all uncommon to see a ragged peon moving through a bare field punching holes in the soil with a pointed stick and dropping a seed into each hole. There is, save in new oases, no fertilizer other than the manure of livestock, no modern farm machinery, no evidence of scientific know-how.

I have visited Brazilian farms so badly eroded that the bones of the earth showed through her skin. The produce was a pitiful demonstration of futility.

The country is larger than the United States, but much of it is unexplored, including areas of forbidding jungle. Most of the people live in the coastal areas where once-fertile lands are rapidly washing away. A plane trip across Brazil is dramatic. For hours you see the interior below, untold acres of soil never turned by man and lush with vegetation, then suddenly the green ends and the yellow coastal area begins. More than 60 per cent of the population is engaged in agriculture, but only 2 per cent of this immense land is under cultivation. Much is in pasture, more in forests.

Agriculture scarcely keeps up with population growth, and a good deal of food must be imported into the land which, properly used, could feed its people and more. As it is, life expectancy in Brazil is probably between thirty-five and forty years. Malnutrition takes a heavy toll. The sixty-five million Brazilians, save for the well-to-do, live on a grossly inadequate diet, heavy with bread, rice, corn, beans, and mandioca. Except for chicken now and then or a little charque (dried beef) there is almost no meat. To buy this food, which gives him some sixteen hundred calories and leaves him weak, the Brazilian spends most of his pitiful income. He does not get enough proteins, calcium, iron, vitamins, or calories. Brazil's index of infant mortality is among the highest in the world.

In the settled rural areas, hundreds of thousands of farm laborers are leaving the land and hastening to the cities, hoping to find a better life. From friends or on crude radios, they have heard of the opulence of São Paulo and Rio de Janeiro and they feel they have nothing to lose by trying to share in the wondrous riches. But the better life, for most migrants, is an illusion. They find themselves, quite likely, living in wretched slums—the spillover of idle humans that stagnates around the growing urban centers of Latin America. As farm labor is siphoned off, food production declines.

Brazilian leaders in desperation have sought to stimulate farm production by financing price supports for certain commodities, by subsidizing exports, by restricting imports of food and fiber, and by providing credit to farmers who wish to expand or improve production. Results have not been encouraging. For instance, in the past twenty years wheat production has increased greatly, yet imports of wheat and flour have also risen.

Most Latin American countries have agricultural conditions like those of Brazil. In many respects the situation is similar to, though worse than, that of the Soviet Union. There, five times as many people as in the United States are engaged in agricultural production, yet our output surpasses that of the USSR. In Latin America, four times as many people are engaged in farming as in the United States, but total production is only about half that of the United States. Latin America is a net food importer. Yet Brazil, alone, is larger than the United States and is probably equal to it in agricultural potentiality.

Allowing for land too poor to cultivate and the extremes in rainfall, Latin America is probably using less than 40 per cent of the land suitable for the raising of food. South America itself has half again as much arable land as Europe and four times as much as Asia. Just under half of Latin America consists of plains, of which nearly 95 per cent is cultivable. Another 33 per cent of the total area is in plateaus and tablelands, of which about 75 per cent is suitable for agriculture. Even the 20 per cent remaining, hill and mountain land, is not totally unsuited to farming.

In general, though not in every country, the population grows faster than farm production. In the past twenty years, agricultural output in Latin America has increased about 32 per cent; population has risen 38 per cent. In 1955–56, the total production of primary crops was some 40 per cent higher than the average annual output for the period 1935–39 but, because of the population increase, production per capita was 4 per cent under the previous average. The inefficiency of old farming techniques may be illustrated by a single fact: In Uruguay, where agriculture is more mechanized than it is in most other Latin-American countries, wheat production per man is ten times as great as it is in Mexico, Peru, and Venezuela.

Unfortunately, the major increases in agricultural production have been largely in export crops—bananas, cocoa, wool, sugar, coffee, meat—whose prices fluctuate capriciously. These increases may be due partly to the fact that United States private capital is heavily invested in production of such commodities. Total United States private investment in Latin-American agriculture approached $700 million before the Cuban seizures of property; of this, 90 per cent was held by twelve companies.

Latin America's precarious economic situation—dominated by overdependence on the production of export crops—calls for far-reaching changes in agriculture. Production of cereals, fruits, milk, vegetables, meat, and some fibers must be substantially increased. Production of some foods, fibers, and coffee must be decreased. Primitive practices must yield to scientific farming methods. Widespread losses of topsoil and plant nutrients must be checked. Nations which spend a high proportion of scarce foreign exchange for food imports have to become more self-sufficient or else develop a diversified foreign trade which will enable them to import food without jeopardizing international balances.

It makes no sense for a nation to grow more coffee than it can sell, and at the same time import wheat which it could grow efficiently; yet Brazil does precisely this. It is pathetic for men, women, and children to toil on hillsides cultivating corn which yields a tenth as much as another readily available variety, but most Andean countries do this. It defies elementary logic for a country to be dependent on the export of a low-grade ore for nearly 70 per cent of its foreign exchange and then be compelled to use a substantial part of that exchange to buy food it could grow domestically—as Bolivia does. And it is anachronistic and inhumane to maintain in agriculture a baron-and-serf relationship that forces workers to live in poverty and impedes national economic growth—as nearly all of Latin America does.

The United States has severe farm problems of its own—but we are involved in the agricultural problems of Latin America, too. We are apt to be overly critical: We are tempted to be scornful of our neighbors and insist that they mend their ways as a condition to receiving help from us. Changes are surely needed, and aid should stimulate them. But we should not be too quick to point fingers, for we have indulged in many of the malpractices now prevalent in Latin America. And we still do.

We, like they, grow commodities we cannot sell. Our southern states fail to grow types of food the people need to improve their diets. These are in part the consequences of federal programs which have tended to freeze obsolete patterns of farming. When we are critical of schemes in Latin America which artificially yield some improvement in farm income but result in the accumulation of unsalable surpluses, we should temper our words. We have only to look over our shoulders at the grain stored in the Midwest.

Much of the cotton land of the United States could more profitably be devoted to fruit, vegetables, milk, and meat production. This fails to happen, however, for several reasons: Southern farmers are experienced with cotton but are strangers to other farm enterprises. Government subsidies make obsolete production tolerable, and sometimes quite profitable. And if sudden changes were made in farming, community services like transportation would become partly obsolete. (Highways and railroads have been built to carry cotton from fields to gins.) Hardships spread like ripples on water. These and other pressures against desirable adjustments win out—here, as other pressures do in Latin America.

What is more, we used outdated and wastefully exploitive methods on the soil for many years. Our scientific and soil conserving practices are a phenomenon of the twentieth century, for the most part.

In the middle of the last century, a few in our country became alarmed about the lack of farm efficiency. They began a movement which led to the passage of the Land Grant Act of 1862, signed by Abraham Lincoln. This was designed to promote efficiency of agriculture and industry. When the new collegiate institutions, brought into being by the legislation, began their work, few trained scientists were available to staff them. So the first task was to develop a faculty. After trial and error, the academicians began suggesting improved practices to farmers. The advice was scorned. Men on the land scornfully called the professors "test tube" farmers. A new generation had to inherit the land before farm opinion altered enough to accept the mandate of the future. Then, in 1894, federal aid induced the creation of a series of agricultural experiment stations and soon research into many phases of crop and livestock production was under way. But not until 1914—less than fifty years ago—was an extension system created to carry the results of research to practical farmers. At that time, knowledge in the laboratory was twenty-five years in advance of farm practice. Today essentially no gap exists between discoveries in the laboratory and the application of new knowledge in everyday farming.

The practices and attitudes of farmers in Latin America are reminiscent of those of United States farmers in the mid-nineteenth century.

I first visited an agricultural experiment station in Latin America in 1953. Flying to Cali, Colombia, we were driven to Palmira on a rugged road in torrid heat. Dust clouds from our auto caravan obscured the scenery. When I arrived at Palmira I could not recognize my companions and could scarcely see at all. But discomfort was soon forgotten, for here was a station which, under the guidance of scientists from Michigan State University, was conducting research into every aspect of Colombian agriculture. Poultry specialists were seeking to discover the breeds best suited to Colombian conditions, the diets most conducive to egg and meat production, the chemicals most effective in controlling diseases, and the management methods most likely to yield maximum profit. Similar work was under way with livestock. Plant breeders were developing hybrid corn and other grains that would produce larger yields, while withstanding unique climatic conditions. Plants never before grown in Colombia were being imported and tested. The Michigan experts had brought together young Colombian scientists who were learning the exacting methods that go with good research, the intention being to turn the work over to them as soon as possible.

Few of the practical farmers of the area visited the station to observe the "test tube farmers." No extension service was available to report the results of research to men and women on the land. Only a few large landowners were curious, but then theirs was already a good life and they were in no particular hurry to change the established order. A few miles from the station, the farming I saw was no different from what farming had been a century before.

A week later, I visited a project at Santa Cruz, Bolivia. Here was new land, never touched by a plow. The area had been made accessible only recently by a new highway. It was about seven thousand feet lower than La Paz, and suitable for a variety of crops. A tiny experiment station had been established and was being supervised by a representative of the International Cooperation Administration. Like all other such projects in Latin America, management would be turned over gradually to local personnel.

The director of the research project—an attractive, olive-skinned young man whose enthusiasm and flawless Spanish were impressive—proudly showed me the first results of his work. He had imported a variety of corn called "Cuban Yellow." From the first plantings he had achieved a yield about ten times greater than was usually obtained from native Indian nubbins. He was excited about the potentialities. It was a pleasure to see a native with such vision and energy. I was with him half a day before I learned he was not Bolivian, but an agricultural agent from the southwestern part of the United States, a graduate of the New Mexico College of Agriculture and Mechanic Arts—a Peace Corpsman eight years before the term was coined.

Some years later—my hopes and curiosity had been at high pitch in the meantime—I asked about the progress being made in the Santa Cruz area. The news was keenly disappointing; the government of Bolivia had not been able to persuade many families to move to this rich agricultural region. This seemed astounding. At that time 70 per cent of all agricultural land was held by 4 per cent of the landowners. The workers were trapped in the sixteenth century. No one leaves home easily but I had thought that these poor families—despairing of a system which provided barely enough to keep them alive and of their inability to offer their children a better lot—would surely rush to the fertile land to build a new and abundant life. But they did not want to move; roots grow deeply over the centuries, and these people were bound to their shabby homes by habit stronger than chains. So the government transferred some of its young conscripts to the area, hoping they would come to like it, see its potentiality, possibly marry girls in the area and settle down after their military service. Conscription met with its usual limited success.

Of all the people in Latin America, Bolivians should rejoice over the opening of new lands and eagerly settle it. Their country was not endowed with much good land. The number of persons per square mile of arable land is nine times as great as it is in Argentina, for example.

I had dark thoughts about the Santa Cruz project. I felt thoroughly annoyed, like a father whose expensive new present has been casually rejected by his child. The International Cooperation Administration had provided funds for the establishment and operation of the experiment station to demonstrate scientific practices that would assure a stable living to farm settlers. It seemed inconceivable that people on the verge of starvation would be so attached to tradition as not to seize this Aladdin-like opportunity.

And then I thought again of some of our experiences here. I recalled that for all our worship of science and jet-like progress in food and fiber production in this century, we were, as late as the 1930s, following practices that threatened future generations. We were mining the land. One hundred and fifty million acres had been completely ruined by our exploitation, a similar amount had lost most of its precious topsoil, and still another hundred million acres were rapidly washing into rivers and out to sea. At first, the answer was indifference; the land seemed endless, and families would ruin one farm, then move into virgin territory and ruin another. Later it was largely ignorance or habit that sustained malpractices. The most memorable incident, because it was relatively recent and immortalized by John Steinbeck, was the dust bowl in our Midwest. The soil was so abused that it finally blew away; I lived in Washington, D.C. at the time and can recall the fine yellow powdery dust of the Oklahoma panhandle settling on the government buildings.

For nearly three decades, beginning early in the 1930s, we spent hundreds of millions of dollars annually in an effort to convince farmers that they should cast aside the customs of their forefathers and farm the earth as nature obviously intended, on the contour. This nationwide effort gradually slowed soil and plant nutrient loss, but by no means wholly solved the problem.

An incident in North Dakota flashed into my mind. At the owner's request, federal scientists had made a detailed survey of a farm rapidly being ruined by erosion. Every soil type had been analyzed to determine its best use and its tolerance to erosion. The evidence had been placed on a large, colored map. Scientists then indicated the terraces, strip plantings, and crop rotations required for the control of erosion. The contour farming plan recommended, among other things, the moving of fences and the removal of several scrubby trees near the farmstead. The trees were in the way of contour plowing. The farmer angrily condemned the entire plan. "My father," he said, "planted those trees when I was a baby, and nobody cuts them down!" He would carry on his farming as before, regardless of consequences. It didn't seem to occur to the man that his father, in planting those trees, had hoped to benefit future generations, but now a similar concern for descendants required that they be cut down or moved. Sentiment and habit are powerful forces.

Six years after my first exposure to the farm problem in Latin America, I went to an agricultural experiment station a few miles north of Veracruz, Mexico. It was financed jointly by the Rockefeller Foundation and the Mexican Government. I arrived in midmorning. All around was a great green expanse. Here was a medley of luxuriant crops, of livestock and poultry waddling in fatness, and of dedicated, starry-eyed men, hard at work. The adviser was an American, in his mid-thirties, who reminded me of the handsome county agent I'd met at Santa Cruz. He had succeeded in bringing to the station a group of young Mexican scientists—plant geneticists, livestock breeders, soil experts—who were well trained and familiar with the practical agricultural conditions of the area. They were fired with missionary zeal.

From my knowledge of such stations—I had been in thirty or more in the United States—I would have guessed this one north of Veracruz to be nine or ten years old. I was amazed to learn that it was only entering the third year.

When the lunch bell rang, we walked to a large tent that had been erected hurriedly on the lawn in front of the main research building. I shook hands with the two hundred practical farmers who had come to have lunch with us. From them I learned that they were regularly in touch with every aspect of the station's research and were applying on their own farms the superior practices they saw developed on this scientific oasis.

Thus in Latin America I observed a drama which duplicated a phase of our own agricultural history: first, in Colombia, scorn of test tube farmers; then in Bolivia a respect for science but a reluctance to give up old ways; and in Mexico, the thrilling climax of almost continuous flow of useful information from laboratory to farm. It took us a century to enact our dream. What was going on in Latin America was squeezed into less than a decade.

With the proper help, Latin America can make headway against its agricultural problems. On my first study mission to Brazil in 1953, the Minister of Agriculture told me that he wished to initiate an improved extension program to carry the knowledge developed in a few experiment stations to individual farmers. He wanted to stimulate the production of new crops and induce farmers to plant improved varieties. He saw the need for better breeds of livestock. They had to drain wet lands and irrigate dry lands, to check soil and fertility losses, and to reforest eroded areas.

Shortly thereafter, the United States helped set up a cooperative enterprise: *Escritório Técnico de Agricultura Brasil-Estados Unidos*, naturally called ETA.

ETA established nearly fifty farm research and demonstration projects. It hired twenty-five hundred Brazilians, instigated the creation of two hundred farm extension offices, and developed cooperative relations with seventy existing organizations—from agricultural colleges to farm credit agencies. Thirty United States technicians were assigned to work with the

119

Brazilians, many of whom were given grants to study scientific farming in the United States.

The members of ETA soon saw that too much land was in coffee, and probably too much in cotton. Soil and fertility losses were rampant. They decided that interior lands, blanketed with native grasses, were suitable for the production of a wide variety of crops. On such lands, Brazil could produce all that was needed to provide a healthy diet for her people.

But science would have to invade the land, for they found that ill-bred, undernourished Brazilian dairy cows produced only a third as much as do dairy animals in more advanced countries. The potato yield was only a sixth as much per acre as in the United States. Beef, poultry, and crop production was found to be equally inefficient.

ETA has now been operating for about eight years. Its main effort has been to mobilize the scientific, educational, and credit resources of the country and to bring these to bear on the problems of individual farms. Results in terms of changing farm practices have thus far been meager, as I have previously said, but the agricultural possibilities of the country have been amply demonstrated. And someday, we may witness a great burst of progress in agriculture like that of the United States early in this century. There are bursts now, but some almost seem to be misfires.

President Juscelino Kubitschek initiated a bold plan to open the interior of Brazil. He built a new capital on virgin land and envisaged a spectacular road-building program that would eventually provide transportation from Brasilia to every section of the nation. Highways would radiate from the new capital city like spokes of a wheel. While at present the construction of this remote city (financed, as I'll point out in the next chapter, with worthless money) appears to have been an act of folly, it may be that in the long future the creation of Brasilia will be hailed as the beginning of a better era. If the opening of the interior induces large numbers to move to it from the coastal areas—especially from ruined farms and from the over-populated cities—if settlers develop family-size economic units and produce food and fiber which will eliminate the need of imports and enrich the diets of the Brazilian people—then Brazil will have made giant strides toward permanent prosperity and political stability.

Irrigation projects have enabled some countries to diversify their agriculture. With the governor of Sinaloa, a state on the west coast of Mexico, I flew one afternoon over a large irrigated area north of Mazatlán, Mexico's main seaport on the Pacific. From the air, the fields of perishable vegetables looked like an old-fashioned patch quilt. As our plane dipped close to the earth, I could see that yields were as plentiful as any in the United States.

But two factors made the project risky. While transportation up the west coast to the United States was available, the Mexican production coincided with that of our southwestern states, thereby eliminating them as a market. The average Mexican family simply couldn't afford to buy the luscious, perishable products from the lands of Sinaloa. Here was another obvious case of the need for *balanced* economic development keyed to effective demand. I have no doubt, however, that the growing prosperity of Mexico will in time make the Sinaloa irrigation project an asset to the country.

Of course, before the problems of people, food, and farms can be solved swiftly, drastic changes will have to be made in the patterns of land settlement and ownership. Of the eight million square miles in Latin America, less than 5 per cent is under cultivation. A higher percentage, of course, is in pasture for livestock. On the farms, ranches, and plantations live more than 125 million persons. Some farmers operate *minifundios* which average only eight acres in size, comprise three-fourths of the total number of farms, but constitute only 4 per cent of the land. Others help run *latifundios*—2 per cent of the farms but nearly 70 per cent of the land. Between these two extremes are the middle-sized, family-operated farms of the United States variety. Clearly agriculture is dominated by the *latifundios*—big, self-sufficient enterprises, the Spanish and Portuguese concept transplanted to Latin America.

Here, again, the United States has had its own experience. In the pre-Civil War era, southern plantations and ranches tended to become ever larger. Some were miniature empires. In the Reconstruction period, most of these were broken into smaller holdings. Efficiency of production declined. But fortunately, the pattern of landownership which evolved was not inimicable to eventual efficiency.

Who in Latin America owns how much land? And what is being done about it? In Venezuela 3 per cent of the landholders own 90 per cent of the land. In Mexico, before the revolution, the same situation existed, and among the owners were many Americans. In Chile, less than 2 per cent of the landholders own 50 per cent of the land.

Mexico insisted upon making its "reform farms" so small that the new owners and their children had to be satisfied with subsistence type of farming at a time when mechanization and other modern farm methods were bringing startling increases in production on farms of more economic size in the United States.

As mentioned in Chapter 2, land reform has been delayed for too long in Brazil where half the private land is owned by only 2 per cent of the landholders. The resulting discontent has nourished Francisco Juliao and his Peasant League in their fight against the government.

Agrarian reform has also become a principal political issue in Colombia. Under a new agrarian reform law, plans call for small owner-operated farms on what is now public domain; for the consolidation into larger holdings of numerous handkerchief-size farms which now yield only poverty; for the division of large land holdings. The entire undertaking is to be financed through a cooperative bank.

In Argentina, immense areas of good land are still held by the government. Land reform is, therefore, aimed primarily at disposal of public domain. Over a period of years, the average private holding has decreased from 2500 acres to about 550 acres.

Fifty per cent of the farmers of Paraguay are classified as "squatters." They have no legal right to the farms they occupy. Reform movements have so far been stifled.

Nearly all of Ecuador's productive land is owned by a very few families —often reported to be 1 per cent of the population. Most of the 2.4 million Indians of the country, most of them illiterate, work on the land, living on less than seven hundred calories a day. Every effort to change this has been stubbornly resisted by rightists who are impervious to suggestions for improvement and by leftists who await violence as their avenue to power.

Uruguay has had modest success with a miniature experiment: It has purchased a number of large holdings, divided these into sixty-acre farms, and sold them on generous credit terms to farmers.

In Chile, nearly four thousand farm families have received holdings of economic size through the help of a government agency.

Most attempts at land reform in the past have been emergency measures to satisfy a discontented population and have been carried out hurriedly, without sufficient knowledge of farm science.

Unfortunately, agriculture all too often has taken a back seat to industrialization. Latin-American leaders have pushed industrialization at the expense of agriculture, causing economic imbalances. This emphasis on industrialization has sometimes accentuated an already difficult balance-of-payments situation, which in turn has led to political instability. People on a near-starvation diet and dependent on imports for much of their food may, if income from exports declines, be threatened with actual starvation. Unrest and uprisings will surely follow.

Through artificial devices, inflation, price controls, and subsidy exchange rates, some governments have discouraged agricultural production and encouraged the use of scarce foreign exchange for food imports. This has been so serious that a few countries which formerly produced enough of such products as wheat and sugar to meet their domestic needs have at times had to import these very commodities.

Ceilings placed on domestic prices of foodstuffs as emergency attempts to control inflation have prompted domestic producers to cut back production, and has made them unable to compete with especially favorable exchange rates for food imports. This has led to some absurd situations—to scarce foreign exchange being used to import food which in turn has been illegally re-exported at a profit for the contraband traders. The ill consequences of manipulating prices and foreign exchange rates have been recognized in most countries and during the past several years stringent corrective measures have been taken. There is clearly no substitute for efficient production. It is fun to play poker, but no one should confuse a card game with the creation of real wealth.

The United States considers the improvement (and reform) of Latin-American agriculture so important that it has become a major element in our foreign policy under the Alliance for Progress. Intimately involved in these problems as we have been for the past twenty years, we have made some inroads.

In Guatemala, the United States began in 1954 to help with a promising program. Half of the nation's land was owned by eleven hundred families and half by the government. Many farmers were *minifundistas*, squatters with no legal titles to the plots they farmed, subject to capricious removal at any time, and constantly at the mercy of tradesmen and petty officials. The United States-Guatemalan effort was to move a great many of the *minifundistas* to fifty-acre tracts on good land on the Pacific slope. In this forested area, five acres were cleared on each farm by the public team, leaving the remainder of the task for the farm family. The farmer was given ownership of the land—a revolutionary step. A rural bank extended credit for seed, fertilizers, fences, farm machinery, and cattle. The average income for these farmers increased more than 50 per cent. Rural clinics, schools, water and sewage systems, and self-help houses have been built. It is an understatement to say that conditions were permanently improved.

Agricultural production has been increasing slowly in Colombia—but it is lagging behind the population increase. More than 63 per cent of the total Colombian population is engaged in farming, but farmers produce only 40 per cent of the gross national product. The United States has given both technical and economic help in land settlement, soil conservation, agricultural engineering, forest management, livestock improvement, farm-to-market roads, irrigation and drainage, and the production of cocoa and kenaf as promising new export crops. A major purpose has been to increase food production and consumption while reducing the nation's dependence on coffee production.

When I visited Bolivia in 1953, the situation was bleak. The price of tin had plummeted (from $1.12 to $.80 a pound), dragging with it an already abominable living standard. My companions and I were stunned by what we saw. The United States moved quickly to send surplus food to the country. And when I returned home, I urged that economic aid be given to buttress the program of technical assistance. A year later, funds were made available to import farm machinery, tools, fertilizers, and insecticides. Roadbuilding machinery was brought in to improve the farm-feeder roads in the mountainous terrain. In three years, the International Cooperation Administration provided nearly $71 million in economic aid for these purposes, after which the flow of such funds began to decline. The total effect of technical and economic assistance was to improve agricultural production both quantitatively and qualitatively. In the meantime, however, the value of Bolivia's mineral exports declined from $100 million in 1954 to $70 million in 1961, so that the economy of the country was in worse condition than it was at the time of my visit.

The United States agricultural assistance program has been expanded every year for nearly twenty years. I had the pleasure of signing, with the President of Chile, the agreement which initiated the program in his country in 1953 and today it is a small but vital force in the country. I have visited cooperative projects in seventeen of the republics. In all, we have helped to improve agriculture in nineteen countries.

In addition, the United States has paid about two-thirds of the cost of maintaining a modern research station at the Inter-American Institute of Agricultural Science at Turrialba, Costa Rica, which is under the aegis of the Organization of American States. The work of the station was considerably strengthened after 1956–57 when the presidential representatives recommended a new system of administration for the program, expanded it by adding a temperate zone station in Uruguay, and made it possible for all the American nations to benefit from it.

From all Latin-American countries, promising young men have been brought to the United States on grants from foundations and through the Agency for International Development for training in our colleges of agriculture. Our colleges have sent teams of specialists to various Latin-American countries, upon request, to help establish and supervise research stations, or to help organize local schools and training institutes. Vocational schools, supported in part by United States funds, have taught men and women how to repair, care for, and construct farm machinery.

Numerous loans have helped to build irrigation projects and processing plants and to import farm machinery. They have financed highways, railroads, and air and water transportation as a direct aid to agriculture, for lacking economical transportation, a coastal industrial area in Ecuador, for example, can import food cheaper than it can ship it from the high sierra region of that country. All-weather highways are especially essential to a diversified, geographically well-distributed agriculture. Latin America has nearly 700,000 miles of roads, but less than 8 per cent are improved. In the planning stage are 350,000 more miles, and loans are being sought both for the improvement of old and the construction of new highways.

Valuable as these programs have been, Latin Americans, aware of their lingering deficiencies, have been less than satisfied. They have wanted us to help finance a system of credit for individual farmers. Many schemes have been proposed, a persistent one being that we should provide funds to a central bank of a Latin-American country which in turn would lend money to farmers for various purposes—dividing large holdings into family-size farms, opening new lands, enlarging current holdings, and purchasing machinery, fertilizers, livestock, and improved seeds.

The first organic legislation which would make feasible financial assistance of this type was enacted by Congress in September 1960, at the request of President Eisenhower. Anticipating new loans under this act, representatives of the Latin-American states, meeting in Bogotá, agreed that they should enact land tenure legislation which would ensure equitable distribution of the ownership of land, create agricultural credit institutions to finance individual farmers or groups of farmers, and impose tax systems and institute fiscal policies which would encourage improved land use in a pattern of private ownership.

Armed with the new United States legislation and the Act of Bogotá, a United States delegation to the Punta del Este inter-American conference in 1961 agreed that the United States would extend massive credits to Latin America during the next ten years in an effort ". . . to encourage, in accordance with the characteristic of each country, programs of comprehensive agrarian reform, leading to the effective transformation, where required, of unjust structures and systems of land tenure and use; with a view to replacing *latifundio* and dwarf holdings by an equitable system of property so that, supplemented by timely and adequate credit, technical assistance and improved marketing arrangements, the land will become for the man who works it the basis of his economic stability, the foundation of his increasing welfare, and the guarantee of his freedom and dignity."

Quite obviously, agricultural affairs in Latin America—and our relationship to them—are nearing a climax. For twenty years, our technical and economic assistance in this field has made steady but unspectacular progress. The people of the United States have known little about it and there has been a disheartening lack of appreciation among the peoples of Latin America. Greater and more controversial issues have obscured what has been taking place. Newspapers and public officials have so dramatized price fluctuations and economic disadvantages that little attention has been given to these simple acts of toil and good faith which have been dedicated to all future generations of Latin America.

I sometimes think of that resentful mestizo farmer I crossed the dusty fields to greet, of the weariness and grimness in his face, and of the millions of other Latin Americans like him. How would they react if they learned of these efforts to help them, if they could somehow understand the promise of our grand new alliance? But most of them don't know, and I wonder if they will have the patience and endurance to bear their poverty until the promised reform comes about—or whether they will finally choke on their bitter wine and seize the future angrily.

10
Wherever poverty is laid to rest, the grave is usually marked with a smokestack.

IN URUGUAY STANDS ONE OF THE MOST BEAUTIFUL hospitals I have ever seen. New and about eighteen stories high, it glistens proudly in the sunlight as a monument to progress and prosperity. The facilities and equipment I saw inside were completely modern, the furnishings were tasteful, and the design was handsome and utilitarian. But only the first two of the eighteen stories were being used—the others were standing idle. The national budget could not provide the funds to hire the doctors, nurses, and medical technicians to pay operating costs.

A university professor in São Paulo told me that an entrepreneur had built a factory to produce gin, only to discover that he could not obtain the foreign exchange to import juniper berries.

When I first visited São Paulo I thought it must be the fastest-growing metropolitan area in the world, and to the best of my knowledge this was true. Reinforced concrete buildings, practical and sturdy, were rising in every part of the city with a speed that punctured my Yankee egotism. In fact, growth was so rapid that I began to have misgivings. I soon realized that São Paulo typified an almost frenetic industrialization which has swept Brazil—and most of Latin America, for that matter. Brazil has industrialized so rapidly that there is not enough power to keep all the factories running. Lacking sufficient hydroelectric energy, coal, and oil, Brazil has been forced to import huge supplies of oil. As some $400 million of its foreign exchange has gone for oil, industries—rationing energy—have had to close down for part of each week.

Latin Americans are convinced that industrialization is the open sesame, the magic key to prosperity. And it is true that wise industrialization could ameliorate many of their economic problems and permit them to supply the needs and wants of their people. But excessive industrialization —that is, industrialization for its own sake rather than for the sound contribution it can make to solid economic progress—is dangerous.

In the United States, Du Pont began as a small powder mill on a river. Most American industry began as humbly, and grew with the decades to its present mightiness. But Latin Americans, seeing Du Pont, want to reproduce quickly its present gigantic complex in their own countries—and they cannot. Some of the factors which nourished our industry do not exist in Latin America, and in any case economic development cannot be achieved in a few short years.

A corporation doesn't grow by itself. An imperative of solid economic growth is balance. Availability of local raw materials and trained man-power is vital. So is adequate productive energy. If cheap fuel is lacking, increased industrialization, raising as it must the demand for imports, can place greater, perhaps impossible, burdens on an already overburdened balance of payments. Economic transportation must be taken into account. High-cost, uneconomic industries that absorb raw materials and other re-sources and make demands on severely taxed transportation and power facilities may adversely affect the entire economy.

Latin Americans often wave aside caution, such as my repeated re-minder in conversations with business leaders that it took the United States several centuries to reach its present stage of economic development. When our constitution was written, 95 per cent of all the people were farming. A good share of the country was a forbidding wilderness. Trans-portation was fairly primitive, as were the few educational institutions. Factories were small, many of them family-operated. Houses were monu-ments to community cooperation. Even by 1862, when Lincoln signed the Land Grant Act to stimulate agricultural and industrial development through the training of young people, 50 per cent of our people were still engaged in low-efficiency farming. Industry had not begun to approach modern dimensions, and when the United States entered the twentieth century, there was not a single industrial research laboratory in the land.

But hard work, frugality, wise management, a careful husbanding and investment of surplus funds, and prudent borrowing enabled the total economy of the nation to expand over a long period of years and then suddenly to attain maturity and efficiency.

Latin Americans do not want to wait; they want to absorb this experi-ence in a decade or two. Misled into believing that the Soviet Union under a Communist dictatorship has done this, they think they can, too. Soviet propaganda has spread the notion that its productivity has been increasing manyfold faster than that of the United States. Many Latin Americans say that if with private enterprise they do not quickly become prosperous, they ought to try a Soviet brand of state capitalism.

This view was forcefully expressed to me by an alert president of a trade union in São Paulo. He had traveled in the United States and was familiar with the responsible position in society occupied by our workers, as contrasted to the new type of slavery imposed upon the laborers in the Soviet Union. But he was convinced that only a rapid economic growth could prevent Latin American workers from wishing to copy what the Soviets claim is their experience.

I pointed out to him, as I had to others many times, that the Soviet Union has created a false image of itself throughout the world. Some persons in the United States have been misled, too, almost to the point of hysteria.

The Soviets contend that their industrialization started after the revolution—that progress has been made only under Communism. But there were many industries in Czarist Russia. The rate of growth since then has not approached the Communist claim. Russian industry today is between fifteen and seventy years behind comparable industries in the United States. Soviet agriculture is unbelievably primitive. The efforts of half the population are needed to provide the people with a meager diet of potatoes, bread, fatty meats, and gravy; fruits, green vegetables, and premium cuts of meat are luxuries, reserved for the new elite. In the United States, far less than 10 per cent of our citizens are engaged in producing an overabundance of food and fiber for the American people, and much for export. Russian housing is deplorable. A distinguished American economist, after visiting Russia, said, "Picture the slums of any major American city and magnify them to occupy nine-tenths of the city—that is the nature of Soviet housing." In terms of living standards, the Soviets have barely achieved a level of welfare comparable to that existing in the United States a century ago—a conclusion sustained by sound statistical evidence, by unbiased reports of scores of foreigners who have traveled in the Soviet Union, and by my own observations there.

Too much of the world has been deluded by Russia's blatant propaganda primarily because of her noisy success with giant propulsion and heavy satellites. A dictatorship can withhold the benefits of production from its people in order to make a few electrifying advances. There can be no doubt that by controlling and channeling the toil of the Russian people, the Communist dictatorship has outdistanced others in hurling heavy instruments into outer space, and at the same time it has developed a military machine of formidable proportions. But people everywhere, including Latin Americans, must scrutinize the true cost of these results: While Sputnik may seem a symbol of man's eternal quest for knowledge and power, its significance is literally "pie in the sky" for the Russian people.

Such facts shatter at least a portion of the image the Soviet Union has projected of itself. The part that remains, however, is still persuasive. By controlling all elements of production, the Communist hierarchy has reached its few, highest-priority objectives. In Latin America, the people—labor leaders, financiers, politicians, and peons—want a jet-speed industrial development which will increase employment, raise wages, reduce dependence on primary products, and yield a new period of prosperity and happiness. Poverty is neither universal nor inevitable. The past must be shaken off. A new era must begin. Does this not require a large measure of control over all phases of production?

Latin-American leaders who offer this reasoning abhor most aspects of Communism. It is economic control that interests them. What some evidently do not see as clearly is that democratic governments, built on systems of private enterprise, can exercise considerable constructive control through taxation, credit, and a host of other mechanisms.

Perhaps the greatest hazard of Latin America's attempt to make a headlong plunge into industrialization is inflation—the maintenance of honest money. Even with our experience and advantage in this country, we are in a constant struggle with inflation. In Latin America, I have seen inflation distort economic development, disturb living standards, destroy confidence in local currency, impair the growth of local savings sorely needed for development, induce the flight of domestic capital to the United States and Europe for investment, and encourage speculation in local real estate rather than wise investment in productive enterprise which would benefit the whole population.

Small factories (potential Du Ponts, if you will) are ruined by inflation. If, for example, a factory owner figures the life of his equipment to be ten years, he sets aside ten per cent of the cost of the equipment each year for a decade. But after ten years, when the equipment is worn out, it may cost five or ten times as much to replace.

Nearly everyone suffers. During the eight years of my travels, the cost of living in the United States increased about 10 per cent. In the same period, living costs in one Latin-American country more than doubled, tripled in another, and increased nearly thirtyfold in still another.

The political instability which shook Brazil in 1961 was partly the aftermath of President Kubitschek's printing-press spree. He literally printed new money to finance the grand new capital (Brasilia), and the salaries of government employees were paid with the same depreciated money. Prices skyrocketed.

The effects on different economic groups were extremely uneven, worst on those with fixed incomes. Such policies cause great numbers of people to wonder whether poverty under socialism would not be preferable to the inequities experienced in their "private enterprise."

The tragedy of Brazil, incidentally, is that it has never approached a realization of its potentiality—the highest in Latin America. It has the major ingredients of growth and affluence: A sturdy, heterogeneous population, vast undeveloped lands, rich resources, some good business minds. Yet Brazil has not adjusted and developed her agriculture. She has not developed her native oil resources as she should, or maintained a sound currency, or promoted a balanced industrial-agricultural complex. Prosperity is possible in Brazil, provided the leadership and the people will tolerate a period of adjustment while past excesses are overcome.

But even as I write, Brazil bristles with violence and antagonisms, caused in part by the effort to fight inflation. Store owners, resisting attempts to hold down the cost of food, have halted its distribution to create the illusion of a food shortage.

Leaders often jeopardize their political positions in trying to maintain honest money (while at the same time trying to promote efficient production). It is notable that some Latin-American countries in recent years—notably all of Central America—have dealt heroically with this problem. They realize that inflation cannot truly be *controlled*—it must be *prevented*. And prevention requires unpopular measures—controlled budget expenditures, taxation, and credit policies to assure that growth in the money supply and in money income does not outstrip growth of production. A number of governments in South America (Colombia, Peru, and Chile) have recently succeeded in keeping budgets balanced and currencies stabilized and convertible while maintaining sound though moderate rates of economic growth. Some have successfully stabilized bank credit expansion—keeping growth within reasonable limits by means of effective central bank policy and judicious enforcement of appropriate requirements on commercial bank reserves.

These general restraints—little understood and nearly always unpopular

—are vital to maintain a sound currency, a balanced economy, and a steady growth in domestic savings for further investment. Such restraints also have a bearing on a nation's ability to attract private capital for industrial development and public capital for auxiliary services.

The task of a wise political leader is of course made more difficult if his predecessor resorted to excesses which for a time falsely gave the impression of prosperity. Juan Perón emptied the treasury of Argentina and pleased vast numbers of people while he was doing so. President Frondizi was compelled to ask the Argentine people to suffer through a period of austerity while difficulties and imbalances were being corrected. A nation on a spending spree is like an alcoholic on a binge—it's easier and more fun to get on it than it is to get off. President Frondizi, as others before him, paid the price of trying to sober a nation to its fiscal responsibilities—and to the basic task of obtaining wealth, not by legerdemain, but by production. And this is one of the bitter ironies of life: It is the masses who are most hurt by inflation (the wealthy generally manage to avert real harm), yet it is the masses who often stifle efforts to halt this evil.

President Betancourt is navigating a perilous course in Venezuela as he seeks to overcome the problems left to him by the unprincipled management of Pérez Jiménez. President Alessandri has led Chile into a program that will not show its good results to the people until two decades of mismanagement of economic, credit, and financial affairs have been overcome—and, as if man-made problems weren't enough, his task has been made doubly arduous by the devastating earthquakes which have rocked that country.

A factory accomplishes little if its goods must be shipped across the country on the backs of mules. Without adequate transportation facilities, efficient industrial growth is impossible.

A cabinet minister in Ecuador once told me that his country had three urgent needs: roads, roads, and more roads. In Ecuador as in other Andean countries, mountainous terrain often isolates rich agricultural regions from industrial centers, making internal traffic and trade difficult and sometimes impossible. Hence the sales of farm goods tend to remain small within a country, and coastal industries are compelled to seek external markets.

In São Paulo, southern Brazil, I found that much of the cement used in massive construction programs was being imported from Germany because it was cheaper to transport it across the Atlantic than to bring it from northern Brazil where it exists in abundance.

For years, Bolivia neglected her agriculture to such an extent that she had to import 50 per cent of the food required to meet the meager diet of the population. Determined to improve this, she found that it would first be necessary to build a highway to open rich farm lands in order to increase and diversify food production and thus save precious foreign exchange needed for industrial growth.

In all Latin-American countries better highway, rail, harbor, inland waterway, and air transportation facilities are needed to develop mining and manufacturing, to increase and diversify agricultural production, and to expedite a rapid exchange of raw and processed commodities among interdependent producing groups.

The demand for power in an expanding economy is insatiable. I have seen in nearly all the American states the spectacle of severe power shortages and potential shortages, even where herculean efforts were being made to develop new sources. And power facilities, especially hydroelectric facilities, are gluttons for capital. It is difficult for countries short of capital to keep up with the demands for power; they must look to the United States and other countries for help.

Private power companies in several countries have offered to expand generating facilities. They have agreed to bring in the necessary foreign capital to pay for imports of generating machinery and distribution materials. But the rates the companies have been permitted to charge for electricity have been frozen at low levels while inflation and exchange depreciation have forced operating costs upward. In such a squeeze, private companies have not been able to finance expansion programs. This in turn has given rise to internal political quarrels.

As I mentioned earlier, a foreign-owned power company in Brazil could not make enough to expand nor to justify seeking additional capital because of the low rates. The resulting power shortage led to the rationing of energy and the closing of factories. This put people out of work and caused hardship in the low echelons of the economy. And, of course, the foreign owners were blamed.

Two major power companies in Mexico were developed by European, Canadian, and United States private capital. Their rates of earning were never enough to finance expansion, and the returns to stockholders were never satisfactory. In 1960, one of the companies sold its interest at a fair price to the Mexican Government. This caused a political storm in Mexico, not because of the purchase itself, but because many influential citizens felt that private interests in Mexico, not the government, should have bought into the company.

I soon became convinced that ownership of public utilities should be in local hands, preferably in private hands, if possible. Even in the United States public utilities are subject to public control which is sometimes whimsically or capriciously administered. It is not different in Latin America. Political leaders wish to keep rates as low as possible to please all users, and especially to provide cheap power that will attract new industries. If the utilities are foreign-owned, the temptation to shift the blame for difficulties to the alien owners is irresistible.

Naturally, electric power alone cannot meet all the energy requirements of an industrializing nation. Coal, oil, and other fuel must be available.

Colombia, Ecuador, Peru, and Venezuela have oil, and both Colombia and Peru have coal resources. Chile has coal mines, some oil, and attractive hydroelectric potentiality. Argentina and Bolivia have oil, and both have made strenuous efforts to develop the resource. President Frondizi broke with tradition by permitting foreign oil companies to help his nation with the immense problems of discovery, drilling, recovery, and refining processes. Previously, foreign oil companies had been stiff-armed in Argentina.

Oil experts have long insisted that Brazil has rich petroleum reserves, but it has been a Brazilian political imperative to exclude large foreign oil companies from the country. For years, Brazil, lacking both the capital and technical know-how to develop its oil resources, imported more than $250 million worth of petroleum products each year. In one year, the cost of imports rose to $400 million. Wheat imports that year cost $150 million. These constituted an unprecedented demand on scarce foreign exchange —needlessly so, since Brazil could have produced both oil and wheat.

Several years ago, I discussed this problem with leading newspaper publishers in Brazil. They told me that in similar discussions with foreigners they had felt that the interest was centered in the welfare of the "oil monopolies" of the world. I convinced them that our concern was for their welfare. There might be, they conceded, a way to let wealthy and experienced oil companies help them solve their problem without violating the traditional view that the mineral riches of the earth belong to all the people—that oil must not be exploited privately for the benefit of a few but by the government for the welfare of all. But they were skeptical, and with justification. For thirty years, in his campaigns and official pronouncements, Brazil's former dictator (then president) Vargas had made the big oil companies his pet whipping boys. He called them robbers and traveled the countryside with barrels of oil on the back of a truck. While ranting against the oil companies, he would dip his hands into the oil and then hold them up, comparing the dripping oil to the blood sucked from the people of Venezuela and Colombia by the oil barons. He had been so successful in his invective that it has been politically impossible for private firms to invest in Brazilian oil. To develop its oil resources, Brazil established a governmental corporation in preference to private companies. Today Brazil produces only one-fourth of her daily requirements.

With the exception of Brazil, Mexico, and Argentina, political geography presents a formidable obstacle to rapid industrialization in Latin America. The countries are small and they have failed to overcome the limitations of size by developing mutually advantageous trade among themselves.

In one Central-American country, a thoughtful political leader asked me: "Have you ever considered what the consequences would have been in the United States if each of your states had been an independent nation, with its own currency and trade barriers, each trying to balance its internal and external budgets each year? Wouldn't each state have had inefficient industries and wouldn't your people have been extremely poor? That is our situation. El Salvador is no larger than Maryland, Costa Rica no larger than Ohio. We must enlarge our market area if, in the industrialized world of today, we are going to achieve any degree of success."

Undoubtedly, our phenomenal success in the United States results in part from the fact that we have long enjoyed one of the largest free-trade areas in the world. Each industry, by trial and error, or by careful planning, has been located where it could produce at the least cost, and with no barriers to trade within the nation. Each could sell in large volume, thus progressively reducing unit costs, while raising wages, improving quality, and financing research to improve old products, develop new ones, and explore and find new markets.

Since our own experience in this regard has been so fruitful, it is strange that our government for a great many years maintained an attitude of indifference, at times of disfavor, toward suggestions for common regional markets in Latin America. In fact, at the economic conference in Buenos Aires in 1935, the United States openly opposed the idea.

For more than a hundred years there were sporadic efforts to develop a measure of economic integration in Central America, but they came to nothing. The United States had no part in the discussions. Beginning several years before World War II, the southern group of South American countries and three nations in the northern portion of South America progressed so far as to enter into formal agreements for the promotion of common markets. Little was achieved, and the United States continued to remain aloof.

When funds of the International Bank and of the Export-Import Bank were loaned for the installation of steel mills and other enterprises in Latin America, some began to realize that new plants could not succeed unless they found wider markets than would be provided in the countries where the plants were being installed. Self-interest called for a re-examination of traditional policy, which led to a change of attitude. We changed in the mid-1950s from indifference to encouragement, and finally to enthusiastic support for regional markets in Latin America.

I was in El Salvador in 1958 just a month after the Ministers of Economy of Guatemala, Costa Rica, El Salvador, Honduras, and Nicaragua had developed agreements for economic integration and the gradual elimination of trade barriers. Panama, much to their disappointment, hesitated. These five countries recognized that each was too small to attract industries that could have a significant impact on their economies. Hence, neither public nor private capital would be available to promote industrialization. They also recognized the political realities: Taking into account past jealousies and suspicions, as well as the current fear that one nation might gain an advantage over another in a completely free-market situation, they were willing to start with a plan that would have made classical economists aghast. By common consent, a new industry would be obtained for one of the five countries and have access to the markets of all, but a second industry would not be developed with this privilege in the first country until each of the others had also established a new enterprise with common market rights. A rubber tire factory in Guatemala, a steel mill in El Salvador, a pulp and paper plant in the forest country of Honduras, a meat-packing plant in Costa Rica, and a textile plant in Nicaragua were being considered.

They planned gradually to reduce tariffs on several hundred commodities. They would also eliminate export taxes and quotas on commodities which comprised somewhat less than half their interstate trade.

Some of my Central American friends insisted that political integration must accompany economic union. While I gave wholehearted support to their first shaky efforts toward economic cooperation, as did Assistant Secretary Rubottom, who was with me, I remained discreetly silent with respect to political union. Central America was at one time unified, so it is not surprising that there are advocates of reunification. But the marked success of the Western European Common Market was a fact before the delicate question of loss of sovereignty to a supra-national agency began to make waves, and my earnest hope was that the two questions would not become intermixed in Central America. The political question—despite its merits—could delay the essential economic reform.

A second encouraging move toward economic integration occurred in 1959, when Peru, Bolivia, Paraguay, Brazil, Chile, and Uruguay reached a tentative agreement to begin a ten-year program of tariff, export tax, and quota reductions. This would mean free movement of about three-fourths of their interzonal trade. By then, the Under Secretary of State, Douglas Dillon, had announced that the United States would support the efforts of Latin-American governments to create regional markets. He had promised that we would "assist financially . . . with a view to permitting enjoyment of the benefits of regional markets through public and private investment."

Six months after this contiguous group of nations had declared in favor of economic integration, President Eisenhower visited four of the countries and said to a joint session of the Congress of Chile: "The principal impetus for any nation's economic development must be its own will—its own dedicated effort. Then, financial and technical assistance from abroad can be extremely helpful. So, too, can increased cooperation between neighbors. Working together, nations can increase trade and reduce costs of production to their mutual benefit. These developments will attract additional credit. . . . The United States, as the largest common market in the world, could not but look with favor on the efforts of other free nations—in Europe, Latin America, or elsewhere—to enhance their prosperity through the reduction of barriers to trade and the maximum use of their resources. We feel that a common market must be designed not only to increase trade within a region but to raise the level of world trade generally."

While several of our ambassadors in Latin America, Under Secretary Dillon, and Assistant Secretary Rubottom had been supporting the concept of economic integration in Latin America—and I had, too, only much more boisterously than they—this was the first time a President of the United States had officially put an end to the indifference of the past and promised new types of cooperation in the future.

The Eisenhower phrase, "not only to increase trade within a region but to raise the level of world trade generally" had far-reaching implications which did not go unnoticed. It has been given two interpretations. The preponderant one is that it was a warning for common market nations not to permit their cooperative efforts to cut off or reduce trade with others. A second interpretation is that the President was suggesting the possibility that the common market could lead to greater and mutually profitable trade with the United States, a goal which might require our participation in plans for economic integration. I'm sure he really meant both of these things. Certainly, the ultimate goal of sophisticated leaders in most of the Americas is to achieve a common market for *all* of Latin America *and with the United States as well.*

The possibility of developing a single common market among all the Latin-American nations has been in the discussion stage for several years. Studies were initiated in the mid-1950s by the Economic and Social Council of the OAS. In 1956–57, the need to increase inter-American trade was considered in detail in the meetings of the twenty-one presidential representatives. They emphasized the need for change and called upon the Economic and Social Council to intensify its studies and find solutions. Later, studies also went forward under the auspices of the United Nations through its Economic Commission for Latin America.

A study prepared for the Subcommittee on Latin-American Affairs of the Senate Foreign Relations Committee questioned whether there is a "natural" economic affinity among all the nations of Latin America. There seems to be, the researchers contended, certain natural regional groupings. Further, they said, since there is a strong political motivation for achieving greater integration of Latin America as a whole, it might be feasible to arrive at a formula which would permit the creation of regional common markets with a broader trade liberalization movement encompassing them all.

Discussing common markets is a lot easier than establishing them. For one thing, in a program of economic integration, the inefficient producers go out of business and the efficient prosper. (Should the United States join the European Common Market, for example, it would probably lose its watch industry, for Swiss and German producers can make watches more cheaply.) In Latin America, where the nations are at different stages of industrial development, the less developed nations fear that their own industrialization will halt. They see themselves left with the role of supplying primary commodities to their more economically sophisticated partners. Experts working on the problem have suggested varying rates of reduction in trade barriers, with advantages for a stated period being given to the less-developed countries.

In 1959, the United States representative on a special committee of the Organization of American States declared: "Regional market arrangements should aim at trade creation and increased productivity through broadening opportunities for competitive trade and should not simply be trade diverting. This means that the arrangements should provide *for trade liberalization in all commodities*—not just those in which members are competitive with nonmembers—and that duties and other restrictions applied by members of a regional market to nonmembers should not be higher or more restrictive after the formation of the market than before."

This plea—that arrangements provide for trade liberalization in *all* commodities—was known to President Eisenhower when he declared in his address to the Chilean Congress that we envisioned an increase in the level of world trade generally. His statement met with mixed reaction in the United States.

No one in the United States objects, of course, to our becoming involved in a trade expansion that doesn't compete with our own producers. Everybody applauds if economic integration enables Honduras to have pulp and paper plants, for we are an importer of newsprint; American dollars buy that newsprint, then come back to us when Honduras purchases our manufactured products. But let someone imply that we should eventually join an economic union which competes with our own economic complex—agricultural or industrial—on the assumption that production should be located wherever in the hemisphere it would most efficiently serve everybody—and alarums and excursions rend the air.

American farmers are militantly in favor of efforts under our Trade Agreements Act to lower duties on non-farm products, for only if we buy abroad abundantly can we sell as much of our massive farm surpluses as we do now. But when lower agricultural duties are suggested, the farmers become firm tariff protectionists. We have high tariffs on wheat and a host of other commodities. We have other trade restrictions, including sanitary regulations, which are sometimes enforced more for economic than for health reasons. Beef is an example. To protect our own herds, we forbid the importation of beef from regions infected with several cattle diseases. Hence, we import no Argentine beef—though huge areas of Argentina are free of anthrax and foot-and-mouth disease which infect herds in other parts of the country.

Our imposition of quotas on lead, zinc, and oil indicates that we are not yet ready to consider all the nations of the hemisphere as members of a community whose economic, political, and social destinies are inseparable.

If nations could start afresh and plan their development from primitive days to economic maturity, it is likely that all would agree to the theory of mutual economic advantage in free trade. But, barring nuclear destruction, we won't be starting from scratch, and the integration of primitive, partially developed, and mature economic societies raises far-reaching political and social problems. Our fear of a hemispheric common market is similar to that of the unevenly developed Latin-American nations which are struggling, because they must, toward regional economic cooperation.

When I made my first study trip to South America in 1953, I heard expressed everywhere—by industrial, agricultural, governmental, and other leaders—the hope that the United States would not favor restrictive legislation which would impede trade. They were deeply concerned about our tariffs and quotas. "We are paying customers," they said, "and we feel, therefore, that the United States should welcome imports from us." They were especially concerned even then about petroleum, wool, lead, zinc, and fish.

Wherever we went, leaders asked that we urge upon our government the need at least for stability in the rules of international trade. They hoped for better than this, but they did want positive assurance with respect to stability. They indicated that their faith in us would be weakened if we failed them in this regard. I officially recommended to our government that "the United States adopt and adhere to trade policies with Latin America which possess stability, and with a minimum of mechanisms permitting the imposition of increased tariffs or quotas. I consider this matter of stability and consistency *the outstanding requirement.*"

Then in the next few years we imposed quotas on lead, zinc, and petroleum and dumped cotton unexpectedly on the world market. When I returned to Latin America, feeling somewhat sheepish, I expected criticism, and I got it. But not as much as I'd anticipated. Latin Americans seemed to understand that President Eisenhower had followed a course made essential by strong internal political pressures, and that the course chosen was less damaging to them than higher tariffs would have been. They recognized, too, that the people of the United States would have to be better informed on all the complex elements of international trade— just as theirs must be—before we could achieve the stable policies which would gradually liberalize trade in all commodities, not just those "in which members are competitive with nonmembers."

Latin Americans strain to burst into this century. They do not strain nearly enough with their archaic agriculture, but they race toward the industrial age of plenty.

Despite trade barriers and lack of regional market mechanisms, despite inflation, lack of local credit, and inability to borrow funds from the United States in the volume desired, Latin America is industrializing faster than most persons in the United States realize.

Data are rudimentary, but a reasonable estimate is that the gross annual output increased about 50 per cent in the last decade, and industrial development was the main contributor. A sobering fact, however, is that economic growth has been accompanied by a momentous increase in population—and the rate is expected to be still higher in the future. Consequently, the per capita output growth is estimated to have been only about 2 per cent a year.

Great variations in industrialization are found from country to country, with growth most evident in Mexico, Brazil, Argentina, Chile, and Colombia.

In Mexico, for example, as James G. Maddox points out in a perceptive study, total goods and services produced have grown at an average rate of more than 6 per cent a year, and—more important—the *rate* of increase in per capita production since 1953 has been greater than that of Argentina, Brazil, or the United States.

All major sectors of the Mexican economy seem to have grown at a fairly steady rate, but industry especially has increased. Roads have been paved and transportation improved. Production of iron and steel, electrical power, cement, petroleum—all basic to an industrial society—has been expanded. The Mexican Government has built the basic foundations of an industrial society by encouraging the inauguration and development of heavy industry.

As a result, Mr. Maddox notes, "not only has the Mexican economy grown at a rapid rate, but also the Mexican people have made rapid material progress." The old patterns of distribution and wealth are finally being altered.

In other countries, too, there are signs of growth. Steel production has burgeoned in Brazil, and achieved moderate success in Chile and Colombia. Refining of metals is increasing, and the manufacture of appliances—such as radios, refrigerators, and washing machines—is on the rise in several countries. The automotive industry is expanding at a surprising rate, particularly in Brazil. Argentina, Brazil, Venezuela, and Mexico are moving up in chemicals, including paint, fertilizers, plastics, insecticides, and pharmaceuticals. A number of countries, unlike Brazil, have become nearly self-sufficient in the production of cement. The construction industry grows with these. Textile processing plants, particularly for cotton, are at last beginning to adopt modern technological methods; the industry as a whole employs more than a million workers and supplies most consumer requirements.

Consumers are becoming more demanding both of quantity and quality, and manufacturers are responding. Vast sums (about $1 billion in 1959) are being put into highways that will make a network, a blood line, for the continent. The goal is to increase Latin America's 688,000 miles of road 50 per cent within a few years.

The circular process is under way: By improving efficiency and output, the Latin-American countries are slowly beginning to meet more of their domestic needs, and they are accumulating modest savings which can finance more industry.

Industrialization began in Latin America when British, French, German, and, later, United States capitalists began to exploit the natural resources of the countries.

For years, some of these enterprisers were indifferent to the welfare of the people of the host country. Their exclusive incentive was profit. This attitude was coincident with the official United States policy of condescension and intervention.

Fortunately, this early attitude has almost wholly disappeared.

I made it a practice to meet with large numbers of United States businessmen who have spent many years in Latin America. In Lima, Peru, for instance, some two hundred responded to an invitation, and we chatted for more than four hours. I have been happy to find that our businessmen in Latin America appear to be deeply conscious of the necessity of carrying on their work for the benefit of the people of the host country as well as for the benefit of the United States stockholders. In most instances, I have been impressed with their highly developed sense of business and political statesmanship. They recognize a dual mission of aiding Latin America and representing the United States. Because of them the age of exploitation may soon be forgotten.

In some countries, United States enterprises are operating with no difficulty and are making good profits. In others, where exchange difficulties persist, they may have trouble in importing essential products or in exporting earnings, even though locally their operations are moderately profitable.

In Rio de Janeiro, the head of Sears, Roebuck told me that when his company first went into business in Brazil, it imported more than 450 different processed items in quantity. Gradually, the company stimulated the development of local, small industries to supply its needs—some mere handicraft industries, others small manufacturing plants hiring a relatively few employees, and a few quite large. Now practically all items handled by the company in Brazil are locally manufactured. Brazilians praised Sears to me, not only for its ingenuity in developing local manufacturing establishments, but also for its policy of keeping earnings in the country for reinvestment.

This friendly attitude toward a United States corporation in Brazil is in sharp contrast to a general view often expressed in Latin America. Many persons would prefer to obtain public loans, rather than private capital, to finance industrial development. They tend to overlook two important facts. First, private funds—if conditions are right to attract private investment—are available in large quantities, as compared with public funds, and can therefore be obtained faster and in greater quantity. Second, private loans and especially private development by the United States enterprises carry with them management and technical skills which are often the difference between success or failure, particularly in the early stages of new developments when local personnel must be trained.

But Latin Americans point out that a private industry owned by citizens of the United States may make large profits over a period of years and then, unlike Sears, Roebuck which has left most of its earnings in the country, may suddenly withdraw all or a part of them, thus causing difficulty in international balance of payments. They feel it is better for them to amortize an original public loan and then retain future earnings for further development.

The Minister of Economy of Brazil, arguing for public funds as a stimulant to industrial growth, complained that an American automobile manufacturer had invested a relatively small sum in establishing an assembly plant. Its rapid expansion thereafter, he said, had been financed from earnings. In a few years, the company was worth ten times its original investment and wished to withdraw much of its capital from the country. "If exchange is available," he exclaimed, "they will take out ten times as much as they invested. Had we borrowed the money at 5 per cent, we could have repaid the original amount plus interest in two years!" Whether the automobile industry would have developed successfully without the initial capital and management experience of the United States company is at least an open question.

Though United States companies abide by all local laws, including tax laws, the people often equate our private enterprises with their own which, they believe, are to a considerable extent responsible for the inequitable distribution of the fruits of production. This is a major basis of their argument that private capital is imperialistic—that it involves foreign ownership over which, it is alleged, the national government—or more precisely, the people—loses control.

I've tried to refute this, as always, by pointing to our own history. From the beginning down to 1878, we drew large amounts of private capital from Europe. Public credit was almost unknown. Private capital from abroad contributed mightily to our development, building railroads and communications systems, establishing new industries, and hastening the expansion of many companies which were struggling in the hope that retained earnings would finance future growth. Foreign enterprises and foreign capital did not impinge upon our sovereignty. We would by legal means have corrected bad situations had they occurred. Gradually, as our exports of goods and services exceeded our imports, we began to liquidate the debt. It took us forty years to do this. *We did not become a creditor country until 1918.*

A good many United States entrepreneurs, recognizing the attitudes of Latin Americans—fallacious as they may be—have sought to join with local investors in establishing and operating industries and businesses. This has worked well in most countries, but not in all. A major United States producer of aluminum had a joint-ownership plan in Mexico but ran into such difficulty with local management and Mexican business mores that it disposed of its interests to Mexicans. A United States public utility found joint ownership unworkable in Mexico. On the whole, though, mixed ownership and mixed management have been successful, and they have escaped some of the criticism aimed at foreign enterprises.

Pioneering efforts by United States companies have often had a chain-reaction effect in the development of the host country. I went to the central jungle of Venezuela shortly after Bethlehem Steel and United States Steel began tapping the rich iron ore resources far back from the coast on the Orinoco River. The area had never before been opened. The steel companies dredged the river for 150 miles, built piers, laid a railroad, and built a highway from the river to the ore deposits. A sizable town grew up at the point of ore shipment. Farm settlements quickly sprang up along the highway. In all, the two companies are reputed to have invested as much as $300 million in the undertaking.

I went to the top of a mountain where, like ice cream nestling in a cone, the richest iron ore on earth is located. Mining operations were just beginning. A few years later, United States Steel alone shipped six million tons of ore, and its goal for the following year was eight million tons.

Immense sums have been paid to the Venezuelan Government, the wages of workers have been well above the local average, good health and educational services have been provided. This initial penetration into a forbidding, untamed jungle is gradually leading to further development—something that probably would not have occurred for many years had it not been for two United States companies.

The National Planning Association, which has made a series of case studies on United States business performance abroad, examined the record of Sears, Roebuck de Mexico. After reporting on how Sears, which originally expected to import most of its goods from the United States, brought about the development of local suppliers for 80 per cent of the commodities sold, the National Planning Association said: "Sears as a merchant has played the same creative role in industrialization as was played a century and a half ago by the Boston merchants in establishing textile and hardware industries in New England. But Sears came into the process relatively later and has played its role faster and with a lighter hand. . . . The effect has been to build up wholly native industries with standards of performance that would have been achieved much more slowly by any other method than that of the well-placed order for goods to be delivered. . . . As for the middle class which is forming due to thousands of impulses—of which Sears payments to small manufacturers and to its own employees form only one—the broad effect of the Sears operation is to hasten the establishment of the middle class by giving a large proportion of the people a much wider choice of goods than they formerly had. Sears has done this by . . . introducing new products, by lowering prices, by supplying more reliable products, by encouraging in customers the process of deliberation and choice through advertising, quality labeling, counter display. . . . These practices have affected not only the Sears clientele, already the largest retail clientele in Mexico, but also a large part of the buying public through the effect of its example on other stores." The Planning Association concluded its report with this sage advice to United States businessmen who might plan investments in Latin America: "You will do better for yourself and for the country that receives you when you send abroad not just capital but the methods and management that are your most valuable stock in trade."

A year after its study in Mexico, the National Planning Association sent researchers to Peru to consider the century-long experience of W. R. Grace & Co. in that country—especially of the effect of the company's widespread activities on Peruvian life. The research scholars found that Casa Grace in Peru, after a hundred years of ups and downs which paralleled those of the host country, today presents an amazing integration of skills, nationalities, and control systems. Organizational know-how and managerial talent of Casa Grace have made a contribution to other Peruvian industries. "Grace engineers have gone to many other companies," they pointed out. "Hundreds of technicians trained in Grace shops have added to Peru's short supply of skilled workers. The distribution and merchandising system has been a pattern which others have followed. As Peru's economy continues to develop, there inevitably will be greater demand for those who have had managerial experience with Casa Grace."

Peter Grace, present head of the W. R. Grace industrial and financial empire, was not, by the middle of 1961, particularly optimistic about additional United States private capital going to Latin America to speed development. He felt that the rate of return from manufacturing enterprises owned by the United States investors in Latin America was considerably less than that of Western Europe. Further, investors were discouraged by foreign exchange devaluation, heavy taxation, and the risk of expropriation. United States businessmen with investments in Latin America had been faced with depreciation in some local currencies ranging from 8 to 30 per cent per year.

Still, during the period of my studies, private United States investment in Latin America had been increasing at the rate of about $600 million a year until it reached a total of more than $9 billion. The expropriation of a billion dollars of United States properties in Cuba, with no intention of payment as provided by international custom, unquestionably frightened potential investors. The two previous major instances of expropriation of United States enterprises in Latin America had been forgotten or excused. Many came to believe that Mexico had been justified in expropriating the foreign-owned oil properties in that country; compensation for them had been arranged by negotiation to the satisfaction of the Roosevelt administration, if not to the former owners. Most citizens of the United States also had felt some sympathy for Bolivia when it expropriated the tin mines of that country, and again compensation had been offered, at least in principle, if not with a realistic formula.

The theft of a billion dollars of resources by Castro was quite a different matter. Were similar revolutions threatened in other countries, and if they developed, would private investments, so eagerly sought in the past, go for naught?

This question was evidently in the minds of the ministerial representatives of the American republics when they met at Punta del Este in 1961, and formulated a declaration to the peoples of America. In the declaration, the ministers promised to stimulate private enterprise, avoid disastrous inflation, guarantee the greatest possible price stability, and maintain adequate bases for economic development. This would be done, they promised, on the principle that free men, working through the institutions of representative democracy, can best satisfy man's aspirations. "No system can guarantee true progress unless it affirms the dignity of the individual which is the foundation of our civilization," they said.

Thus, while the ministers did not mention Cuba, or its denial of human rights, or its flagrant disavowal of international custom, nonetheless by indirection they assured the peoples of the hemisphere that the normal procedures of democratic society, so flagrantly flaunted by Cuba, would be observed and strengthened. Such procedures permit expropriation but only with adequate compensation.

The members of the United States delegation obviously and properly accepted this assurance in good faith—indeed, they joined in the declaration. They also accepted the reasoning of our southern neighbors that public capital is especially essential at this stage in Latin-American development. In the Declaration of Punta del Este, the United States pledged "to provide a major part of the minimum of $20 billion, *principally in public funds*, which Latin America will require over the next ten years . . . in order to supplement its own efforts."

11   We can only pay for the past, but we can invest in the future.

"MONEY," SAID JEAN JACQUES ROUSSEAU, "IS THE SEED of money, and the first guinea is sometimes more difficult to acquire than the second million."

Money is indeed the seed of money, and this was, at least until the period 1958–60, the guiding philosophy of United States economic aid to Latin America. As a theory, it makes good sense. Latin America needs immense amounts of money if it is to join us in the prosperity of the twentieth century—more than we can ever give in direct aid.

Money, more than anything else (without minimizing the importance of human determination), is needed to break the impervious circle which squeezes and confines Latin America in its present underdeveloped condition. Agriculture must be vastly improved, industrialization must be planned and pushed, education must be made available to all, health services must help people become hardy and productive. But which of these things comes first? How can you provide education and health services without funds? How can you get funds without a healthy industry? How can you industrialize without an educated citizenry and agricultural efficiency to keep them fed?

Money is certainly the wedge, the beginning, but it must be money that goes to work for the nation, money that breeds new money. Desirable as parks, art galleries, new office buildings, and luxury apartments may be, they do not produce money. On the contrary, they can absorb large amounts of domestic and foreign capital without contributing appreciably to productivity. On the other hand, irrigation projects, power plants, highways, railroads, mines, manufacturing plants do produce money, which goes to build more productive enterprises to produce more money. And as new money grows from seed money, some of it is channeled into education, health, housing, consumer items. This is how the United States became prosperous, and this is how the United States long expected Latin America to seek prosperity.

It was only natural, therefore, for United States and international lending institutions to insist for a great many years that their loans be used primarily for productive purposes and be repayable either from tax revenues or from the earnings of enterprises meriting the loans.

Private and public lending institutions also insisted that a major share of the capital needed in Latin America would have to come from Latin America itself, that is, from its own seed money. Some countries, notably Argentina and Colombia, seemingly have used few of their *public* funds for productive investment. Others, like Mexico and Venezuela, have devoted as much as 50 per cent of their public revenues to this purpose. For Latin America as a whole, about 25 per cent of all public funds have gone into investment.

I would estimate that about 75 per cent of the total private and public investment in Latin America during the past ten years was provided by the Latin Americans themselves, including the earnings of foreign-owned enterprises which were kept in Latin America. In other words, in the past decade, perhaps 25 per cent of the capital used to expand industry, agriculture, and social institutions has come from abroad. This net inflow has been negligible in some years, as in 1950–51, and high in other years, as in 1957–58, when it totaled nearly $1.75 billion.

More than two-thirds of this outside money was private, less than a third public. There was a discernible upward trend in the flow of both types for nearly a decade, a trend which was chopped down, so far as private funds are concerned, when Castro confiscated foreign-owned enterprises in Cuba.

It soon became obvious to me that all of the countries needed more capital than was available to them, and I was surprised and puzzled to discover that our lending institutions had more funds available than were being loaned. Why wasn't this money flowing to Latin America faster?

I discovered some of the reasons in visits with two Latin-American Presidents.

In mid-1953, I went to an Andean country which vigorously had been seeking Export-Import Bank loans to finance airport construction. I had done my homework by reading the documentary material on these applications. Obviously, land transportation is difficult, expensive, and some-times tortuous in the mountainous areas of the west coast of South America. One may travel on a train a couple of days from a coast city to an interior capital, high in the Andes; the same trip by air takes an hour. So airport construction seemed a reasonable need and I was ready to hear more about it. But airports weren't mentioned. I met with industrial, labor, and agricultural leaders, and they talked convincingly of the need for a highway system that would tie the coastal and high sierra regions together; public loans, they said, were desperately needed for this purpose. I talked to government officials, ready at the drop of a syllable to encourage them to follow through, in normal channels, on their application for funds for airports, but they too talked only of the need for roads and public funds to build them. Finally I chatted with the President, and he too talked of roads. I gently mentioned to the President the official application for air-port loans, but he dismissed this with a wave and went on about roads being the highest priority need.

Upon my arrival in a Central-American country in 1958, I was escorted at once to the office of the President of the republic. He was a scholarly, slender, attractive man in his early fifties. He had a quick, charming smile, but he wasted little time on pleasantries. He wanted to talk about his coun-try's urgent needs.

Succinctly, he outlined his priority program. There were six projects de-pendent upon loans from the United States: power development, food processing, transportation, education, health, and irrigation. We talked for two hours without interruption. I became impressed with his knowledge of economic conditions and his conception of how economic growth could be speeded in his country. As I rose to go, he asked me to talk the next day with his cabinet in order to learn the details of what he and his as-sociates had in mind.

In midmorning of the next day, the entire Cabinet came to the United States Embassy for a three-hour conference. This harmonized with previ-ous experiences. Usually my associates and I would meet with the Presi-dent and his Cabinet in a room of the government palace and then, after several hours of discussion, the President would excuse himself, leaving his ministers to go over project details.

And so, as I sat down at the conference table with the ministers, I was prepared to hear more details about the proposals the President had dis-cussed with me the previous afternoon.

When they began talking I could barely believe my ears. I trust I con-cealed my astonishment when, in the first few moments, it became evident that the ministers had views quite different from the President's. They suggested seven projects, only one of which had been mentioned by the President. The President's six proposals would cost $35 million in a two-year period. The projects presented by the cabinet would cost about $30 million in a three-year period.

I cite these incidents not to ridicule, but because they are fairly typical, and because they suggest why capital doesn't flow southward as freely as it should. I suspect that had the President of the United States, in mid-nineteenth century, been called upon to submit to European creditors a comprehensive development program with priorities, he, too, would have had difficulty being logical or consistent. But United States development involved thousands of individual decisions among private investors, lenders, and borrowers, relieving the central government of the responsibility for either success or failure. Since Latin-American governments are assuming a high degree of responsibility for economic progress, they cannot afford to be vague or mistaken; they must be as precise and accurate as possible.

Some of the American republics have not mastered the type of economic analysis and planning that might help them obtain large loans, public and private. Since lending institutions cannot satisfy total needs overnight and borrowing countries cannot absorb too much credit hurriedly without serious dislocations and repercussions, each nation must have a development plan. It must assign priorities to each project. Timing and coordination are especially important: One loan, launching a successful enterprise such as a new highway into virgin forest country, may make feasible a second development loan, perhaps for a paper mill. The first loan would undoubtedly be public; the second might better be private.

The cardinal requirement in development planning is to guide the flow of investment funds. The government can directly control the direction of public funds, and this area is substantial in Latin America, which relies more on public ownership and operation than we do. Our general philosophy is that all productive enterprise should be privately owned and operated unless it is found to be more efficient as a monopoly, in which event it is either publicly owned (highways) or publicly controlled (public utilities). Latin America, while relying substantially upon private initiative, is more chary because it has failed to spread benefits widely. Thus, an average of 35 per cent of new investments in Latin America is governmentally controlled, and this has a powerful influence on total development.

Latin-American governments also influence the direction of private investment by controlling credit policies, foreign exchange, taxation, price controls, and capital imports. As I have pointed out, the Brazilian entrepreneur built his gin factory then was unable to get scarce foreign exchange to import juniper berries. Because Latin-American countries frequently import more than they export (in monetary value), they must restrict the use of exchange reserves they accumulate for essentials, like fuel, food, manufacturing equipment, and so on.

The substantial control which Latin-American governments have over the direction investments take emphasizes the imperative need for careful analysis and over-all planning. Yet, as I learned in visiting the two Presidents, so deficient are some of the Latin-American nations in this regard that they cause confusion among the lending institutions by presenting conflicting requests or by suddenly shifting their priorities in loan applications.

One notable effort to overcome these deficiencies began in Brazil early in 1953. Brazilian and United States technicians worked together for a long time analyzing Brazil's economic potentiality, its needs, its credit capacity, and the highest-priority projects. The work was competently done. Unfortunately, however, Brazilian officials thought the joint planning was a commitment on the part of the lending institutions to finance the proposed projects. This, of course, was not and could not have been true. Final decisions would have to be made by the public and private agencies from which the funds would be requested. The Brazilians were furious and made no effort to hide their anger. I was singed by it on arriving in Brazil just as the joint study commission was completing its work and the members were arguing. "The kind of technical advice you received is as good as money," I said in an attempt to mollify my peeved Brazilian friends. But they were more concerned with what they felt was our abrogation of an understanding than with what they might get if they submitted the jointly prepared projects to lending institutions.

In my first official report to the President in 1953, I suggested that the United States should, if requested, give technical help to each Latin-American nation in determining how its resources, including its borrowing capacity, could make the greatest contribution to economic development. The purpose, I said, was to establish priorities of need, to develop project plans in ways that satisfy lending institutions, and to do this within the credit worthiness of the nation. I especially urged that technical help be given in planning for the coordination of public and private loans, pointing out that public loans for transportation, power, and harbor development, for example, would lay the foundation for industrial and agricultural growth, thus encouraging private enterprise, both domestic and foreign.

Some technical assistance was given to governments by the International Bank, and studies made in Latin-American countries by the Export-Import Bank indirectly had this effect. But in general, I found that the lending institutions had misgivings about providing help in planning for fear that, as in Brazil, the host governments would consider the technical assistance to constitute firm commitments for loans.

This problem came up for consideration in the committee of presidential representatives early in 1957. The twenty-one representatives unanimously agreed that countries in the process of economic development would have to prepare national programs that gave a clear idea of the nature of the problems to be solved, the priorities to be given to the various projects, and the best ways to carry them out. They recognized that some of their countries were not able to develop "bankable" projects—a term invented by them, meaning worthy of bank loans—because such an undertaking required "theoretical and practical knowledge that at times is not available in a particular country, or not available to an extent warranting the possible cost." In short, they didn't have the "know-how." The complex problems involved, the representatives felt, were almost insuperable, unless specialized technical assistance could be given. They therefore recommended to the Presidents of the American republics that through the machinery of the OAS there be created an inter-American technical committee "to assist the government of any country, at its request and on a reimbursable basis, in the study and preparation of 'bankable' projects for the purpose of furthering the economic development of the country or region concerned." They also recommended the creation of statistical and other research services within the OAS to make both national and hemispheric planning more fruitful and reliable. (Interestingly, this 1957 recommendation for a group of technical experts who would be available to help each nation in development planning was not too different from the proposal to establish a committee of nine "wise men" which provoked warm debate at the 1961 Punta del Este meeting.)

By 1958, however, when I was preparing an additional report on inter-American affairs to the President, I felt that serious deficiencies still existed in the area of economic research and planning. By then, I was preparing a strong recommendation that the United States reverse its traditional policy against the creation of an inter-American Bank, and I suggested, therefore, that the Bank, when established, should be given funds for regional and national planning in Latin America. Technical help given by either a special committee of the OAS or by an inter-American Bank (in which the borrowing countries themselves participated) would not face the danger of misunderstanding and seemingly prior commitment which had retarded our unilateral help.

There are a few basic bits of technical information needed about money, as well. Too many of the key officials in Latin America simply do not know the rules and regulations of lending institutions. This is another major reason why funds do not flow to Latin America as freely and as fast as they should.

I know of cases where this lack of sophistication in fund raising has resulted in disappointing failure. A Minister of Commerce, for example, had gone to Washington to support his government's application for a project loan. At that time, the World Bank, which had the application, could not make a "soft" loan (a loan for local expenditures which can be repaid in local currency). When his application was denied on the grounds that the loan could not be amortized in "hard" currency, the minister was disappointed, frustrated, and angry. He went home empty-handed. Unfortunately, he did not transfer his application to the Development Loan Fund, which had only recently been established. Assistant Secretary Rubottom had been battering his head against a stone wall in trying to get the Development Loan Fund to make some of its resources available to Latin-American countries, but the officials of the Fund at that time seemed to be preoccupied with other areas of the world. The project which was proposed by the Minister of Commerce was so meritorious that Fund officers would have had a difficult time in making a negative decision on it, and this would have helped not only him, but might well have created an understanding among Fund officials of Latin-American problems sooner than actually occurred.

The Development Loan Fund was created primarily to replace grants with loans. It was given broader authority than that possessed by the Export-Import Bank and the World Bank. It was prepared to make loans for local currency expenditures, and could authorize repayment in local currency. It could, in other words, make "soft" loans. Such loans are not "soft" in the sense that they are unsound or are grants in disguise. No responsible person would favor having an agency of the United States Government make economically unsound loans. A loan should be genuine, with repayment expected. A grant should be a grant. Otherwise the whole field of international credit could be undermined, and the people of our country would demand the abandonment of an offending credit institution.

There can be no doubt that "soft" loans are needed in Latin America. Like other underdeveloped regions of the world, Latin America not only suffers from a shortage of domestic savings, but is able to maintain foreign exchange balances only through the net importation of new capital. This is easy to understand. People with barely enough money to subsist don't put money into bank accounts and, as I have said, the wealthy of Latin America often prefer the safer investments in banks of Europe and the United States. But, more fundamentally, Latin America, largely an agricultural society (and not a very efficient one as I have said), generally imports more than it exports. This is inevitable in an evolving society which wishes to progress faster than would be possible with locally generated savings. Indeed, its rising population rate forces Latin America to hurry onward just to keep from slipping behind. Hence, sound development projects which can be financed on a basis of reasonable amortization may require loans involving both domestic and foreign capital. Further, until underdeveloped countries, including those of Latin America, can increase their productivity and exports, which will assure favorable balances of trade, they may lack dollars or other borrowed currencies to meet repayment schedules, even though they could meet their obligations in local currencies.

There is quite an array of lending institutions, each fulfilling a special purpose. It is therefore not surprising that prospective borrowers sometimes become confused when they submit project applications. The International Bank for Reconstruction and Development makes governmentally guaranteed loans to finance many types of development projects. Its policies are not determined by the United States, but by an international board. The International Finance Corporation, allied with the International Bank, can make loans for private developments. A recently established development agency, associated with the World Bank, can make "soft" loans. The Export-Import Bank makes loans of many types, the major requirement being that the loans involve dollar expenditures and that they be repaid in dollars. The Development Loan Fund, a newer United States credit agency, was designed to replace grants with loans; it has broader authority than the Export-Import Bank and can, as I have indicated, make loans for local currency expenditures and permit them to be repaid in such currency. The Agency for International Development makes loans in Latin America under special circumstances. The newest credit institution, The Inter-American Bank, makes both "hard" and "soft" loans. And, in addition, there are of course many important private lending agencies.

Only a trained borrower is completely at home in this financial complex. Further, a development program for any country may require the cooperation of several public and private institutions, not only in determining the credit capacity of a nation, but also in timing loans in such a way that each supports the other.

Prior to the creation of the Inter-American Bank, I thought the difficulty posed by lack of understanding of the rules and policies of lending institutions by borrowers could be overcome by the creation of an informal committee which would endeavor to help borrowers route their applications, properly prepared, to the agency most likely to give it favorable consideration. I was delighted to find officials of the public lending agencies receptive to the idea. But before such an arrangement could be made, the United States, to my great joy, notified the leaders of Latin America that it was prepared to consider participation in a new inter-American development institution, an offer which was in response to a suggestion persistently advanced by Latin American leaders for many years. The new inter-American institution would maintain informal methods of credit coordination among all relevant public and private credit institutions, and provide a permanent source of information and advice in this regard to member nations seeking loans. I had recommended this to the President, and I think it will eliminate what for years has been a serious deficiency.

A third reason why loans have not flowed to Latin America in greater volume may be found in the attitudes of the heads of the lending agencies. Naturally they follow normal banking procedures. They wait for someone to ask for money. Then they respond strictly on a businesslike basis. The World Bank could probably follow no other procedure. But the Export-Import Bank, the Development Loan Fund, the Agency for International Development, and the Treasury are agencies of the United States, and in my judgment should, within the aims of our foreign policy, take considerable initiative in helping Latin-American countries develop project applications worthy of their support. I strongly recommended in 1958 that these agencies become creative in using credit as a means of helping Latin America achieve its economic goals. I suggested that our lending institutions, with the cooperation of the World Bank, if possible, inform the republics of Latin America that (a) they stood ready, as a cooperative group, to consider sympathetically the extension of sound, well-timed loans in support of practical development plans, and (b) they would meet jointly with delegations from each applicant country to determine how credit resources might best be employed to help the nation proceed effectively with its economic program.

My eagerness to increase the flow of credit did not by any means deprecate the constructive good which had been done in Latin America by the World Bank and by United States lending institutions. At that time, World Bank loans to Latin America amounted to about $150 million a year, and loans outstanding were about $800 million. Forty per cent of all Export-Import Bank loans over a period of years had been made to Latin-American nations; in all, the Bank had authorized $3.5 billion of such loans, and its outstanding commitments were then $1.8 billion. The Congress had just increased the lending authority of the Bank from $5 billion to $7 billion, making substantial sums available for lending. I wanted to speed up the use of these funds.

A fourth deterrent to capital flow pertains only to private credit. Foreign private capital to Latin America, from the United States and other developed countries, can under proper conditions play a greater role, good as the record has been. Private capital always faces choices: opportunities in the home country, investment possibilities in other developed countries, or undertakings in underdeveloped ones, including Latin America. Each decision requires a judgment about political and economic stability, fair and equitable treatment, possibility of earnings, and assurances as to the remittance of dividends. Private capital in Latin America has faced and made choices, too. Unfortunately, the decision has often been to invest outside Latin America at the very time that additional capital, both local and foreign, was needed at home.

The United States has encouraged its businesses to invest in Latin America by two methods: First, under appropriate conditions, an American company in Latin America need pay only 38 per cent in corporation taxes, rather than the prevailing rate of 52 per cent in the United States; second, under treaty arrangements with an individual country, a corporation may deduct from the United States taxes, as if actually paid, the tax forgiveness of the host country.

It is abundantly clear that such devices have only a limited usefulness. Latin-American countries must *attract* private capital—by permitting opportunities for a fair profit, by assuring reasonable provisions for the transfer of earnings and amortization payments, by maintaining equitable labor and management laws and regulations, and by eliminating fear of discriminatory treatment, expropriation, and government interference in management. Some countries have already made such provisions, as indicated by the $9 billion of United States private capital in Latin America and the net increases in such investment of $600 million a year until Castro came along.

A fifth deterrent to the flow of funds from the United States to Latin America is political and philosophic, rather than economic. The difficulty arises from varying concepts about private and public enterprise.

We believe that the competitive enterprise system is the most productive and the most protective of freedom. While we have a high degree of socialized activity in the United States—more than a fourth of our national income goes into security, agricultural, educational, welfare, and a multitude of community services—the important point is that most of our productive enterprise is private; usually, only services are public.

Our dedication to this concept was one reason why no United States institution would extend public credit to Pemex, the Mexican oil monopoly. There was another reason: United States private capital had invested heavily in oil production in many countries—in the Middle East and in several Latin-American countries, especially Venezuela—and it was feared that if the United States officially granted funds to an expropriated and publicly-owned enterprise in Mexico, it might touch off a series of expropriations in countries where we had oil interests. It was believed that the constant need of oil-producing countries or enterprises for additional credit, and their belief that sources of credit would dry up if these enterprises became public, was the real deterrent to expropriation.

When the late Henry F. Holland was Assistant Secretary of State for Inter-American Affairs, he told me many times that he would never advocate a loan for Pemex. But the United States did engage in a bit of Machiavellian action with Mexico. It extended more than a hundred million dollars in general credit to the Mexican Government, knowing that Mexico might adjust its own budget in such a way as to have the new funds finance services which were not objectionable to us and thus free internal funds for Pemex.

In Latin America, our insistence that productive enterprises normally be privately financed—and for years I was vocal in this respect—has been grossly misunderstood. Some Latin Americans see this as our way of exploiting them. They feel that our concern is for the welfare of United States private enterprisers, not for the welfare of the people of Latin America.

This philosophic problem became acute during the Marshall Plan aid to

Europe. Certain European countries, too, place greater reliance on socialized enterprises than we do. Many in the United States, including influential members of Congress, insisted that no Marshall Plan funds go to promote socialism or to any enterprise already in public ownership. Their demands, after acrimonious debate, were overruled. Such a policy, if actually executed, would have two dangers or shortcomings. First, if unilaterally enforced by us, it would be interpreted as a form of intervention. Second, it would violate a fundamental policy of the United States—perhaps our most cherished policy: Our belief in free choice. President Eisenhower challenged Khrushchev to let this policy become universal: Hold elections in every country under the auspices of the United Nations, he suggested, and then let us abide by the results. We will respect the right of any nation to be democratic, socialistic, or communistic, he said, so long as it is a true expression of the will of the people.

It is a knotty problem for our country, dedicated as it is to total freedom, including economic freedom, to have its tax-supported agencies lend funds to other countries for a type of organization that seems to us to be contrary to the best interests of that country, and a sharp departure from our philosophy about such matters. But we must temper our reasoning not only by honoring the policies of non-intervention and free choice, but also by recognizing that private enterprise in Latin America is not always the enterprise we know here at home. Frequently it is an opportunity for the privileged rich to get richer—at the expense of the underprivileged.

The Kennedy administration in mid-1961 seemingly began a reversal of policy by making a public loan to Pemex. I do not criticize this. If the lending institution was convinced that the loan would promote sound economic development in Mexico and would be repaid on schedule, then it was right in making the loan.

I shall not confuse my conviction about what is best for our own society, on the one hand, with what, on the other, is a sound policy for making loans to countries that subscribe to a somewhat different philosophy. Indeed, we have extended credit and made gifts to Yugoslavia and Poland. Why then should there be criticism of public loans to public productive enterprises in Latin America?

Because the flow of credit to Latin America is so important for its economic development—though for many other reasons, too, as I shall indicate—I recommended to President Eisenhower that a Committee on Inter-American Affairs be established and directed to advise the Secretary of State on all matters of hemispheric importance, including credit problems. I felt the members of the council could bring to the President creative ideas for strengthening relations, improving aid programs, and emphasizing by its very existence the importance which the government and people of the United States attach to fruitful partnership with the American republics. To comprehend the relevance of this suggestion to aid programs, one must consider how day-by-day operations of our government are conducted.

The public imagines that United States foreign policy is established by the President and then is faithfully executed by the State Department and other agencies of the government. This may be true when we face a grave crisis in Berlin, Laos, Suez, or Formosa. But in the routine operations of our far-flung and complex federal government, things are quite different. The continuing implementation of a broad foreign policy—the business of putting real flesh on the bones—is a tremendously complicated and tedious undertaking, requiring wisdom, a lot of patience and, above all, a coordination of many federal and sometimes private activities.

The President may determine and all federal officials may agree that strengthened economic relations with a particular Latin-American country will contribute to our own national welfare. No one could quarrel with such a broad judgment. Everyone, too, may favor a policy of economic cooperation and stability in the rules of international trade between the United States and the country concerned. But to bring the general policy into the realm of meaning may require a dozen or more public and private decisions which are arduous to coordinate. The Assistant Secretary of State for Inter-American Affairs may know precisely what needs to be done on specific issues, but he does not control the agencies of action. He must try to persuade them to do the right thing at the right time. He will appeal to the President for intervention only when crucially important matters are involved. This is one of the inevitable consequences of big government.

The Assistant Secretary may, within established policies for stockpiling for security purposes, try to induce the General Services Administration to purchase a particular ore whose world price is abnormally low; the Administrator of that agency will make the decision and it may be negative. (Certainly it would be negative today, now that our stockpiles are overflowing.) The Assistant Secretary may feel that the World Bank should make a development loan for the expansion of transportation and power facilities, but the decision is outside the sphere of authority of the United States Government. He may believe that the Export-Import Bank should quickly extend certain short-term loans; in this instance, not only the

Bank, but occasionally the Secretary of the Treasury may have to be consulted. The achievement of the program may require changes in the laws and policies of the country concerned; the Assistant Secretary can do no more than point out the facts to the appropriate ambassador; this would likely occur in a situation where private capital was being asked to cooperate in a new enterprise and the existing laws of the host country were unattractive to private capital. The Assistant Secretary might, in the midst of his negotiations, learn that the Tariff Commission was about to recommend an increase in duties on commodities imported from the country; he could only ask the Secretary of State to appeal to the President, who has limited legal authority under rigidly specified conditions to overrule the recommendations of the Commission.

Even if the Assistant Secretary were successful for a time in getting all that he advocated, other circumstances might arise to thwart his efforts. There could be, at the time of his negotiations, a vigorous two-way trade between the United States and the country he was seeking to help. But the country might, for domestic reasons, alter exchange rates and thus adversely affect the level of trade. This action could injure United States traders; this, in turn, could cause private and public lending institutions, which had previously agreed with the Assistant Secretary, to change their minds, or at least await further developments.

This hypothetical situation does not exaggerate what actually goes on almost daily in the State Department. In an effort to overcome some of the more exasperating phases of this ramified and diffused decision-making process, the Assistant Secretary of State for Inter-American Affairs has maintained an inter-agency committee which brings to his office from time to time representatives of some twenty agencies to consider developments in United States-Latin American relations and to assure mutual understanding in the hope that unity of action will result.

I had these circumstances in mind when I recommended to the President that he create a new Committee on Inter-American Affairs with the Secretary of State as chairman and the Assistant Secretary for Inter-American Affairs as vice-chairman. The other members, I thought, should be drawn from the general public—persons known to be deeply concerned with and knowledgeable about Latin-American affairs. I believed that such a group could not only advise the Secretary of State and President on general matters in the Latin-American area, but also could be influential in helping coordinate the thinking and actions of the many federal agencies whose daily decisions vitally affect hemispheric relations.

Six months later, the President's National Advisory Committee on Inter-

American Affairs was established. Christian A. Herter was then Secretary of State. Douglas Dillon was Under Secretary, and R. R. Rubottom, Jr., was Assistant Secretary for Inter-American Affairs. The other six members were drawn from the fields of education, labor, industry, and business.

From our first meeting with the President, and in all subsequent sessions, we of the Council gave attention to every aspect of inter-American relations. Some of our research and discussions centered on economic affairs and the need of Latin America for credit, and on the desirability of lending institutions, especially the new Inter-American Bank, helping Latin America overcome the impediments to the flow of funds which I have been discussing.

But Secretary Herter, Doug Dillon, Dick Rubottom and I were by now completely convinced that more funds would not by themselves help very much. For the historic social injustices which had been kept dormant for several hundred years, but had been gradually coming to the fore and had been much on our minds from mid-1957 onward—and especially since my trip with Rubottom to Central America—were causing an inflammation throughout the hemisphere, Castro's true purposes were becoming clear in Cuba and, reminiscent of Stalin, he was trying to foment revolutions in Panama, the Dominican Republic, Venezuela, and Guatemala.

We were quite aware that while the "seed money" philosophy was still valid and that orthodox policies had not outlived their usefulness, nonetheless Latin America would not evolve in freedom, as we all wished, unless an immediate attack were made on the stultifying and mortifying social stratifications. We realized fully that a hungry man in a mud hut with a life expectancy of less than forty years found little consolation in the promise that things might be different a generation hence. He and all like him were weary of poverty, hardship, and promises. They wanted bread, houses, hospitals, schools. And their resentment at their failure was all the greater by the affluence which a relatively few of their fellow citizens enjoyed and with whom, under Communist encouragement, they equated us of the United States.

We saw what needed to be done. But how could we—in the interest of our own good relations in the hemisphere as well as for sheer humanitarian reasons—induce the leaders of Latin America to cast aside the methods of centuries, and open at once better opportunities for the masses, without plunging the United States once again into a policy of outright interventionism with all the ill consequences that would flow from such action?

This was the dilemma. I shall never forget how O. A. (Jack) Knight, a labor leader who knew more than any other living American about the attitudes of the workers of Latin America; Walter J. Donnelly, Vice President of United States Steel, living in Venezuela, a former United States Ambassador, and favorably known throughout the hemisphere; Charles A. Meyer, Vice President of Sears, Roebuck, whose company had set such good examples in its work in several of the Latin-American countries; Kenneth Holland, once Assistant Director of the Office of International Information and Cultural Affairs of the State Department and now President of the Institute of International Education, and well informed on all such matters in Latin America; Dana G. Munro, Professor of International Studies at Princeton, a former Minister to Haiti, and a deep student of Latin-American history—I shall never forget how these men, along with Herter, Dillon, Rubottom, and me worked long hours in session after session to find the right answers. We knew that a start of a sort had been made when the Inter-American Bank was established. But it was only a start.

From these discussions among ourselves and with President Eisenhower, and from the President's trip to several of the Latin-American countries early in 1960, we found an answer. The stage was set for a new approach to helping Latin America advance economically while bringing social justice to the masses of the people.

Book III

To United States policy planners, it began to appear that problems in Latin America were a tangled skein, uncountable and inextricably bound together. Traditional faith in economic aid as a panacea was badly shaken, for the orthodox approach of providing massive amounts of "seed money" to shore up the Latin-American economies was seemingly getting lost in the tangle. Only a new approach could unravel the bind.

During the Eisenhower administration, it became clear that for our aid to be meaningful both to the republics and their peoples, social reform was imperative. This was the starting point, but a rather unpromising one, for it implied that we should intervene and demand reforms. Having learned from history that unilateral intervention is doomed to failure, the United States worked assiduously for the complex and improbable alternative of collective intervention. Fortunately, United States leaders convinced the Latin Americans themselves to tie strings of social reform to our economic aid.

In the late 1950s, under President Eisenhower, long-standing United States policies affecting Latin America were reversed and the foundation for a fruitful partnership was laid. On this foundation a new edifice, an Alliance for Progress, was built.

Those who now view these unprecedented efforts as a negative response to Castro Communism are ignoring the facts, for our policies began to change before Castro became a prominent figure in the hemisphere. When he displaced Batista in 1959 (to the delight of most of the world, including Americans) our new approach to Latin-American affairs was well under way.

Now two revolutions smolder in the hemisphere: the Alliance for Progress and Castro Communism. One is dedicated to democracy, justice, and economic growth; the other, conceived in bloodshed, is dedicated to violence, totalitarianism, and the destruction of human freedom. The former will take time; the latter can come with the dawn. They cannot survive side by side. Latin Americans must choose between them.

12

We cannot change history, but we can act so that our children won't want to.

OUR PRESENT DECLARATIONS OF HONORABLE INTENTIONS as we seek to help Latin Americans achieve a better life are often obscured in their minds by the grim echoes of history. The child is the father of the man, they feel; leopards do not change their spots. And in the eyes of many Latin Americans, the United States is the fat, rich uncle who, having made his fortune by exploiting others, now strikes the pose of benefactor.

We must convince Latin Americans that our concern for their welfare is deep, abiding, and genuine, that it is not simply a negative and grudging response to Castro Communism, that it is not merely a gambit in the cold war. The long and fearsome shadow of our past behavior precedes us in our hemispheric efforts and makes the task a formidable one.

But even as history indicts us, it reveals an enlightening evolution of our relations with Latin America. It is not important for Latin Americans to excuse our past actions, but it is imperative that they view the entire sequence of history and recognize that our present policies and attitudes are very different from what they once were. If they are to judge us, it should be, in all fairness, not on what we did but on what we do. The momentum of change may have increased in the past several years as the tension in the world has increased, but the policies themselves have been shaped by a long-maturing concern for and interest in Latin Americans.

The change can be seen at a glance. We began early in the nineteenth century with a big-brother attitude which grew into a patronizing imperialism. Imperialism was eventually displaced by a policy of juridical equality of states, and concurrently we turned our efforts from exploiting Latin America to assisting in its development. From a rigid policy of making loans only for projects that would produce income, we moved to a policy of helping the peoples of Latin America build homes and hospitals and schools. We passed from a period of open intervention through a phase of absolute non-intervention into our present and sensible support of collective intervention in behalf of social justice and rising levels of well-being for the peoples of Latin America.

Recent policies become clear and significant when viewed in the perspective of history. The Act of Bogotá in 1960 and the Charter of Punta del Este in 1961, which developed in the Eisenhower and Kennedy administrations, are truly historic turning points in hemispheric relations. But these represent a fourth period in the long history of inter-American relations and they are preceded by three others which extended from early in the nineteenth century to late in the 1940s.

The first era of inter-American relations—*the big-brother era*—began with the Spanish-American wars of independence and continued to the opening of the twentieth century. It was marked by a condescending attitude in the United States and varying degrees of Yankeephobia in Latin America.

The liberation of South America from Spain began April 19, 1810 when wealthy creoles of Caracas, Venezuela replaced the Spanish captain general with a junta. This touched off wars that would last fourteen years and culminate in the liberation of Venezuela, Colombia, Ecuador, Peru, and Bolivia.

Two heroes emerged in the wars of independence. They remain symbols of courage and patriotism throughout Latin America. Simón Bolívar was twenty-six when he led the rebels in the Caracas revolt. Five years earlier, in Rome, he had climbed the Aventine Hill to vow before God that he would not rest until he had freed his country, Venezuela, from the Spanish yoke. To the south, a quieter, self-effacing, but no less courageous rebel, Jose de San Martín, carried the banner of freedom through Argentina, Chile, and Peru.

The victory over the Spanish in Caracas in 1810 was short-lived. Two years later the Spanish retaliated and dealt a crushing blow to the rebels at Puerto Cabello. Francisco de Miranda, Bolívar's superior in the revolt, was defeated and fled to La Guaira, where he planned to sail for London. Bolívar set sail for Curaçao, and from there went to New Granada (now Colombia), where he fought the Spanish under Antonio Nariño. But

Bolívar was eager to return to Venezuela and resume the battle there. In March 1813 he went home, formed a volunteer army, and slaughtered the Spanish. In October 1813 he was solemnly acclaimed the "Liberator of Venezuela." Three months later, he became the dictator.

But Bolívar's problems were not over. In September 1814, after a series of Spanish attacks, he admitted defeat and fled once more to Colombia. Here too the Spanish were winning, and Bolívar's presence did not help turn the tide. He fled to Jamaica where he tried in vain to persuade the British to aid his cause.

Hubert Herring, in his brilliant history of Latin America,* describes Bolívar during this six-month exile: "He had moments when he thought the revolution was dead, that his life had been futile. He was now only thirty-two, but he was old beyond his years. His face was pale, but his black eyes still burned; he was far from beaten. He spent the days in writing. In his famous Letter from Jamaica, he poured out his diagnosis of the ills of Spanish America and the possible lines of its redemption. He wrote to his unnamed (and probably non-existent) correspondent: 'We are threatened with the fear of death, dishonor, and every harm; there is nothing we have not suffered at the hands of that unnatural step-mother—Spain. The veil has been torn asunder. We have already seen the light and it is not our desire to be thrust back into darkness.'"

For the next two years Bolívar sought support for a return to Venezuela. In March 1816, equipped by the President of Haiti, he landed on the northwestern coast of Venezuela. He spread his tail feathers, crowed menacingly, briefly stirred a lethargic populace, and sailed back to Haiti.

The tide turned during the years between 1817 and 1820. Soldiers of fortune from England, Scotland, Ireland, and Germany swelled his ranks. By February 1819, Bolívar controlled enough of Venezuela to proclaim independence and form a congress. On June 24, 1821, he defeated the Spanish at Carabobo and assured freedom for Venezuela—though it took two more years to rid the country of all Spanish forces.

Even before he had won in Venezuela, Bolívar marched off to New Granada, defeated the Spanish at Boyacá, and entered Bogotá as the Liberator. Then he turned toward Peru, the last great Spanish stronghold in South America. (En route, he would stop at Quito, Ecuador, to crush the Spanish.) Bolívar was on his way to meet his equal in courage and patriotism: San Martín.

San Martín did not emerge as a hero until well after Bolívar had

* A History of Latin America. New York: Alfred A. Knopf, 1955.

begun his crusade. The struggle for freedom had started in the south in the same year that it began in the north: In 1810, Buenos Aires broke with Spain. San Martín did not take command, however, until 1814. And then, rather than obey a political order to attack upper Peru (a move he thought was doomed to failure), San Martín resigned his post. He shrewdly garnered the position of governor of the Province of Cuyo, claiming that his health demanded the climate and clear air. His real reason was to plan for the liberation of Peru, without which Spanish America could never be free. San Martín planned to assemble a force, cross the mountains to Chile, defeat the Spanish there, and proceed (with greater forces) to Peru. He projected a step-by-step approach for the eight years that followed.

From 1814 to 1817, San Martín built an army. Then in January 1817 he began the arduous and perilous journey across the Andes into Chile. Although the trip took a heavy toll of his forces, San Martín caught the Spanish unaware and routed them. By April he had wrested Chile from Spain's grip.

San Martín was a patient man, austere in his integrity. He shunned the acclaim of the Chileans, refusing even their gifts of appreciation. For two years he prepared for the next step. By 1820, he was ready to move against the Spaniards in Peru.

An odd assemblage of ships commanded by a disgraced British admiral carried San Martín's forces to Pisco in southern Peru. Cautious as always, San Martín chose not to meet the Spaniards in full tilt at their Lima stronghold. In Pisco he waited, recruiting volunteers from reluctant Peruvians. To jibes from overeager patriots, San Martín explained his caution: "I do not seek military glory, nor am I ambitious for the title of conqueror of Peru: I only wish to free it from oppression."

To do this, it soon became evident that he needed the help of Bolívar, who was in Ecuador. Bolívar offered the help; San Martín accepted and agreed to a secondary role.

Bolívar was as boastful as San Martín was humble. When they first met, Bolívar toasted the "two greatest men in South America: General San Martín and myself." San Martín responded: "To the early end of the war; to the organization of the republics of the continent and to the health of the Liberator of Colombia." For reasons never fully documented, but somewhat obvious, the two patriots did not join forces. San Martín quickly and quietly left for Europe to return thirty years after his death to be honored with a ceremonial burial in the cathedral in Buenos Aires.

Once more the dominant figure on the stage, Bolívar prepared to liberate Peru. In September 1823 he marched triumphantly into Lima.

The curtain came down on the drama more than a year later when Bolívar's forces under Sucre met the Spaniards on a high plateau near Ayacucho. There, though heavily outnumbered, Sucre defeated the Spanish and virtually won Spanish-American independence.

The United States had won favor with the leaders of the new republics in Latin America. We had shunned the safer course of supporting Spain. Instead, we had begun lending moral support to the rebels as early as 1810, by sending "agents for seamen and commerce" to the republics where juntas were organized. In 1811, even a few consuls were sent. The people of the United States were with the patriots, and guns and munitions found their way south to rebel armies. In 1822, the United States formally recognized Gran Colombia, Argentina, and Mexico; in 1823, we granted formal recognition to Chile, and in 1824 to Brazil and Central America. The United States was the first nation to welcome the new republics to the free world, and this had a sobering effect on Spain's plan for reinvasion. Then in 1823, President Monroe warned the European nations to stay out of the hemisphere, and Latin-American leaders were exultant.

What an opportunity opened to us at this early stage in our relations with Latin America, and what an Alliance for Progress might have accomplished then! As it was, Latin-American gratitude to the United States waned quickly. The Monroe Doctrine, helpful as it was, had been the expression of the big brother looking after a weaker member of the family. Latin Americans sensed but did not initially object to this patronizing relationship. Then Henry Clay and John Quincy Adams made it clear that the Doctrine involved no commitment for armed support of the new nations in the event of a Spanish attack, and Latin-American leaders began to suspect that it was to be interpreted only for the benefit of the United States.

In the middle of the nineteenth century, the big brother to the north became aggressive. On March 2, 1836, United States settlers in Texas declared their independence from Mexico. Four days later, General Santa Anna slaughtered 187 Texans at the Alamo and stirred the United States to fury. Sam Houston defeated and captured Santa Anna a month later and won independence for Texas. The following year, the United States recognized Texas in an open and hostile affront to Mexico.

Mexico demanded the reconquest of Texas. The United States, embroiled in the slavery question, debated annexation and feared that

Britain would take Texas if we did not. In 1843, Mexico warned that annexation meant war.

Manifest Destiny was becoming a heady brew in the United States at that time. Texas was annexed in 1845. But this was not enough. California lay like a ripe fruit within our reach. So President Polk bluntly offered to buy California from Mexico and infuriated the Mexicans. When they refused, he ordered General Zachary Taylor into the disputed area between the Rio Grande and the Nueces River. There was no recourse but war.

It was a short war and a disastrous one for Mexico. The Treaty of Guadalupe Hidalgo in 1848 separated Mexico from half of her former domain. In cash and cancellation of claims, Mexico received about $18 million for this territory. We were assured of title to Texas and received all but a part of what is now California, Arizona, New Mexico, Nevada, Utah, and part of Colorado. Mexico lost more as well: She suffered economic collapse, a shattering loss of face, and the sickening revelation that she was prostrate, impoverished, and saddled with corrupt leaders.

Almost immediately a feeling of shame grew in the United States. The big brother was a bully. Latin America looked on with concern. The victory won in the Mexican War is costing the United States considerable goodwill even today.

After our Civil War, noticeable improvement in inter-American relations began. Cultural intercourse increased. Domingo Sarmiento, writer, educator, and later President of Argentina, developed an affinity for North American life after an extended stay in the United States, and his views impressed the peoples of the young American nations.

Secretary of State William H. Seward's warning to Napoleon that the United States was prepared to help Mexico evict Maximilian and French troops from this continent restored to some extent confidence in the Monroe Doctrine. Coincidentally, mushrooming French and British investments in Latin America engendered distrust of Europeans. (In the 1870s and 1880s United States investments were comparatively small, save in Díaz's Mexico.) Then came an intellectual reaction against European customs which were blamed by such men as Sarmiento and José de Victorino de Lastarría of Chile for the lack of progress in Latin America.

Meanwhile, North American business interests were being persuaded to support an Inter-American Customs Union by Secretary of State James G. Blaine. United States industry was booming and the search for new markets and new sources of raw material was becoming intense. Blaine was reacting to Europe's domination of the Latin-American market. He also feared that the late-nineteenth-century rash of Latin-American boundary disputes and wars might tempt European nations to intervene. Blaine was eager to establish machinery for mediation; he called the first Inter-American Congress in Washington in 1889. Though well attended by most of the new Latin-American republics, it accomplished little at the time. But it did pave the way for today's Organization of American States and was, in fact, the apogee of inter-American relations between the 1820s and 1930s.

From the closing years of the nineteenth century to the early 1930s, the big brother became *the meddling uncle*. The United States intervened repeatedly in Latin-American affairs and earned for itself a lasting resentment on the part of Latin-American leaders and intellectuals.

As the nineteenth century ended, European powers were spreading their empires through Africa, the Middle East, and Asia. The United States, emerging as a world power in its own right, feared that Europe might expand into the Western Hemisphere. Besides, Americans had no wish to be left behind in the scramble for wealth and power. A profound psychological change swept the country. Industrialists with expansionist ideas led the way (followed eagerly by Americans charmed with a new sense of power) toward our divine appointment: The United States succumbed to imperialism, though of a milder variety than that of the British and French. The natural flow for our empire was to the south—into the strategic Caribbean.

The domineering relationship which the United States was to develop in the Caribbean could be foreseen as early as 1895, when President Grover Cleveland belligerently pressured Great Britain into accepting his particular settlement of a dispute over British Guianan and Venezuelan territory. Our incredible audacity shows in the ultimatum delivered by Secretary of State Richard Olney:

"Today the United States is practically sovereign on this continent, and its fiat is law upon the subjects to which it confines its interposition. . . . It is because, in addition to all other grounds, its infinite resources combined with its isolated position render it master of the situation and practically invulnerable as against any or all other powers."

In 1895, Theodore Roosevelt, champion of Manifest Destiny, wrote to Henry Cabot Lodge: "This country needs a war." Three years later we instigated the Spanish-American War, to the delight of our population, and drove the Spanish tyrants from Cuba. In doing so, we adorned our imperialism with the wreath of liberty and viewed it as a holy crusade. Latin America did not share our vantage point and saw it only as blatant intervention. The northern relative was now not only resented; the meddling and greedy uncle was feared and despised.

In 1902, our policy toward recently liberated Cuba caused Latin Americans to believe that we had fought the Spanish-American War only to replace Spain as ruler of the island. The Platt Amendment to the treaty which we forced Cuba to sign heightened Latin-American animosity toward us. It subordinated Cuba to the status of protectorate of the United States and gave us the right to intervene in Cuba if we felt its independence, or its internal order, or its financial sovereignty was threatened. The Roosevelt Corollary to the Monroe Doctrine claimed the right of the United States to intervene in Latin-American republics to prevent intervention from outside the hemisphere. To Latin Americans it was simply a legal justification for a general policy of intervention which could affect every nation in the hemisphere.

Actually, our insistence upon the Platt Amendment had some legitimate justification. We were genuinely concerned for Cuba's stability and special support from the United States seemed to be a prerequisite to Cuban economic development, political maturation, and freedom from further European intervention. But the United States was also motivated by a concern for the property rights of its citizens in Cuba and by an infatuation with the concept of expansionism.

If, during the heyday of its interventionism in Cuba, the United States had initiated even a reasonable degree of social justice, universal education, and true democracy—which it seems to me it was in a position to do—all succeeding developments in our relations with Latin America would have been far different from what they proved to be. There would surely never have been a Batista or a Castro. And Cuba, as a neophyte democracy, could have been a stimulant to peaceful social change in the other Latin-American republics. Hemispheric hostility might have changed to warm friendship.

But the "world of what might have been" is, by its very nature, shaped by hindsight. The leaders of those days were no doubt doing what they thought to be the proper thing. The concept of social justice was not then foremost in official or popular thinking. A priceless opportunity was missed, but our present judgment of these leaders should be tempered by the realization that tomorrow will reveal opportunities we are missing today because one or another concept has not yet occurred to us.

Never one to be bound by inhibition or criticism, Teddy Roosevelt next moved bluntly but effectively to his pet project—the Panama Canal. The Isthmus of Panama was then part of Colombia. When Roosevelt could not persuade Colombia to sign a treaty granting him canal rights, he supported a Panamanian revolt by using the United States Navy to prevent Colombian troops from landing to suppress it. A few days after the revolt, he recognized the rebel government, and less than a month later, the Roughrider had obtained his treaty rights in return for support of the new government. Riding roughshod over Colombia's sovereign rights won us new enemies in Latin America.

Roosevelt further offended Latin America in 1904 when he applied the Roosevelt Corollary of the Monroe Doctrine to the Dominican Republic. The United States had made itself responsible for the payment of debts of some $30 million which various Dominican governments had contracted irresponsibly with Great Britain, France, Germany, and Spain. The creditor nations had become concerned about repayment, and Roosevelt feared their intervention. He established a customs receivership in the Dominican Republic, took over all customs houses, and collected the duties. More than half of these import revenues went to pay the republic's debts.

To Latin Americans Roosevelt's actions were hardly surprising: Disregarding their feelings, he had grabbed a canal zone and was now taking control of island republics so that he could protect shipping lanes that would in time converge on the canal.

William Howard Taft's administration did nothing to change the image of the United States. Taft also established customs receiverships—in Nicaragua and Honduras. And following another Roosevelt precedent, Taft sent troops to occupy Nicaragua to protect American lives and property rights. (Roosevelt's marines had occupied the Dominican Republic in 1908.) Our dominance in the Caribbean, Central America, and Panama grew. And ill will in Latin America grew with it.

In 1913, many Latin Americans applauded the elevation of Woodrow Wilson to the presidency. Here was a man of a political party different from Taft's and Roosevelt's. One of Wilson's earliest pronouncements as President emphasized the importance of inter-American cooperation and understanding. Surely the United States policies would change for the better.

But Wilson made matters much worse. In an effort to build democratic institutions, he repeatedly meddled in Latin-American internal affairs. Such a policy would have been unfeasible even in nations where social and economic conditions permitted the growth of Wilsonian democracy; in the virtually anarchic nations of the Caribbean, it led us into calamitous situations.

Wilson first tried to apply to Haiti and the Dominican Republic his theory that direct guidance by the United States could develop democratic governments in an orderly fashion. He attempted to help his favorite political parties through moral and material aid—and failed dismally. Leaders resisted his aid; it was as a kiss of death in their countries. By 1915, Wilson had to send troops to Haiti to restore internal order, protect United States interests, and assure democracy. The occupation lasted for nineteen years, during which time the United States appointed the leaders, foisted a constitution on the country (drafted in Washington), made Haiti essentially a protectorate of the United States, and for the first time gave white foreigners the right to own Haitian land.

If Latin Americans could not see the good in Wilson's idealism, it was because their view was obscured by the blue uniforms of United States marines on their soil.

Wilson also succeeded in creating hostile attitudes among revolutionary leaders of Mexico, despite the fact that he helped keep the revolution alive by causing the downfall of the reactionary regime of the brutal Huerta. For a brief period, Wilson was praised in Mexico, but when he put pressure on the more progressive regime of Venustiano Carranza (partly in response to Villa's forays into Texas), Mexican anger became violent. Wilson wanted Carranza to govern in harmony with his own democratic and institutional beliefs. Not until the United States entered World War I did Wilson give full recognition to the Carranza Government, which he had helped come to power three years earlier.

Wilson's recognition policy was a sharp departure from historic precedent. Traditional policy requires that, to merit recognition, a regime need only maintain internal order and abide by international obligations. Wilson added a new ingredient. He would only recognize regimes that passed a test of "constitutional legitimacy." The policy did not work. Even when several nations seemingly accepted Wilson's preconditions, actual democracy did not result. Elections were rigged, elected officials were coerced, and other ways were found to circumvent the "democracy." Wilson's recognition policy served only to expand the practice of intervention.

Economic factors began to bear on inter-American relations in the post-Wilsonian period when Latin-American producers became more dependent on markets in the United States. Our tariff policy of the 1920s was aimed at protecting domestic producers. Many Latin-American countries were hurt. Congressional representatives from the western states successfully fought down efforts to reduce the import tax on copper, for example

—a reduction which would have helped Chile. Argentine beef was refused admittance to this country in 1927 when a "sanitary" embargo was placed upon it, technically because of the foot-and-mouth disease threat on the Pampas. Doubt of our motives arose, however, when disease-free zones were not exempted from the embargo. Then Cuban sugar was so heavily taxed that its share of the United States market was cut in half.

The Smoot-Hawley Tariff Act of 1930 raised our tariff walls against Latin America in the midst of an economic depression and provided Yankeephobes with valuable evidence in support of their contentions that the United States sought only to exploit their economies. Latin America, they charged, was to be kept in a colonial status to the United States—a mere supplier of cheap raw commodities not produced in the United States.

Soon another source of friction developed. Private investment capital grew into importance during the 1920s. By 1930, private United States investments in Latin America had reached $5 billion, thus for the first time rivaling British investments there. Many of the companies in the early stages of their penetration into Latin America did not have the concern for local development and welfare that is now so evident in the activities of our businesses abroad. Indeed, businesses domestically were only beginning to display the social conscience which is now characteristic of them. The responsibility of businesses to promote better social and economic environments in a host country—while making money—remained a concept largely unborn. The impression created in Latin-American minds in the 1920s is still a major though unjustified obstacle to mutual understanding.

As economic matters continued to increase significantly in inter-American affairs, the United States again resorted to forceful intervention. Although Charles Evans Hughes, Harding's Secretary of State, had withdrawn our forces from Nicaragua in the summer of 1925, Secretary of State Frank B. Kellogg of the Coolidge administration felt it necessary for the interests of American lives and property to send them back. In his justification of this reinvasion, President Coolidge added fuel to the flames of Latin-American fury by telling Congress that "the person and property of a citizen are a part of the general domain even when abroad."

This new imperialistic adventure was magnified by demagogic Latin-American politicians who used invective against the Yankees to divert attention from emerging social and economic problems at home. And thus an era which had opened in goodwill closed in a spirit of enmity and carping criticism. Our experience in intervention and imperialism had not been a happy one; further, as I shall indicate, the lingering effects of interventionism caused the United States to delay longer than it might otherwise have done in fostering programs of internal social reform in Latin America.

In the third period of inter-American relations, the meddling uncle became the *good neighbor*. President Franklin Roosevelt's Good Neighbor policy replaced intervention and imperialism with mutual respect and juridical equality of states.

At the Montevideo Conference in 1933, Secretary of State Cordell Hull affirmed that no nation has the right to intervene in the internal affairs of another. He qualified the pledge by stating that the United States would base its non-intervention policy on considerations other than the Montevideo declaration until such time as its terms could be more fully defined. Even this qualified expression of the Good Neighbor policy was joyfully accepted, however, for considerable groundwork for it had been laid by four enlightened Americans. While nothing can or should detract from the significance of the radical departures from the fateful policies of Theodore Roosevelt and Woodrow Wilson which were instituted by the Franklin Roosevelt administration, much guidance was derived from the actions and attitudes of Secretary Charles Evans Hughes, Secretary Henry L. Stimson, President Herbert Hoover, and Ambassador to Mexico Dwight W. Morrow. Their work was transitional.

The movement toward a foreign policy more acceptable to Latin America was initiated by Charles Evans Hughes, who discarded most of the Wilsonian prerequisites for recognition. He reinstituted the traditional practice of recognizing governments which could maintain internal order and discharge international obligations, save as the policy applied to Costa Rica, Guatemala, Honduras, El Salvador, and Nicaragua. Here the Wilsonian concern for democratic procedures was maintained because these nations were signatories of a treaty which pledged common non-recognition of any regime coming to power through violence. Not only did Hughes deem it inadvisable for the United States to weaken this attempt to reduce the number of revolutions and *coups d'état* which had plagued that region, but he also shared the concern of previous administrations for a measure of control over the sensitive area. Kellogg and Stimson maintained Hughes' divided policy, for the most part. Only when the Central-American republics abrogated the treaty in 1934 did Cordell Hull extend to them the pre-Wilsonian recognition criteria.

Hughes withdrew our armed forces from the Dominican Republic in

1924 and, as previously mentioned, removed them temporarily from Nicaragua. Through vexing times, he maintained a moderate attitude toward Mexico.

But it was Dwight Morrow who deserved most of the credit for restoring Mexican goodwill after Wilson's heavy-handed meddling. Morrow was a banker with J. P. Morgan & Co., and knew as much about people as he did about banking. Sent to Mexico City as ambassador in 1927, Morrow decided to do what he could to improve relations between the two countries. He dispensed with protocol and diplomatic niceties and dealt with President Plutarco Elías Calles man to man. Calles was despised by most Americans for his flagrant defiance of United States interests and his dictatorial regime. But Morrow won Calles and the two became friends. Morrow used his influence to persuade Calles and other Mexican leaders to conduct their social reforms, especially their land reform, with enough regard for North American interests to prevent a rupture of diplomatic relations. He liked Mexicans and sought the company of journalists, teachers, businessmen, farmers, and people from all levels of society.

In December 1928, a memorandum issued by Under Secretary J. Reuben Clark took much of the sting out of the Roosevelt Corollary to the Monroe Doctrine by re-emphasizing the Doctrine's anti-European nature and not mentioning any rights of unilateral intervention by the United States. In 1928, Herbert Hoover, in a fine display of personal diplomacy, made a pre-inaugural goodwill tour through South America and won plaudits from the Latin-American press. Stimson arranged for the withdrawal of our forces from Nicaragua by January 1933.

For several reasons it remained for the Administration of Franklin D. Roosevelt to become recognized as the architect of inter-American cooperation. First, the Democratic party was thought by Latin Americans to be more concerned than the Republican party with the welfare of the common man and to be anti-business in outlook. Latin Americans not only disliked North American businesses themselves but, through their concern about their own economic disadvantages, had identified themselves with "underdogs" in the United States. In this philosophic exuberance they overlooked the fact that Woodrow Wilson, the most persistent interferer of all, was a Democrat. They identified the evils of North American policy with Republicans.

Second, the Republican party was committed in the early thirties to the high tariff trade policy established by the Smoot-Hawley Act. This policy was not conducive to smooth relations with nations whose economic well-being depended substantially on the accessibility of markets in the United States. Hull, a Democrat, on the other hand, induced the Congress to pass an Act which authorized reciprocal trade agreements, and Latin America foresaw benefits flowing to them under the new program.

A third factor was more obscure. It is difficult to assess the true effect of personalities on history. It must be recognized, however, that the three chief figures of the Good Neighbor policy—Franklin Roosevelt, Cordell Hull, and Sumner Welles—played important personal roles in the development of better inter-American relations. Roosevelt's dynamism, flamboyance, self-confidence, oratorical abilities, and colorful phrasings may not have been appreciated by all of his fellow citizens, but to Latin Americans these personal mannerisms evoked admiration. His continued concern for hemispheric problems, coupled with his drive for social change in the United States, harmonized neatly with the desires of the masses in Latin America. Hull's chief personal contribution came early in the period when, before the Montevideo Conference of 1933, he introduced himself to the various delegates in a warm, informal manner in his hotel. Gone was the stereotype of the haughty, condescending Yankee diplomat. Although Hull's attitude toward Latin America is thought to have been made more tolerant by pressure from Roosevelt and Welles, he rarely strayed from the confines of the policy and almost always acted in the highest traditions of the Good Neighbor. Sumner Welles had an all but catastrophic beginning. In Cuba, in the early days of the Administration (before the Montevideo Conference), Ambassador Welles became personally involved in Cuban politics. He threatened armed intervention and delayed recognition in order to place in power the faction he thought could best govern the country. Welles' pressures—some of them extreme—brought the Cuban Army and Batista into Cuban politics. For a harrowing period it seemed to Latin Americans that the new Administration would behave no differently from its predecessors. Resentment was discernible, the general failure of the Cuban policy was quickly noted by Roosevelt and Hull, and Welles was recalled during the Montevideo Conference. Evidently Welles realized his mistake, too, for subsequently as Under Secretary of State he assumed a commanding position in inter-American affairs. Capably, coolly, gravely, he managed the day-to-day mechanics of the Good Neighbor policy. His consistency in principle and deed earned him the respect of most Latin Americans.

The era began, then, at Montevideo with a qualified pledge that the United States would not intervene in the internal affairs of the other American republics. The pledge lost its qualification three years later when, in response to Latin-American pressure, Hull signed at Buenos Aires a new treaty which without reservation pledged the American nations to a policy of non-intervention. Latin-American nations felt that at last they had achieved true equality with the United States and that this meant the cessation of all diplomatic, economic, and military interference.

This was a broader interpretation than the one prevailing in Washington at the time. Bryce Wood in *The Making of the Good Neighbor Policy*† states that the expense and ineffectiveness of the Nicaraguan intervention, as well as the ill will engendered by it, had caused the Roosevelt administration to turn away from *armed intervention* as an instrument of national policy, but concern in the early 1930s for the protection of the lives and property of our citizens abroad did not lead us to adopt the completely non-interventionist views of Latin-American leaders. The Roosevelt administration soon discovered, however, that diplomatic and economic pressures on the internal policies of the Latin-American nations did not effectively protect our private interests and individuals, nor did they encourage a spirit of genuine cooperation. So a policy of reciprocity was conceived: The United States would behave in ways known to be favorable to Latin America and then hope Latin America would reciprocate by treating our private citizens with fairness and by joining with the United States in economic and defense agreements as war clouds appeared in Europe.

As Wood skillfully details, our policy, steadily moving toward reciprocity had reached the point in 1938 that we could use mild economic pressures in an attempt to insure just repayment for North American oil holdings expropriated in Mexico by President Lázaro Cárdenas. We accepted expropriation as the legal right of the Mexican Government, never considered the use of force, and finally agreed to a Mexican proposal for the method by which the amount of repayment should be determined. The restraint exhibited by the State Department was noted and approved throughout Latin America. The final settlement, made in 1941, was accomplished by international negotiation between equals, a feat that would have been unlikely a decade before.

When war clouds appeared over Europe, the State Department became concerned primarily with national defense. The strategic importance of Mexico (Mexico's attitude had a profound influence on policy decisions in the other Latin-American republics) was an important consideration in our soft attitude in conducting the oil negotiations. Gone was the idea that the State Department should be a "collection agency for bondholders and

† New York: Columbia University Press, 1961.

bankers" (to use Wood's phrase). This new willingness to treat Latin-American nations as equals evolved just in time to encourage the hemispheric solidarity that was vital to the Allied prosecution of World War II.

At the same time, United States businesses found they had to act on their own to prevent discrimination by Latin-American governments. Such actions on rare occasions took the form of bribery, but usually businesses took enlightened steps of a popular nature to achieve their end, such as providing better living facilities for workers, educating workers' children, paying taxes, raising wages, and encouraging sound economic development.

United States businesses quickly learned that this approach provided a more persuasive deterrent to unfair treatment than had the big-brotherly protection of the State Department. Indeed, our businesses set standards of good citizenship which have not as yet been emulated by all indigenous enterprises in some of the Latin-American countries. I can say confidently, on the basis of personal studies, that most United States business leaders in Latin America have become true statesmen and fine examples for their Latin-American business associates.

In addition to these changes in policy, the Roosevelt administration provided Latin America with other tangible proof that our attitude had changed. Naval and marine forces were withdrawn from Haiti in 1934, to complete our withdrawal of armed forces from the Caribbean. In the same year, the Platt Amendment was abrogated and Cuba achieved full sovereignty. Treaties which had given the United States control over certain internal affairs of Haiti and the Dominican Republic were allowed to expire in 1936 and 1940, respectively. In 1936, a new treaty with Panama ended its status as a protectorate of the United States.

Meanwhile economic problems pressed for attention, but the Good Neighbor policy did not achieve distinction in this area of relationships. The crash of 1929 and the ensuing depression wreaked havoc with inter-American trade. Reciprocal tariff reductions made by the United States with Latin-American nations helped some, but by 1938 Latin American-United States trade was only half what it had been nine years before. Much of that trade had been diverted to European nations, mainly the Axis powers, which had profited from our high tariff policy.

Our aid programs, which became large in the Eisenhower years, began modestly in 1938. The Export-Import Bank began making loans to Latin-American nations for public works and similar purposes. In the next two years, the bank committed loans of some $200 million to Latin-American governments.

In 1938 the United States sent a few trained technicians to Latin America to assist in economic development. Recipient governments paid the salaries of the technicians—a practice which was altered later.

By this time, the State Department was preoccupied with the gathering storm in Europe. What would be the attitude of Latin America?

The fruits of the Good Neighbor policy had ripened quickly. The meddling uncle was forgotten (at least for the moment) and every Latin-American nation, save Argentina and Chile, took its place in the line of defense beside the Allies. In January 1943, Chile broke relations with the Axis powers; a year later, Argentina did the same.

During the war, Latin-American nations, except Argentina, effectively suppressed Axis subversion and espionage, and even Argentina cooperated by ending its direct telegraphic communication links with Germany and Italy. Locations for air and naval bases were offered to the United States. Bases in Brazil proved to be of immense importance in the provision of logistic support for Allied campaigns in North Africa and for the anti-submarine campaign in the Atlantic. The War Department had to turn down volunteer contingents from several Latin-American nations because of the impracticability of training and indoctrinating small bodies of foreign troops, but Brazilian soldiers fought with valor in Italy and Mexican pilots flew against the Japanese.

Latin America quickly became the primary source of strategic raw materials. Prices of these commodities were kept down by price controls in the United States and by the heroic efforts of Latin-American laborers, who worked longer hours without significant raises in pay.

Reciprocally, we shipped scarce machinery to Latin America and increased our economic aid, chiefly through the Office of the Co-ordinator of Inter-American Affairs and a lend-lease program. The Co-ordinator of Inter-American Affairs was able to generate a substantial amount of good-will through a modest assistance program which concentrated on improving health and sanitation, cultural relations, and basic economic capabilities, including agriculture. Lend-lease was important to Brazil, which received most of the $260 million in goods we sent to Latin America. (One State Department officer contended that we did a good job of providing Latin Americans with consumer goods at fair prices, but that local profiteers increased the prices exorbitantly. Of course we received the blame.)

As World War II approached its climax, several developments interrupted the smooth functioning of the Good Neighbor policy. Our leadership of inter-American affairs in the State Department changed four times in two years, and Latin Americans became confused by what seemed to be changing attitudes and policies. When the United States began planning in 1944 at Dumbarton Oaks for a postwar world security system, consultations were held with the British, Russians, and Chinese, but not with Latin Americans. Brazil was consulted but others were thoughtlessly ignored. Latin Americans began to fear that the system of hemispheric consultation was being scrapped.

Despite the chagrin thus engendered, it was possible to lay the basis for an inter-American security system at a meeting in Mexico City in 1945. The agreement developed there—the Act of Chapultepec—declared that a system of multilateral sanctions, decided upon after consultation, would be used to meet threats of aggression, both internal and external to the hemisphere. It left open an important question: Would unanimity or a mere majority be required to impose sanctions?

In 1945, the behavior of our ambassador in Argentina once again raised the specter of United States intervention. The internal Argentine situation which led to the crucial incident had begun in 1944.

When a group of Argentine officers, including Juan Perón, overthrew President Edelmiro J. Farrell, Cordell Hull sharply criticized the new regime and brought out from the storehouse of ineffective diplomatic tools the old weapon of threat of non-recognition. However, a conciliatory atmosphere developed and Spruille Braden was assigned as Ambassador to Argentina in May 1945. As the Argentine presidential election of February 1946 approached, Braden launched verbal attacks against Perón. The State Department published a book which listed wartime Nazi activities in Argentina. This direct interference in Argentine politics was roundly denounced in Argentina and throughout Latin America, and in October 1945 Braden was reassigned. Unhappily, the policy identified Perón with Argentine nationalism and greatly increased his popular support.

Following Perón's election, a meek policy of conciliation toward him was adopted. Then new outbursts of criticism were leveled against the United States—this time for being pro-dictator and anti-democratic. The dilemma of what attitude to maintain toward Latin American dictators was upon us.

This vexing problem was intensified by a new social and economic ferment in Latin America. Modern communication media were beginning to reach all the people, even in remote mountain hamlets. Progressive parties in Latin America were emerging. The historic concern about intervention by the United States became somewhat obscured as fears arose regarding the feudalistic nature of Latin America's social order. Some felt the United States could be a valuable ally in overcoming this grave internal problem, especially by not supporting dictators who ruled by sufferance of the elite. Others felt the United States should adhere strictly to the policy of non-intervention but should provide massive amounts of public and private loans, to democratic and dictatorial regimes alike.

Economic problems swelled like a balloon, and essentially obscured all other issues. Postwar prices of Latin-American raw materials declined and prices of goods imported from the United States increased. The United States poured recovery funds into war-torn Europe at an amazing rate while Latin American problems went, it was felt, largely unnoticed. Europe received more than $28 billion between the end of the war and 1950. Latin America obtained in the same period about half a billion dollars, mostly in loans. This, it was charged, was discriminatory, lacking in appreciation for what Latin America had done during the war, and indicative of our relegating Latin America once again to a secondary role in our plans for the future.

Criticisms of North American private capital were also intensified by some who felt it was slow in returning after its wartime displacement (most of the reduced amount went into Venezuelan oil and iron ore). Contradictorily, others charged that our private capital was exploitive. Demagogic politicians, including leftist leaders, again created the image of the grasping Yankee imperialist. The press became filled with vituperations: Latin America was being reduced to a colonial status economically by the Octopus of the North; the economies of Latin America were being crushed; United States leaders were concerned only with Europe, Greece, Turkey, and Korea; Latin America was being neglected.

Despite the overwhelming preponderance of economic issues which worked violently and in a sea of misunderstanding against inter-American goodwill, the nations of the Western Hemisphere signed two important treaties during the latter part of the 1940s.

The Inter-American Treaty of Reciprocal Assistance was concluded in Rio de Janeiro in 1947. The principle of collective security was reaffirmed: An armed attack on one nation of the hemisphere would be considered an attack on all signatories. The deficiency of the Act of Chapultepec was overcome—the problem of voting procedure was resolved. Two-thirds of the signatory nations could determine the steps to be taken against an aggressor.

In April 1948, in Bogotá, the Charter of the Organization of American States was adopted. Delegates from all the American republics created a permanent institutional framework for inter-Americanism. At this same conference, however, leaders of the Latin-American nations failed to persuade the United States delegation headed by Secretary of State George C. Marshall that a large and continuing aid program was needed in their countries. They were advised to rely upon their ability to attract private credit and private investments.

And so the third period in inter-American relations ended in an atmosphere very different from that of its beginning. Franklin Roosevelt, Hull, and Welles had opened the era with dramatic and noble moves which had essentially eliminated imperialism and interventionism. They had established firmly the concepts of mutual respect and juridical equality of states. So great was the momentum of goodwill thus engendered that it had been possible, despite our ineptness at Dumbarton Oaks and the violation of non-interventionism in Argentina, to create new instruments for collective security and a permanent organization dedicated to inter-American cooperation. But as vast and complex problems of economic relationships and of internal social threat became paramount toward the close of the era, new antagonisms toward the United States rapidly developed. These newer issues would dominate the Latin-American activities of the Eisenhower and Kennedy administrations and make it essential for the good *neighbor* to become the good *partner*.

13   Compromise is less a sacrifice of principle than an ad-
        mission of fallibility.

PRESIDENT EISENHOWER'S INTEREST IN LATIN AMERICA
began when he was a student in high school. While I, nine years younger
than he, was absorbed in Horatio Alger and Motor Boy books, he was
reading, for sheer pleasure, every history available in our home and in the
Carnegie Library of Abilene. A few dealt with the Americas, and he became fascinated, especially with the problems and opportunities in Argentina. Had he not been admitted to West Point, his serious intent was to
migrate to Argentina and make a career for himself there. The possibility
of doing this was renewed when, in football and equestrian exercises at
West Point, he seriously injured a knee. Continuing with a military
career came into question. But he remained in the military and so did not
visit any of the Latin-American nations, except Mexico, until 1946 when
a goodwill trip to Brazil, Uruguay, Mexico, and other nations rekindled his
interest and exposed him to their postwar problems of development.

After he took office, President Eisenhower had the Korean War to contend with, as well as manifold other international crises, and the prospects
for an early goodwill trip through the hemisphere were bleak. In late
March 1953, he asked me to begin the series of study trips which absorbed
much of my time and thoughts for eight years.

"I want you to tell the leaders of Latin America," he said to me, "that
one of the main goals of this Administration is to strengthen relationships
between our countries. You may emphasize that while I am President the
United States will consistently maintain a policy of non-intervention, juridical equality of states, and free choices of peoples." He used the phrase

good partners. My brother felt most deeply about the old concept of the free choice of peoples; he believed it to be one of our most fundamental concepts and, much later in his Administration, he would challenge Khrushchev to permit free elections in every country of the world and to abide with us in whatever the result. He knew that the Latin Americans remembered, and not pleasantly, our imperialism and interventionism of the past, and he hoped that we could prove by word and deed that this was a new era and that we could be trusted to work for the common good.

In his instructions, the President said: "I want you to get a broad view of the conditions which affect the total relations of the United States with the republics of Latin America. Keep an open mind and consider what we can do, what policy changes or programs will be necessary, to unify the republics of this hemisphere."

I plunged at once into a series of briefing sessions in the Departments of State, Treasury, Agriculture, and Labor. I also had long discussions with officials of the Export-Import Bank, the International Bank, and other lending agencies. From these agencies, and with the approval of President Eisenhower and Secretary Dulles, I selected the men who would be associated with me in the forthcoming studies. We soon decided that the great economic problem which dominated all others was that of the changing relationship between raw commodity prices and the prices of industrial goods.

It was natural, therefore, for us to think primarily about what could be done to help. We realized the need for industrialization in Latin America as a way of reducing her dependence on the export of primary commodities. So we considered what, if anything, the United States could do to speed industrialization. We knew that agriculture had to be made more diverse and more efficient. And we knew that if Latin America was to develop an efficient agriculture and a successful complex of industry, the people would have to have better education, better housing, better diets, better health services, and better managerial training.

President Eisenhower knew that economic conditions had become paramount. He knew this from his general knowledge, but he also knew it from specific and recent incidents. He had scarcely sat down in the presidential chair when he learned that the Truman administration had committed the United States to a $300 million balance-of-payments loan to Brazil. Also, President Truman had all but promised a loan for the development of copper mining in Peru—as I recall it amounted to about $140 million.

In 1953, United States private investment in Latin America was about $6 billion, public loans and investment about $1 billion. The President indicated that he hoped we could speed the flow of credit. Of course, the United States could not force private funds to flow faster; the Latin-American nations would have to attract them. But the government could increase public loans and investments.

So we set out to visit the ten republics of South America in the summer of 1953 with the thought that much could be accomplished if we could find the general methods to speed orthodox economic assistance. We would not try to pass judgment on particular projects in this or that country—that was the business of full-time State Department and International Cooperation Administration officials. Instead, we would seek to develop the knowledge and perspective which might justify changes in our own policies and programs that would lead toward greater prosperity in Latin America—toward that "Good Partnership." Perhaps we were naïve, or simply caught up in the overwhelming desire to improve the world, for we began in high spirits and high hopes as on a crusade. President Eisenhower and John Foster Dulles saw us off at the airport, lending prestige to our mission.

On this first study trip to South America, my associates and I learned a great deal. We conferred with more than two thousand government officials, businessmen, politicians, students, teachers, farmers, and union leaders. Conversations ranged the political spectrum, from visits with arch-conservatives and ultranationalists to meetings with ultra-liberals and internationalists.

Many of my experiences have been discussed elsewhere in this book to illustrate the problems of misunderstanding, agriculture, credit, industrialization, price-fixing, and so on. Hence, a few highlights of this first trip are given here only to demonstrate that none of my conversations with Latin-American leaders even hinted that the problem was more than economic, that the orthodox approach to Latin America's problems was inadequate.

For nearly a month before we left, the United States Information Agency had given to the Latin-American press pictures and biographies of every member of our party, and these were prominently displayed to herald our coming. (Further, every move we made in each country was carried by the press of all ten countries and also in the press of the other ten republics not being visited. The only press that gave scant coverage was our own.)

When we arrived at the Venezuelan airport, which is at sea level and about ten miles from Caracas, a thousand persons were there to greet us, headed by the Foreign Minister and other dignitaries. It may be interesting to describe the diplomatic imperatives: I would descend from the plane first, greet the Foreign Minister, present him to my wife and the other members of my party. The Foreign Minister would then take me down the line to meet the host-country dignitaries, after which I would greet the United States Embassy staff in a second line—all very formal. Next, I would be escorted by the Foreign Minister to the honor guards who were there to play the two national anthems; one was always expected to inspect the troops.

Invariably about twenty cars would be on hand to transport the party: the Foreign Minister and I in the first car, my wife and his wife in the second; several cars for the United States Assistant Secretaries and their counterparts, and so on down the line. The caravan always proceeded directly to the United States Embassy, where champagne would be served, after which the Foreign Minister and his associates would leave, and we would prepare to make our first call. That first call was always on the Foreign Minister. Then we would pay our respects to the President of the republic. Usually, the President would give a dinner and the Foreign Minister a luncheon in our honor. And I would give a return luncheon for the Foreign Minister and other dignitaries; occasionally the President came to the luncheon. It was all very proper and a bit stiff, but friendly.

After arriving in Venezuela, we drove from the airport to Caracas over a new broad highway which cut through the mountains. Everywhere in the city there were signs—stretched across the streets, in store windows, and on billboards—reading "Welcome Milton Eisenhower." Several hundred thousand persons lined the streets, waving homemade American and Venezuelan flags.

Calling on the dictator, Colonel Marcos Pérez Jiménez, was a unique experience, and it would have been even if it were not my first official visit to a head of state outside of the United States. We were met at his place and escorted by his assistant to the outer office of the dictator. There we were joined by the Foreign Minister whom we had left only a few minutes before. We waited about five minutes—which seems to be the custom— and then were shown into a massive, sumptuously furnished office. He was standing at the far end, and we had to make quite a march to reach him. He stood unsmiling in his colorful uniform, heavily weighted with decorations. Short, stocky, balding, and richly colored in the face, Pérez Jiménez was the very epitome of authoritarian dignity; he wore it like his uniform.

The dictator stepped forward and, without waiting to be introduced, took my hand and welcomed me to his country. Then came the protocol of the divan, which had been explained to me by Jack Cabot. The head visitor is always escorted by the President of a Latin-American country to a divan and seated on it to the extreme right. The President may sit immediately to his left, or in a chair facing the visitor. Other members of the delegation are seated according to rank.

I said, quite formally: "Mr. President, I am here as a representative of my brother, President Eisenhower, on the first stop of a long journey. We hope to gather much evidence about United States-Latin American relations and about the impact our many programs are having in these countries, so that upon our return home we may consider whether changes in our policies and programs would lead to a firmer hemispheric partnership. We hope to visit with your ministers, and with industrial, educational, and other leaders in Venezuela. While our program is filled by previous arrangement, we shall, of course, make any adjustment which would suit your convenience."

Pérez Jiménez was just as formal and spoke as if he were carefully considering each word. He expressed his pleasure at our coming and pointed out that Latin America as a whole must speed its development. Venezuela, he said, was in a special position, for its sales of oil and iron ore gave it a favorable balance of trade. He was using the income, he explained, to promote the educational, agricultural, and industrial development of his country (which was something of an exaggeration, as I later discovered). Pérez Jiménez made no suggestion of loans to his country. During this fifteen-minute meeting, he invited me to accompany him on a visit to a military installation and to lunch with him the following day.

After leaving the presidential palace, I was given a panoramic glimpse at the new Caracas. Pérez Jiménez was using many of his oil and iron ore dollars to rebuild the central section of the city, mainly for government offices. It was the most grandiose plan I have seen anywhere. Our hosts insisted that we stop at a new hotel under construction. It was about eighteen stories high, and from the penthouse they proudly pointed to a mammoth swimming pool below which was being built by the hotel. They said: "It is the largest swimming pool in the Western Hemisphere and probably in the world."

"You brag like Yankees," I replied. And they smiled and took this as a compliment.

Later, we started down a long construction ramp from the top of a new library building and the Chief of Protocol of the Venezuelan Foreign Office whispered: "The workers have gathered at the bottom of the ramp. Perhaps you would be willing to say a few words to their leader?"

I glanced down. There stood several hundred men, ranging in age from about sixteen to fifty. They were clad in tattered clothing and their shoulders were sagging as if they were physically supporting the magnificence about them.

As I approached, the leader stepped forward, not a trace of a smile on his lips. His bearing was as dignified and formal as Pérez Jiménez's had been. He nodded and said in formal Spanish: "I take great pleasure in greeting your Excellency."

Sometimes one reacts spontaneously, and good consequences may follow. I forgot momentarily that I was in a foreign country with mores different from ours. Grinning, I pushed out my hand and used the informal greeting, "*¿Qué tal?*" ("Hello! How's everything?") My hand was seized in a hearty grip, a big smile invaded his lips, white teeth glistened, and in surprisingly good English he said, "How are you, Dr. Meel-ton?" (Either "Dr. Meel-ton" or just "Meel-ton" soon became my sobriquet throughout Latin America.)

As we chatted, I sensed a change among the workers. Their eyes began to sparkle; expressions became expectant. So I went down the long line, shaking hands with each man—every handclasp a punishing physical, but rewarding spiritual, experience.

As a result of this fortuitous occurrence, doors were miraculously opened to me, so much so that my original schedule had to be altered repeatedly. For in addition to prearranged appointments with governmental and other leaders, requests for appointments poured in from labor leaders, representatives of small, normally unrecognized groups, members of opposition political parties, market women, and others. From them, I learned facts and attitudes that I could not otherwise have come to understand. Many of these I have mentioned earlier.

In long and serious discussions the next day, my hosts never departed from the theme of industrial and agricultural development. This strengthened my belief that our unresolved problems in Latin America were largely economic, as our briefings in Washington had indicated.

I kept my date with Pérez Jiménez at a military school outside of the city; it was a sort of Venezuelan West Point. After an elaborate luncheon with many toasts, Pérez Jiménez asked me to join him on a tour of the post. Ordinarily when such a thing happens, the President would put his guest in his own car and escort him to the places to be visited. Instead Pérez Jiménez and his wife got into his car and raced away. I was puzzled about what to do, for this was not on the program. The Foreign Minister came up to me and suggested that I go with him. Soon we arrived at a firing range where the President was waiting for me. He proudly showed me what was going on and then launched into a rather angry statement about the United States military policy. He said he had been trying in vain to buy planes and ships from us. He was not asking for a gift; he had the dollars to pay cash. Why he should encounter procrastination he simply could not understand, for he had been told that the United States wanted all Latin-American nations to get military equipment and supplies from us, rather than from other countries, so that all men could be trained with standardized equipment. I told him I would look into the matter when I got home, but went on to say that our policy was to discourage Latin-American nations from spending too much on arms, feeling that they needed all the funds at their disposal for the development of human resources and the economy.

"It's as simple as this," he said, "either the United States will promptly sell me what I want or I will get it from Britain, France, or other countries. Then my men will not be trained with standardized equipment as you would wish."

(I did report this conversation to Secretary Dulles when I got home but did not follow through to learn what happened. Once we refused to sell two cruisers to Peru. She then bought them from Britain. Whereupon Chile, pretending to be in danger but actually not wanting Peru to have the prestige of naval superiority, cried loudly that she too needed additional ships.)

Following this brief talk, Pérez Jiménez and his wife again drove off, and again the Foreign Minister came to my rescue to say that I was to join the President at the headquarters of the military post. There the dictator greeted me anew and led me through the buildings. I was astonished at what I saw: famous paintings in every room, oriental rugs on floors that were polished like mirrors, crystal chandeliers, great windows with silk damask drapes—a truly regal atmosphere. I could readily see that Pérez Jiménez was trying to keep his army as happy as possible. I knew that he had buildings full of political prisoners, that there was an undercurrent of political unrest, and that many of his enemies were in exile. So I understood his proclivity for sumptuous military living.

On our way from Caracas to Bogotá, Colombia, we flew over farms, ranches, and villages. We could spot great *latifundios* with their clusters of buildings where the lords of the manors resided, and the sprinklings of huts in various parts of the empires where the peons lived. I must with some shame confess that at this stage what I was seeing from the air—miserable huts, dilapidated villages, only an occasional schoolhouse, great cattle ranches—did not impress upon me the full significance of social stagnation in Latin America. Nor did this problem come up in conversations with Latin Americans on this first trip.

In Colombia I met with the new President, General Gustavo Rojas Pinilla. He had taken power in a bloodless revolution at a time when the people were weary of the long civil war which had been raging. Rojas did not seem to want to be President. He was a mild sort of fellow, not what one would expect of a military leader or a dictator. He told me that he would hold elections within a year and that he would not be a candidate. Obviously he changed his mind, perhaps because power has such a hypnotic influence. He may have thought, as so many have, that no one else can wield power quite so well as he and that he owed it to the people to lead them—whether they liked it or not. Or possibly, it was nothing so philosophical: He may have liked power and the prerogatives it yields.

Nothing I heard in Colombia—in Bogotá, or the industrial city of Medellín, or the agricultural country around Palmira—changed my mind that the real problem in Latin America was economic.

In Ecuador I met with President Velasco Ibarra, a very tall, slender man who looked German. He was a spellbinder before crowds, but quiet face to face. At a fabulous dinner which he gave for me, he leaned over and said: "I'm told you get bored with speeches."

I smiled and replied: "I only make them because I have to."

"So," he said, "we'll do away with them tonight. We'll merely lift our glasses to one another." Very considerate, I thought, for a man who really loved to orate.

What I saw and heard in Ecuador reinforced my view that the orthodox approach to Latin America's problems was the right one. By now I was meeting the cry that we were spending billions in Europe, none in Latin America; that we thought other areas of the world more important to us; that we had cheated Latin America when we bought from them at low prices during the war and then had sold to them at high prices when goods became available after the war. I did my best to answer these unjustified charges (as I have pointed out earlier in this book). But it is interesting to note that not a soul even intimated that we need do any more than speed assistance in the form of loans.

Bolivia was in real trouble when I arrived. The price of tin had fallen sharply and people were starving. President Paz Estenssoro urged me to have the United States send emergency food supplies. In response, I made my first call home and spoke to Secretary Dulles, asking him to ship surplus food to Bolivia if possible. We did.

Paz Estenssoro told essentially the same story as the other presidents:

Latin America's need for funds for rapid industrial and agricultural development. In retrospect, it is surprising that this revolutionary (to many in the United States he was Communist) did not even hint that the orthodox approach of financial aid was insufficient.

In Peru, I met for long discussions with President Odría—a dictator, but not like Perón or Jiménez, as he demonstrated when he turned the government over to the elected-Manuel Prado in 1956. President Odría urged us to recommend that the United States move massive amounts of credit to the Latin-American republics and to maintain stability in tariff and other rules affecting international trade.

Before leaving Peru, I called an all-day meeting of my associates to sum up what we had learned so far and to develop an outline for the report I would prepare when we got home. I was aware by this time that we were not gathering all the data we should, so I suggested that thereafter our party should divide up the chores. Andy Overby would call on the Ministers of Finance, bank presidents, business leaders, and others to obtain an up-to-date picture of such problems as international balances or imbalances, credit and inflation, local interest rates, and so on. Sam Anderson, an expert in international trade, would visit the Ministers of Commerce, private importers and exporters, and others to develop information on production problems, industrialization, exports and imports, laws relating to trade. Jack Cabot and I would carry the load on political and social problems, and I would personally do all I could to get a current picture of agriculture and education.

Further, since no matter how hard we worked we could only cover limited areas, I suggested the outline for my report, the idea being that we could then concentrate on obtaining the information to flesh it out.

The outline began, following an introduction which would state the purpose of our trip, with a section on the importance of Latin America and the United States to each other. We agreed to gather additional data on the economic, political, cultural, and even military interdependence of the American republics.

Second, I suggested that we state succinctly and emphatically the basic concepts which guided our nation in its relations with Latin America and also guided us in carrying out our assignments: mutual understanding, mutual respect, juridical equality of states, mutual security, and mutual goals.

The third section would analyze our findings on the trip with respect to these five requisites to good relations.

By now I was becoming convinced that the section dealing with mutual understanding would be of highest importance, for the resolution of all other problems was dependent on doing away with harmful misconceptions. Of next importance would be the section on economic development, for surely here was Latin America's crucial need. We should evaluate basic resources, population growth, dependence on primary commodities, agricultural production, transportation, power and fuel, industrialization, the menace of inflation, the need for capital, the need for better management, and the need for stability in the rules of international trade.

The final section of the report would be my personal recommendations. We agreed that we would jointly write or at least agree on the factual phases of the report, but that I personally, after full consultation with them, would take sole responsibility for the recommendations.

We took time to visit the Inca ruins high in Cuzco and Machu Picchu (the most spectacular place I have ever visited). We went to Machu Picchu on a narrow-gauge railway, the single engine car being more like a streetcar than a railroad car. The tracks ended at the foot of the mountain and we transferred to an old rickety bus which was to take us up the serpentine road to the mountaintop. The road was unpaved, naturally, and there were no guardrails along the side. At times, as the bus climbed, the turns were so sharp that we had to back and start several times to get around them. The sheer drop at such a point might be thirty-five hundred feet. Truly I was so frightened that I determined I would not ride that silly bus down; I would walk. But the sight at the top was worth the fright. How the Incas ever got rich topsoil and tremendous cut stones—measuring ten feet on each side—to the top of the mountain no one knows.

I had struck up a conversation with a senior from Princeton while roaming around the Inca ruins. He, too, had been highly nervous on the way up, and I rather think he was stalling up there trying to figure out a way to get down without riding the bus. He suggested that since we had so much to talk about we take the bus down, but keep talking and never look out the window. This we did—and it worked. But if I ever visit Machu Picchu again, it will be with a motorcycle or walking shoes.

In Chile, President Carlos Ibáñez del Campo and his ministers concentrated on the need for a method of stabilizing primary commodity prices—particularly copper—and the need for additional credit.

In Santiago I had one of the most revealing conferences on the trip. Thirty democratic labor leaders spent an afternoon with me. They first wanted to talk about Communism. Many Chilean labor leaders were at that moment in the Soviet Union, at Soviet expense, undergoing indoctrination. These men argued that the United States must bring large numbers of democratic labor leaders to the United States to see for themselves how the whole private enterprise system works and how our workers had attained dignity and influence in our democratic society. I accepted their recommendation with enthusiasm and later put it in my report.

Then they talked about economic conditions and repeated much of what government officials had emphasized. They complained about low wages, but said nothing about the need for any sweeping social change.

Then came Argentina (I have given a full account of that visit elsewhere) and Paraguay. By now, I had talked with five dictators. So my next stop in Uruguay was, in contrast, a joyous breather. The air seemed fresher, the sun brighter, the auto sirens louder, the fluttering flags crisper.

Relations between Argentina and Uruguay were badly strained. Political refugees from Argentina were congregating in Uruguay. This made Perón furious. He threatened to cut off all trade between the two countries. Uruguayans were fearful, but were staunchly supporting the government in its defiance of Perón.

When, after the usual motorcade into the city and a call on the Foreign Minister, I entered the chambers of the Presidential Council, I was met at the door and ushered immediately to a side room. There on a pedestal was a beautiful bronze piece by Belloni, one of Latin America's most eminent sculptors. It was of a Gaucho on a wildly bucking horse; the impression of action was so strong that I felt the Gaucho should be shouting. I was truly overcome when this magnificent piece of Uruguayan art was presented to me by the Council. Later, I gave it to Pennsylvania State University.

The Chairman of the Council escorted my colleagues and me to an impressive conference room, where members of the Council and we were seated, facing one another. At each place was a handsomely bound copy of the constitution of Uruguay. The Chairman opened the book in front of him, summarized a few sections, and then read others in full. He was impressing upon us that Uruguay is a democratic model among the American nations.

But, inevitably, we turned to economic matters. Wool tops have long been exported to the United States, a prime earner of dollars. Shortly before my visit, the United States had raised the tariff on wool tops and the members of the Council were provoked about this. I therefore pointed out that under our tariff laws, the United States must, if a foreign country subsidizes the export of a commodity to the United States, place a countervailing duty on that commodity. The United States had refrained from doing this for nearly a year following Uruguay's employing export subsidies as a means of increasing sales, hoping to induce Uruguay to remove

197

the subsidy; finally, with no further excuse for delay, we had raised the tariff on wool tops. We regretted this, but we had no choice: Our law was quite clear on the point.

The remainder of our conversation followed the normal pattern: the imperative need for economic development, the desire of Uruguay to obtain long-term loans at low rates of interest to speed her development, a plea for more liberal trade rules, and the urgent necessity of finding a solution to fluctuations in the prices of primary commodities.

In the dozen or more conversations my colleagues and I had in Uruguay with governmental officials, bankers, educators, and trade union officials, not a whisper was heard about a possible responsibility on the part of the United States to encourage social change in those Latin-American countries which enjoyed far less freedom than the people of Uruguay.

At last, weary but a little wiser, we came to Brazil. In Rio, we called on President Vargas. He was a short, oldish, roving-eyed man. His vivacious and attractive daughter was at his side constantly, and I soon concluded that Vargas, long dictator but then constitutionally elected president, was not well. What information I wanted came from government and other leaders. I arrived (as mentioned previously) in the midst of an angry quarrel between Brazilian leaders and economic analysts from the United States—when Brazil jumped to the conclusion that an offer to help the country develop economic priorities was a commitment for lending institutions to finance these priorities.

I met with the publishers of leading newspapers in Rio and São Paulo and we had frank, off-the-record discussions about Brazilian problems. They were economic. The country was constantly suffering a shortage of foreign exchange, was importing wheat and oil, both of which could be produced there, and was laboring under a multitude of economic restrictions. I argued that Brazil would benefit by allowing private interests to develop its oil resources, but these men did not believe it was possible because of Vargas' tirades against the oil companies.

Brazil was the last stop on the trip, and during the five days there I saw things which finally set me thinking beyond the scope of our planned report. Perhaps it was cumulative, and Brazil merely brought it into focus, but I had become more and more aware of the gap between the privileged few and the oppressed masses in Latin America. One experience in particular impressed itself indelibly in my mind.

We had driven to one of the largest *fazendas* (farms) in Brazil. It was truly an empire, owned by a tremendous fellow about forty-five years of age. He was handsome, jovial, even exuberant. Like a feudal lord, he owned all that he could see. Five thousand families lived on his land, and all of them worked for him. Before lunch, he showed us how the coffee beans were brought in for drying, turning, more drying, grading, and bagging for shipment. Then he led us to a beautiful spot in a fruit orchard where a massive barbecue had been prepared for us. The tables were loaded with several kinds of barbecued meats, vegetables, many different fruits, milk (a rarity), and sweets of all kinds.

We were all hungry, and we turned to the meal with delight. But even as we ate, I noticed the peons laboring in the fields a short distance away. They were thin, ragged people, older than their years. They already seemed exhausted, but they had many more hours to toil under the broiling sun. They had probably had a handful of beans for breakfast and would have the same for lunch. Their diets, typical of Brazilian laborers, were heavy with starches, short in proteins, minerals, and vitamins—totally inadequate to sustain them. I found that I was no longer hungry for the sumptuous feast before me.

I have given this abbreviated account of my visit in 1953 because I want to emphasize as strongly as I can that both United States and Latin-American leaders were then thinking solely in terms of orthodox economic aid to Latin America as the solution to perplexing problems. By the end of the trip I personally had become painfully aware of the need for social reform—for misery, poverty, ill health, and illiteracy obviously haunted the land like evil specters. But except for an uneasiness and a feeling of compassion, I did not relate this to what we were doing and should do officially, except to hope that our efforts might aid countries improve production and thus provide funds for internal social development. Certainly instigating internal social change did not seem to be the responsibility of the United States. Had I not reaffirmed to many groups in every country that this Administration would adhere strictly and honorably to the Franklin Roosevelt policy of non-intervention?

When we got home, I met at length with high officers in the International and Export-Import Banks, and in the Treasury, Agriculture, Labor, and other Departments. I did this because I wanted to report faithfully and quickly what I had seen and learned; I wanted to try out the recommendations I would probably make and win support for these recommendations, for I had long before learned that many officials have the power to paralyze action if they disagree with it.

These conferences, sandwiched between university duties, took several months, and so my formal report did not reach the President until November 23, 1953. Of course, before then, I had made an oral report to Secretary Dulles and my brother. Indeed, both had met us at the airport on our return, and we had driven directly to the White House where we spoke for an hour. Later, I met with the Cabinet and in about thirty minutes summarized what I had found and what I felt should be done.

When my report was received, it was placed before the National Security Council, the top coordinating agency for foreign affairs. After detailed study and discussion, the report was approved and therefore became accepted foreign policy.

The recommendations were grouped into sections: To strengthen understanding and mutual respect, which I felt was a key to the future, I suggested ten specific actions or programs that should be undertaken or strengthened. Under the topic, economic cooperation, I recommended that we maintain stable trade relations with Latin America, gradually liberalizing the rules; that if for security reasons we maintained a stockpiling program, we should purchase ores from Latin America on price declines, thus providing a modicum of price stability; that we consider amending tax laws in such a way as to remove all obstacles to foreign private investment in Latin America; that we greatly increase the flow of public capital to Latin America; that we provide technical help to improve development planning in the Latin-American nations; that we make food grants, as in Bolivia, to help meet emergencies; that the technical cooperation program be expanded that we work to bring about an expansion of the activities of the Organization of America States in economic and social areas; and that we work through the International Monetary Fund Board in an effort to check inflation.

I concluded by urging the Administration, the Congress, and the people of the United States to take a long-range view as we considered how we might strengthen our economic relations with the nations of Latin America. "Working together," I said with optimism and perhaps naïveté, "the nations of the hemisphere can, if history should so decree, firmly stand against any enemy in war, and prosper mightily together in times of peace."

The Senate Foreign Relations Committee and the House Foreign Affairs Committee asked me to report to them, and I accepted on the condition that my remarks be completely off the record. I had served as the President's personal representative and my report was exclusively for him; any recommendation to Congress should come from him. Both committees agreed and I spent a delightful two hours with each. At the conclusion of each oral report, the congressmen asked constructive questions. If, at that time, my analysis was wrong—namely that we should work hard to eliminate serious misconceptions while at the same time speeding economic aid to our southern neighbors—the members of the two committees did not so note. Neither they nor I saw what was to emerge later—a surging, swelling, revolutionary demand, not just for aid, but for rapid social revolution in country after country. Had I, on this first trip, talked only with government and industrial leaders, I could be charged with having missed a great opportunity to spot fairly early the growing resentment among the masses. But I had been among the people, too—workers, teachers, students, farmers—and had heard not a whisper of what was to come.

Most of my recommendations, I am happy to say, were put into effect.

All during 1954, 1955, and the early months of 1956, I made speeches up and down the land in an effort to develop understanding of Latin America among the people of the United States. I also had frequent discussions with the ambassadors of the ten countries I had visited and also with Ambassador Manuel Tello of Mexico, who had become a good friend.

I continued to work with the State Department staff, particularly with the Assistant Secretary for Inter-American Affairs. Jack Cabot went to Sweden as United States Ambassador and the late Henry F. Holland came in as Assistant Secretary. Cabot was very much the Harvard man, highly articulate, well informed, bilingual, gracious, and courageous. He often made Latin Americans angry by his candid speech, but they always respected him. Holland was different—a bilingual Texas lawyer who thought like a lawyer. He was precise and logical. Undoubtedly, he was devoted to promoting better hemispheric relations, but he was also looking for a new approach to problems, something that would make a unique impression and prove to the Latin Americans how very important we considered them to be.

About this time, the regular five-year Inter-American Conference was held in Caracas. Because of pressing university duties, I could not attend. Secretary Dulles headed the delegation and induced the conference to pass a charter-type resolution which condemned any possible intrusion of Communist imperialism into the Western Hemisphere.

Meanwhile, the flow of private and public credit was showing a gratifying increase.

In this interim period from 1954 to early 1956, my life became rather complicated and I had to neglect my Latin-American duties to some extent. The President had suffered a heart attack. Naturally, I gave all the help I could, though being careful not to assume any authority, for I recalled the difficulties that developed when Mrs. Wilson seemingly took over many governmental responsibilities when the President was ill. But I was frequently traveling between Denver (where my brother was) and Washington. On one trip to Denver, Secretary of Agriculture Ezra Taft Benson and I happened to be on the same plane. The press at once carried a front-page, top-headline story which claimed that I was essentially dictating agricultural policy and Benson was merely a front man. After all the care I had taken in my activities never to bypass responsible government officials, this kind of nonsense was almost too much to bear.

I also went to Key West where the President was supposed to be resting. Kubitschek had recently been elected President of Brazil and before his inauguration flew up for a breakfast meeting with President Eisenhower. He talked of a program to be called "Operation Pan-America," which was the formation of a massive development fund with the United States putting up the bulk of the capital. He made no suggestion of reform or the need for it.

In 1956, the Presidents of the American republics met in Panama. President Eisenhower had had a serious ileitis operation, but he was determined to attend the meeting. His entrance into Panama City was greeted with such enthusiasm by the hundreds of thousands who lined the streets that a White House aide who was in a car with me exclaimed, "You'd think he was running for President of Panama!"

Despite the weakness he still suffered from the ileitis operation, President Eisenhower held individual conferences with all of the Latin-American Presidents to discuss with them a proposal he planned to make in a plenary session of the meeting. In the course of these visits, the Presidents of the Central-American nations urged him to visit them and to send me on a study trip like the one I had made to South America. The President assured them that one of us would make the trip as soon as possible.

President Eisenhower, in his formal address, said:

". . . in all of these matters, our nations act as sovereign equals. Never will peace and security be bought at the price of subjecting any nation to coercion or interference in its internal affairs . . . may it not be that we can now look forward to a new phase of association, in which we shall dedicate to individual human welfare the same measure of noble effort that heretofore has protected and invigorated the corporate life of our nations? . . . I believe we can help one another. The possibilities of our partnership are not exhausted by concentration in the political field. Indeed our Organization has already begun to apply the principle that material welfare and progress of each member is vital to the well-being of every other . . . we can do more . . . each of us, as President of an American Republic, should name a special representative to join in preparing for us concrete recommendations for making our Organization of American States a more effective instrument in those fields of cooperative effort that affect *the welfare of the individual* (emphasis mine). To those representatives of ours we could look for practical suggestions in the economic, financial, social, and technical fields which our Organization might appropriately adopt. . . . So earnestly, my friends, do I believe in the possibilities of such an organization for benefiting all our people, that in my own case and with the agreement of other Presidents in this Organization, I shall ask my brother—Milton Eisenhower—already known to nearly all the Presidents here—to be my representative in such an organization.

". . . let us join to find ways which will enable our people to combat the ravages of disease, poverty, and ignorance. Let us give them, as individuals, a better opportunity not only to pursue happiness, but to gain it."

So here was my new assignment. From his informal discussions with the other Presidents, my brother knew his proposal would meet with enthusiastic approval. The stage was set—somewhat inadvertently—for the initiation, almost imperceptible at first but reaching a crescendo in 1958, 1959, and 1960, of dramatic and beneficial changes in United States-Latin American relations.

This new task did not come at a propitious time. Only six weeks before I had notified the Trustees of Pennsylvania State University of my intention to resign, for wholly personal reasons. I had been very fond of the faculty, students, and alumni of Penn State and had thought I would never leave there. When my wife died, a year after our trip to South America, I carried on without undue interruption. But as my daughter Ruth prepared to go to Swarthmore, and I looked forward to being alone in an eighteen-room house, I was possessed by a desire to leave. In the meantime, and before I had decided to leave Penn State, I declined an invitation from the Trustees of Johns Hopkins University to become President there. I planned only to help President Eisenhower and perhaps take a tour around the world.

While still in Panama, I received a long-distance telephone call from the late Carlyle Barton, then the lovable and distinguished chairman of the Board of Trustees at Johns Hopkins. He said: "The Trustees of the

University have just unanimously elected you President. There are dozens of newspapermen waiting outside and I would like an answer from you before confronting them."

I even surprised myself a little by accepting on the spot. But I warned Mr. Barton that I was not certain just when I could assume my new duties.

Early in September 1956, I visited Johns Hopkins to prepare for my assumption of the presidency of the university and simultaneously laid plans for the first meeting of the twenty-one presidential representatives of the American republics to be held in Washington, D.C. As the representative of the President of the host country, I would be chairman of the group.

Then another complication arose. Henry Holland, who with President Eisenhower and me had conceived the whole idea of this new effort to strengthen the Organization of American States and have it work for individual betterment, suddenly announced that he would resign as Assistant Secretary of State for Inter-American Affairs to enter private business in New York. He simply could not afford financially to remain in government.

I was frustrated. Holland had carefully thought through the types of problems we should bring up and that the other representatives were likely to raise. He had been in communication with our ambassadors in all of the countries and was better prepared to counsel then anyone else. At my urging, he promised to come to Washington often during the months in which the presidential representatives would be working, but he would no longer have an influential voice in Latin-American affairs.

His Deputy Assistant Secretary of State was Roy R. Rubottom, Jr., one of the ablest and most forthright men I have ever known. Rubottom was bilingual and knew Latin America thoroughly. He had served in several of the republics and had also been head of our economic mission in Spain before coming to Washington as Holland's deputy. He was rather young, governmentally speaking (forty-four at the time); I suppose this is why he was named *Acting* Assistant Secretary, for he surely had all the talents and leadership qualities the post demanded. This was a most unfortunate arrangement at the very time that a crucial international conference, which presumably was to blaze new trails, was about to get under way. Henry Holland could do no more than give me personal help. Rubottom, only *Acting*, could not launch out into new areas and policies—an "*acting*," as Washington knows, never can. So from the moment the conference opened it was almost a foregone conclusion that we would have to develop ideas and programs within current policy. Had things worked out differently, it is conceivable that this meeting would have spelled out the great revision of United States policy which was so desperately needed and which was soon to come.

We worked from September 17, 1956 until mid-May, 1957. In that period the representatives had three full-dress, prolonged plenary sessions, with four working committees and one special committee sandwiching meetings in between. I was glad that Johns Hopkins, in Baltimore, was so short a drive away. As it was, I was working from twelve to eighteen hours a day on university and government business.

The unanimous report of the presidential representatives dealt constructively with new ways in which the Organization of American States could contribute to Latin-American development—in health, education, student and teacher exchanges, mutual understanding, statistical services, industrialization, credit, nuclear energy, transportation. But, as I look back on those arduous eight months of plenary and committee sessions, I am sure that the most significant contribution of the representatives involved the crucial social problem in Latin America.

It was during this conference that my own views about our role in Latin-American affairs (which had been evolving subtly since 1953) began to crystallize. I was stimulated to reach certain convictions by Pedro Beltrán of Peru, who made an eloquent plea for United States help in social development.

What we were doing in Latin America, he said, was well and good, but it was not enough, and it was doing too little for the people who needed housing, better diets, education, and health services. He urged that we finance such social projects in Latin America.

President Eisenhower, addressing the other presidents in Panama, had stressed the *welfare of the individual*. This was based on his great sympathy for the downtrodden and did not at that time foreshadow a change in our policy or an awareness of a ground swell for social reform. But I had been reflecting more and more on the injustices I had seen in Latin America and the absolute absence of any mention of this in my talks with Latin-American leaders. Still, I took it for granted that the correction of social injustices was strictly a Latin-American problem and that if we tried to do anything unilaterally about it we would bring the hemisphere down around our ears with screams of intervention.

Now, Pedro Beltrán was *asking* for this kind of intervention. And as a means of financing it, the old proposal of an Inter-American Bank—resisted so adamantly and so long by the United States—was being renewed. I was deeply moved by Beltrán's pleas and was impressed by his logic. I saw that loans to governments for social improvement projects might bring about a modicum of reform, for recipient governments might have to revise tax laws to begin collecting from the rich in order to meet interest and amortization payments.

And so, as I have said earlier, I argued far into the night with United States officials that we give up our historical position and endorse this proposal for an Inter-American Bank. For twenty years—under Roosevelt, Truman, and Eisenhower—Latin-American nations had been asking for the bank with the thought that it would have a board of directors predominantly from Latin-American nations that would be more sympathetic to meeting their needs. It might surround loans with certain conditions which could bring about some slight change in the rigid social structure of Latin America.

I pointed out in my confidential talks something of which Dick Rubottom, I, and others had become aware: Some of the severest criticism of the United States was coming from countries which received the most aid from us, such as Brazil. We interpreted this to mean that the aid was not generally thought to be benefiting all the people—indeed, that it seemed to the masses that it was being used to sustain the prevailing order which exploited them.

My arguments were not wholly in vain. Unfortunately, Secretary Dulles was abroad; Douglas Dillon had not as yet become a key figure in Latin-American affairs, and Dick Rubottom was, remember, only *Acting* Assistant Secretary. Further, Latin-American leaders had not at that time indicated awareness of their own great responsibility for fostering social reform. Had not Beltrán failed to suggest that the starting point for social change had to be in Latin America?

The countries themselves obviously needed to begin tax reform, land reform, reduction of military expenditures, increases in spending for education, health, and low-cost housing. None of the Latin-American leaders made this point; they were concerned only about more money from abroad for social projects.

Even so, high officials of the State and Treasury Departments began to give more sympathetic consideration to the possibility of creating an inter-American development institution, but this was not made evident to the presidential representatives. Three months were to pass before new words on this issue would be spoken.

In mid-May, in a most impressive ceremony in the Pan American Union, the twenty-one presidential representatives met to sign our completed document. We had achieved unanimity—but only because I had insisted on postponing a decision on the Inter-American Bank.

It may seem strange that I could have done this, believing as I did that an immediate decision was needed. However, I had no choice but to support United States policy or resign. Friends have suggested that I should have gone directly to the President. Even in retrospect, I do not think so.

In the first place, my own ideas were new and ill-formed. I was moved as much by emotion as by cold analysis and full comprehension of all the factors involved. The heads of the principal lending agencies, Samuel C. Waugh of the Export-Import Bank and Eugene R. Black of the International Bank, were men of long experience. It simply would not have done for me to go to my brother with a half-formed idea, for he would have had to call in his highest and most responsible advisers and they obviously would have favored sticking to our current policy. But most important of all, I had been assured by State Department and Treasury officials that this and other sticky problems would be fully discussed at the forthcoming Inter-American Economic Conference in Buenos Aires. In August 1957, these promises were kept. At Buenos Aires the United States for the first time indicated a willingness to study the possibility of joining in the formation of a hemispheric development institution.

Scarcely was the work of the presidential representatives completed than I was off again.

President Ruíz Cortines of Mexico had come to The Greenbrier Hotel at White Sulphur Springs, West Virginia early in 1956 to meet with President Eisenhower and Prime Minister St. Laurent of Canada, and I had participated in the discussions. During the meetings, President Ruíz Cortines had said to me:

"Your distinguished brother and I have become friends. I want him to come to Mexico, and I have told him so, but I realize his world responsibilities are pressing and will prevent him from coming for a year or more. And so I would like you to come as my personal guest and as his brother. No doubt the trip will have to be official, as your other trips to Latin America have been, but we will keep everything as informal as possible. I'm told you do not like to waste time on formal banquets and speeches. But I do want you to come and talk about common problems."

Then, his eyes twinkling mischievously, he added that he had already spoken to President Eisenhower and had obtained enthusiastic approval.

I accepted without qualification. The trip to Mexico, in August 1957, was highly rewarding. I talked at length with President Ruíz Cortines and his Cabinet and learned a great deal. We chatted informally and candidly about bilateral and hemispheric problems. President Ruíz Cortines was obviously proud of the fact that he had pushed rapidly ahead in trying to have Mexico's growing economy benefit all of the Mexico people. I was greatly interested in the evolving Mexican revolution and the lessons it might hold for other Latin-American nations. Ruíz Cortines recognized that most other Latin-American countries had not begun a program of reform, as Mexico had done in 1910, but he felt that change was in the air, and that it could be brought about by peaceful means.

I told him that I felt the United States stood ready to help those countries which wished to bring about social change, but I saw no way in which we could take the initiative. He stated forcefully that any initiative in this regard on our part would be construed as intervention and would be disastrous.

The trip was not all work, but even some of the play had good results. We went fishing at Acapulco, using the President's special boat. I caught a 125-pound, 13-foot sailfish, not a record, but a respectable catch. Ambassador Manuel Tello also got a sailfish. My daughter Ruth, who went along as my hostess, caught a couple of 10-foot sharks. Each time a fish was caught, a flag of appropriate color was run up a tall flagpole. On our way back to shore, one of the men gaffed a tremendous turtle and kept it. Ruth insisted that a special flag be run up for the turtle, but the dismayed captain protested that there was no such identifying flag. Ruth removed her multi-colored kerchief and insisted that the captain hoist it; he did. As we neared port, with about fifteen flags flying—one never before seen in Acapulco—several hundred persons rushed down to the dock at the Club de Pesca. When they discovered that a turtle was the object of that strange flag, they roared with laughter.

Only a week before, the press of the United States had carried banner headlines and long stories about a "disastrous" earthquake in Mexico City and Acapulco. Tourist travel to Acapulco—its lifeblood—declined greatly. Actually, damage had been slight. Our press carried pictures of the good catch we made that pleasant day, and almost at once tourist travel returned to normal. No doubt this was wholly coincidental, but local leaders gave me credit.

I was no sooner back from that trip than we began planning another, this one to Central America and Panama. The Presidents of these six countries had renewed through diplomatic channels the invitation they has informally extended to me in Panama City. Dick Rubottom felt that the trip was vital and the President and the Secretary of State agreed. We planned the trip for the summer of 1958 and soon included Puerto Rico in the schedule because Governor Muñoz-Marín wanted me to help celebrate the sixth anniversary of the island's Commonwealth status. I was delighted, for I had made a detailed study for the Department of Agriculture in Puerto Rico in 1938 and was eager to see for myself the remarkable changes that had been made. Because of my new interest in social reform, I was particularly anxious to see Puerto Rico's self-help housing, which had been prominently reported in our press.

The year 1958 was an important one in Latin American-United States relations. Subsidies on cotton and quotas on lead and zinc aroused Latin-American ire against us. All records were broken by the flow of private and public capital to Latin America. Douglas Dillon, then Under Secretary of State for Economic Affairs, was taking special interest in Latin America. Thomas C. Mann had arrived on the scene as Assistant Secretary of State for Economic Affairs. Dillon, Mann, and Rubottom quickly recognized the need for changes in our policies. They began setting up commodity study groups, beginning with coffee and cotton, to learn what could be done to stabilize prices. They had agreed that the time had come for us to take the lead in creating an Inter-American Bank, thus discarding a century-old policy. We all felt that the United States should begin promoting the development of common markets in Latin America—another reversal of standing policy.

As we planned our trip to Central America, we had in mind different objectives from those of our first trip. We knew now that no matter how voluminous the flow of credit might be, no matter how successful we might be in helping promote economic growth within the prevailing order, this would not be enough. The masses did not benefit from prosperity; the gap between them and the privileged only widened.

It was as we were making final plans for our trip that Vice President Nixon was stoned and jeered by angry mobs in Peru and Venezuela.

We were deeply concerned for him and for the consequences of all this on our relations with Latin America. And we were worried about the effect of Nixon's experiences on our own scheduled trip.

I am convinced that the Vice President unwittingly set the stage for his trouble when he was in Montevideo. I had been there much earlier, and in conversations with students had learned that there were some with extremely leftist views. Our conversations had been spirited but amiable.

Mr. Nixon met unexpectedly with university students in Montevideo.

After a bit of initial heckling, he overcame his opposition with such candor and skill that he won an ovation. At that moment, the extremists, including adroit Communist leaders, determined to humiliate him before his trip was completed.

Word was flashed to Buenos Aires. A group of Communists and Perónistas succeeded in snarling traffic as Nixon was being driven to the inauguration of President Frondizi (his main reason for making the trip). The purpose was to delay him and thus embarrass the United States. On my two trips to Argentina, before and after the Nixon visit, I had encountered some good-natured heckling from Perónistas, but they were obviously merely having a good time, for when I walked among them, they made anti-American remarks, pretending not to know I was there, and then smilingly turned to me and shook hands. I am therefore convinced that the Buenos Aires incident involving the Vice President was not, as the press generally said, a spontaneous expression of anti-Yankeeism. It was a maliciously planned move of a tiny minority.

In Lima, the Vice President may have made a mistake. I had been there, too. The University of San Marcos, oldest university in the Western Hemisphere and today noted for the liberal views of its faculty and students, conferred upon me an honorary doctorate. As I left the ceremony and walked through a group of several thousand students, a few young men on an upper balcony began whistling. I glanced up. They were good-naturedly jostling each other. I did not know that a whistle in Latin America meant disapproval, so, naïvely, I waved my hat to the balcony whistlers. This unsophisticated gesture proved to be fortunate. The entire student body began to cheer, and the whistlers laughed a little sheepishly. But when Nixon arrived in Lima, plans made in Montevideo and transmitted to Communists and leftist students of San Marcos had reached a stage of dangerous determination. The Vice President would be greeted with showers of tomatoes and stones. He was informed of this. Evidently fearing that he would be charged with cowardice if he did not follow his original plan, he walked into real trouble. The extremists thus achieved their first reprisal for the victory Nixon had won in Uruguay. But they were by no means satisfied, for press reports praised the Vice President for his courage and strongly condemned the student minority for insulting a distinguished visitor.

The Nixons arrived in Caracas only a few months after Pérez Jiménez had been overthrown. A temporary junta was in power and was anxious to create an impression different from that of the fallen dictator. Hence, security forces which are in evidence for any foreign visitor of standing (even for me) were not present in anything approaching normal numbers. In the excited disorder that followed the ousting of Pérez Jiménez, Communists and extremists found their opportunity. By violence, they sought to overcome completely the favorable impression the Vice President had made in his first verbal encounter with their forces. On my own trip to Caracas I had had no difficulty.

I am not analyzing here why extremists exist in Latin America. They do, in abundance, as they would anywhere where there is discontent and injustice. I am contending that it is erroneous to say that the peoples of Latin America had suddenly come to a point of explosion because of any failure in United States policy, as was widely suggested at the time. The indignity to Nixon occurred first because he had outwitted the Communists and other extremists and they sought revenge; secondly, conditions for an insulting attack were favorable; and third, since Nixon was a leading political leader of the United States, he was an ideal target, as contrasted to my associates and me who had been traveling throughout the continent before the incident, and continued to do so afterward, without insult or physical harm.

It was also suggested shortly after the Nixon incident that Caracas crowds were angry because the fallen dictator, Pérez Jiménez, had found temporary asylum in the United States. It should be recorded that the junta which seized power from Pérez Jiménez issued him a diplomatic passport and asked the United States Ambassador to grant him a visa for immediate flight to the United States. The object was to get the dictator out of the country quickly, but it would have helped if the junta had explained this to the people.

In one respect, at least, I now wish that I had been subjected to a Nixon-type incident in the early period of my missions to Latin America (though I confess I would have wanted it to be of a much milder variety). Had this occurred, I probably would have realized sooner than I did that extremists, seriously at work in all the republics, were persuading the people mistakenly to identify the United States and even our substantial aid exclusively with the privileged of their countries.

But back in 1958, I had no such wish. Special intelligence reports from the countries we were to visit, especially from Guatemala and Panama, were ominous. It appeared that we, including my daughter, might encounter the same kind of violence that Nixon had met on his trip.

My brother, Foster Dulles, Rubottom, and I were deeply disturbed. We now faced the kind of decision Nixon had: Should we avoid trouble and look like cowards and, more important, show the Communists that they could interfere with normal foreign service procedures—or should we go in and risk indignities and a blow to the nation's prestige?

Secretary Dulles said: "I'm concerned for your safety, Milton, but you have to go. We cannot let rabble-rousers dictate how we conduct foreign policy." President Eisenhower agreed, and so did I.

We had no trouble on our trip. I have thought about this, and am sure there were reasons. Most Latin Americans were ashamed of what had happened to Nixon, and the people and leaders viewed my trip as an opportunity to erase much of the harm that had been done. Security forces were strengthened, perhaps too much, for there was no evidence of anyone's trying to initiate trouble. And then, as I have mentioned, Nixon was a political leader, game for the Communists, while I was an educator.

Anticipating trouble, the United States press sent a flock of reporters along—the first time they had shown such deep interest in my activities. When nothing of sensational news value occurred, the reporters, as noted earlier, filed stories about the bristling security guards which were shielding me from the danger that lurked around every corner. I was disgusted. (Interestingly, United States reporters had been critical of the lack of sufficient security forces on the Nixon trip.)

Just prior to my trip to Central America I had been on vacation in Wisconsin. The State Department called me off my favorite lake to say that the trip had been moved forward several days, and since I could not drive back to Washington in time to make the schedule, the Air Force was sending a small plane to get my daughter and me. I induced a friend to drive my car back. We arrived in Baltimore in the evening, packed late at night, and the next morning boarded a plane in Washington for Panama.

Senator Proxmire of Wisconsin made a silly but vicious speech in the Senate, criticizing President Eisenhower for sending a government plane to bring my daughter and me back from a vacation. The story was carried throughout the United States and in the papers of all of the countries I was to visit.

I was surprised, shocked, and furious. I had adopted the practice early in 1954 of never accepting a cent from the federal government. Like any-one else, I was entitled to expenses and even a consultant's fee, but I had decided I would not submit an expense account. The only thing I accepted from the government was transportation. All else I paid for my-self. I resisted the urge to strike back and said nothing. Then to my pleasure, David Lawrence came out with a long syndicated column, tear-ing into Proxmire. How he knew of my policy of accepting no money from the government I do not know, but his article was accurate. Proxmire did not apologize, but evidently he was receiving critical letters from his constituents, for about a week after his original speech, he placed the Lawrence article in the Congressional Record.

Throughout the trip that summer, I took a good deal of friendly ribbing about the Proxmire story. This pleased me, actually, for it showed that my relations with the leaders of Latin America had achieved such friendly terms that they could bring up the incident and josh me about it.

Our first stop was Panama. Things were seething when we arrived. The economy was weak and highly vulnerable. Plagued from its beginning with boom and depression, it was then in a low period. The government was fearful of uprisings. Students and leftists were hurling threats. The United Arab Republic Embassy was trying subversively to promote a "Suez situation." And the country, like a parched prairie in late summer drought, seemed on the verge of being inflamed.

Our relations with Panama, which are determined largely by three treaties and by the daily operations carried out under them, are watched with interest by most of the Latin-American nations, and especially by the west coast countries, for they are concerned with inter-American trade through the Panama Canal.

The treaty of 1903 gave the United States, in perpetuity, control over a ten-mile-wide strip that bisects the country. The language of the treaty was definite. The United States was given absolute jurisdiction over the Canal Zone *as if it were sovereign*. Other provisions of the treaty essentially made Panama a protectorate of the United States.

A treaty of 1936, approved by the United States Senate in 1939, canceled many of our rights in the Republic of Panama, and ended our guarantee of her independence. Our jurisdiction over the Canal Zone was not altered.

Another treaty, in 1955, was designed to solve numerous problems. We guaranteed to provide equal pay for equal work regardless of the nationality of the Canal Company employees, to increase annual payments to Panama, to build a bridge linking the two sections of the country separated by the Canal Zone and, *if feasible*, to purchase from Panama or the United States all supplies needed to operate United States enterprises in the Zone. The phrase "if feasible" precipitated a major international quarrel.

The same oppressive conditions and gross inequities flagrant in other

Latin-American republics exist in Panama—but here there is a ready-made, built-in scapegoat: the alleged profit-making owner of the Canal Zone, the United States.

Panama's economy is based more upon commerce than upon production. From the days of the earliest explorers, Panamanians have lived—miserably, to be sure—on the expenditures of travelers crossing the isthmus. Panama probably receives three times as much in income from the operations of enterprises in the Canal Zone as it does from all its exports.

A high official said to me: "You in the United States inherited vast mineral wealth, rich agricultural lands, and unlimited opportunity. Africa was given gold and diamonds. The Middle East is rich in oil. God gave Panama nothing but a waterway. We must make a living from our resource, as others have from theirs."

And that's the rub. Panamanians generally feel the United States is exploiting their one God-given asset for its own benefit. They believe we have made vast profits from the Canal while they have received nothing. This is the most serious kind of misconception that I have referred to in previous chapters, for the fact is that the Canal has been a financial burden to the United States. The Canal debt to the United States treasury is in excess of $450 million. Revenues have not been sufficient to retire the debt. Indeed, the Canal Company pays the Treasury interest only on $350 million of the indebtedness. Any income above operating costs is spent on Canal improvements. Furthermore, the United States initially paid Panama $10 million for jurisdictional rights and now pays to Panama an annual rental of nearly $2 million—either from Canal Company income, or State Department appropriations.

Panama benefits from the $50 million spent yearly in the Canal Zone and from tourism, made large by the Canal. Indeed, the per capita income of Panama is higher than it is in fifteen other Latin-American republics.

Even so, the hordes of underprivileged, living on either side of the Zone, see only a narrow strip of land which represents a nation of undreamed of riches. And this wealthy interloper makes "untold profits" from Panama's resource. The privileged elite do nothing to disabuse the people of this fallacious notion.

In the summer of 1958, several specific issues reached the boiling point. The Canal Company was paying equal wages for equal work, as agreed by treaty, regardless of the nationalities of the employees. Thus, truck drivers, janitors, and other unskilled and semi-skilled workers were paid about 30 per cent more than they would have received for comparable work in the Republic of Panama (though considerably less than such workers receive in the United States). About 95 per cent of such workers were Panamanians; only about 5 per cent were other nationals, including United States citizens. The highly skilled jobs—engineers operating the great locks, for example—were filled mainly by United States citizens, with Panamanians in only about 5 per cent of such positions; wage scales matched those of the United States. This seems to me to be a feasible wage policy, but the government of Panama vigorously contended that the treaty of 1955 meant that all wage classifications would be comparable to those in the United States. If we agreed to this in Panama, similar demands would be made everywhere in the world where the United States maintains military or other installations. Costs would skyrocket by many hundreds of million dollars a year, and difficulties would arise from the creation of new privileged classes in the host countries.

Panamanian leaders were further exercised by what they deemed to be a flagrant violation of that treaty provision which required the governor of the Canal Zone to purchase all supplies, *if feasible,* either from Panama or the United States. At that time, the governor (who is also president of the Canal Company) was buying from Panama about 90 per cent of the beef required for Zone residents; a few choice qualities, not available in Panama, came from New Zealand or Australia. New Zealand and Australian beef was cheaper than that from the United States. The governor argued that the "if feasible" phrase was intended to cover just such a situation. Panama insisted that the practice was an act of bad faith.

A similar act of bad faith, Panamanians contended, was the sale of luxury goods, such as perfume and jewelry, in Zone commissaries. Such items, they felt, should be purchased in the Free Zone.

While these issues simmered, Panama's leaders turned their fire on a major issue: the raising of Canal tolls. During my 1958 visit, Panamanian officials earnestly insisted that the tolls be raised and annual payments to Panama be substantially increased. Tolls have not been changed since 1914 when the Canal was opened. Since all other goods and services had gone up, Panamanians insisted, tolls should, also.

The press suggested that Panama should receive 50 per cent of Canal revenues. If the intent was for Panama to be paid half of the net receipts, then there would be no real cause for controversy, for there are no net profits. If, however, the demand was for half the gross income, then it was tantamount to asking the United States Treasury to subsidize Panama further to the extent of about $50 million a year.

It is not easy to change canal tolls. Agreements and relations with other maritime nations are involved. In fact, only 30 per cent of the traffic through the Canal is United States traffic; the other 70 per cent is foreign traffic (though some of it involves United States ships). In essence, we are simply providing a global transportation facility for the majority of shipping. Panama Canal tolls are roughly comparable to those of the Suez Canal and are slightly higher than those of the St. Lawrence Seaway.

But far and away the hottest issue in Panama in 1958 involved a question of national sovereignty, hence of national pride. Panama wanted its flag flown in the Zone as an acknowledgment of its sovereignty— a demand it had been making for nearly twenty years. There is no doubt that Panama has titular sovereignty over the Zone. The 1903 treaty provides that the United States shall have jurisdiction *as if it were sovereign*; the United States, therefore, is not the sovereign power. For example, the status of the Zone could be changed only by a mutual Panama-United States agreement to amend the organic treaty.

For several days I discussed these issues with members of the Panamanian Cabinet, our ambassador and his staff, and the governor of the Canal Zone. The President of the republic, Ernesto de la Guardia, a former student at Dartmouth and a good friend of the United States, accompanied Dick Rubottom, Ambassador Julian F. Harrington, and me on an all-day fishing trip. We had ample opportunity to probe the details of the problems. In addition, President de la Guardia outlined Panama's need for capital to finance schools, roads, piers, and, above all, housing. He was especially interested in a project I had previously explored with the governor of the Zone and with representatives of Panamanian employees of the company. Some thirty-five hundred of these employees wished to build low-cost houses in Panama City; monthly payments to cover interest and amortization could be deducted from their salaries, making the loan from the United States for the total cost a fairly safe investment, since the United States was the employer. While this would be only a modest start in correcting the deplorable housing situation in the city, it would demonstrate our concern and might temper somewhat the passionate views about sovereignty, rental payments, wages, and flags.

The governor of the Zone and the United States ambassador did not agree on what should be done. The ambassador felt that some concessions in Zone-republic relations should be made. The governor felt that these relations were good—that Panama was looking to the Canal Company rather than to its own resources to improve the economy. He suggested that we should be exceptionally generous in helping to stimulate agricultural, industrial, and social improvements in Panama. And this, he contended, would relieve the pressures on the Zone and the Canal Company.

Technically, this affair was beyond the scope of my general mission. Throughout the trip I tried earnestly to confine my studies and conversations to truly hemispheric problems, to those facts and circumstances which most extensively affect total inter-American relations. I failed. My hosts invariably raised questions of bilateral concern. Since the Assistant Secretary of State and our ambassador to the host country were nearly always present in visits with Chiefs of State and cabinet members, I could occasionally relax as they probed these specialized questions. But after such visits, when my colleagues and I retired to the United States Embassy, the ambassador normally would not permit me to remain aloof. He would argue that problems only *seemed* bilateral, that in fact they usually had hemispheric implications. And of course, he was right.

I felt quite strongly about the situation in Panama and decided to speak candidly as soon as I returned home. I left Panama with a feeling of impending disaster weighing heavily upon me.

Our next stop was Tegucigalpa, Honduras. Conditions in this country were especially bad. Annual per capita income was $150. Honduras had only a third as many highways as Costa Rica, and only a twentieth as many as El Salvador. Illiteracy was high and schools were few. My talks with President Ramon Villeda Morales and his Cabinet stressed the need for more aid.

In Costa Rica, I had two extremely interesting experiences, one sad, the other most pleasant. Shortly after I arrived, the Minister of Health, a beloved figure in the country, died. I attended the funeral services in the church and was escorted to the front pew to sit beside President Mario Echandi Jiménez. After the service, the President took my arm and led me from the church. He took me to the street and into a funeral procession immediately behind the hearse. It is the custom there for the mourners to walk behind the hearse to the cemetery. As we began the solemn trek to the cemetery three miles away, my mind was on the intelligence reports I had read in Washington. About two hundred thousand people lined the streets, and the President and I were escorted by one security agent.

There was not one untoward incident.

On a happier note, I was invited to address the National Assembly, a privilege usually reserved for Chiefs of State. I spoke generally of our policies with regard to Latin America, indirectly answered the main criticisms of us (price-fixing, our greater concern for Europe, for example), and ended with a promise that the United States would continue to look for ways to be helpful. I received a standing ovation, especially from the young visitors who filled the gallery. (Where was the violent anti-Yankeeism so readily reported during the Nixon trip?)

I was able to meet with former Costa Rican President José Figueres, one of the real fighters for democratic freedom and social justice in Latin America. He is an enlightened man, realizing that the primary problem separating the United States from Latin America is a lack of understanding. Figueres made an eloquent plea for exchanges of students, teachers, and leaders. In a long discussion about Latin-American dictators, Figueres showed great sympathy for our dilemma. He recognized that the United States had been forced into a position of leadership which it had not sought, and that it did not like dictators. When he said we should not have decorated Pérez Jiménez (he was right, of course), I reminded him that when we had opposed Perón openly in 1945 our opposition had made him a hero among his people. Then Figueres made a most amazing statement:

"Perón," he said, "was elected through his own demagoguery. The United States was right in opposing him, but you didn't persist long enough. You should have kept on opposing Perón." Figueres obviously felt that some unilateral intervention was needed.

We were in Nicaragua from July 21 to July 24. Only 11 per cent of the land was under cultivation, though an additional 27 per cent was arable. Of the population, about 70 per cent was mestizo, 5 per cent Indian, 17 per cent white, and 2 per cent Negro. The average per capita income was $180. President Luis Somoza was the first President who did not talk about economic matters.

His assassinated father Anastasio had been a dictator, and so the son was eager to show me that Nicaragua was progressing rapidly toward democracy. He insisted that I visit with opposition political leaders and opposition press editors so that I could be assured of the trend in Nicaragua. He had had the National Assembly adopt a constitutional amendment making it impossible for him or any close relative to run again for the presidency.

President Somoza's Minister of Education made a special plea to me and to Dempster McIntosh, managing director of the Development Loan Fund, for money for education. He said that from 1951 to 1958, Nicaragua had increased the number of schools from less than 1100 to 2045; the number of teachers from 2375 to 3750, the number of students from 68,000 to 115,500. The educational budget had risen from $7.7 million to $35.5 million, and President Somoza had even reduced the military budget in order to find more money for education. But much, much more was needed. He particularly wanted loans that could be repaid in local currency; here was the kind of loan that could be made from an Inter-American Bank or from our own Development Loan Fund.

It was in Nicaragua that I lost my temper for the first time on my official trips. A large group from the University Club came to see me. One vicious-looking character seized the floor and gave his associates no chance to speak. He was obviously an out-and-out Communist, for he followed the Party line and used the typical jargon. Usually, I was able to maintain my composure, but this time I did not. I lashed out at him and said that if he, an educated man, really believed the propaganda he was spouting then I felt sorry for him and the educational system which had produced him. I took his points one by one and refuted them. That night I received a letter from the club commending me and saying that the man in no way represented their views.

We flew to Puerto Rico on July 24, where I spoke to an audience of one hundred thousand on Commonwealth Day, July 25.

"Our record is impressive," I said. "The Philippine nation is independent by its own choosing. Alaska is on the verge of statehood by its own choosing. Hawaii is seeking statehood and no one doubts that her aspiration will be realized. Puerto Rico is a Commonwealth within the United States system by its own choice. That is the record of the United States. What a reversal of human history it would be if Hungary could be free and independent, by its own choice; instead her leaders are brutally slaughtered for no greater crime than the God-given right to re-establish institutions compatible with their belief in . . . human dignity. . . . And how greatly world tensions might be relieved if all would agree that each of the nations of the Middle East had the inherent right of free choice." (The Lebanon crisis was then upon us.)

In Puerto Rico I traveled around the island to study self-help housing projects, industries, agriculture—the same places I had visited in 1938. The change was unbelievable. Average per capita income had increased five-fold since I had made studies there just twenty years before. It is impossible to compare Puerto Rico with independent Latin-American nations, however, since it is in a privileged situation; for example, it sets its own tax rates considerably below those in effect on the mainland, and ships goods free of duty anywhere in the United States.

El Salvador is called the prime example of inequality, with considerable justification. It has a few fabulously rich families, but the people are very poor. I visited schools, low-cost housing projects, farms, and ranches. At a dinner, the President, Don José María Lemus, said to me: "My main principles are honesty in government and better living conditions for the people. Neither I nor any of my ministers is dipping into the Treasury, as so many Latin-American leaders have done. This might happen again in the future, but not during my Administration. The three biggest problems in El Salvador are housing, education, and public health and these are really a single problem. We have undertaken a bold program to solve these problems, but we did not anticipate the world economic depression. We need help."

President Lemus told me that he favored the economic union of Central-American states as a means of providing all the five countries with a broader market and freer trade. Later, at the headquarters of the Central American Organization, which is working valiantly for a closer association of the five republics, I spoke out strongly and constantly about the desirability of developing a common market. I honestly believe that the people of Central America can easily double their incomes when a common market is fully operating.

Guatemala was our last stop, and I was eager to be getting there. My party and I were weary of traveling and living out of suitcases. The trouble in Panama was still on my mind.

Perhaps the most interesting experience was a visit from the market women, who are quite famous. They openly defied the government during the short Communist period in Guatemala, and got away with it. These women are small capitalists. No matter how meager their resources, they own their own little shops, or markets, or tiny domestic industry (probably in their homes), and they prize their freedom.

The women knew that we were building highways which would eventually benefit the economy of the entire country; that we were helping to resettle farmers on land which they would own and operate; that we were helping with health, education, and other things. But, they said, the people generally have the impression that our aid goes to a relatively few individuals, strengthens the rich, and does nothing for the poor. Could not the United States do something that would obviously benefit all the people, and let them know about it?

I asked what this could be, but they had no suggestions. They had, however, put their finger on a crucial issue, for by now I had come to realize that while all we were doing in Latin America was in fact for the benefit of all, this was not understood. The Communists had an easy time misrepresenting our motives and actions.

I had many talks with Guatemalan leaders and they listed a tremendous number of urgent needs, ranging from promotion of tourism, to highway construction, to education. Unfortunately, Guatemala suffers from under-nationalism (a reverse of most Latin-American nations). There is almost an absence of patriotism among the people, and it is easy to see why. A large percentage of the population is comprised of unassimilated Indian peoples. Guatemalans were subjugated during the great Mayan period that extended for a thousand years before the Spanish conquest. Three hundred years under Spanish rule did not revive their spirit. Since gaining independence, they have suffered a series of dictatorships of the most authoritarian kind. Only recently has there been a degree of freedom, and the people are not yet ready to accept the responsibilities of it. There is little concern among them about the future of the nation.

As we boarded the plane to depart for home, my associates and I were completely worn out. Our nerves were shot from tension, anticipating Nixon-like incidents. So when we were well in the air, we all burst into hearty cheering, had a few drinks, and sat back to breathe.

When we arrived home, I turned at once to the crisis that I was sure was developing in Panama. I agreed generally with ambassador Harrington that the United States must make some concessions, so I talked at length with the Secretary of the Army, who serves as the President's representative in supervising the Governor of the Canal Zone. I thought we should recognize Panama's titular sovereignty by flying the Panamanian flag in selected locations, at least on ceremonial occasions. The State Department had agreed. I urged that, even though the prevailing wage scales were already higher than those for similar work in Panama, we should grant additional modest wage increases at once. And I felt that we were needlessly creating an issue by purchasing beef outside of the United States and Panama—regardless of what was meant by the "if feasible" in the 1955 treaty. I wanted a team of experts to go to Panama to explore the possibility of loans for industrial and agricultural development and diversification. And, most urgent of all, I thought the United States should initiate a program of low-cost housing, starting with the thirty-five hundred Canal employees; no precedent would be established, for, I pointed out, these men and women were employed by a United States Government corporation.

I repeated these recommendations in the State Department.

I repeated them to the head of the Development Loan Fund and urged a cooperative effort by the Fund and private credit institutions in initiating the housing experiment.

I repeated them, in short, to anybody who could act—and who would listen. I had been a bureaucrat myself long enough (in an earlier period) to know that the rustle of paper is the most deafening sound in the world, but I pounded desks and raised my voice anyway because I was convinced that there would be the devil to pay in Panama, probably on the next Independence Day, unless we made a good showing before then.

I found support in State, particularly in the need to quell emotional issues by flying the Panamanian flag at some point, either regularly or on ceremonial occasions. But when Congress got wind of this there were violent protests, as there were from the Secretary of the Army and the Governor of the Zone. They saw flying the flag as the first step; next Panama would want police power in the Zone; soon, we would be without complete jurisdiction and the efficiency of the Canal operation and its readiness for security action might be jeopardized.

As I have previously said, I never used my privileged position or my family relationship to evade traditional channels. My assignment in Latin America had not been to try to find solutions to one country's problems; that would have rudely displaced our regular diplomats and endangered the President's delicate and continuing relations with his governmental associates. But I was sorely tempted this time, and I have always regretted that I did not go directly to the White House.

Unsuccessful in convincing federal officials of the worthiness of my recommendations, I alluded to some of them softly in my official report to the President which reached him on December 28, 1958. In this report I said, "Many leaders of Latin America point out the need for social development. They contend that the lack of housing constitutes their most serious single social problem. They hope a method can be found to make credit available for home, hospital, and related construction. . . . Health conditions are substandard. Ill individuals are not productive . . . better housing would improve health, attitudes, and productivity."

This part of my report was approved by the appropriate members of the Cabinet. But I went on to urge that we experiment with low-cost housing projects in Panama, not only to help alleviate a threatening situation there but also to discover a workable pattern for wider application. Under Secretary Dillon coordinated the government-wide review of my report before its publication and transmittal to the President. Reluctantly, after receiving strong disapprovals from the lending agencies and the Treasury Department, he suggested that I modify the housing recommendation. So I altered the offending section.

On housing in Panama, I merely expressed the pious hope that private capital would help. On the larger issue, I adhered to the long-held orthodoxy that it would be preferable to increase the tempo of economic development so that wage earners themselves could build and finance their homes.

"The problem of housing finance is, however, much more difficult," my revised report said. "There are situations where extremely low productivity of the worker and low levels of income do not permit the worker to pay the economic cost of adequate housing. Even in advanced countries, housing makes very heavy demands on savings, and absorbs a large share of the income of workers. The choice is then between subsidizing housing for the individuals concerned or—and this is, of course, a long-range solution—raising productivity and improving the level of income in order to permit the worker to buy or rent adequate housing. While the second is clearly the better course, it is, as I have mentioned, a long-run solution. As to subsidizing housing in one way or another, this is a decision for each individual government."

I did what I did against my own wishes, but because I knew that the entire report would suffer if I disregarded the objections of the federal officials. I did not want to jeopardize the other recommendations which I felt to be of immense importance.

The final report, approved by relevant agencies prior to its transmittal to the White House, was not wholly shortsighted, however. It was right in that the Latin-American nations themselves should long ago, and certainly by that time, have so revised their economic and social systems that (a) a far greater share of the rewards of production would go to the masses of the people and (b) local savings could be developed to meet at least the local costs of social development. In that event a substantial attack on the deplorable housing problem would have been possible through their own national authorities. In such a situation even orthodox aid from us which stimulated production would have directly helped with social progress.

The final revised report was wrong, however, in that the threat of revolution was rising, most of the Latin-American nations had not brought about changes to achieve economic justice, and the time had come for the United States to take the initiative in stimulating change. (Perhaps we needed a new definition of "non-intervention"—one which recognized that he who pays the piper at least has some say in calling the tune. I think the United States is correct in attaching conditions to its loans and grants—so long as these conditions are honorable.)

The follow-up on the Panamanian problem is significant enough to detail here. Early in October 1959, Secretary of the Army Brucker asked me to meet with him in his office. He had received disturbing reports from Panama—something about Panamanian students and some political leaders and others marching on the Zone on the coming Independence Day to hoist the Panamanian flag. I sighed inwardly in despair. It appeared that the Government of Panama would not try to prevent this "invasion." In fact, the government was thought to be encouraging the movement. Secretary Brucker then outlined a program of eight or nine actions which he felt we should and could take, without violating principle or provisions of existing treaties. I tried to appear placid as he repeated a plan nearly identical to the one I had urgently proposed thirteen months before.

I knew now we were fighting time, and since I was spending the weekend at the White House I suggested to the Secretary that I report our conversation to the President. He readily agreed. I paused only long enough on my way to the White House to clear the procedure with the Secretary of State.

It was a Saturday evening when I spent an hour telling the President about each of the issues involved and suggesting what might be done and what would probably happen if action were not taken. Early on the following Monday morning, he summoned to the White House the top men of the State, Treasury, and Army Departments, and of the Development Loan Fund and the Export-Import Bank. In the meeting a nine-point program evolved, and a rush tag was placed on each action.

For all his power, the President of the United States is not a magician. It takes time to set up low-cost housing projects or to establish equitable new pay scales, or to prepare and process applications for development loans. And so, before the President's orders could be executed, Panama boiled over. Two thousand Panamanians "invaded" the Zone. In Panama City, the United States flag was torn down from the United States Information Office and trampled. Fortunately, no one was killed.

In most of the world, Uncle Sam wore a hangdog look. More importantly, perhaps, we were confronted with a new dilemma.

If the programs being rushed through the federal mill were now implemented, it would appear that they were undertaken in response to the attack. Too often I had heard in Latin-American countries that "the way to get action out of the United States is to stir up trouble or threaten to turn to Moscow for help." And so it was necessary to wait. A few months later, when relative calm prevailed, elements of the program began to be put into effect. The flag was flown—without untoward incident. Wages were raised, so that unskilled and semi-skilled workers, mostly Pan-

amanians, received nearly 40 per cent more than comparable workers in the
Free Zone. The Governor of the Canal Zone was directed to stop buying
beef from New Zealand and Australia—to buy *all* supplies from Panama
and the United States. Luxury items were removed from the commissaries.
A start was made on housing. Feelings in Panama quieted, for the time
being.

In September 1961, President Roberto F. Chiari of Panama wrote
President Kennedy a long letter. He said that relations between the two
countries had been improved, but that, in justice to Panama, further modi-
fications in treaty arrangements and economic matters should be made.
President Kennedy thereupon created an Advisory Commission to study
the problem, preparatory to discussions that might lead to possible treaty
revisions.

A few days after President Kennedy's reply reached President Chiari,
the Panamanian National Assembly passed a resolution calling for a new
treaty which would set a date for the United States to relinquish full
jurisdiction over the Canal. The Assembly suggested, among other things,
that in the transitional period Panamanian sovereignty over the Zone be
affirmed, that Panama receive a "fair" share of Canal revenues, that mixed
Panamanian-United States courts be set up in the Zone, that Panama
be given exclusive jurisdiction over the waterway's terminal ports, that the
Panamanian flag be flown on all public buildings in the Zone and on ships
using the Canal, that "effective equality" of treatment for Panamanian
workers in the Zone be established, and that arbitration be used to settle
disputes between Panama and the United States.

Whether the Assembly resolution is purposely excessive to provide a
negotiating advantage, I do not know. Nor did President Chiari's subsequent visit to this country seem to shed much light on the problem.

I have no doubt that United States-Panamanian relations are going to
be changed, perhaps after a series of jarring experiences. To improve our
own posture in the republic, I would have the President of the United
States make an immediate administrative change: Our representation there
should be unified.

Our ambassador in Panama has no control over Zone affairs and has too
little influence on Zone-Panama relations. He can report his views and
recommendations to the Secretary of State, who in turn can report to the
President. The President may then call in the Secretary of the Army, who
supervises the Governor of the Zone. While this circuitous process is under
way, the Governor of the Zone is most likely talking with high Panamanian
officials, including the President of the republic. He is probably visiting

with Panamanian businessmen, addressing Rotary and other clubs, and meeting a steady stream of important Panamanian visitors at his headquarters. What he thinks and advocates often become lead stories in the press—under banner headlines.

In some respects, the governor, in his capacity as president of the Canal Company, feels he is more responsible to Congress—to which he must go each year for appropriations—than he is to the Secretary of the Army and the President. The Congress has been adroit in making itself felt in Canal Company administration.

The United States desperately needs a *single voice* in Panama. And that voice should be the ambassador's. The President should direct that he, and only he, hereafter maintain formal and informal relationships with the government and people of Panama. The Governor of the Canal Zone should confine his activities to the internal administration of the Zone, and as president of the Panama Canal Company he should direct its operation in harmony with existing policies. He should not negotiate with anyone outside the Zone, save in the presence of the ambassador, and then he should be, in effect, a technical advisor to the ambassador. The governor should of course be free to report anything he wishes to the Secretary of the Army and the President; but in Panama there should be no doubt in anyone's mind about who speaks for the United States. All "playing off" of one high official against another should cease.

The question of jurisdiction over the Zone is complex, and in time will have to be faced realistically. Much thought has been given in the United States to the future of Canal management, first after the Suez crisis, then after the violence in Panama, and now in response to President Chiari's requests. No one can be so farsighted as to know what may happen in the next twenty-five years, or whether a change of status in Canal government and management may be required. We should, however, be prepared; we should carefully plan alternative lines of action.

I doubt that a treaty guarantee of rights in perpetuity can be sustained. What seemed felicitous to Panamanians in 1903 (when Teddy Roosevelt's "big stick" won them their independence from Colombia) may be unacceptable to their great-grandchildren tomorrow. Our stubborn insistence upon the legality of the original guarantee might in itself be cause for revolt and bloodshed. Many situations, from a Suez-type incident to a changing political climate in the hemisphere, might make amendments to the 1903 treaty seem attractive to the United States.

As a precautionary and economically justifiable move, I would begin at once a program of Canal debt amortization. This would require higher tolls. Debt retirement itself might be a persuasive argument for postponing the question of jurisdiction for a number of years. When the Canal debt is paid, we would at least be in a position to accept a change without forfeiting the heavy investment the United States taxpayers have in the Canal.

Both Adlai Stevenson and Harry Truman have proposed that the Canal be placed under the jurisdiction of the United Nations or the Organization of American States, but this requires Panama's consent. At present, Panama opposes the internationalization or inter-Americanization of the Canal.

Others have suggested that we gradually train Panamanians in preparation for a joint United States-Panamanian management, or possibly the transferring of jurisdiction to Panama. The former may be the most reasonable course to follow. The latter would be opposed by maritime nations and possibly by the Andean countries of Latin America which fear that shipping costs would be increased unwarrantedly as a means of improving Panama's income.

Although the Assembly resolution calls for the eventual transfer of the Canal to Panama, I am sure that many thoughtful Panamanians prefer that we retain considerable responsibility, for they believe we can manage the enterprise more efficiently. Those who hold this view prefer to seek greater rewards from increased tolls. Personally, I would, in addition to using part of the income from higher tolls to retire the debt, increase the annual cash payments to Panama—perhaps to $5 million or more a year.

Regardless of what happens in the jurisdictional area, we should be scrupulously careful henceforth to buy supplies only from Panama and the United States. Present wage policies should be maintained, but every effort should be made to train Panamanians for the skilled jobs which command United States wage rates. We should not make further concessions on the flag issue and, by an exchange of letters between the two governments, should record the mutual understanding that the Panamanian flag in the Zone is only a recognition of Panama's titular sovereignty. All United States lending agencies should give special attention to economic and social improvement in the Republic of Panama. The Inter-American Bank should be persuaded to give high priority to social reform and development.

I have often wondered how many Panamanians would agree with a forceful statement made to me by a leading Panamanian educator: "If I were President of the Republic," he said, "I would oppose the internationalization of the Canal, for I would rather negotiate with a single power. I don't think I would press for nationalization even if the United States were willing. The main reason for nationalization would be to increase Panama's income, but some day soon another canal must be built, and if Panama tried to obtain too large a return from the present waterway, it would force maritime nations, or one of them, to make a new sea-level canal, possibly through Colombia, large enough to handle all traffic." I couldn't have agreed more. The educator continued: "In any event, even high tolls would not yield all the revenue needed by my country for social and economic development. This raises the serious question of how rapidly a growing population—already one million—on this small isthmus, which is smaller than your South Carolina, can possibly prosper. So, as President, I would look at Puerto Rico and the privileged status it has as an independent Commonwealth within the American system. I would wonder whether it might not be worthwhile for my country to give up a little sovereignty—total sovereignty is a myth anyway—in order to achieve a similar status. After all, the moment the Canal bisected my country, some such privileged status became a moral obligation of the United States and a right of Panama's. Do you think we could persuade the people of the United States to this view?"

I did not attempt to answer his question.

14   A man with a home, a full stomach, and children in
        school is a poor revolutionary.

My report to the President following the study
trip to Central America had not reached the President until December
1958—partly because I had held a series of policy discussions with officials
when I got home and partly because I had been consuming a good deal
of time trying to get my views on Panama and low-cost housing included.

I wrote more urgently than I had before about the need to promote
understanding, and to this end, I emphatically renewed my recommendation for national commissions in all countries. I urged that we increase
still further the flow of credit—and to make credit more useful, I suggested
a series of moves which would lead to better planning in each Latin-
American country, to the establishment of project priorities, and to better
coordination among the lending agencies. But the most important recommendation I made in the field of credit was for the immediate creation of
an Inter-American Development Bank, with a governing board representing all the American republics and with authority to make both hard and
soft loans.

Shortly after my Central-American trip, Under Secretary Dillon had
appeared before the Inter-American Economic and Social Council and
announced United States support for the creation of this family institution. Hence in my report I could write with confidence on the outcome.

I pointed out that the new bank should complement, not supplant, the
lending activities of existing institutions, but should, indeed, become the
focal point in coordinating all loans to Latin America.

Assistant Secretary Rubottom and I were convinced after our Central-

American trip that all the financial help in the world would not build good relations for us or promote stability in Latin America unless there was also a crescendo of social change in country after country. Instead, hatred of us would increase, for we were mistakenly identified, partly as a consequence of adroit Communist propaganda, with the oligarchists, the privileged.

Dillon, Rubottom, and I saw the establishment of the Inter-American Bank as a major first step out of a dilemma. While it would only be a start, a bank which the cooperating nations themselves controlled could attach conditions to loans, and these conditions, in the field of tax reform, for example, could be a stimulation to social reform. And, if loan conditions were deemed to be intervention, at least it would be in collective form and not intervention by the United States. (Years before, the International Bank had refused to make loans to Latin-American countries unless they first agreed to settle their obligations to other countries. This made some countries angry, but the condition was fulfilled.) Further, we were only responding to a request the Latin-Americans had been making for two decades, and so this could not be something we foisted upon our neighbors.

Shortly thereafter, the Inter-American Bank was authorized and some of the responsibility for future lending policy was transferred from the United States to an agency in which the recipient nations had to make critical decisions.

With this move, United States policy toward Latin America had altered much more than was generally recognized at the time. Still not identifiable, and unnamed, the foundation for the Alliance for Progress was nevertheless being laid. And it is important to emphasize that this was occurring *before* and just after Castro overthrew the despotic Batista in Cuba. The charge which redounds in Latin America today that the change in our policy toward Latin America—our efforts to lift the people out of poverty under the Alliance for Progress—was solely in response to the threat of Castro Communism, is patently untrue. Castro Communism was well concealed when these things were happening. Fidel was a hero in the hemisphere. There is no doubt that subsequent policy changes were hastened by the threat of revolution, for as I have said, we began to see clearly that our constructive efforts were not really getting through to the Latin-American people—that they were being bluntly and maliciously misinterpreted. And so Herter, Dillon, Mann, and Rubottom, working with the President, speeded the monumental task of turning the giant edifice of foreign policy.

The 1958 report to the President dramatized another change in orthodox policy—it pushed strongly for the United States to promote common markets in Latin America. I have mentioned previously that the United States in all previous administrations had been opposed to common markets, so this, too, was a genuine change to the long-time benefit the peoples of Latin America.

In some respects, I think the most significant part of the report was the recommendation that the President create a high-ranking committee on inter-American affairs. I gave two reasons for my suggestion: to upgrade inter-American affairs in a way that would be universally recognized, and to bring outside views to bear upon policy formation.

The President created the National Advisory Committee on Inter-American Affairs with Secretary of State Herter as chairman and Rubottom as deputy chairman. Dillon also always sat in and I identified the other members in Chapter II.

In February 1959, at the time the President and the Secretary of State were moving to set up the committee (a month after Castro came to power in Cuba and while he was still being applauded throughout the hemisphere), the United States presented to a special committee of the Organization of American States a number of suggestions for social development. Foreshadowing the Act of Bogotá, the proposals called for an increased flow of credit, better development planning, increased trade, intensified efforts to promote common markets, and *the beginning of social change through the financing of low-cost housing*.

Just about this time, President Eisenhower flew to Mexico to visit President Lopez Mateos. Rubottom and I accompanied him. It appeared that all of Mexico had journeyed by bus to the small seaside resort of Acapulco. Half a million persons lined the streets, laughing, waving flags, and shrieking "I like Eeekee!"

We met and talked for two days. The two Presidents came to understand each other very well. It was here that President Lopez Mateos suggested that he and President Eisenhower maintain constant, direct liaison, and that I be named for that purpose. Bob Hill, our ambassador to Mexico, agreed enthusiastically to the arrangement. Had I been ambassador, I might have been reluctant, for such liaison is obviously an ambassador's responsibility. But Ambassador Hill and I had become good friends and he knew that I would not abuse my privilege; thus there was no obstacle to this unconventional assignment.

General attitudes could not have been more propitious. Several of the ministers in the Lopez Mateos Cabinet, when I undertook this unique task, had lived or visited extensively in the United States. They, like their President, shunned the ever-fashionable anti-Yankeeism and indicated by word and action their desire to strengthen bilateral relations. Ambassador Antonio Carrillo Flores—a member of a distinguished Mexican family—was the intelligent, respected representative of his government in the United States. As Finance Minister in the Cabinet of Ruíz Cortines, he became recognized as a leading financial figure in the hemisphere. He is a charming gentleman with many friends in the United States, and I can perhaps describe him best by saying that he is more like an enthusiastic, outgoing Midwesterner than any Latin-American I have known.

And so, in the summer of 1959, I went to Mexico again. It was a useful trip, as my previous visits to Mexico had been. I traveled more than five thousand miles and never had more than one security officer with me; even he was unnecessary.

One day as I was traveling by bus north of Veracruz—the schools were closed for the summer—I saw hundreds of youngsters rush from a school-house toward the highway. Then I noticed that they were waving home-made paper United States flags. I had the bus stopped. I got out and stood at attention as the young people, ranging in age from six to ten, sang two verses of "The Star-Spangled Banner" in English. They had gathered from a wide area when they heard I would be passing that way. Their faces were solemn—painfully so—as they sang. But at the conclusion, they broke into cheers, broad toothsome grins on their faces.

This was a delightful "extra" of a profitable visit. I spent many hours talking with President Lopez Mateos and members of the Cabinet about serious matters.

The abiding concern of a Mexican President and his associates naturally must be the welfare of their own people. But Mexico's interdependence with the United States is so extraordinary that her national welfare is substantially linked to her relations with the United States.

It is obvious that our government, regardless of the party in power, wants to maintain exemplary relations with our nearest southern neighbor. We ought to be able to achieve the detailed understanding that cements true friendship. We have an opportunity to set a model for the larger community of nations to emulate. Our investment in Mexico approaches $900 million and is rising; we have a large two-way trade; tourist travel is heavy, and more of our students study in Mexico than in any other country; large numbers of Mexicans work in the United States.

But despite friendship and vital interdependence, perplexing problems mar our relations. They are not crises, but they are potentially serious and should be resolved. They range from boundary disputes and fair distribution of boundary waters to the control of animal diseases and the regulation of civil air traffic; from the difficult problem of territorial waters and the adjustment of private claims to the possible development of joint defense plans and economic difficulties caused by our marketing surplus agricultural commodities and restricting the importation of lead and zinc.

The age-old question of territorial waters comes up in most high-level discussions. Most maritime nations recognize that national sovereignty extends only three miles into adjacent waters. The United States has tried to persuade all nations to accept the three-mile limit, for under this concept some thirty-five or forty straits and similar waterways are open to world traffic, a fact of crucial importance in planning for free-world security. If territorial waters were extended to six miles, many of the waterways would lose their international character. A twelve-mile limit would restrict freedom of the seas in this regard to relatively few.

Mexico claims its territorial waters to be three marine leagues, or 10.35 miles. It contends that in the Treaty of Guadalupe Hidalgo of 1848 the United States recognized this, and then verified it in the Tidelands Case of 1960, when our Supreme Court found in favor of Texas in a dispute over the right to exploit oil resources of the continental shelf.

The problem is complicated by the fact that shrimp are abundant in the waters bordering Mexico, and United States shrimp fishermen are active in these waters. We feel they are operating legally so long as they remain three miles from the Mexican shore, but under Mexican law, they are thieves if they come inside the three-*league* limit. Often they are arrested and fined in Mexican courts. On at least one occasion, gunfire developed. In the Mexican press, United States shrimp fishermen are called pirates, and the Mexican people do not understand why a rich country like the United States permits its citizens to rob them of a valuable resource.

The United States proposed a compromise: For purposes of shipping, the two countries would agree to a territorial limit of six miles, while at the same time tacitly accepting traditional rights of exploiting water resources for a distance of twelve miles. Mexico rejected the suggestion. To understand why, one must remember a few critical aspects of history.

History also holds the key to another troublesome problem—the Chamizal, a tract of some six hundred acres in the suburbs of El Paso. The Rio Grande has shifted its course rather capriciously from time to time, thus altering the Mexican-United States border. As a consequence, sovereignty over the Chamizal came into dispute. In 1910, the question was submitted to an arbitration commission of three. A year later, the Canadian and the Mexican members declared that about two-thirds of the area belonged to

Mexico, one-third to the United States. The United States refused to accept the decision, claiming that the arbitration commission had exceeded the mandate given it by the United States and Mexican Governments.

A half-century later, the question is still unresolved. The area is now occupied, partly by sub-standard developments, but also by some expensive installations. Occupancy is partly American, partly Mexican. The Chamizal issue is often passionately discussed in Mexico and Texas. To Mexicans, our refusal to accept the majority decision of the arbitration commission is a flaming reminder of the land hunger we dramatically demonstrated on several historic occasions.

From time to time, the United States has suggested possible bases for negotiation. Mexico has declined to negotiate, insisting that the United States must first acknowledge the arbitration award of 1911. In 1962, after a visit to Mexico, President Kennedy in a press conference said of the 1911 arbitration decision, "the United States backed down and did not accept the award." And he indicated that he and President Lopez Mateos agreed that the time had come for both sides to give ground and find a solution. The two leaders said they would instruct their agencies to study the problem and recommend a solution.

Mexico's view on the Chamizal and territorial waters is not unreasonable. Neither is the attitude of the United States. Compromise by both sides would seem to be required. But for Mexico, the lingering effects of history have been controlling and thus an acceptable accommodation has not been found. This historic influence began many years ago.

The United States supported Mexico in its fight for independence from Spain, but immediately afterwards began meddling in Mexico's internal affairs. Our ambassador openly advocated a republican form of government for Mexico and thus alienated the friendship of Mexican conservatives who favored a monarchy.

"Moral imperialism" became a byword in Mexico in the 1820s and 1830s and it poisoned Mexican-American relations. Undaunted, our ambassador, noting the rapid colonization of Texas by Americans, suggested that the territory be sold to the United States. Such a gross miscalculation of the Mexican frame of mind about territorial integrity and national sovereignty led to the firm conviction that the United States was the imperialistic enemy of Mexico.

In 1836 Texas became independent, a fact which the Mexican Congress refused to recognize. When sentiment rose in the United States for annexation of Texas, this was taken in Mexico as proof indisputable of the imperialistic designs of the "Colossus of the North."

Trouble continued throughout the late 1840s. Anti-American feeling was sedulously cultivated by the dictator, General Santa Anna. General Zachary Taylor's forces defeated those of Santa Anna, but it was not until General Winfield Scott marched from Veracruz and occupied Mexico City that Mexico grudgingly acknowledged defeat.

In the resulting Treaty of Guadalupe Hidalgo, Mexico relinquished all but a part of what is now New Mexico, California, Texas, and Arizona —more than half of her original territory. It was in this treaty that the Mexican position on territorial waters originated. The treaty established the boundary between the two countries in the middle of the Rio Grande *and for three leagues beyond its mouth*. The United States has since contended that the three-league clause pertained only to the question of international boundary, not to the broader question of territorial waters. Mexico strongly takes the opposite view.

In 1853 Santa Anna, again dictator of Mexico, sold the Messilla Valley in southern Arizona (the Gadsden Purchase) to the United States for $10 million. This alienation of national territory by Santa Anna was bitterly resented by Mexicans.

During the War of Reform and the French intervention, the United States indirectly helped Mexico and relations improved. Then came the long dictatorship of Porfirio Díaz, from 1877 to 1880, and from 1884 to 1911. The despot, to obtain funds for his own use, encouraged foreigners, including Americans, to acquire ownership of 40 per cent of Mexico's resources. More than 95 per cent of the people of Mexico were left without land resources of any kind, even for burial. This laid the basis for serious future trouble.

Then we sent to Mexico an ambassador who constantly intervened in Mexican internal affairs. He supported Huerta against President Madero, and to this day, some Mexican scholars insist that our ambassador was implicated in Madero's assassination.

When Woodrow Wilson entered the White House, his anger was turned against President Huerta. Wilson's attitude seemed to be "democracy or else." His assumption that we had a moral right to interfere in Mexican affairs to establish democratic institutions was contested by Mexicans. They again shouted charges of "moral imperialism."

Venustiano Carranza, with arms from the United States, defeated Huerta, but could not control marauding Mexican bands. We assumed this chore and in 1916 General Pershing pursued the bandit Pancho Villa into Mexico—and this, again, was viewed as a violation of Mexican sovereignty. Carranza fed the flames of anti-United States hatred.

To a long list of difficult situations, there was now added the explosive question of property rights of United States companies and nationals. Under the new Mexican Constitution of 1917, the revolutionists began laying the foundations of economic democracy. This upset powerful United States interests and eventually resulted in the expropriation of oil properties by President Cárdenas. Cárdenas also seized nearly forty-five million acres of land owned by wealthy Mexicans and United States citizens and distributed it in small parcels to Mexican nationals.

Despite mutual irritations caused by expropriations, Mexico supported the United States in World War II. The problem of expropriated property was settled by negotiation. President Roosevelt went to Monterrey to visit President Avila Camacho, and in a public address declared that "the epoch of exploitation of resources and people of one country for the benefit of one group in another has now definitely passed." Mexican antagonism began to wane.

Mexico's development quickened appreciably under President Alemín. Then came the period of President Ruíz Cortines and President Eisenhower, both of whom worked assiduously for strengthened friendship. President Ruíz Cortines visited the United States, encouraged friendship for this country, worked for economic improvement in his own country, and insisted that the benefits reach vast numbers of Mexican people— a policy which commanded the admiration of everyone in this country.

Cooperative efforts—including an exchange of presidential visits—were continued during the Eisenhower and Lopez Mateos administrations. Our part of this friendly partnership is now being carried on by the Kennedy administration.

I present this minute history as a reminder that the United States on many occasions intervened in Mexican affairs, displayed a patronizing attitude toward the Mexican Government, and came into possession of vast areas once claimed by Mexico. (Mexico's attitude toward the United States was also far from exemplary.)

Fortunately, the Mexican people and their leaders are incurably friendly and lovable. They are willing to forgive much of the past. They will work with us earnestly for improved relations. But historic influences are still such that any political leader of Mexico who today suggested ceding a single inch of Mexican territory to the United States would, in all likelihood, be immediately overthrown.

Hence, in the dispute about territorial waters, Mexican leaders feel they cannot agree to any compromise which would reduce their country's legal claim to less than three leagues beyond her land boundaries. Similarly, the

Chamizal problem cannot be settled unless the United States first recognizes the validity of the arbitration award of 1911, which upheld Mexico's claim to a substantial part of that small piece of real estate.

I am proud to have hundreds of warm, intimate friends in Mexico. But even to me, whom I believe they trust, they caution that more years of stable, mutually helpful relations must pass before they can be sure that we would not again violate their sovereignty or invade their territory in time of crisis. (During World War II, for example, Mexican leaders became incensed over a rumor that the United States, alarmed over the Japanese threat in the Pacific, might have to move into Mexico to provide an adequate coastal defense. I was assigned to track down the completely false rumor, but had no success.)

Time is gradually erasing the scars of history. I had substantial proof of this when I later undertook a delicate assignment in Mexico for the National Aeronautics and Space Administration. The successful development of Project Mercury required a control station on the west coast of Mexico, for from this station would come the signal to bring our orbiting astronaut back home should trouble occur on the first pass around the earth. Our ambassador to Mexico warned me that the assignment must surely fail, pointing out that he and his predecessors had not been able to persuade Mexico to install radar and other devices for the common defense of the two countries. Mexico was one of the few nations of the hemisphere with which we did not have a military agreement; all efforts to develop one had fallen flat.

Project Mercury, while under civilian control, had military overtones. It seemed likely that Mexican misgivings about our military power would frustrate my efforts. Only one man in Mexico could possibly give me a friendly hearing, so I went directly to President Lopez Mateos. The details are probably still classified, but I can say that I explained the project fully to the President. At his suggestion, I also briefed Foreign Minister Manuel Tello and Dr. Nabor Carrillo Flores, Rector of the University of Mexico and head of Mexico's Atomic Energy Commission. I came home feeling optimistic. Months passed with no word from Mexico. Then, when President Lopez Mateos came to this country to visit President Eisenhower, I talked privately with him on a boat ride to Mount Vernon.

"We are, Mr. President, on a very tight schedule," I said. "We must have an answer as soon as possible."

"I have not forgotten," he replied. "This has been constantly on my mind. I have a suggestion. If this is truly an international effort, why do you not staff the Mexican station not only with your own people, but also with ours and with scientists from other countries—and also assign a few of our people to some of the other foreign stations?"

It was a splendid way of demonstrating that the installation was part of an international scientific effort—not a United States military project—and I therefore gave President Lopez Mateos my word on the spot that NASA would concur. (Indeed, Dr. Keith Glennan, head of NASA, and I had discussed this possibility and he enthusiastically favored it.) As the world now well knows, official Mexican approval was forthcoming and the station at Guaymas, Mexico has played its part in Mercury flights.

Historic attitudes are changing. If we always send to Mexico men of the stature of Dwight Morrow, Francis White, and Thomas Mann; if Mexico sends to the United States distinguished diplomats of the caliber of Manuel Tello and Antonio Carillo Flores, and if the attitudes and decisions of our government continue to be as they have been for the past thirty-five years, then gradually the relations of Mexico and the United States can become a model for the hemisphere.

To this end, I hope the United States will accept the 1911 arbitration decision in the Chamizal dispute, trusting to the fairness of Mexican officialdom thereafter to reach with us an agreement which protects the dignity and rights of both nations. I also hope the problem of territorial waters will be resolved. I would have us accept the Mexican view that its sovereignty extends for three leagues into adjacent waters, respecting her full rights thereto, including fishing, oil, and other rights, and simultaneously enter into a new treaty which establishes the right of United States ships to cruise these waters in harmony with the freedom-of-the-seas concept. Most important, I trust we can convince the Mexican people generally that we shall never again violate their sovereignty.

In addition to our long talks about bilateral problems such as these, President Lopez Mateos and I discussed candidly and informally the whole concept of hemispheric solidarity and the means of building a dependable partnership. Castro was now beginning to reveal his true colors, and the spirit of revolution was becoming almost tangible throughout Latin America. The people, sleeping like a giant in the earth for centuries, had suddenly awakened to historic injustices and were crying for justice. My Mexican friends felt strongly that each nation had to find its own way of achieving social reform, as Mexico had done. The United States, they insisted, should remember propriety and act only in response to requests for assistance from individual countries. I was to see again, when Castro had goaded us into pushing for collective condemnation of his Communist regime, the unbending attitude of Mexican leaders with regard to United States intervention.

I hurried home, not only to report to President Eisenhower on my visit with President Lopez Mateos, but to meet with the National Advisory Committee on Inter-American Affairs, which was about to hold a series of crucial meetings with President Eisenhower and Secretary Herter.

Advisory committees are sometimes ground up in the wheels of bureaucracy; ours was not. The President had given us carte blanche to investigate whatever we felt to be relevant, and Secretary Herter and Assistant Secretary Rubottom had put the resources of the State Department at our disposal. We got all the ideas and facts we asked for—from the State Department, from the Development Loan Fund, from other lending agencies. The committee, with the full participation and creative leadership of Herter, Dillon, and Rubottom, was coming to grips with the problem of stimulating social change. There can be no doubt that Castro's wicked influence in the hemisphere was spurring us onward, but we felt strongly that what we were now considering was far too important to be distorted by emergency adaptations. We realized that since mid-1958 our government had been moving carefully in reshaping its attitudes and policies. Prudent decisions were more important than hasty, noisy action.

We had no thought of recommending that public or private credit or technical and other aid to Latin America be reduced. Rather, we wanted a procedure and legal authority which would permit the United States to help bring about social reform in ways that would not bring charges of unilateral intervention.

At the beginning of 1960, Secretary Herter worked with Dillon and Rubottom to set up a special technical group to draft suggestions for an inter-American conference to be held nine months later in Bogotá. These were to be hemispheric declarations, and the Secretary fully intended that our delegation to Bogotá have in hand specific suggestions in nearly every field: tax reform, land reform, tax administration, and so on. Such documents are not prepared overnight; a great deal of research and policy study are involved.

At about the same time, the President at last got his wish to visit Latin America. Because time was limited, he traveled only to Brazil, Uruguay, Argentina, and Chile, taking with him the Secretary of State, the Assistant Secretary for Inter-American Affairs, and the members of the National Advisory Committee on Inter-American Affairs.

The trip was a notable one, both in improving Latin-American understanding of our programs and policies and in helping President Eisenhower crystallize his own views with respect to a new and bold step he would take later.

In a television address to the people of the United States before his departure, he said: "Early tomorrow I start a journey to several of our Latin-American neighbors . . . to learn more about our friends . . . to assure them again that the United States seeks to cooperate with them in achieving a fuller life for *everyone* in this hemisphere, and to make clear our desire to work closely with them in the building of a universal peace with justice. . . . It is vital for national partners to develop better understandings and to improve common programs. The bonds among our American republics are not merely geographic; rather they are shared principles and convictions. Yet even among close comrades, friendships too often seem to be taken for granted. . . . So I shall reaffirm to our sister republics that we are steadfast in our purpose to work with them hand in hand. . . .

"This will be a busy trip," the President continued, "for our neighbors' problems are many and vexing; the lack of development capital, wide fluctuations in the price of their export commodities, the need for common regional markets to foster efficiency and to attract new capital, the need to improve health, education, housing, and transportation—all these are certain to be subjects of discussion in each of the countries I visit."

Then the President promised to restate throughout his trip the basic principles and attitudes that govern our country's relationship in this hemisphere, namely, non-intervention, mutual respect, juridical equality of states, rapid and widespread economic progress, the rule of law, the triumph of liberty, and the fight against Communist subversion.

Millions of persons, in city after city, greeted the President with frenzied enthusiasm, indicating again that despite all difficulties, disappointments, and misunderstandings, we were all still members of a family; on occasion we could surmount family quarrels and give vent to deeper emotions of friendship. While the press of the United States gave top headlines to the ninety pro-Castro students who waved banners and threw tear gas bombs in Montevideo, and to a few small but futile incidents elsewhere, the trip was one gigantic triumph after another. This was reassuring. It indicated that a reservoir of goodwill left a little time for action.

As the trip proceeded, and the President received ovations from the joint sessions of the Congresses of Brazil and other countries, he did in fact repeat time and again the policies which he had said on his departure were inviolable. But he also kept adding to them.

In Brazil, he said: ". . . the first responsibility of leadership in any nation is to work for the welfare of its own people, its own land," and he pledged United States aid in this effort. Turning from economic matters to the charge that the United States wished to dominate other countries, he exclaimed: "We . . . hold . . . the burning conviction that relations among sister nations must be characterized by mutual respect . . . by respect for each human being, regardless of his race, creed, or color, and a willingness to help one another promote the *well-being of all our peoples.* . . . We do not wish to prosper at another's expense."

President Eisenhower gave open endorsement to President Kubitschek's idea of Operation Pan America. "The high purpose of this imaginative proposal—" he said, "to attack the problem of underdevelopment by cooperative effort—is one which the government of the United States endorses."

Later that evening, in a toast to President Kubitschek, President Eisenhower said, "On this trip with me . . . are Secretary Herter, Assistant Secretary Rubottom, and the citizen members of the United States Advisory Committee on Inter-American Affairs. The fact that these gentlemen are accompanying me symbolizes the high importance we of the United States attach to good relations with all the nations of Latin America."

The reference to the committee was more than an after-dinner pleasantry. On the plane trip from Brasilia, the President had begun to discuss with us the need for some dramatic move—some "upheaval"—that would shake the historic structures of the Latin-American nations into a form that encompassed and rewarded *all* the people.

In Argentina, where President Frondizi was struggling to overcome the excesses of the Perón dictatorship and to establish the foundation of steady progress, President Eisenhower expressed his pleasure that the United States had already put vast credits at the disposal of the Argentine Government as an expression of confidence in its efforts to shore up the nation's economy. He said he hoped the blessings of such an advance would benefit *all* the people. Before a joint session of the Argentine Congress, he said: "It was once possible to think of democratic freedom as a matter of purely national concern. But now in a world of exacting interdependence, freedom must be fostered, developed, and maintained cooperatively among many nations. Hence, across national boundaries, among peoples and governments, a constant increase in mutual understanding must prevail.

Based on that understanding, political, cultural, and economic cooperation will succeed, with benefits for *all*."

He was constantly emphasizing the theme of having the benefits of economic progress reach the masses. At Bariloche, Argentina, in the heart of the majestic Andes, he endorsed a statement which President Frondizi had made before the United States Congress thirteen months earlier: "When there is misery and backwardness in a country, not only freedom and democracy are doomed, but even national sovereignty is in jeopardy." And in a joint statement, the two Presidents declared that "economic progress and improved living standards facilitate the development of strong and stable political institutions."

He told the people of Chile that we want to see the undernourished and unhappy people of the world given the opportunity to enjoy the "blessings of bread, peace, and liberty."

Addressing a joint session of the Chilean Congress, President Eisenhower strongly supported a move initiated by President Alessandri for a reduction in arms expenditures by Latin-American nations (then totaling $1.5 billion a year). He pledged United States aid in protecting Latin America against any attack and urged that the funds saved in the military cutback be spent for social improvement. Also, he praised the progress being made by Chile and its neighbors in the formation of a common market and promised wholehearted cooperation.

In Santiago, President Eisenhower received a letter. It was an urgent communication from the President of the Federation of Students, dealing in part with the Cuban-United States situation which had worsened with each passing month. The Federation had a membership of twenty-five thousand drawn from the seven Chilean universities. The leaders of the Federation had been elected by free and secret vote and represented a wide range of political views. They explained that they were Christians, anti-Communist, pro-democracy, and liberal in their outlook.

President Eisenhower took their letter seriously and was dismayed, for it indicated a wide misinterpretation in Latin America of our attitudes and actions on many problems, including our stand on expropriations in Cuba. Many of their statements indicated that they felt this was the main issue between Cuba and the United States.

"Has the United States become a satisfied nation, one which fights for the maintenance of the prevailing order in the world and in Latin America?" they asked. "This dangerous image is becoming accepted more every day. If this is true, we must respectfully say to you that the United States will have little or nothing to offer the younger generation and the immense multitude of the poor, who compose 90 per cent of the Latin-American population. And we will have little or nothing to expect from the guidance and genius of North America."

In the United States and Western Europe, it made sense to fight for the prevailing order, they argued, because social order represented values widely shared: Personal freedom, social justice, real equality in the law, high cultural, scientific, and technological levels, and satisfactory standards of living. But to defend the existing society in Latin America meant only maintaining the privilege of a thin layer of the population which controlled the power and wealth, surrounded by an ocean of poor people.

This was blunt talk, and the students made the most of it. They continued: It would be a mockery to pretend that such a situation reflected the Christian or democratic order for which the immense mass of starved, illiterate, uncultured people should hope. If the injustices that existed were all that Christianity and democracy could offer, no one should be surprised if in desperation the best children, soon to be leaders, should turn to Communism.

"The United States apparently finds its best friends . . . to be those . . . to whom the prevailing order in this starved and illiterate America means the right to enjoy a standard of living which would be envied by the multimillionaires of the United States," they said. "But they are not the friends of the United States. They are the friends of their own privileges, which they aspire to identify with North American interests in order that they themselves may be supported by the United States."

They urged the President not to defend the former prevailing order in Cuba or the prevailing order elsewhere in Latin America, but to encourage by all legitimate means those who fought for the creation of a new social order—one which would be closer to Lincoln's definition of "government of the people, by the people, for the people."

While they did not give unqualified "adhesion" to the Cuban experiment—excesses were evident to them—nonetheless they were strongly in favor of Cuba's agrarian reform. They contended that the reform under way was more moderate and more generous with old landowners than that carried out by General MacArthur in Japan, or the agrarian reforms supported in full by the United States in Egypt, India, Israel, Pakistan, and South Vietnam.

"Why this difference?" they wanted to know. "Is it because seven North American companies on the island own two million hectares of land? If this is the reason . . . how can anyone escape the dangerous conclusion that North American private investment is the worst threat to free national decisions and social progress?"

The students expressed confidence in President Eisenhower as a world leader, but feared that in the Cuban situation his innermost instincts might be suppressed by pressures from powerful financial interests in the United States.

The students presented their arguments to the President by letter shortly before he was to leave for an informal talk to the American Embassy staff and members of the Chilean-American groups in Santiago. He hurriedly dictated a note of acknowledgment and then turned to me.

"Milton, I want you to talk to these young people this evening. Try to make clear our attitudes toward Cuba. Emphasize that had Castro carried out his original promises for freedom and democratic justice, he would have our firm support. They seem not to realize that the tyranny in Cuba is now the worst ever experienced in this hemisphere. And tell them that I shall have our ambassador here reply in detail to their letter as soon as possible." He hurried off to his engagement, obviously disturbed by the letter. He was deeply moved by the students' sincerity, but shaken by their erroneous impressions of our attitudes.

When he rose to speak in a crowded auditorium a few moments later, he could not put the letter from his mind. He mentioned that the students had written to him "in the most respectful and even affectionate terms," but then went on to explain errors in the students' analysis of United States relations with Cuba and other nations of Latin America.

Before individuals who do not carry great responsibilities in the world spread information, they should be sure of their facts, he said slowly and with emotion. They should read history carefully.

"These students happen to be people I am interested in more than any others in the world," he went on. "The young people of today, with all of their opportunities for learning [and] the certainty that they are going to take over the responsibilities of government, of business, of the social order . . . these are the people in whom we must be interested."

If the United States is to help, he continued, all of us must have genuine understanding of one another, our purposes, our methods. The United States makes mistakes, but "our heart is in the right place. I believe in these young people, but I do hope they will come to their conclusions on the basis of fact." He emphasized that the United States wants every American republic to become economically, politically, and socially strong. If for no other reason, we would want this because our trade with each country would increase as each nation improves its economy. But we would also want it just as one wants to see members of his family succeed. And we would want it because we know that only strong nations in our divided world can be sure of retaining their precious freedom.

Late that night, Dick Rubottom, Ambassador Walter Howe, and I met with the President of the Student Federation. We tried to convince him and his colleagues that we fully understood and sympathized with the need for basic reform in Cuba and other countries, but we insisted that reform must be achieved by legal and democratic means—and certainly without the intervention of an extracontinental power. We told him that a reply from Ambassador Howe would reach him soon.

The reply was prepared in the State Department and sent to the Student Federation over the signature of the ambassador. It was essentially a white paper on United States policies toward Latin America. Indicative of the importance attached to the exchange was the fact that the ambassador's letter was nearly six thousand words long. It emphasized three points: First, while the people of the United States had developed a political and economic system appropriate for themselves—though subject to constant adjustment and improvement—they did not seek to impose their system on others, recognizing the right of each country to evolve and enjoy its destiny free of foreign intervention. Second, the United States did not consider itself a "satisfied nation." The progressive income tax, social security systems, free schools, and other social programs in the United States had brought about a wide distribution of the national income; and younger generations abroad should realize that these advances had been made through the will of the people themselves, that the "prevailing order" in every country was only a situation of the moment subject to change through the will of its people. Third, it was our desire to help each country improve the lot of the common man—to make the prevailing order more equitable—but we would never do this by inciting violent revolution. To do so would be the most arrogant kind of colonialism, repugnant to the American people. It must be understood that the United States is not opposed to land reform and other social changes in Cuba or elsewhere—quite the contrary—but we expected social change to be carried forward legally and democratically. Finally, it must be understood that the United States could not intervene unilaterally in the affairs of another nation, no matter how inequitable the prevailing order might be.

I dwell on this correspondence with the Chilean students because I think they spoke eloquently for the discontented masses of all the Latin-American countries. The crucial point to note, I believe, is that they viewed the Cuban revolution, with all its frightful excesses, as the beginning of a program of reform that would lead to the social justice they felt was denied them in their own country. Furthermore, they felt that our insistence upon identifying Castro with the international Communist conspiracy was a mistake, or at least a smoke screen to obscure the real problem. (They must know better by now.) They replied, in a letter to Ambassador Howe shortly after hearing from him, that "The threat of Communism is merely a reflection of the most important question of our time: the poor in the world (that is to say, 80 per cent of the human race in Latin America) want bread, education, homes, health, security, dignity, freedom, and hope. The order under which they live denies them these things. But we all know that poverty is no longer a misfortune, but an injustice, an act of immorality against the divine order. . . . We are Christians and supporters of democracy. There are impassable barriers separating us from Communist ideology and methods, but no one should claim to be deceived: the West has been successful in spreading throughout the world a certain scale of values that symbolizes civilization. If Christianity and democracy fail in the coming ten or fifteen years in giving work and bread, dignity and security, to the poor, the fiery breath of Communism will cover the entire earth."

Students do not speak for governments, but in Latin America they often speak for humanity. I was convinced then, and firmly believe now, that the letters from the Chilean Student Federation revealed more sharply, clearly, and poignantly, the true situation in the Latin-American countries—and the relevance of that situation to our relationships with Latin America—than any official document released by a foreign office, any speech by a Latin-American President or Minister.

It is too bad, however, that the letters also revealed ghastly misunderstandings of United States external and internal policies. They showed an almost complete lack of comprehension of the patient approach we had used in dealing with Castro.

As I shall explain more fully in the next chapter, the United States had faced an all but insoluble dilemma in its relations with Cuba. We could not move against Batista without violating the sacrosanct pledge of nonintervention. When Castro's revolutionary forces began to make headway, we halted the export of arms to Batista. Then, on January 1, 1959, Castro won his fight; the United States was among the first to recognize the new regime. But almost as soon as he gained power, Castro began to emulate Batista with bloody orgies of revenge and suppression of freedom. He seized both United States and Cuban properties with no thought of compensation. He vilified the United States, calling it "a vulture feeding upon humanity." In frequent marathon television diatribes, Castro paraded a host of vile and false accusations against the United States. Through all of this, the United States resisted the urge to retaliate. The State Department and President Eisenhower insisted upon a policy of unprecedented patience—so much so that my Mexican friend said we lost face in Latin America. Even as we were on the trip, Chilean newspapers published a State Department statement endorsing Cuba's right to institute social reform by legal means. But patience was in vain. As President Eisenhower spoke to multitudes in Latin America, Castro intensified his vilification of the United States.

The Chilean students were either ignorant of all this, or unwilling to accept the full truth, perhaps blinded by a sense of injustice. But they were destined to witness, in the months following their letter to President Eisenhower, Castro's betrayal of his own revolution, his boastful embracing of Communism, and his subversive attempts to plunge all of Latin America into the web of Moscow's conspiracy.

The last stop on President Eisenhower's trip was Montevideo. There he took account of the criticism often heard throughout Latin America that in the postwar era the United States had done more for other areas of the world. The people of the United States, he said, have known holocausts of anxiety, suffering, and great human tragedy three times in this century, yet had not turned inward to indulge in self-pity. Rather, in a way unprecedented in history, we had given of our substance in repairing the material damage done by war, and had extended the hand of friendship and economic aid to all who wished to progress in freedom. These efforts required the people of the United States to impose upon themselves the most burdensome taxes in the history of the nation, and caused us to forego many internal improvements which cried for attention. Our efforts to be helpful to others had even threatened our financial situation in the world, due to a serious imbalance in international payments. But, even so, the aid flowing to Latin America would continue and increase. In the whole complex of world cooperation, we attached no greater importance to solid, abiding partnership with any area of the world than we did with that of the American republics.

He then used words close in meaning to those which the Chilean students had expressed to him: "I believe it is the duty of every nation, no matter how large or small, how weak or strong, to contribute to the well-being of the world community of free men. For a time, perhaps, some can supply only certain skills or personal or spiritual support. The important consideration is that we should all accept a common sense of responsibility for our common destiny. *I am sure you hold the concept, as we do, that every human being, given an opportunity to do so, will make his contribution to the general welfare. You must feel, as we surely do, that hunger and privation must be eliminated from the earth by the cooperative efforts of peoples and of governments of goodwill."*

Cynics say that a trip of this sort may have an immediate emotional effect, but is of no lasting value. I do not believe this. Every one of the thirty-two brief talks and formal addresses the President made on the trip was carried, usually in full, not only by the press of the host country, but by newspapers, radio stations, and television stations throughout Latin America. For months afterwards, evidence poured in to show that our policies and programs had become better understood and that much ill will toward the United States had been dissipated. The impact it made on young minds, on the rising generations, is incalculable.

But the most significant development on the trip did not at the time come to public attention. As conference after conference was concluded, the President spoke earnestly with the Secretary of State and the members of the National Advisory Committee on Inter-American Affairs of the imperative need for immediate social change in Latin America. He had seen enough to convince him that the choice was between rapid peaceful action and violent revolution, between reform in freedom and dangerous moves toward Communist dictatorships. He had been particularly inspired by a visit to a low-cost housing project in Santiago. The government had provided land, utilities, and foundations for nearly five thousand homes. The people themselves were building their houses, mostly of large wooden blocks which fascinated the President. He walked among thousands of low-income families, talked with them, and visited in their homes. They showered him with flowers. Some hugged him. He was reminded of pioneer days in the United States when friends in communities joined in building their primitive dwellings.

Later, when I discussed with him the substance of my conversation with the Chilean student president, he kept referring to the self-help housing project.

"You know," he said, "I'll bet these people will not be in these houses in a few years—they will be building better ones. We've got to find a better way to help. These people want to help themselves. That is worthy of our support—and we should do something about it soon."

"I'm glad you've had a chance to see this project," I said. "It could be duplicated in every community of Latin America."

"I wish that world events would have permitted me to make a trip of this sort sooner—and not just to four countries but to twenty," he answered.

Back home, Secretary Herter, Under Secretary Dillon, Assistant Secretary Rubottom, and the other members of the National Advisory Committee on Inter-American Affairs plunged anew into consideration of the delicate problem: How could the United States encourage social change without violating the Good Neighbor concept of non-intervention?

On April 20, 1960, in an address in the Pan American Union, Secretary Herter hinted at things to come: "If we support the premise that the dignity of the individual in a free society is strengthened when he acquires his own home, so must *we also recognize the importance of land ownership to the man who works the land*." He saw this as a problem that challenged the Organization of American States and all its members.

Three months later, from his summer office at Newport, President Eisenhower said he would propose a new program for Latin America, and in August 1960 he sent to the Congress his strong recommendation for a substantial change in United States lending policies with respect to Latin America. The purpose, he said, was to "help our Latin-American neighbors accelerate their efforts to strengthen the social and economic structure of their nations and improve the status of their individual citizens." He urged that the new legislation be enacted before the Economic Conference of the American Republics which was to convene at Bogotá on September 5, less than a month later.

On August 15, 1960, Under Secretary Dillon appeared before the Foreign Relations Committee of the Senate in support of the President's recommendations. He stated the situation straight out: "While there has been a steady rise in national incomes throughout the areas, millions of underprivileged have not benefited. . . . Improvement in the standard of living of the great majority of the population has been disappointingly slow. . . . The distribution of national incomes in many countries has been far from equitable, with the bulk of the income going to a very small portion of the population. . . . The low level of both general and technical education has severely limited the productivity of the average Latin-American workers. In some countries, progress has been impeded by out-dated economic, legal, and social institutions. . . . Where obsolete institutions exist, the result is not only to prevent the best utilization of the country's resources but to deny a large part of the population an opportunity to share equitably the growth of the national product."

He explained that we would continue to extend credit to Latin America through existing institutions, but that this was not enough. *Needed was the authority to attack social stagnation.* (Rubottom and other members of the Committee on Inter-American Affairs silently but fervently applauded.) Among other things, he said, we wished to assist the development of "aided self-help" housing (such as the President had seen in Santiago). The Latin-American governments would assist in acquiring land, the prospective owner would provide the labor, and we would give technical assistance and help finance the cost of materials.

Under Secretary Dillon warned that the existing frustration and social unrest bred over centuries of injustice threatened momentarily to erupt in violence. The Eisenhower administration, he said, envisaged an immediate assault on these problems by the nations of the hemisphere working together, each carrying its share of the burden. In behalf of the President, Dillon asked for an initial authorization of $500 million to make a start on social problems, and $100 million for special aid to Chile for relief of earthquake victims.

Acting in record time, the Congress enacted Public Law 86-735 on September 8, 1960.

Two days before the Congress had completed its work on the Act, Under Secretary Dillon was in Bogotá addressing a special committee of the Organization of American States. The greatest task of our time, he said, is to raise the living standards of the great masses of the people. He reviewed the ways in which the United States was already aiding Latin America, then pointed out that we were now prepared to add a wholly new and additional fund for social development. *"The United States,"* he said, *"is prepared to devote over the years ahead large additional resources to the inauguration and carrying forward of a broad new social development program for Latin America dedicated to supporting the self-help efforts of the governments and peoples of Latin America."*

Vigorously keeping the initiative, the United States had circulated before the delegations met a draft agreement—the culmination of nine months of hard work. It proposed the establishment of an inter-American program of social reform. It called for an attack on social problems through the improvement of conditions in rural life, better use of farm land, better housing and community facilities, and the modernization and improvement of education. It suggested that Latin-American nations modernize their tax systems, make more effective use of land resources, and modernize credit institutions.

The Inter-American Bank would administer the funds for social development and would make hard and soft loans. (Now all the pieces were tidily fitting together.) Progress would be reviewed annually and new programs would be proposed as needed.

On September 12, 1960, all the American republics, save Cuba, proclaimed the Act of Bogotá.

By that time Public Law 86-735 was in effect and it was known that substantial funds would be available under the right circumstances. The real significance of the Act of Bogotá, therefore, was that Latin-American nations agreed *to act cooperatively in solving social and economic problems.*

The Act of Bogotá, a truly historic document, outlines specific measures to be taken in the field of social reform. If the measures are carried out faithfully by the nations of Latin America, the whole human society of our neighbors will begin a process of far-reaching change. This will mean, in turn, that the aid we extend—public and private, orthodox and unorthodox—should, if humanity has not become entirely cynical, transform the misgivings about us among the Latin-American people into joyful and wholehearted friendship. From what I have seen of Latin America, I think chances are good.

And so, with the Act of Bogotá and Public Law 86-735—only four days apart—the Eisenhower administration made its final effort to reshape our policy toward Latin America into a positive and constructive force for benefit of the masses of the people. These final actions completed the construction of the foundation for the Alliance for Progress.

If mistakes in policy, program, or judgment were made during the Eisenhower years—and I'm sure there were some—they were primarily errors of timing. Perhaps if I had jumped the chain of command to the White House in 1958, the violence and ill will in Panama could have been prevented or at least lessened. If President Eisenhower had been able to visit Latin America earlier, he no doubt would have seen then more quickly than I did the blunt weight of injustice balanced so precariously on the thin edge of revolution; it had taken me four years to cast off the past and to see the awful dimensions of the future. Indeed, all of us concerned with Latin-American affairs were slow in proposing changes in traditional policies relating to price stabilization, common markets, credit mechanisms, and social change. No doubt we adhered longer than we should have to the Good Neighbor concept of absolute non-intervention. All of us, for too long, hurried through the maze of tradition—a malady common to busy men burdened with responsibility.

On the other hand, I am not sure, even now, that traditions, attitudes, and policies evolved over a period of a century and a half can be rudely altered overnight. New policies not only require painstaking research and creative thinking; they must gain acceptance, and creating the climate for acceptance also takes time. But if we were guilty of slowness of pace, it must be recorded that more constructive changes in basic foreign policy affecting Latin America were made during the Eisenhower years than during any previous Administration—and most of them, one sees with the wisdom of hindsight, might better have been made long before President Eisenhower took office.

In the two Eisenhower administrations, twice as much public and private credit flowed to Latin America as in any previous eight-year period. In some countries, the increase was fivefold, and emergency aid to Bolivia, Guatemala, Haiti, and Chile prevented outright collapse.

The capital of the Export-Import Bank was increased by $2 billion—so much so that it had more funds available to lend than Latin-American countries requested or received.

The Organization of American States, which had demonstrated its vitality and effectiveness in political and security matters, assumed a new, more positive role in economic and social affairs.

The Development Loan Fund was created to provide additional aid to Latin America and other underdeveloped areas, and to make soft loans —a sharp departure from traditional policy.

Largely through the efforts of the United States, two new agencies were created in the International Bank for Reconstruction and Development: The International Finance Corporation, authorized to lend money to private enterprises, and the International Development Association, designed to speed economic growth in less developed areas, including Latin America, by lending international funds repayable on other than conventional terms.

The Inter-American Development Bank, long desired by Latin-American nations and repeatedly rejected by previous Administrations, was brought into being with the authority to make both hard and soft loans (and here was an essential mechanism for a collective attack on social injustice).

Funds to finance technical assistance and related activities were substantially increased and the cultural exchange program was tripled.

Whereas previous Administrations had opposed even discussion of methods that might stabilize the prices of Latin America's primary commodities, the Eisenhower administration initiated the creation of the commodity study groups, sanctioned the coffee stabilization plan of the producing nations, and committed the United States to helping find feasible methods of solving the critical problem of changing price relationships.

The Eisenhower administration vigorously supported common market developments for the entire Latin-American area and for regional groupings, whereas previous Administrations had either opposed such plans, as at the Buenos Aires Economic Conference, or had declined to discuss the problem.

In response to urgings by the United States, the American republics, meeting in Caracas in 1954, declared their opposition to the entrance of international Communism into the hemisphere. At Santiago in 1959, they reaffirmed their determination to protect democratic institutions, free from totalitarian influence. At San José in 1960, they asserted their determination in this regard—Cuba, naturally, dissenting.

A long-standing dispute with Mexico about the welfare of the Mexican migrant workers in the United States was satisfactorily settled.

A special conference in New Orleans, which brought together more than one thousand businessmen from the American republics, greatly stimulated United States private investment in Latin America—a beneficial movement which continued until Castro Communism frightened potential investors.

Nearly half a billion dollars worth of surplus foods and feeds were donated or sold to Latin-American countries for local currencies, these funds then being used to finance various internal development projects.

A greatly increased effort to eradicate malaria from the hemisphere was financed largely by the United States.

And in Public Law 86-735 and the Act of Bogotá of September 1960, the basis for aid to speed genuine social reform and economic growth in Latin America was solidly laid.

It is fair to say, I think, that on the foundation of mutual respect built by the Franklin Roosevelt administration, the Eisenhower administration promoted more constructively, more consistently, and more voluminously the sound development of Latin America than did any previous United States Administration. Further, when President Eisenhower left office, only a third as many dictators held power as when his first term began.

The record is eloquent testimony to our concern for Latin America and to our willingness to aid in its ascent from poverty.

But while this vastly increased effort has paved the way for social reform, it has not assured us of a happy resolution of the crucial problem. Unrest in Latin America has intensified. Criticisms of us, most of them unwarranted, have continued and, in some areas, increased. Danger of bloody revolution in country after country has heightened. Traditions inherited from history have become more and more obsolete, intolerable, dangerous.

The legacy to the Kennedy administration, then, was mixed: It contained all the authority and agreements needed for a great thrust forward, the buds of a new harvest of goodwill, the promise of a new era; but it also included, in Cuba, the embryo of disaster, the spark which could inflame the hemisphere.

15   History sadly reveals that those who grasp freedom
with violence too often crush it.

IN 1958, A NEW FLAMBOYANT PERSONALITY ROSE IN THE
Western Hemisphere: A young and romantic rebel, filled with zeal and a
lust for battle, was seriously challenging dictator Fulgencio Batista's rule
of terror in Cuba. Dr. Fidel Castro had gathered round him in the Escambray Mountains a ragtag band of more than a thousand tough and
dedicated rebels, pledged to overthrow Batista and establish freedom and
social justice in the Caribbean isle. Castro had become a hero not only in
Cuba, but in the United States and all of Latin America. His courage
and defiance caught the hemisphere's imagination, and his guarantee of
free elections within a year after Batista's downfall had made him a
symbol of a noble revolution.

The New York *Times* practically deified Castro. Here was a youthful
savior who would create ideal democracy in Cuba, perhaps sprinkled with
a bit of socialism. He was "the most remarkable and romantic figure to
arise in Cuban history since José Martí, the hero of the Wars of Independence," wrote Herbert L. Matthews. "He has courage, dynamism, and
leadership." (Interestingly, Juan Perón had these same qualities and was
at once the most attractive and the most ruthless man I ever met.)

The mass media of the United States echoed the *Times* in praise of the
bearded rebel. The American people watched unfolding events with
sympathy and eager anticipation. Castro was even more popular in
Latin America; he won the people *and* their leaders. The President of one
Central-American country was so smitten that he ordered a planeload of
arms flown to Castro in the mountains after a serious setback at the

hands of Batista's armies, exclaiming: "I feel sorry for that young man." At this point, public opinion in the United States and Latin America was one.

Fidel Castro had been a latent revolutionary even during his student days in the late 1940s. He espoused radical causes and demanded, among other things, the nationalization of United States-owned power and telephone companies. (Later, in 1958, he would tell a United States correspondent: "I am still the same revolutionary but I have had time to study the political and economic factors. I understand that some ideas I used to have would not be good for Cuba. I do not now believe in nationalization.")

On July 26, 1953, Castro led an unsuccessful revolt against Batista's Moncada Barracks in Santiago de Cuba. His courage and determination were far outweighed by his inexperience and clumsiness as a fighter. His rebellion was instantly crushed. Castro and the survivors of his followers were imprisoned. At his trial, he defied Batista and demanded the social reform so desperately needed in Cuba. Unimpressed judges sentenced him to fifteen years in prison. In 1955, a confident Batista made his greatest political error and declared general political amnesty.

Freed from jail, Castro made his way to Mexico and prepared for his return to Cuba. From wealthy Cubans who had fled Batista's tyranny, he received money and encouragement. His band trained in the hit-and-run tactics of guerrilla warfare. On December 2, 1956, he and his small, hard-core rebel force landed in Cuba and were met by Batista's troops. Only Fidel, his brother Raul, Che Guevara, and a few others escaped. They fled to the forbidding jungles of Sierra Maestra to lick their wounds and recruit disgruntled farmers to their cause.

For two years, Castro did more flouting than fighting. Constantly moving to stay one step ahead of his pursuers, he perched in the mountains and scolded Batista like an angry bluejay. His defiance and elusiveness embarrassed the dictator, and Castro became a symbol of rebellion to a people who had long salved their misery with a growing lust for revenge. In April 1958, after sixteen months of sabotage and threats, Castro vowed total war against Batista. But he was premature in his pledge. Batista hounded the rebels and crushed the general strike which Castro had called in Cuba. The ragged revolutionary force lay low until the end of the year.

By December, Castro was strong again. He controlled one-third of Cuba and occasionally left the mountains to attack cities. Batista's twenty-nine thousand soldiers were humiliated. On Christmas Eve, a priest went into the mountains with an urgent message for Castro: General Eulogio

Cantillo, commander of Moncada Barracks (where Fidel's first rebellion failed), wished to talk with him. Batista's troops, unable to defeat Castro, were ready to join him. A week later Batista fled to exile in the Dominican Republic and to the sheltering wing of brother dictator Trujillo. His army surrendered to Castro.

Nearly nine months before Castro's victory, the United States banned the shipment of arms to Cuba. Officially, this gave the United States a position of neutrality toward the contending forces. Later, the policy of military aid to Batista up to March 1958, and the refusal to provide arms to Castro, were to be harshly criticized throughout the hemisphere, even in the United States. (Later still, this left-handed support for Castro would be attacked with equal vigor, creating for the hapless government officials a typical "damned if you do and damned if you don't" dilemma.)

Hindsight is a glorious privilege, often revealing belated wisdom. For many years, and regardless of the political coloration of the United States administration or of the recipient governments, we had been entering into military compacts with Latin-American nations. To provide for the common defense of the hemisphere, it seemed prudent that the relatively small military forces in Latin America should be trained in the use of standardized weapons. Second, it had been demonstrated repeatedly that a failure on our part to provide sufficient arms for internal security would only cause Latin-American nations to buy them, even over our protests, from other countries—including countries hostile to us. Third, we unquestionably had become preoccupied with the maintenance of military strength among all nations that would oppose imperialistic Communism, and our overriding purpose in this regard may have made us less critical in our judgments than we might otherwise have been.

We were contributing to the military potentiality not only of Cuba, but of most of the Latin-American republics. Mexico, which staunchly refused to enter into a military pact with us, limited its acquisition of arms from the United States to relatively small purchases. Our arms went to governments of varying degrees of democracy. We helped train Latin-American military personnel. Often the men we trained became defenders of democratic institutions, as in Argentina where military men overthrew Perón —though later they grossly marred this good record. Others, unfortunately, often led palace revolts. During the long period of military assistance—it is still in effect—many dictators fell; a strong trend toward democratic institutions was discernible throughout most of Latin America.

In retrospect, however, one cannot but wish that we had halted our arms shipments to Batista earlier than March 1958. I do not agree with those who have argued that we should have openly given arms to Castro. Surreptitiously, Castro got military supplies from private groups in the United States, Venezuela, Mexico, Costa Rica, and other countries. But for the United States to have armed him officially would have been considered an offensive violation of the policy of non-intervention, and in the light of subsequent events would have truly made fools of us. Strict neutrality was the only possible policy, in a contest between a Batista and a Castro.

But Castro triumphed in any case. Bearded and bold he came down from the Escambray Mountains and marched upon Havana. Straggling farmers, hesitant shopkeepers, and timid bureaucrats, urged by the prevailing political winds, joined his ranks and made them legion. Before the conquering hero, the black-hearted Batista fled. The revolution was won.

The United States and Latin America cheered with the jubilant Cubans in that memorable January of 1959. With Batista gone, freedom would return. Schools would be built. The land would belong to the people. New houses would spring from the earth. Beaches would be opened to all people. Graft, gambling, and prostitution, which had become principal "industries" in Cuba, would be eliminated.

In the midst of the rejoicing, officials in our State Department were cautious and perplexed. While the United States joined the parade of governments granting recognition to the new regime, experienced diplomats held their breath, feared the worst, and prayed for something better.

Months before Castro's victory, two events caused some of us to have misgivings about him and his future intentions. Several United States citizens had been taken captive by his mountain forces, and Castro had arrogantly declared that he would deal with these "captives" as he saw fit. Then with a foolish recklessness (that was to characterize him and later cost him much of his support), Castro threatened to cut off the water supply to the United States Naval Base at Guantánamo Bay. Further, his heady intoxication with power, his rambling and egocentric frothing, his wild-eyed messianic posture stirred troublesome memories and provoked apprehensive premonitions that Cuba might again be ruled by a man so seduced by power that the social reform and freedom he so loudly promised would pass like fading, hollow echoes. I recall how shocked some of my friends were when I said, in September 1958, that the difference between Batista and Castro was merely Tweedledum and

Tweedledee. I did not, I confess, suspect his affinity for Communism, nor did I foresee the vicious attacks he subsequently would make upon the United States.

In April 1959, the American Society of Newspaper Editors invited Castro to come to the United States. I was greatly disturbed by this. Only the President of the United States may appropriately invite the head of a foreign state, as Castro in reality was, to visit this country. Our government had no intention of extending such an invitation. Whether due to arrogance or naïveté, the invitation from a private group, newspaper editors, was a violation of the Logan Act which forbids private citizens to arrogate foreign affairs to themselves. But Castro came and received a warm welcome from the editors and enthusiastic greetings from students on several university campuses.

President Eisenhower did not see him. But while he was in Washington, Castro had a two-hour closed conference with Vice President Nixon. Mr. Nixon asked him when elections would be held in Cuba. Castro explained that the Cuban people did not like elections, for they always got bad government by such a procedure. He struck his chest for emphasis, saying: "The people want me, Fidel Castro!" He had begun to conceive himself in Batista's image.

From memory, the Vice President dictated a dozen pages to record this revealing conversation. I saw it in confidence two days later. It was the first official hint of what was to come. On the basis of the Castro personality and self-worship revealed in that interview, one could predict an increased tempo of executions after brief military mock trials of hundreds of "revolutionists," suppression of freedom of the press, blind hatred and punishment of anyone who opposed him, seizure of property, ousting of his own officials who to the slightest extent disagreed with him. Tweedledum had replaced Tweedledee. All these things, and more, occurred.

Castro's betrayal of his own revolution shocked the people of the United States. Public praise changed to condemnation. The press of Latin America joined us to the extent of cautiously questioning his motives, but the people, captivated by his promise of social reform, did not waver in their enthusiasm and support. Castro cells were organized in many countries—cells eagerly infiltrated by Communists. The mass judgment of the United States and Latin America began to diverge.

Castro christened his regime with blood. He had probably killed only about 450 of Batista's soldiers at the front during the war, but he was well on his way to killing more than that at the execution wall. In an orgy of emotion and vengeance, Castro executed several hundred fellow

Cubans after drumhead court trials: "If Americans don't like what is happening," he shrieked to the mobs that egged him on, "they can send in the Marines; then there will be two hundred thousand gringos dead."

This was the same Fidel Castro who had declared on August 1, 1958: "The victories we have won in arms, without murder, torturing, or even questioning the enemy show that attacking human dignity can never be justified."

This was the same Fidel Castro who said in solemn wisdom: "If any war of cruelty is stupid, it is never so much so as in a civil war where the fighters will have to live together some day, and the victors will find themselves before the children, wives, and mothers of the victims."

And this was the same Fidel Castro who insisted from his mountain lair that "The example that our combatants are giving must be held up as an edifying stimulus for our future generations, as against the shameful and depressing examples given by the murderers and torturers of the dictatorship."

The hate for Batista and his henchmen was understandable, and so, to some degree, was the cry for revenge. But the merciless and haphazard slaughter which marked Castro's infant regime appalled the civilized world. Many people, unwilling to believe they could have been so wrong, rationalized that this was simply a bad phase in a good movement. Others shrugged and talked of the hot blood of Cubans which could feed a lust for revenge indefinitely. They quoted an old Spanish proverb: "Have patience and you will see your enemy's funeral procession." Nothing so dignified as a funeral procession in Castro's Cuba: Busloads of men were driven to newly dug trenches and shot at the foot of their mass grave—not even an original method, as many Jews could point out.

In these early tumultuous months following Castro's victory as a revolutionary leader, four distinct issues emerged: Was Cuba at last to enjoy democratic freedom, or to suffer still another tyranny even worse than Batista's? If tyranny was to be the unhappy lot of the people, would it be solely at the hands of their own leaders, or would it be imposed from Moscow? Would Castro expropriate and pay for property as sanctioned by international custom or would he simply steal it? Would Castro, either as democratic leader or dictator, deliver on his promises of social reform which had won him the support of his own people and Latin America generally?

As events unfolded, the people of the United States concerned themselves largely with the first three of these issues, though not indifferent to the need for social reform. But most people in Latin America—nearly all of the underprivileged and a few of the leaders—cared mainly about the fourth, almost to the exclusion of the first three. And so, in our reasoning and attitudes, we parted company with our neighbors to the south.

Soon the second phase of the revolution—Castro Communism—became evident. Said our State Department in a white paper: "Never in history has any revolution so rapidly devoured its children. The roster of Castro's victims is the litany of the Cuban revolution." Dr. José Miro Cardona, who had spearheaded many groups opposed to Batista and was Castro's first premier, soon had to flee to the United States, later to head a council in exile which would work for the overthrow of Castro. Dr. Carlos Manuel Urrutia Lleo, first provisional president under Castro, was arrested because of his opposition to Communism. Two-thirds of the original members of Castro's revolutionary cabinet were ousted; some went to prison and others fled the country. Men who had organized anti-Batista movements, fought with Castro in the jungles and hills, persuaded Cuban labor to back Castro, supported in the press his early efforts for reform, represented him in embassies in the United States and Latin America—these and hundreds of others who had been loyal to Castro during the revolution had to go into exile, or to jail, or to the execution wall. Ernesto "Che" Guevara, a Communist physician from Argentina, and brother Raul Castro, a confirmed member of the international Communist conspiracy, became the dominant advisers of the premier.

Then the Communist party of Cuba, which had once supported Batista and had dismissed Castro as of no importance, became the sole political party. Castro Communism was born. Dr. Osvaldo Dorticos Torrado, an avowed Communist, was elevated to the presidency. Raul took charge of the armed forces, and Che Guevara became the dictator of economic affairs. Trade unions, university faculties, students, professional groups, civic and farm organizations were remolded to harmonize with the Communist pattern of central control and rigid obedience.

Guevara rushed to Moscow to declare Cuban solidarity with the Soviet Union. Mikoyan traveled to Cuba to assure Castro that the Soviet Union would lend Cuba economic and military assistance. Castro and Khrushchev embraced for photographers after a United Nations meeting in New York. Khrushchev threatened to rain missiles on the United States if it dared attack Cuba. The Soviet Union began shipping arms to Castro. (Today, the military forces maintained by Castro with Soviet help are probably fifteen times as large as those which were at the command of Batista. Save for the United States, they are the largest in the hemisphere.) Finally, when the mask had worn absurdly thin, Castro removed it with a flourish to reveal the Communist beneath. He openly admitted that Cuba was now a "socialistic" state. The banners of Lenin came out from under the olive green fatigues to drape the streets of Havana and provide a grim shroud for liberty. Khrushchev had spawned.

At this stage, opinion in Latin America became clearly ambivalent. The great sea of underprivileged, with no vested interest in the established order of their own countries, and many students and mature intellectuals, continued to praise the Cuban revolution. However, leading newspapers, Latin-American presidents and cabinet members, and other knowledgeable men were disillusioned, frightened, or hostile. Editorials recalled that in Santiago, Chile in 1959, Cuban had agreed that free elections, freedom of information, human rights, and hemispheric economic cooperation should be fostered and protected, whereas now these and other promises were being flaunted.

A parade of Latin-American governments withdrew recognition from Castro's Cuba. At San José, Costa Rica, in August 1960, the foreign ministers of the hemisphere condemned the threat of foreign intervention in the affairs of the hemisphere and the acceptance of such intervention by one of the members of the Organization of American States. The United States had failed to get a more specific condemnation of Russia and Cuba, but Raul Roa, the Foreign Minister of Cuba, stomped out of the conference anyway. Stung, Castro attacked the Latin-American Presidents who had once supported him, and brushed aside the Organization of American States as an inept and ineffectual institution, a mere tool of the United States.

The attitude of the foreign minister of Mexico, Manuel Tello—an intelligent, conscientious friend of the United States and a true Mexican patriot—indicated, at the conclusion of the San José conference, a fear that now gripped some of the leaders of Latin America. He issued a public statement indicating that for Mexico, at least, the declaration of San José was not to be construed as a criticism of Fidel Castro or of the Cuban revolutionary government.

I have known Manuel Tello for many years. I admire and am fond of him and his family. I know that he is dedicated to the strengthening of democratic institutions and to all sound measures that will promote hemispheric solidarity. Why then did he feel called upon to issue such a statement: that the members of the OAS were not collectively censuring Castro and Castro Communism in the Declaration of San José? Suffice it to say here that while Mexico has made remarkable progress, and has striven to spread the rewards of increased production to all of its people, there is still unrest. The poor, the underprivileged, the restless and unhappy find leadership in General Cárdenas, former President of the republic and bitter foe of the United States. It should be noted that in Mexico former Presidents exert great influence, and every Mexican President to follow Cárdenas has shown in numerous ways that this "anti-yanqui" is somebody to be reckoned with. Foreign Minister Tello must have felt that public opinion in Mexico would not solidly support an anti-Castro, pro-United States declaration. Similar fears, though of varying degree, were evident in other countries.

Our Congress, the Executive departments, and the American people became impatient with Latin-American leaders. Here, we felt, was an obvious violation of the 1954 Declaration of Caracas that "the domination and control of the political institutions of any American State by the international Communist movement, extending to this hemisphere the political system of extracontinental power, would constitute a threat to the sovereignty and political independence of the American States, endangering the peace of America, and would call for a meeting of consultation to consider the adoption of appropriate action in accordance with existing treaties." Or, more bluntly, we must prevent Communism from getting a toehold in this continent or we're all liable to perish. The Caracas Declaration is, in effect, a policy statement supplementing the Rio Treaty of 1947, which provides for collective security: An attack on one is an attack on all. Although the United States delegation to San José argued strongly for collective action against Cuba, it succeeded only in getting the vaguely phrased Declaration of San José.

A few days after Foreign Minister Tello had drained the pale blood from the Declaration with his statement in San José, I met a Mexican friend who had been an intimate associate of President Ruíz Cortines.

"Why did Mexico abandon us in our opposition to Castro and the Communist influence in this hemisphere?" I asked him. And before he could reply I reminded him rather sharply that "Whenever a Latin-American nation wants something from us, we hear engaging declarations about the common destiny of the peoples of the hemisphere, the desirability of all of us acting in concert, and the need to share with one another in the true Christian spirit." I was uncorking a magnum of irritation. "But when the United States is in trouble or in a ticklish situation and needs the support of Latin America, what happens? We find ourselves intensely lonely. You know as well as I do that Castro is a danger to all of us, and you also know that the only effective way to deal with him is for all of us to act together through the OAS. But we got precious little cooperation. And even the few fine phrases of San José were repudiated by Tello."

He had listened calmly and his reply was utter simplicity: "Castro has not insulted us," he said. "If he had, we would have at once withdrawn recognition. He has repeatedly insulted you, and we wonder why you were so hesitant in making your decision in the face of the insults he has heaped on you. In short, Milton, you lost face in Latin America."

This was undoubtedly part of it, but not all. I pressed him to explain the failure of the nations to act together, as called for by numerous treaties and the Caracas Declaration. He replied that the general pronouncement of the Foreign Ministers at San José was quite sufficient; all action was entirely up to the Government of the United States.

In many ways, I think this was, so far as public opinion in the United States was concerned, a low point in hemispheric relations. (The nadir of Latin America's view of us was yet to come.) Our people's depression was reflected in the press, in Congress, and in statements of government officials. We felt deserted by some of our best friends. Many failed, I am sure, to realize that other forces were at work in Latin America which could no longer be ignored by the privileged classes and leaders in power. Long-smoldering discontent was being inflamed by the newly established cells of Castro's workers—cells financed by Cuban embassies and through these embassies by the Soviet Union and her Eastern European satellites. Latin-American countries other than Cuba were on the brink of revolution. It was not surprising that such support as the United States received in San José, Bogotá, and Punta del Este, from 1959 to 1961, was of a tepid political nature; nor was it surprising, I suppose, that where financial aid was concerned they were enthusiastic in anticipation.

After the executions, and after the ideology showed itself, the economic aspects of the Castro revolution tended to sharpen and deepen the divergencies in judgments as widely expressed by the peoples of the United States and Latin America.

When Castro seized power, the book value of United States investments in Cuba, public and private, was about one billion dollars. The market value was much higher. These investments had been built up over a number of years, beginning in the period of Spanish colonialism and continuing during ensuing regimes, especially during the dictatorship of Batista. American and Foreign Power and the International Telephone and Telegraph Company owned power and communication networks. Freeport Sulphur Company, through its Moa Bay Mining Company subsidiary, became a rival of the two United States utility companies for size.

The United Fruit Company had expanded its land holdings to nearly 275,000 acres. The United States Government owned the nickel mining and processing plant. Hotels, gambling establishments, sugar mills, and even bathing beaches were owned by United States, Spanish, and other aliens. In general, it is estimated that United States individuals and companies owned or controlled 80 per cent of Cuban utilities, most of the mines and cattle ranches, nearly half of the sugar lands, most of the sugar mills, and a high percentage of oil refining plants. Although Cuba reaped immense benefits, its desire to reduce foreign ownership greatly is understandable. A few Cubans were also large owners of income-producing property, and here, too, one can sympathize with the Cuban desire for more widespread ownership.

When he visited Washington, D.C. in April 1959, Castro told the American Society of Newspaper Editors that he had no intention of expropriating or confiscating these properties. He invited further private investment in Cuba.

At that time, United States economic relationships with Cuba, including our purchase of more than 50 per cent of her exportable sugar, meant about a billion dollars a year to Cuba's income. And about $40 million of the annual earnings on United States investments in Cuba were being reinvested there.

One of Castro's first official moves after he returned to Havana from Washington was to begin a program of land reform. Three-fourths of all land was held by 9 per cent of the landowners. The land was to be divided into 70-acre farms and distributed among the peasants. These extensive holdings would be paid for initially with national bonds bearing 4½ per cent interest.

But the promise of compensation was soon forgotten. Lands were confiscated. Hotels and similar properties were seized. Mines, sugar mills, and other plants were first placed under government "managers" and then taken into public ownership. Castro did not even pretend any more that he would pay for his expropriations. With each theft, his invectives against the United States increased in ferocity.

In July 1960 we halted our imports of sugar from Cuba; in October 1960 we placed an embargo on all exports to Cuba, excepting food and medical supplies.

Finally, in January of 1961, after a series of provocative moves, Castro ordered the United States Embassy staff in Havana reduced to eleven persons within forty-eight hours and made charges that our embassy people were working against his government. We had suffered indignities seldom before heaped on a nation by any power, large or small. Now the United States withdrew recognition from the Castro regime, turned our affairs over to the Swiss Embassy in Havana, and warned Americans in Cuba to come home.

This rupture cost Cuba much of the one billion dollars a year she realized from her relations with us—equal to the book value of our private and public investments in island properties. We had been paying Cuba some $360 million a year for sugar, including a premium of two cents a pound above the world price. United States companies in Cuba had been paying $75 million a year in taxes, more than double that amount in higher-than-average wages, and six times that amount for local goods and services. United States tourists had been spending between $50 million and $75 million a year in Cuba.

Some of the expropriated properties—sugar plantations, mines, utilities, industrial plants—continued in operation, of course, but economists estimated that Cuba's total national income, even after allowing for the limited Communist trade which developed, was reduced by half. This meant that the average per capita annual income, in round figures, dropped from $380 to $190.

Communist promises to fill the economic gap were only scantily kept. The Soviet Union, Poland, and other countries took some of Cuba's sugar, but only a small part of this was paid for in negotiable currency, and then only at the world price, not the premium price we had paid. Much of the Communist payment was in tanks, guns, ammunition, and other expensive hardware.

The upward surge in industrialization—a trend that could have made Cuba less dependent on her sugar and tobacco—came to a halt. Price fluctuations, persistent target of anti-yankeeism, continued.

To divert the attention of peasants and other low-income people from the worsening financial situation, Castro increased the pitch and frequency of his anti-United States propaganda. In frenzied shrieks, he warned of an impending invasion of Cuba and organized a Cuban militia of gun-toting men and women to guard the beaches. The jargon of his tirades sounded more and more familiar: "imperialistic," "colonial," "robber barons," "fat capitalists." Meanwhile, he proceeded with a program of nationalization of properties owned by the Cuban rich. He took over about $1.5 billion of agricultural, bank, insurance, and other Cuban-owned properties.

As unemployment mounted, Castro increased his militia and inducted the idle workers into his armed forces, paying them only enough for subsistence.

It is fair to say, I think, that the economic phase of the Castro revolution met with a mixed reaction in the United States. Most people were angry. Owners of property in Cuba were incensed, and looked to the State Department to do what it could to retrieve their losses. Some, however—recognizing that the great disparities in human welfare which had long existed in Cuba could not continue, any more than they could in other Latin-American countries—piously hoped that Castro's excesses would in time diminish in favor of more moderate legal action, as they had in the Mexican revolution many years before. Those who held this hope realized that United States-owned companies paid the highest wages in Cuba, contributed generously to the national budget, and often provided schools, hospitals, and other services; but they pointed out that an inequitable distribution of the rewards of production threatened stability, regardless of the philosophy of the men in power.

All groups in the United States, however, pointed out (and felt deeply about it) that corrective action did not require the brutal and amoral methods employed by Castro. Large land holdings could have been broken up by several methods—by progressive taxation, by long-term loans to farmers, or even by legal expropriation with just compensation. Corporation taxes applicable to manufacturing, mining, hotel and related enterprises, could have financed promised social reforms, including schools, low-cost housing, and health services. Legal methods could even have retained the support of entrepreneurs who could have helped expand industry, improve and diversify agriculture, and contribute to higher living standards of the people.

Castro, the lawyer, was familiar with the legal methods of expropriation, nationalization, land distribution, and general social reform. He knew of the Mexican experience in social change for he had lived there during his exile. President Cárdenas had expropriated foreign-owned oil properties and payment was eventually determined by negotiation. Vast land holdings, partly American- and partly Mexican-owned, had gradually been taken over by the government with just compensation, and the land distributed to the farmers. (The process of land reform is still under way in Mexico. On several trips to that country, I visited with American landowners at our embassy. They had come in not to protest the expropriation of their ranches, but only to ask that they be given more than the sixty days allowed them by the government to move from their land.)

The rapid evolution from Castro's promise to protect foreign investments, to a program of expropriation with compensation in bonds, and finally to outright banditry, coincided with the rise in influence of Guevara and brother Raul. It was when the Communist philosophy completely captivated Fidel that morality was discarded. In a five-hour monologue over Radio Havana in December 1961, he declared: "I always believed Marxism was the correct doctrine. I am Marxist-Leninist and I will be Marxist-Leninist until I die." Even those who had deluded themselves into believing that Castro was a fanatical—but pure—revolutionary were now forced to face the truth, for there was nothing equivocal about Castro's mentors. "Morality," said Lenin, "is that which serves to create a new Communist society." And he also said that "a Communist must be prepared to make every sacrifice and, if necessary, even resort to all sorts of schemes and stratagems, illegitimate methods, and conceal the truth." When Castro later shipped two thousand Cuban youngsters (including his own son) off to the Soviet Union to be educated, Cuban mothers reacted to him as though he were another Herod, and hid their children. Lenin had said, "Revolution is impossible as long as the family exists." The children who remained in Cuba's schools were well taught by Castro's Communists, and fourth-graders learned to chant a little jingle:

"I swear to you, Uncle Sam,
    that one day in Algiers or Siam
    We will bury close together
    the dollar and the Ku Klux Klan."

Gabriel Almond, after studying many case histories of ex-Communists, stated that "for a fully committed Communist, lying, misrepresentation, and brutal actions, if done in the service of the Party, are the fulfillment of ethical obligations, mere incidents on the road to salvation." And Lenin had written that "the will of a class is at times best realized by a dictator."

Thousands of Cubans fled from Castro's totalitarian rule, just as thousands before them had fled from Batista's. They came in great numbers to the United States and many migrated to Central America. Unofficial estimates put the number of fleeing Cubans at two hundred thousand— many of them middle-class, but also a significant number of professionals, which left a serious gap in Cuba. A third of the physicians have fled, as have half of the agricultural engineers, more than half of the certified public accountants, nearly half of the electrical and civil engineers, and a sixth of the pharmacists. The United States supplied the refugees with food and clothing and made efforts to get them jobs. They organized into factions to nurse their hate and plan for revenge. Several groups talked of invading Cuba to overthrow Castro, but they were so badly divided among themselves that this for a time seemed unlikely.

In the summer of 1960, however, the idea of an invasion began to take root among many of the refugees. By this time, my role in the government was approaching an end. My knowledge of the subsequent invasion is therefore second-hand, gathered from discussions with career officers in the State Department, watching and reading, and from visits in Florida with a few Cuban educators.

I do know that President Eisenhower did not have any plan to sponsor an invasion of Cuba. He recognized that the day might come when an invasion by Cuban refugees would be irrepressible so far as they were concerned. So he approved of the Central Intelligence Agency's organizing the Cuban disparate groups of refugees in the United States, giving them clothing, and arranging for their military training. There was no secret about this. Stories of these developments were carried in our press, particularly in Florida.

As the months passed, it became clear that a decision to invade Cuba, if such became necessary, would be taken after President Eisenhower left office. No sooner was President Kennedy in office than the possibility of an invasion increased. Refugees, United States officials, and an increasing number of Latin-American leaders became disturbed by a report that Castro was to receive large shipments of Soviet jet fighters early in 1961. The success of any refugee attack would be jeopardized by the jets. Furthermore, Castro had been crushing resistance in Cuba with awesome effectiveness, and internal resistance was essential to any attempt to overthrow the dictator.

In the face of this threat, all refugee groups in the United States put aside their differences and united under Dr. José Miro Cardona. Richard M. Bissell, Jr., a CIA Deputy Director, became responsible for the invasion operation. He had organized and run the U-2 operation.

An invasion plan began to take shape. It called for an amphibious landing of Cuban refugee troops on the southern coast of the island near the town of Trinidad. The exile force had built a shabby air force of obsolete B-26s, which were no match for Castro's air force. To succeed, the invasion needed air cover and the destruction of Castro's planes. The exile air force, it was decided, would make several preliminary bombing runs to destroy Castro's planes on the ground. The odds for success were good. If, for any reason, Castro's planes got into the air during the invasion to harass the exile B-26s, a few tactical jets from a United States carrier lying close by could put them out of action. The Joint Chiefs of Staff gave the plan a good chance of succeeding. According to reliable reports, never disputed, President Kennedy told CIA to go ahead. He warned, however, that he might call off the plan at any time before the point of no return—which was set at one day before the invasion. D-day became April 17; the point of no return was noon, Sunday, April 16.

The Cuban invasion illustrates dramatically the natural conflict between the military and political phases of foreign policy. When President Kennedy ordered the invasion plan ahead, it was militarily sound. When he reserved the right to call it off, he was indicating an uncertainty that was wholly political.

Early in April, President Kennedy reviewed the invasion plan with political and military advisers and received the first major denunciation of the whole idea. Presumably, J. William Fulbright, Chairman of the Senate Foreign Relations Committee, felt the venture was wrong and ought to be aborted. His counsel was not taken, but it may have been influential in the emasculation of the plan which followed.

With political considerations weighing heavily upon him, President Kennedy made a decision which virtually doomed the invasion: There would be no air support from United States planes at any time and the invasion plan could include only two preliminary bombing runs against Castro's planes by the exiles' air force, one on April 15 and one on the morning of the invasion. Later, the President deferred to the State Department and changed the landing area from the populated town of Trinidad to the deserted Bay of Pigs—a move no doubt designed to shield as much as possible our hand in the plot.

By April 10, the Cuban brigade was being assembled and equipped for action. On April 12, from a point hundreds of miles from Cuba, the convoy was en route. On Saturday, April 15, the exiles' B-26s hit Castro airfields and destroyed a part of his air power.

For three months, Castro had been spreading invasion hysterics on the island. Armed militiamen and women bristled around Cuba and stared out to sea. In the United Nations, Cuban Foreign Minister Roa charged repeatedly that the United States planned armed intervention in Cuba. Ambassador Adlai Stevenson disputed this. And even on the morning of the invasion, Secretary of State Dean Rusk denied any United States invasion of Cuba. (Technically, of course, he was correct.)

Sunday evening, after the first successful attack by the refugees' rickety B-26s, Bissell received an urgent message from the President. The second strike at the Castro airfields was to be canceled. *This was the final blow.*

The exile B-26s that were to provide air cover for the landing would have flown nearly five hundred miles to get to Cuba and they would have fuel enough for less than an hour of cover over the beaches. Bissell consulted with another CIA Deputy Director, General Charles P. Cabell, who made a new proposal to the State Department an hour or so before the scheduled landing. He asked that the United States carrier U.S.S. *Boxer* supply air cover if it became essential. The request was denied.

What happened at the Bay of Pigs is tragic and humiliating history. The Cuban refugees waded ashore—right into Castro's heavier firepower. Castro's remaining airplanes sank the refugees' supply ships in the Bay of Pigs. Even so, the exiles fought on and established a small beachhead.

On Monday, in the face of impending, dismal failure, Bissell was told that the exile B-26s could attack Castro's airfields at will, though nothing could be done before Tuesday. This was a strange, inexplicable second change of signals. Meanwhile, what remained of the convoy had assembled and salvaged as much ammunition and supplies as was possible. Chances of their getting ashore were slim with Castro's remaining planes certain to find them on Wednesday morning.

At this point, after tortuous strategy sessions, the President authorized United States air cover from the U.S.S. *Boxer* for precisely one hour over the beaches. This would allow for the landing of the supplies and for a strong strike by the exile air force. A slight chance of success existed.

The plan collapsed when the exile B-26s arrived over the beaches ahead of schedule—before the *Boxer's* jets had taken off. The confusion on time was not surprising, considering the frequency of changes in the basic plan. Castro's jets made mincemeat of the B-26s and turned on the supply ships. All that remained to do was to rescue as many exile invaders as possible from the water and leave the remainder of the invasion force to its fate.*

* This narrative account, a summary of interpretative newspaper and magazine reports and numerous conversations, contains the possibility of minor error, for the full truth about the Cuban invasion will not be known until the State Department is authorized to issue an authentic and complete statement on all aspects of the fiasco. The only comment made by a member of the Cabinet appeared in the press on January 21, 1963: Attorney General Robert F. Kennedy was quoted as maintaining that while responsibility for the failure of the invasion rested with the President—for he personally had approved the invasion plan—it was not true that the President had "reneged at the last moment" on promised air cover. The Attorney General said that United States air cover had never been promised (he did not say it had never been considered and tentatively approved), and that the second air attack by the exiles' B-26s was not canceled, but only postponed. In answer to the question as to why United States planes were not used when defeat was imminent, the Attorney General indicated that difficulties in Berlin, Laos, and Vietnam made it inexpedient to commit United States air forces to the Cuban conflict.

The United States was ridiculed throughout the world. It had been involved enough to be blamed for the invasion, but it had not been involved enough to assure success.

The Soviet Union, if it felt the need to use coercive power (as it did in Hungary), would carry through to victory, regardless of world opinion. Indeed, the only reason for employing physical force (and it is not of itself a justification) is to win completely. But the United States had paralyzed itself and doomed the Cuban freedom fighters with a kind of strategic schizophrenia. So the Soviets sneered and chuckled. Latin Americans were shocked by our failure and by "this blatant intervention in the affairs of a sister republic" and were sure that our major concern was to recover some of the United States property losses in Cuba. They also blamed our lack of restraint on our zeal to combat Communism regardless of other values that might be sacrificed. Our allies were critical, too, reminding us satirically that we had opposed the British-French-Israeli police action in Egypt. Neutrals were horrified by this power confrontation in violation of the United Nations Charter. And the people of the United States were sickened and disgusted by our half-intervention and identification with such a terrible failure.

In the long history of the United States, this was our worst-planned, most capriciously managed action—and our most humiliating defeat.

It was at this point that Latin America's view of the United States reached a new low.

Had Castro exercised reasonable restraint thereafter, he might have continued to win the support and sympathy of the underprivileged masses of Latin America. But he was in an exultant mood. He had just crushed an invasion. His position was now secure. He became exuberantly and expansively boastful. Speech followed speech. Then on May 17, in a talk to Cuban farmers—who were disgruntled by the failure of the revolution to better their lot—he said, probably in jest, that he would gladly trade the 1214 prisoners he had taken for five hundred tractors which would help develop the agricultural resources of Cuba. This almost fortuitous and seemingly insignificant statement proved to be a bombshell. It was to do far more to make his supporters in Latin America suspicious of him than had the logic of our appeals, or his suppression of freedom, or his brutal methods, or even his open support of Communism.

His reckless proposal initiated one of the most amazing and muddled incidents in the history of inter-American affairs. It precipitated long and furious debates in every country of the hemisphere, especially in the United States.

Within twenty-four hours after his offer, the press, labor leaders, university students, and governmental leaders in most of the Latin-American nations began condemning Castro for the attitude he so recklessly had revealed, namely that tractors were more important than human beings— that he would gladly trade men for machines. Here was startling proof to educated and illiterate alike that our contentions about Castro had been right. He had adopted the Communist philosophy that only goods are sacred, that people are barterable, that a Communist end justifies any means, and that, as in the Soviet Union, the reality of the divine spirit was rejected in favor of a wholly materialistic absolutism.

It is strange, perhaps, that Castro's true philosophy and intentions, which had been apparent to us for more than a year, had not previously penetrated the mind of the Latin-American masses. Then a simple but crude offer to trade men for machines tipped the scales.

Few dictators are immune to criticism. Stalin may have been. Khrushchev is not; he desperately seeks public applause, becomes enraged by every slight or criticism. Perón and Pérez Jiménez, hypnotized by their own greatness, sometimes became uncontrollable, as fury, instigated by criticism from abroad, engulfed them. So did Castro. He began to lie as all Communists do: He had not offered a trade; he was demanding indemnification for damages done his country by the invasion. But the first information that had reached the people persisted. Castro's stock in Latin America started on a sharp decline.

16

Disregard for human beings is the first qualification of a dictator.

I BECAME INVOLVED IN THIS STRANGE AFFAIR QUITE SUD-denly. On Friday evening, May 19, at about seven o'clock, I was sitting in my library at home with a few friends when my telephone rang. The White House operator, whose voice I readily recognized, said that President Kennedy was calling. I was surprised. Having run errands for four Presidents—two Republicans and two Democrats, beginning with Herbert Hoover—I might have been expected to be available to the new Administration. But I had strongly opposed the election of President Kennedy. Indeed, I had bitterly criticized him for having, in his presidential campaign, represented the United States before the world as a decadent, second-rate power when in fact it was and is the strongest military, intellectual, and moral force in all human history. I had also spoken out sharply about his misrepresentation of United States-Latin American affairs. I therefore assumed that my intermittent public service of thirty-five years was ended, at least for the next four years.

When the operator put President Kennedy on the phone, he came immediately to the point. "I want to ask you for some help," he said.

I find it nearly impossible to refuse the President of the United States any request, and I replied instantly: "I'll do whatever I can."

He explained that Fidel Castro was sending ten prisoners to the United States to negotiate for the release of more than twelve hundred of their compatriots who had been captured in the abortive Cuban invasion. The United States Government felt a moral obligation to help these men. It could not deal with Castro, however, for we had withdrawn official recog-

274

nition of his regime. The President, therefore, wanted to establish a committee of private citizens for the sole purpose of raising private funds to buy the tractors that Castro demanded in exchange for the captives. In this way, Americans could perform an act of justice. The late Mrs. Franklin D. Roosevelt and Walter Reuther had agreed to serve on the committee and now he was seeking two Republicans. He wanted George Romney, President of American Motors, and me to help. He would explain the matter to the American people the next day. And our committee would meet with the Cuban prisoners on Monday.

In the few moments while he spoke, many things flashed through my mind. Undoubtedly we were partly responsible for these men being in Castro's prisons. Even though Castro's cynical proposal was a form of international blackmail, we could not in good conscience desert the freedom fighters whom we had helped get into this mess. Further, here was a dramatic opportunity to demonstrate to the world that we truly do put human values above all other considerations. Finally, from long experience with the Latin-American people, I was sure that a humanitarian response on our part would help overcome much of the scorn they felt for us as a result of the invasion itself. (I did not know that even as I spoke the University Students Association of Central America, meeting in Panama, was justifying my confidence by drafting a resolution denouncing Castro.)

I told the President I would help.

When I returned to my guests, my mind lingered over the conversation with President Kennedy. I was somewhat apprehensive about mounting the world stage to perform in a drama that might be quite significant and was bound to be highly emotional. I felt an odd sense of foreboding. However, I reasoned that so long as the people understood that the decision to negotiate with Castro was a governmental one and that the committee's only responsibility was to raise funds, there could be no real difficulty.

At about eleven o'clock that evening, Walter Reuther called me. He expressed satisfaction that I would serve on the Tractors for Freedom Committee. We discussed details of the meeting with the prisoners scheduled for Monday in Washington, D.C. Then he read to me a telegram which he suggested we send to Castro and release to the press the next day. It simply announced to Castro that our committee had been formed to raise funds for five hundred agricultural tractors in exchange for the Cuban captives, and it said: "We make this proposal not as a response to a demand for political ransom, but out of common humanity." Reuther pointed out that the State Department had no objections to the telegram's being sent. Then he said something that was to keep me awake most of the night.

"As I understand it," he said, "this is to be a wholly private effort and we aren't to mention that the President has asked us to undertake this."

"Now wait a minute, Mr. Reuther," I replied, "private citizens cannot meddle in foreign affairs. We must have the President's authorization for this." For us to have dealt with Castro without government authorization would have been a violation of the Logan Act.

"We have no worry on that score," Reuther answered. "I talked this over with Richard Goodwin, who is Special Assistant to the President, and everything is all right. In fact, the State Department is going to help us in every way it can. We've even been assured that we will get tax-exempt status." This would allow donors to deduct their gifts from their incomes in computing taxes.

But I was not satisfied. Early Saturday morning before the President reached his office, I called his press secretary, Pierre Salinger.

"I want to obtain additional information about the responsibility of the Tractors for Freedom Committee and obtain assurance that we will not be in violation of the Logan Act," I said. "I have called you because I do not wish to bother the President."

Mr. Salinger had not heard about the President's plan but said the President would soon be in his office and would call in a few minutes. The call came for Goodwin. He assured me that the President's statement would make clear that the work of our private committee was in further-ance of official foreign policy and would not, therefore, violate the Logan Act.

"May I say publicly that the committee's work is sanctioned by the government?" I asked.

"Of course," he answered.

I did just that in a statement to the press that morning. The afternoon papers carried my statement, announcing that I had been requested to join a committee to raise money to buy the freedom of Cuban captives. The telegram we had sent to Castro was quoted, as was my comment that our work was sanctioned by the government. There was no mention of a statement by President Kennedy.

I kept an ear tuned to the news for the rest of the evening, hoping to hear the President's explanation. It did not come. And I found small con-solation in a comment by Joseph Reap, press officer for the State Depart-ment, which said: "The government will give most sympathetic consider-ation to the expeditious issuance of the appropriate licenses to export bulldozers if the group is able to work out an exchange agreement."

Because Washington had lapsed into its typical weekend trance, the only other comment I heard from the capital came from Florida's Democratic Senator George A. Smathers, who said to reporters that he would contribute to a fund drive. He added: "It is a queer twist of history that the world now is watching the trial of another man who proposed the trade of human lives for machines. The cold offer of one million Jews in return for ten thousand trucks which Adolf Eichmann made sixteen years ago has been repeated on a smaller scale by Fidel Castro."

Sunday, May 21, as I remember it, was a day of anticipation and phone calls. I talked with Mr. Reuther and Mrs. Roosevelt to arrange our meeting in the Statler Hilton in Washington for the next morning. (When Romney declined, the President requested Joe Dodge, former director of the Bureau of the Budget in the Eisenhower Administration, and a Detroit banker, to become the fourth member of our committee, but he would not be available until later in the week.) We also drafted another telegram to Castro, stating that we were prepared to meet with the ten prisoners, now in Miami, and negotiate with them for the proffered exchange—unless Castro advised us to the contrary. A smattering of newspaper editorials and phone calls from friends, generally supporting our fledgling effort, failed to still the nagging doubt that had begun after my Friday night talk with the President. And Sunday's news carried no word from Kennedy.

At eleven o'clock the next morning our committee met for the first time. Mrs. Roosevelt was named honorary chairman, Reuther and I, co-chairman, and Dodge, treasurer. Mr. Kennedy's assistant and personal representative in this matter, Richard Goodwin, was also present and briefed us on the government's involvement. He assured us of every cooperation: The Secretary of the Treasury would arrange for tax exemption on gifts; the government had arranged transportation for the prisoners; we could be assured that our fund-raising efforts had the full approval of the government; the Logan Act was not at issue.

We made several phone calls—to initiate our legal incorporation, to obtain formal tax exemption, and to obtain licenses to export the tractors to Cuba. We then agreed that our committee should be greatly expanded for the fund-raising effort; so we sent telegrams to fifty prominent citizens of both parties inviting their participation.

We had sandwiches sent up to the suite and worked through the lunch hour until the ten prisoners arrived at one o'clock. They were clean-cut young men, neatly dressed in new United States Army khakis. Their spokesman, Ulises Carbo, was a graduate of a college in Connecticut and spoke precise and fluent English. Mr. Carbo repeated Castro's offer to trade the 1214 prisoners for 500 "bulldozers." This led to much discussion about the type of equipment Castro was demanding. His original offer had used the word "bulldozers," but it had been made to farmers in a context that could only mean he wanted agricultural tractors. The prisoners repeated that he wanted bulldozers, but they could not say for certain just what Castro would accept. They pointed out that he had been irritated by the use of the words "trade" and "exchange." He insisted that he was demanding indemnification. The whole affair began to take on ominous overtones.

We gave the prisoners a letter stating that we would undertake to raise the funds for five hundred agricultural tractors for Cuba on the condition that we receive a list of the prisoners for verification. We also decided to send a committee of agricultural experts to Havana to work out the details on the type of tractors to be traded. We repeated this in a cable to Castro.

Meanwhile Fidel had been muddying the waters with demands over the Havana radio. He now offered to exchange the prisoners for twelve hundred "political prisoners" in the jails of various countries, rather than for tractors. He also threatened to call off the negotiations and execute the captives if the United States continued to refer to the deal as an "exchange." He said the tractors were an "indemnity." He specified, also, that the "political prisoners" he wanted must include Pedro Albizu Campos and Francisco ("The Hook") Molina. The former was serving a sentence for an armed attack at the Blair House during the Truman administration, and the latter was convicted of fatally shooting a Venezuelan girl in a New York restaurant during a fight between pro-Castro and anti-Castro Cubans in the fall of 1960. The Cuban Premier said he would drop all claims to indemnification if we exchanged prisoner for prisoner.

Perhaps more perplexing was Castro's demand, by radio, for D-8-type super tractors built by the Caterpillar Tractor Company or a similar type built by International Harvester and other companies. These heavy construction tractors cost up to forty thousand dollars each and are of little use to farmers.

In a story in the New York *Times* by John W. Finney the next morning —reporting on our meeting and the press conference held immediately afterwards—I read several things which shook me deeply. The story said: "Mr. Reuther emphasized repeatedly that the committee effort was being undertaken on a 'non-governmental, voluntary basis' to gain the release of the freedom fighters. . . . Although the Administration was carefully refraining from seeming to participate in the negotiations, it obviously had 'sanctioned' the committee's efforts, as Dr. Eisenhower put it. . . . Mr. Reuther repeatedly avoided giving a direct answer when asked whether he had been in consultation with President Kennedy about sending the tractors. He would only say that the committee had had discussions with Administration officials, particularly the State Department, about the legal problems and had received, in effect, a 'green light.'"

I was beginning to be angry. President Kennedy had not explained our position as mere fund-raisers in support of a governmental policy as he had led me to believe he would.

Then the first rumblings of criticism that would soon engulf the Tractors for Freedom Committee were heard on Capitol Hill: Senator Barry Goldwater and Indiana's Senator Homer Capehart denounced our effort as giving in to "blackmail." It seemed crucial to me that the President speak out at once.

Before he did, on Tuesday, May 23, the lid blew off.

Congress was furious and demanded that Secretary of State Dean Rusk say whether the Administration approved of our efforts to trade tractors for prisoners. Members of the President's own party were foremost among the critics. From his influential position as chairman of the Senate Foreign Relations Committee, J. William Fulbright said he did not think the government should "lend itself to that kind of a blackmail operation." Wayne Morse, chairman of the Senate Foreign Relations Sub-Committee on Latin America, declared that "it is a dangerous thing to countenance" voluntary committees whose operations are bound to have "repercussions on our foreign policy." Congress and the public saw us strictly as four private citizens—do-gooders, no doubt—who had decided to take important foreign policy matters into our own hands. There were cries that the Logan Act be invoked. Others charged that the tractors might eventually be used to kill American citizens, as scrap iron to Japan had been used in building up the Japanese war machine in 1941.

President Kennedy remained silent, despite hints in the newspapers that he was involved. Letters, telegrams, and phone calls flooded my office in such volume that I had to prepare a form letter to reply. I held a press conference in Shriver Hall on the Johns Hopkins campus and expressed my surprise and disappointment at the wave of violent criticism. I feared that it would impede the committee's effort to raise funds. I predicted that reactions in Latin America would contrast sharply with the criticism here at home. Despite the strong temptation, I could not bring myself to state flatly that President Kennedy had requested my participation in this undertaking. This was something he must do himself and even my great discomfort could not justify, in my mind, my revealing his role. I did say time and again that our every act was "sanctioned by the federal government."

I knew from long experience, of course, that the President of the United States is subject to constant pressures about which most of us know nothing. I realized it was unfair to judge him without knowing exactly what motivated him. I had been told that he would make clear to the public the government's role in our effort. Not only had he remained silent; he had apparently not bothered even to call in congressional leaders from both parties to brief them on the plan—an action which might have done much to forestall criticisms in Congress.

My chagrin solidified into a sudden frustration. I was considering more than my own position and that of the university which I represented; I was thinking of the adverse effect that opposition in the United States would have on the committee's effort to raise money and on the attitudes of Latin Americans who had begun to admire our unselfish and humanitarian response.

At this point, I considered resigning from the committee. Only the dreadful thought that my resignation might contribute to—or seem to contribute to—the failure of our effort stopped me. I did not want on my conscience the fate of those 1214 Cuban prisoners who perhaps faced death due to our fumbling management of the invasion.

On Wednesday morning, Tad Szulc, writing in the New York *Times*, began a story this way: "President Kennedy was reliably reported tonight [Tuesday, May 23] to have personally asked three [four] prominent private citizens last week to organize the tractors-for-prisoners exchange with Premier Fidel Castro of Cuba." At last, I thought. Then, later in the story: "However, White House officials disclaimed any knowledge of such a Presidential request. They insisted the Administration was in no way involved in the negotiation between Cuba and the Tractors for Freedom committee for the release of more than 1,200 rebels captured in last month's unsuccessful invasion."

Throughout the day, criticism from Congress and the public continued to mount. Senator Capehart's anger took the form of a proposed resolution that the Senate oppose the committee's effort. House Speaker Sam Rayburn said that the government "is out of it and is going to stay out of it." Senator Thomas J. Dodd, Democrat of Connecticut, accused the Tractors for Freedom Committee of "irresponsible meddling in foreign affairs." Newspaper editorials generally deplored the idea of dealing with Castro in this "inhuman barter."

The afternoon papers carried a statement by President Kennedy. I turned to it eagerly. Then my heart fell. It was not the one I had been waiting for. He called upon Americans to contribute funds and said, speaking of the prisoners, "If they were our brothers in a totalitarian prison, every American would want to help." He also said, "The United States government has not been and cannot be a party to these negotiations . . ." and the government is "putting forward neither obstacles nor assistance to this wholly private effort . . ."

Now I had to face the awful truth. Though the President had personally asked me to help, and though I had understood this fact would be proclaimed to the public—our task being only to raise funds—I now realized, in chilling clarity, that the President intended to maintain the fiction that all aspects of the case, from negotiation to critical decision, from raising funds to actually freeing the prisoners, were private. What, then, about the Logan Act? Was the government's posture assumed because of the unpopular reaction to the trade? Or was the intention from the first to keep the government aloof? Could I possibly have misconstrued the President's conversation with me, and Goodwin's repeated assurance that our activity was fully sanctioned by the government?

The President's press statement poured fuel on the flames. Senator Goldwater described the President's remarks as "lending the prestige of the government to this surrender to blackmail." And he added: "We shall be lucky if he [Castro] doesn't wind up demanding 500 hydrogen bombs rather than 500 tractors." Senator Everett McKinley Dirksen, Senate Minority Leader, said that prisoners in Red China should be freed before dealing with Castro. Senator Bourke B. Hickenlooper of Iowa supposedly went to Kennedy to urge him not to endorse the committee.

Then the assurance we had received of tax exemption turned out to be hollow. In the face of increasing congressional anger, Mortimer M. Caplin, Commissioner of the Bureau of Internal Revenue, indicated that he had issued no ruling, would probably consult Congress before reaching a decision. And Senator Fulbright added "It seems strange that this qualifies as a tax exemption." Speaking for a very small minority, Senator Jacob K. Javits, a New York Republican, defended the Tractors for Freedom Committee for calling Castro's bluff.

I wondered what the Cuban emissaries thought of this sound and fury as, on May 27, they left for Miami in preparation for their return to Cuba and prison.

Despite the heavy criticism, Americans were sending gifts to post-office box "Tractors for Freedom" in Detroit. Several thousand letters, some of them no doubt critical, had piled up. Walter Reuther issued a statement thanking donors for their generous support. We had not yet actually launched a fund drive, for we still awaited word from Castro. We had no funds and no staff. The letters lay unopened in the "Tractors for Freedom" box of the Detroit post office.

The New York *Herald Tribune* on Thursday, May 25, revealed in a story based on a prepared statement by Assistant Press Secretary Andrew T. Hatcher at the White House, that "President Kennedy called Mrs. Roosevelt initially after being informed that she was forming a fund-raising committee. The President then called Mr. Reuther . . . and when it 'became evident that this would be a bi-partisan committee, the President was requested to call Milton Eisenhower.' "

Exactly a week had passed since President Kennedy had called me. It seemed like a year. I had been bombarded with viciously critical letters and phone calls. An old schoolmate from Abilene telegraphed: "Dear Milt stop why not capitulate and give the entire United States to Castro stop I am humiliated and shocked stop are you trying to become the most unpopular man in the midwest stop you have almost succeeded stop." I was cheered by the "almost."

A letter from Joe Dodge on Friday warned of a new explosive element in public thinking. He was receiving charges (as others were) that our efforts would help build up Castro's military machine. Bulldozers and tractors could be used to build missile sites, fortifications, airports. He suggested also that Russia or Red China, both of whom were suffering agricultural difficulties and could use tractors, might end up getting the tractors we sent to Cuba.

This was the only aspect of the whole fiasco that did not worry me, and I telephoned Joe Dodge to tell him so. I had consulted a high military authority on this very point. Cuba had 22,500 wheel tractors and 3000 caterpillar tractors in use on its farms. If we shipped 500—say 450 wheel tractors and 50 of the caterpillar variety—we would be adding only 2 per cent to Cuba's supply. I was assured that this would have no military significance whatsoever.

Although Congress continued protesting (Democratic anger was somewhat muffled by the President's endorsement, except for that of a few, like Virginia's Senator Harry F. Byrd, Chairman of the Senate Finance Committee, who spoke against tax exemption), our committee was beginning to learn unofficially of the reaction in Latin America that was now coming in—and it was better than I had dared to hope. In Brazil and Bolivia, public demonstrations were staged in support of our effort. Fund-raising groups were springing up throughout Latin America. In Uruguay, eight mass circulation papers started a fund to buy tractors. Fifty-three Argentine deputies of President Frondizi's party condemned Castro's cynical offer.

Editorial opinion was violently anti-Castro; it likened him aptly to Hitler. In Honduras, a former Communist and Castro supporter formed a committee to raise funds for tractors.

But the Latin-American reaction was nearly lost in domestic frothing. A statement by a group of Republican party leaders called the exchange "another loss in prestige, another blow." Americans seemed to agree. The mail to senators and representatives was at least four to one against us. According to the *Herald Tribune*, letters to newspapers around the country were critical. Governor Paul Fannin of Arizona expressed the hope that the people of Arizona would "not contribute a dime." A New Jersey citizen wrote Representative Peter Frelinghuysen, Jr., "When Nikita remarked that he would bury us, I didn't think that we would have to supply the equipment." The Indianapolis *Star* editorialized: "If the United States wants these men back let us simply go and take them."

Former Vice President Nixon joined the fray with a statement urging the President to withdraw his approval of the committee's efforts. Speaking to a group in Oklahoma on Saturday evening, he said: "Human lives are not something to be bartered," and added that the whole deal was morally wrong, helpful to Cuba, a violation of our embargo against Cuba, and a bad precedent for other dictators. Evidently hoping to spare my feelings a bit—we had been close friends for years—he added that his criticism was directed at the President, not at the committee.

On this dismal note, ten Cuban prisoners, honor-bound to return to Havana after a week, left Florida to join their imprisoned fellow freedom fighters.

By May 30, Latin-American reaction had been officially assessed by the government and found favorable. Edward R. Murrow called a special news conference to report the findings of the United States Information Agency. "A groundswell of criticism against Fidel Castro's offer to barter prisoners for tractors is rising throughout Latin America," he intoned in his familiar way. "Virtually the only overseas comment favorable to Dr. Castro's offer has come from Cuba itself and from the Communist-bloc countries."

Disgust and disapproval with Castro's ransom demand was evident in nearly every one of the Latin-American republics. *La Prensa* in Argentina said: "In Cuba there are no gas chambers in use; but they have been replaced with the execution wall." Bolivia's *Presencia* called the offer "another move in Castro's tragic circus." A newspaper in São Paulo, Brazil, reported so many calls from readers that it was contributing a tractor to the fund. Other Brazilian newspapers likened Castro to Hitler. In Bogotá, one newspaper said: "There is no doubt that the American people will give all they can to show the world that in this continent the spirit of liberty and Christianism stands generously with solidarity." *Diairio de Costa Rica* in San José said Castro "is possessed by devils, a Marxist, an atheist, and inhuman." Chilean women organized to raise money for tractors. *El Telegrafo* in Guayaquil, Ecuador, said, "Even though this is filthy blackmail, I believe the simoids should be given the machines they want because it might be tomorrow that they would want to trade Roa for a still." A national committee called the "Colon for Liberty" was formed in El Salvador to collect one colon (forty cents) from each citizen to buy tractors. An organization of Mexican farmers proposed that Mexico send Cuba, in exchange for prisoners, some seventy-five Russian and Czech tractors, sold to Mexico years before, which proved unusable. These are only samples of the wave of comments which Murrow found were sweeping the hemisphere. The response made some Americans pause—even wonder if perhaps they were witnessing a rare event: an out-and-out propaganda victory for the United States.

Hubert H. Humphrey of Minnesota led the President's counterattack in Congress. He said on the floor of the Senate: "One reckless statement by the Cuban dictator gave us the opportunity to dramatize and highlight the basic difference between a free society and a dictatorship." He scored Nixon, claiming, "He is morally wrong. . . . He flies squarely in the face of the whole Judaic-Christian heritage." And he advocated "that the United States government, as its expression of support for the committee, take the leadership in the Organization of American States to condemn the mass arrests, imprisonments, and executions in Cuba, and to insist that the Cuban regime release all of its political prisoners."

All were not mollified, however.

Barry Goldwater, sharpening his criticism of the President, piqued Mrs. Roosevelt to reply that the committee to raise funds for tractors had been functioning before Mr. Kennedy got involved. (If this were true, it was surely news to me, as I have related.)

Memorial Day was a busy one. The committee met in the Hotel Roosevelt in New York to complete legal incorporation. We agreed on several important points: First, that a list of additional committee members would not be released until approved by each member (I felt strongly that this should be a bipartisan group, and many conservatives had chosen not to become involved); second, that, at my insistence, a formal appeal for funds would not be launched until Castro agreed to our proposal of farm tractors for prisoners; third, that the committee meet with a group of agricultural experts to prepare a list of precise specifications of the tractors we would provide; fourth, that no large bulldozers of war-making potential be sent to Cuba—only farm tractors.

And then, to my subsequent sorrow, we appointed as executive secretary of our committee John J. Hooker, Jr., a young Nashville attorney who had worked in the Kennedy campaign, was a friend of Robert Kennedy's and Richard Goodwin's, and had come east to offer his assistance. Mr. Hooker explained that the Attorney General had asked him to help the committee. Bobby Kennedy, he said, wanted us to make Hooker our executive secretary. As his first assignment, Mr. Hooker was to talk with Edward R. Murrow about getting help to promote our fund-raising efforts, when and if they were launched, and to contact leading citizens who might be willing to become members of our committee.

The next day, June 1, the committee received a cable from the ten prisoners in Havana, stating that they had delivered our message to Castro. They urged that we send a delegation to Havana to negotiate.

Mr. Reuther and Mr. Dodge met with five agricultural experts in Detroit on Friday and prepared a tentative list of the equipment we would be willing to exchange for prisoners. The list was sent to Castro in a cable which also pointed out that since we had had no official word from him since our inception, we would expect to hear from him by noon on June 7.

I wrote Joe Dodge and reaffirmed my belief (which he shared) that we should send Castro only *agricultural* tractors—that if Castro demanded larger bulldozers or failed to meet our June 7 deadline, our committee should disband. Walter Reuther had indicated to Dodge that several banks might be willing to advance a million dollars so that we might start buying tractors. But Dodge and I were opposed to accepting credit at this point. By now there were more than fifty thousand letters in the post-office box at Detroit, but of course we had no way of knowing how much money they contained. (I did know that one friend of mine, a former United States Ambassador, had mailed a check for twenty-five thousand dollars; a Johns Hopkins trustee had sent five thousand dollars.)

Joe Dodge and I again agreed that we would not permit an announcement of any additions to our committee until we had a politically well-balanced list. At that point, only twenty-five persons had accepted our invitations, and most of these were "liberals." Our view was that only if the effort were truly a non-political, non-partisan one did we have a chance of raising the essential funds.

Over the weekend, Joe Dodge and I were in constant communication. What course all of this would take we could not foresee. Our efforts, so patriotically (perhaps naïvely) undertaken at the request of the President, had resulted in a gigantic propaganda war that could seriously effect United States prestige in Latin America and throughout the world. We patently could not afford another fiasco like the invasion. Although the Latin-American response to our work was gratifying and European press comments were generally favorable, too, the harsh criticism at home was now being reported worldwide, especially in Latin America. We feared that the inconstant admiration of the Latin-Americans might wane.

And there were practical problems. What if Castro accepted our offer and an angry American public refused to provide the $3 million or so we needed to buy the tractors? (We had no government funds; I, as did the other members apparently, paid personally for travel, phone calls, and so on.) What if Castro prolonged the affair until an opening gave him the propaganda advantage?

Of strictly personal concern to me was the possible effect of my reluctant participation on the university which I represented. This had been on my mind for some time. I felt that Johns Hopkins might be hurt by my involvement in this emotional circus. The reason was obvious: A great private university, dedicated to the highest standards of quality, must keep flowing into it great numbers of annual donations from alumni, industries, foundations, financial institutions, and friends. Most such persons and corporations were evidently violently opposed to what the committee was trying to do.

I therefore met with the Executive Committee of the Board of Trustees of the university, reviewed what had happened, and suggested that it might be better for Johns Hopkins if I resigned the presidency. The Trustees unanimously insisted that I remain. This warm vote of confidence was the one high point in the entire experience.

On Tuesday, June 6, the committee's executive secretary, John J. Hooker, Jr., earned his first headline by releasing the names of additional committee members to the press *without* consulting the committee. I was incensed. We had specifically ordered that the list be withheld until approved by each of us. Hooker's list was anything but non-partisan. I called Reuther, since the release came from his office in Detroit, and learned that he was in New York, that the release had been sent by Hooker to his office by teletype. I then discovered from Washington newsmen that Hooker had called them to his Mayflower Hotel room and briefed them on what he planned to do.

Shortly after midnight, still seething over Hooker's deliberate insubordination, I received a copy of a cable from Castro. His response was sheer propaganda and hedged on details. He repeated his demands for indemnification. Then he stated that he could not negotiate by cable and suggested that either Mrs. Roosevelt or I meet with him in Havana.

At this point, I sent President Kennedy the bitterest letter I have ever written. I informed him that I could serve as a member of the Tractors for Freedom Committee only so long as I felt the committee could help the country. I told him of how his representative, Hooker, had arrogantly disobeyed the committee's directive. Then, turning to more important matters, I wrote: "The public should have been told from the first, and should even now be told that the foreign policy decision was governmental —only fund-raising being private. But now the response from Castro, in his cable of today, indicates that he will not negotiate with respect to tractors. He insists that we accept the principle of indemnification for damage done in Cuba, and that he will accept only what the ten prisoners with whom you asked us to meet told us he wanted, namely, heavy D-8-type bulldozers which are war materiel, possibly for trade with the Communist bloc. He has attempted, by flamboyant countercharges to broaden the matter to include negotiation for the exchange of prisoners for prisoners; those he mentions in the United States are imprisoned Communists or criminals. On all these points, *our private committee is not a competent agency*. These demands, if recognized at all, call for serious attention by appropriate government officials and by them alone. Our committee cannot properly carry on an exchange of cablegrams with Castro on such matters without stepping beyond the grounds of the single fund-raising task you asked us to assume."

The letter continued: "On this fundamental point, Mr. Reuther and I are in disagreement. He believes we should continue our cablegram discussions with Castro. . . . My belief is that if we did so we would be moving into the area of governmental responsibility."

I urged the President to make clear to the public that our committee was asked by the federal government only to raise funds for tractors, and publicly to relieve us of our assignment unless Castro limited his negotiation to the question of trading agricultural tractors for prisoners.

Knowing how mail is handled in the White House, I addressed the letter to the President but by covering envelope sent it to the President's assistant, Richard Goodwin, and asked him either to give it to President Kennedy or to brief him on it, but to make sure that my strong feelings were made known. I was never told which alternative he chose. By telephone Goodwin frigidly informed me that he had met my wishes.

Then I wired Walter Reuther that "since our committee was established at the request of the President for only one purpose, namely to raise private funds to finance purchase of agricultural tractors, I feel strongly that we cannot assume obligations of carrying on negotiations on any other matter or engage in a propaganda duel by cable with Castro. Only if I am asked directly by the President to assume an additional function would I consider broadening the present responsibility."

I spent much of June 7 on the telephone discussing Castro's cable with the committee and the press. By the late afternoon the committee had not agreed on a reply.

The evening papers carried Castro's suggestion that Mrs. Roosevelt or I go to Havana. I received a call from the mother of one of the prisoners. She said she and other mothers begged me to go to Cuba, and she added: "Forgive us for asking more of you. We know you have done so much for which we are thankful. We will pray for your success." This crowned my feeling of helplessness.

Dodge called me early the next morning to tell me that he had suggested to Reuther that any answer to Castro's cable be delayed sufficiently to prepare a carefully considered and coordinated reply. He felt we should not offer to send committee members or technical teams to Havana and that we should not modify our June 2 cable in any material degree. Under no consideration would we give in to demands for heavy bulldozers usable for and divertible to any non-peaceful Communist-inspired purposes. We agreed.

After talking with Dodge, Edward R. Murrow, and others, I was convinced that we should not reply to Castro without government sanction and direction. I sent a message to Reuther to this effect and suggested a meeting of our committee early the next morning in Washington.

Meanwhile, my letter to Mr. Kennedy had found its way to the desk of my friend, Secretary of State Dean Rusk. He called to thank me for writing. He agreed wholeheartedly that our committee should restrict its activities to the single narrow field of fund-raising and assured me that the State Department would guide us in our actions thereafter.

Reassured by this call from Secretary Rusk and by his personal approval of a proposed message, I agreed finally to another cable to Castro: It restated our original offer and dismissed most of Castro's reply as propaganda. We said we were prepared to ship one hundred agricultural tractors to Cuba within two weeks, provided he would then release one-fifth of the prisoners. We offered to send our agricultural experts to Havana, to arrive on June 12.

That night on the Jack Paar television show, Barry Goldwater heaped scorn on the committee and heralded a new blast of criticism from Congress and the public.

On June 9, Joe Dodge wrote to Walter Reuther: "What I feared might happen as a result of last night's cable to Castro is beginning to happen." He pointed out that many people were angry that our committee would attempt to continue negotiations after Castro's insulting reply. (The public of course did not know that our cablegram had been approved by the government.)

Disappointed that no member of our committee would come to Cuba, Premier Castro nevertheless agreed in a message, on June 10, to meet with our agricultural experts. They made clear to him in a cable the following day that they would discuss only technical matters.

Some months earlier, my daughter and I had made plans to go abroad June 15 to visit my son and his wife. As my involvement with the Tractors for Freedom Committee became more and more complex, I feared I would have to cancel these plans. But I had been living night and day for more than three weeks in a virtual nightmare and desperately needed rest.

From the moment of the public announcement (that the Tractors for Freedom Committee had been formed), my office was deluged with mail. Phones rang continually, at all hours of the day and night. Events repeatedly overtook us, and orderly planning was virtually impossible. Decisions requiring the agreement or consent of all four members of the committee had to be made one after another, and so we had to neglect other important duties to be available by telephone or to attend hastily called meetings—midday in New York, midnight at a hotel in Washington, one evening at my home. New problems arose so quickly, decisions had to be made so rapidly, that in many cases we barely had time to pen notes on the backs of envelopes of what we must do next. During this frenetic period, I ate many sandwich lunches at my desk, and got my sleep in catnaps. It was a grueling period, made no easier by the fact that we were constantly subjected to vitriolic and unrelenting criticism. My office estimated that in the first few days only one in every ten letters had a kind word to say for the committee's effort and of course none, at this point, knew that the President had asked us to undertake the task. Later on, a few more letters and calls offered support or sent contributions (which I forwarded on to the post-office box in Detroit). But it is fair to say that there was no peace for any of us that hot summer. The whole project seemed interminable, exhausting.

Overnight we had found ourselves in verbal combat with a most unscrupulous rascal, adept at dirty tricks and infighting. Castro responded to our genuine expressions of humanitarian concern with nothing but ranting lies and deceitful propaganda. This was most discouraging, for it soon became clear, at least to me, that Castro would not negotiate in good faith. And yet we could not give up. We believed from what the prisoners told us, that once we relaxed our interest in the 1214 freedom fighters they were doomed; he might "free" them and then liquidate them quietly, one by one, or, when their imprisonment and suffering had demoralized them completely, he might trade them "freedom" in return for making pro-Castro lecture trips throughout South America.

All four of us had gotten more than we had bargained for: With an impossible effort to negotiate with a ruthless dictator before us, from behind we were beset by ridicule and misunderstanding of our motives on the part of the American press and public. My frustration in this situation was almost overwhelming.

Everything considered, I decided I would adhere to my original schedule; so I gave my proxy to Joe Dodge and asked my friend and university associate, Keith Spalding, to attend all committee matters and keep me informed. On June 15, I left for two weeks, but I was no further from the strain and turmoil than the telephone—which rang in Bermuda with annoying frequency.

The day I left, our four agricultural experts returned from Havana with Castro's impossible new demands. Now these were for $28 million in cash, credits, or tractors (in contrast to our offer for $3 million worth of tractors). To me, this meant the end of the whole affair.

On Monday, June 19, Keith Spalding substituted for me at a meeting with our agricultural experts in the Statler Hilton Hotel in Washington. The experts reported that they had met alone with the prisoners and had found them in poor condition. They were sleeping twenty in a room, and some were having nervous breakdowns. (I fear too many people forgot during those hectic days that beneath all the furor were decent human beings with families, and dreams, and a great longing to be free men.) The experts told of a meeting with President Dorticos, who restated the Cuban position and discussed the cables which had been exchanged. Then they met with Cuban technicians, who confined themselves to trying to prove the need for heavy equipment. They wanted it, they said, for bringing virgin lands into production and for clearing forests for roads. Finally the committee of experts met with Castro. He was sorry that the group could not discuss broad-range political and other problems. He offered to free the prisoners and renounce damages if his "political prisoners" would be freed. He talked of compensation rather than indemnification, but would not budge from the $28 million figure.

The experts found Castro irrational at times; he repeated himself frequently and stated that he had reached his maximum position which was not for bargaining. Thereupon, after promising not to talk to newsmen, he held a three-and-a-half-hour press conference.

Later that evening Castro joined the experts at dinner—in the hotel—unannounced. (Typically, he had rounded up everyone in the lobby to provide an audience and had marched into the dining room.) The experts repeated that they were authorized only to deal with the types and sizes of agricultural tractors stipulated in the June 2 cable. The committee felt that Castro might accept these terms if we refused to compromise; they saw evidence that he was short of food, had butchered his breeding stock, and was worried about public opinion.

After the experts had concluded their report to the Tractors for Freedom Committee and excused themselves, the members wrestled with the problem of what to do.

Walter Reuther felt that a last specific offer should be made with a forty-eight-hour deadline.

Mrs. Roosevelt, after expressing her disapproval of the invasion, unhappiness about the present situation, but deep concern for the prisoners, insisted that any wire to Castro must make clear that his demands for $28 million were impossible, wholly outside his original proposal. Nor, she felt, did the committee have the authority to deal with it.

Joe Dodge felt the same concern for the prisoners and their families but was wary of sending another cable. He also repeated his fear that the bad publicity our effort had evoked might make it impossible to raise even the few million dollars needed to buy farm tractors.

Keith Spalding informed the committee that I was opposed to restating our offer to Castro. So the committee adjourned without reaching a decision.

Barry Goldwater now said that a group of citizens in the District of Columbia would seek a court order barring the export of tractors to Cuba.

I talked by radiotelephone with Keith Spalding several times in the next few days.

White House personnel favored a reply to Castro, restating our original offer, he told me. They felt that by increasing his demand to $28 million and reducing the number of prisoners he would release to 1173, Castro had made a serious blunder. They wanted a chance to demonstrate to the world that he was playing a cynical game with the lives of these men.

Reuther, Goodwin, and others felt that we should state our position so unequivocally that Castro could only reply "yes" or "no," Spalding explained. This seemed impossible to me. No matter what we said, I was convinced, Castro could answer, "I have told you that I cannot negotiate by cable. Send Mrs. Roosevelt or Dr. Eisenhower to Havana, and I will make an agreement on the spot." Faced with such a response, we would again be on the defensive, with no prospect of success. It was by now abundantly clear that the prisoners would never be exchanged for farm tractors and that Castro was merely using the affair in a hope of achieving a reversal of the propaganda loss he had initially suffered in Latin America.

Joe Dodge was by now adamantly holding out against another offer to Castro. On June 19, he received a call from, among others, Allen Dulles, Director of the Central Intelligence Agency, and was informed that a "last chance" cable would help expose Castro in a most dramatic way. But Dodge still hesitated.

In talking with committee members and government officials, Keith Spalding emphasized again and again my feeling that Castro had no intention of releasing the captives and therefore that we should bring the matter to a prompt and honorable conclusion. This much we owed to the prisoners. That night, Keith called to tell me that Dodge had reluctantly agreed to a final cable. At once I telephoned Secretary Rusk and, assured by him that the message had his approval, I consented. The cable was sent.

The "last chance" cable was unequivocal. We restated our original offer of 500 agricultural tractors for 1214 prisoners. We gave Castro a deadline of noon, June 23, to accept; if he rejected the offer, our committee would dissolve. It was "fish or cut bait."

For the next few days, we just waited. I could not enjoy even the sunshine of Bermuda.

On Friday, June 23, at 11:26 A.M. (thirty-four minutes before the deadline), Fidel Castro rejected our offer. "Your committee lies when it states that Cuba has changed its original proposal," his cable began. He covered the tired ground of indemnification, $28 million, an equal number of "political prisoners," and the "cowardly invasion" of Cuba. He termed our final offer "ridiculous." And he concluded, to our dismay, with the promise that he would "authorize the delegation of prisoners to go to the United States again and explain the facts to the American people." Here was proof that he wished to keep his foot in the door, that he was still looking for a propaganda victory.

The Tractors for Freedom Committee issued a press release which began by stating that it "deeply regrets that Dr. Fidel Castro has seen fit to renege on his offer to exchange 500 tractors for the lives of some 1200 freedom fighters." It concluded: "As a result of Dr. Castro's action the decision of the committee is to disband and return all contributions without putting them to the use for which they were so generously, genuinely, and unselfishly intended." (By this time more than seventy thousand unopened envelopes were being held in the Detroit post office. These envelopes were never opened. We did not have the funds to pay a large clerical staff to open them, account for the funds, and carefully return them to the donors. So we arranged, at the mere cost of postage, to return the letters unopened.)

The emotional, difficult experience was apparently over. My feelings were mixed. I still felt angry about what had been a needless misconception of the American people; I sorrowed for the abandoned prisoners but, at the same time, could not but sigh with relief that the counterfeit bartering was at an end. This sense of relief was a bit premature. There was an anticlimax which could easily have given Castro another chance to turn the negotiations to his own advantage.

Hurrying to keep the issue alive, Castro sent the Cuban prisoner-emissaries back to Florida the next day. They were astonished to learn on arriving that our committee had disbanded. Obviously, Castro was fighting desperately to win back the initiative. He saw a propaganda advantage in portraying the richest nation in the world haggling over the price of the prisoners' lives.

The ten Cubans, having arrived at Key West on a Costa Rican ship, were promptly taken into custody by the Immigration Service and housed in a hotel where they were permitted to see their relatives.

At this point, Sunday, June 25, young John Hooker re-entered the picture. Ignoring the fact that the Tractors for Freedom Committee had ceased its efforts, but speaking as its executive secretary, Hooker went to Key West and conferred with the prisoners. The press found this to be highly newsworthy. Apparently Hooker made the trip at the request of a government official (perhaps the Attorney General, certainly with the consent of Richard Goodwin).

After a full night of talk with the emissaries, Hooker reported that they were authorized to spend as much as a month raising the ransom for themselves and their compatriots; that they or fellow prisoners might be sent through Latin America to propagandize for Castro; that Castro might now accept the original offer, if it were made once more. The prisoners were, Hooker said, frightened and desperate men.

On Monday evening, Richard Goodwin telephoned Keith Spalding to discuss the alternatives that now seemed to be open to the government: First, the Cubans could be deported, but this was a bad alternative for it would require that they be arrested; second, the prisoners might be induced to go back promptly with a promise that a ship with one hundred tractors would anchor outside Havana Harbor within ten days to test Castro's response and, if successful, the other four hundred tractors would follow.

Goodwin felt the second alternative would be an act of good faith which would thwart Castro in his attempt to seize the propaganda initiative. But since the United States Government had no intention of dealing with the prisoners, he felt the Tractors for Freedom Committee should reform to execute the plan. This was the third time the committee was being asked to "go the last mile"—and not in mere money-raising, but in serious policy negotiation.

I do not really know what I would have done at this point if the President had personally asked me to participate in what Goodwin was suggesting. It may be that nearly three decades of dutiful responses to presidential requests would have overridden my own firm conviction that nothing more of a constructive nature could be done. But the President did not call.

On Tuesday, I received a long-distance call from Secretary Rusk. Calmly and candidly we discussed the matter. He did not protest my decision that it was in the best interest of the United States that the committee remain defunct.

Hooker, meanwhile, by talks with the prisoners and the press, had given the impression that a new approach to Castro was in prospect. On Wednesday, he was quoted by the Associated Press as saying he was hopeful there would be a decision by the next day on whether the committee would reconstitute itself to renew negotiations. He also said, according to the press, that he had been in touch with every member of the committee. Certainly he had not called me. We had not talked with one another since my denunciation of him to the President. He also must have known that I would not be a party to further discussions. The same report quoted Frank Winn, in Walter Reuther's office, who said that he knew of no contact between Reuther and Hooker, and that he knew of no plan to re-form the committee. Joe Dodge told me he had received no call.

The same day, President Kennedy—for the first time speaking in terms of decision about the affair—told a news conference that it was all up to Castro now. The United States, he said, would not change its position. But not until Friday, June 30, two days later, did Hooker accept the decision and announce that he would break the news to the waiting prisoners.

And so ended the most exasperating, frustrating, and enervating six weeks of my life. Even now I am not sure I can assess the experience objectively or accurately. Several things are obvious: Castro's inhuman proposal that men be traded for machines did more to discredit him in Latin America than anything the United States could have done; the real victims in this sordid affair were not nations but the captives themselves —men tormented by the hope of freedom and crushed by the inevitability of their fate; the incident lost its original humane focus and became a propaganda struggle which the United States desperately needed to win; the American people demonstrated again their unique generosity (despite all the criticism, a grocery store owner pledged 10 per cent of his day's receipts, a shipping company offered free transport for tractors, a tractor company offered to produce them without profit; thousands of people sent in contributions); some Americans, however, displayed a shortsightedness and a callousness, as did a good many of their leaders, though I must temper this criticism by saying that had they been told the truth from the beginning their attitudes might well have been different; finally, Castro clearly demonstrated his adherence to the Communist dictum that life is governed by a materialistic absolutism and that lies pave the road to salvation so long as they serve the Communist cause.

The Tractors for Freedom episode helped to overcome to some extent the loss in prestige the United States had suffered in the abortive invasion at the Bay of Pigs. This was not enough, however, to convince Latin Americans of our noble intentions. Too many of the masses still believe that our first concern in all relations with Castro has been to protect American property rights and to restore the social order that prevailed in Cuba before the revolution; that our second concern has been not really freedom and democracy for the Cuban people but a crushing of Castro Communism, which they view as a passing phase—one which will change later, as the Mexican revolution did, when democratic forces triumphed to serve the people. Thus, while Latin Americans have applauded President Kennedy's Alliance for Progress, they unfortunately have viewed it as a purely defensive response to a revolutionary threat in Latin America as personified by Castro; some refer to it as "Fidel's bonus." Whether we can convince them—the facts are here to see—that the Alliance is a positive, humanitarian, forthright offer on our part, conceived before Castro Communism, to promote the welfare of all the people in Latin America—including the underprivileged—remains to be seen. They should see the Alliance as a genuine but peaceful method of achieving the very social reform which Castro promised, but has not redeemed, in his revolution. It is crucial that we convince them of this.*

The young Uruguayan intellectual had said to me in 1960: "You of the United States are to blame for the rise of Castroism. . . . You seized the island from Spain and opened it to your robber barons who plundered most of its basic resources. You forced the Cubans to produce a single crop so that, in turn, they could get industrial products only from you. You allied yourself with the Cuban leaders who crushed the common people."

This view is even today widely held among students and the masses in Latin America.

The modicum of historical truth in this gross misrepresentation is just sufficient to make the entire charge effective in Communist propaganda and to mislead Latin Americans who have read history superficially or with colored lenses.

The United States had no decisive influence on internal Cuban developments from early in the sixteenth century, when settlement began, until 1898 when Cuba was freed from Spain. In that long period, sugar production became the major means of livelihood, with tobacco production a highly advertised but bad second. From the first, the Spanish overlords created great *latifundios*, as they did in other Latin-American lands, and instituted most of the political, social, and cultural institutions and mores which persisted until quite recently. Intelligent leaders in Cuba in this period sometimes warned of the dangers inherent in extreme dependence on a single primary commodity, but those who controlled the destiny of the island were impervious to all suggestions. Spanish colonial rule was characterized by tyranny, incompetence, corruption, and poverty. These were "normal"—a way of life.

While much of Cuba's sugar and tobacco were sold in the United States, and consumer and capital goods were purchased with these earnings, no reasonable person, Uruguayan or otherwise, can claim that this was a design either of the United States Government or of its people.

Spain, noting this growing trade, imposed taxes and other restrictions

---

* Late in 1962 most of the prisoners were finally released and flown to the United States. Castro's original offer to trade prisoners for tractors would have involved a cost to us of about $3 million. His later indemnity demand to us was for $28. The ultimate cost of food and medicine which were used to free the prisoners was $55.9 million, not counting shipping costs.

on the trade. This enraged the Cubans, as "taxation without representation" had angered our forefathers. They began to fight for their independence, the last colonial group in the hemisphere to do so. The cruelties of the Spanish in the Cuban war of independence, late in the nineteenth century, were forerunners of Hitler's mass executions in World War II: Scores of thousands of Cubans were starved in prison. American reaction was quick, mostly in revulsion against the excesses of the Spanish, but no doubt also because Cuba, ninety miles from Florida, seemed a natural ally if not a dependency of ours. United States participation in the conflict helped win freedom for Cuba—and for Puerto Rico and the Philippines.

For four years following the victory over Spain in 1898, the United States maintained military rule in Cuba. This seemed essential, for the former colonials had had no experience in self-government. Our military control was honorable: Local governments, the courts, and other public agencies were improved. Progress in agriculture, education, health (especially in a campaign to eliminate yellow fever), transportation, trade, and general living standards was noticeable but not notable. There was little if any serious thought given to changing inherited social customs. The Cuban people themselves did not then seek such change. Most of them wanted independence—only large landowners objecting—and they got it, with qualifications, in 1902. The limitation on independence was the Platt Amendment to our treaty with Cuba. This amendment, drafted by Secretary of War Elihu Root, approved by the United States Senate, and accepted by Cuba in its new constitution, gave the United States numerous rights, the most important of which was that of intervening in Cuban affairs if we felt the new nation's independence were threatened, or if the Cuban Government seemed to us unable to maintain internal order.

In the ensuing years of quasi-independence, Cuba suffered the indignity of numerous interventions by the United States, saw most of its own Presidents promise honesty and reform only to fatten their own pockets, lived in fear of slaughter by military and guerrilla leaders, and came to accept betrayal as an inevitable condition of government.

While the Platt Amendment did not have any direct bearing on the social structure of the nation, one can, with hindsight, reason that the United States could have induced Cuban dictators to institute programs of progressive taxation, honest tax collection, land reform, local ownership of numerous productive enterprises, mass education, and health and housing programs. Had the United States been so wise and foresighted as to have done this, it is possible (at least it is an interesting speculation) that future relations between the United States and the other American republics might have taken a different and happier course. Cuba had the same evils, the same human misery, the same coterie of privileged, the same need for widely beneficial economic development as did its sister nations in the hemisphere.

But in the early part of this century, neither Latin America nor the United States was imbued with a passion for economic democracy and egalitarianism (of the Franklin Roosevelt variety). We were still entranced with the frontier spirit, and Latin America was preoccupied with its hatred of our interventionism and with a desire to develop faster within the prevailing order.

Cuba's excessive dependence on sugar exports (one of the complaints of my Uruguayan friend) was intensified in 1903 when President Tomás Estrada Palma worked hard and successfully to obtain, by treaty, a substantial reduction in our tariff duty on Cuban sugar. At once, sugar production on the island began a spectacular advance, the expansion being financed mainly by United States private capital; large amounts of Cuban sugar lands and many sugar mills were purchased by United States citizens—perhaps as much as 70 per cent of all such lands and mills. Most assuredly this was not an effort of the United States to keep Cuba in a colonial status. Indeed, farmers in the United States complained that our tariff concession was a too-generous response by our government in an effort to be helpful in ways desired by the Cuban Government.

During the presidency of José Miguel Gómez (1909–13) it was not the United States Government which forced the Cuban President to grant vast concessions to speculators. It was the popular but inept President himself who so ravaged the Cuban treasury that he openly sought new funds (some of which he kept for himself) by granting special concessions to both Cuban and American gamblers, speculators, and playboys.

In the thirty-two years of Cuba's quasi-independence, United States private investment in Cuba increased, but in nearly every situation, from the expansion of public utilities to increases in sugar and tobacco production, from hotel construction to tourism, it was Cuban leaders that did the begging, entrepreneurs that did the responding.

President Herbert Hoover, harassed by Cuban uprisings, recognized the futility of our interventions under the Platt Amendment, but it remained for President Franklin Roosevelt, with the help of Sumner Welles, to bring about in 1934 the abrogation of the offending addition to the treaty.

Just before this was done, however, Sumner Welles made what must be regarded as a serious mistake. He went to Cuba as ambassador in

1933 when that country was in turmoil; mobs were rampant; business had ground to a halt. Welles threatened military intervention, and participated in the imposition of what was, ironically enough, probably the best regime ever organized in Cuba. It was headed by Carlos Manuel de Céspedes, an honest and able man. But the regime lasted twenty-four days (a dramatic example of the futility of intervention by a foreign power). Even many of those who helped overthrow the offensive Gerardo Machado and wanted an honest and liberal government resented what they believed to be a ruling group chosen by the Colossus of the North. It was then, as I have recounted elsewhere, that Batista, a mere sergeant, shoved aside his military superiors and seized power.

In the first ten years of his dictatorship, ruling first through hand-picked henchmen, and later in his own name, Batista brought a measure of prosperity to the island. To retain power, he used the same technique which I saw employed by Pérez Jiménez in Venezuela and Rojas in Colombia—granting military leaders every privilege, showering them with sumptuous quarters (including Persian rugs) and making them the aristocrats of the nation. But always, of course, the military leaders were kept dependent on the continued goodwill and largess of the dictator.

Some students of Cuban history have referred to Batista in commendable terms for what he did from 1934 to 1944. He deserves praise in one sense only—he was better than the Cuban people had usually experienced before. He possessed all the attributes of the arrogant and cruel dictator which later became universally evident, but his initial popularity and firm support of the military made it unnecessary for him to resort to the excesses which characterized his subsequent rule. He did not, of course, refrain in this period from profiting personally from all official and private transactions in the country. Every gambling house and lottery, every person wanting an export permit, every foreigner who purchased property in Cuba—these and hosts of others—paid tribute. When he turned the presidency over to his "elected" successor and retired from public life in 1944, ostensibly for good but probably with every intention of returning at a propitious time, he was one of the wealthy men of Latin America. Ten years before he had been a sergeant, with no resources save a big body, infectious grin, commanding personality, and shrewd mind.

For the next eight years, the Chief Executives of Cuba either fomented or tolerated the ascendancy of graft, corruption, lawlessness, and economic inequities. Cubans, nostalgically, began recalling that during the "good" Batista regime bandits had been kept under control; workingmen remembered that their wages had risen and working conditions had improved; children and parents recalled that the educational system had grown in size and quality. It no longer seemed to matter that Batista had enriched himself. There had at least been an enforced and endurable order.

In a bloodless revolution, Batista came triumphantly back to power, receiving acclaim not unlike that which greeted Castro on January 1, 1959. Now legality, which had appealed to him before (as it always did to Hitler) was scorned. A whimsical tolerance of opponents, evident in his first decade of power, was replaced by a cold refusal to permit opposition. Newspapers were closed and others opened at will; they could exist only if they supported Sergeant Batista. Political enemies, real or imagined, were executed, jailed, or banished (as in 1960 under Castro). The various schools of the university could remain open only if Batista was satisfied with faculty and student attitudes.

Within a year, the inevitable occurred: The Cuban people began to react violently against the rapacity and corruption of the government, the callous brutality of the police, and the failure of Batista to do what he had done before—grant some benefits to the masses. But not for several years would Batista flee from the scene of his triumphs and sadistic rapacities.

Throughout his two regimes, Batista courted Americans lavishly, seeking capital, always capital. He basked in the growing prosperity which foreign investment brought to the island, even as Cubans generally saw the ownership of resources become concentrated in fewer and fewer hands—both foreign and Cuban favorites of the dictator.

It must be clear, even to the Uruguayan intellectual who spoke so passionately to me, that from 1934 onward the United States had no more opportunity to bring about social change in Cuba, without again turning to disastrous interventionism, than it did to promote internal reform in the other Latin-American republics. Over a long period, we had missed two possible opportunities in this regard. After 1934, we did not get another chance. By 1957–58, when those of us who were deeply concerned about social inequalities and rumblings of revolution south of the Rio Grande began seeking a means of promoting reform without unilateral intervention, there was nothing uniquely different to be done in Cuba. The attack on the entire problem obviously had to be cooperative in nature and hemispheric in scope. Much of the initiative had to come from the Latin-American nations, no matter how hard we prodded or fretted, or stood ready with technical skills and cash to help.

The only calm statement that can be made of the Castro regime, aping as it has all that was bad in the Batista dictatorship and adding the ruthlessness and imperialism of Communism, is this: It speeded our efforts to find an acceptable path to collective action in support of political and social progress.

Fortunately, the terrible mistakes made in the Cuban invasion, and the clumsy fumbling displayed in the tractors for prisoners deal, have not characterized other efforts of the Kennedy administration in the Latin-American area: From the moment that President Kennedy called the ambassadors of the Latin-American republics to the White House early in 1961 to formulate an alliance, our efforts to seek justice for the under-privileged of Latin America through collective action have been constantly and earnestly pursued.

17

Latin Americans must choose between a peaceful but revolutionary alliance for progress and bloody revolution. If they choose wrongly, it may be their last free choice.

IN HIS INAUGURAL AND STATE OF THE UNION ADDRESSES, President Kennedy spoke generally of a bold new program to unite the Western Hemisphere in progress. He called it an Alliance for Progress.

In February, he sent two task forces of financial and agricultural experts to Latin America. George S. McGovern, director of the Food for Peace Program, led one and his deputy, James W. Symington, the other. These two groups visited many of the Latin-American republics to offer grain, seed, and other surplus foods and to spur land reform.

Then, in March, President Kennedy held a unique reception for Latin-American ambassadors in the White House. The occasion was ostensibly social. But before the occasion ended, the guests were led to the beautiful, impressive East Room, sparkling in gold and white. They were seated. The President faced them. And then he spoke earnestly about inter-American affairs. He became more specific than he had been in the Inaugural and State of the Union Addresses, proposing now a ten-year program that would be a vast cooperative effort "to satisfy the basic needs of the American people for homes and work, land, health and schools."

The President attached conditions to his offer: For the first time, a Chief Executive of the United States openly and emphatically told the Latin-American countries that our aid would be of limited value unless they themselves vigorously initiated programs of social reform and used our aid to advance those programs.

His offer was substantial. To help finance social development, he would ask the Congress to appropriate the $500 million authorized in Public Law 86-735 of the Eisenhower administration. Financial help by the older, orthodox agencies would be continued and increased. He would commit the United States to ten years of such support, but did not at that time name a sum. (Subsequent events indicated that funds from all sources external to Latin America would be about $20 billion during the decade of the Alliance.)

The President declared: "Political freedom must be accompanied by social change. For unless necessary social reforms, including land and tax reform, are freely made—unless we broaden the opportunity of all our people—unless the great mass of Americans share in increasing prosperity —then our alliance, our revolution, and our dream will have failed. But we call for social change by free men—change in the spirit of Washington and Jefferson, of Bolívar and San Martín and Martí—not change which seeks to impose on men tyrannies which we cast out a century and a half ago."

This was a clear warning to great landowners, military cliques, and other privileged groups that massive aid from us would be forthcoming only if historic structures, laws, and customs began to dissolve and blend into a dynamic program that demonstrated a genuine social conscience—a concern for the welfare of the common people in Latin America.

A few years earlier, talk such as this would have been condemned angrily by Latin-American leaders as "imperialism," "dollar diplomacy," and the "yankee big stick" wrapped, perhaps, in fine silk. This kind of talk was reminiscent of United States intervention in the late nineteenth and early twentieth centuries.

But times were different now. Many Latin-American leaders were frightened. It had become increasingly apparent to them that without social change, violent revolutions were inevitable. Modern communications had eliminated isolation. The underprivileged now knew, as the Chilean students had said, that poverty is not a misfortune, it is an injustice, and that the gap between rich and poor was neither universal nor immutable. Spurred by this awareness, people throughout Latin America were prowling palace courtyards, surly and insistent in their demands for a better life. Students spilled from the university campuses to riot in streets, topple monuments to egotism, and stone public offices. Labor leaders and their fellow workers paralyzed already sluggish economies by striking. People faced with a life of empty misery cared little for danger; they demonstrated a chilling willingness to spill blood—their own or others—to get what they demanded. The rickety and dangerous seat of the presidency became more shaky and more perilous as leaders walked a tight wire between the few privileged and the countless poor. And there was Fidel Castro in Cuba, inspiring and inciting violence, and pledging to establish in Cuba exile governments of all the nations that opposed his revolution.

And so President Kennedy's words fell on ears made receptive by constant listening to the rumble of revolution. Further, at Bogotá, representatives of nineteen of the republics had themselves publicly recognized the crucial problem and had solemnly declared their determination to cooperate in finding solutions. Now, President Kennedy could repeat their words and insist upon collective action without risking a charge of unilateral intervention.

The specific proposals made by the President actually were not new, but his firm support of policies and programs developed over a period of years was highly important. He endorsed evolving plans for common markets, calling them a step toward greater competitive opportunity. He supported commitments made by the previous Administration to help find practicable solutions to the economic instability caused by violent variations in primary commodity prices. Distribution of surplus foods, begun to Latin America eight years before, would be increased. We would continue to support and help establish additional research agencies on a regional basis. We foresaw an expansion of programs in teacher training, especially in the sciences.

The President added a new and dramatic tone to the whole program. He lent to it a spirit of urgency and promise. He gave it a battle cry—*"Progreso, Sí! Tiranía, No!"*

President Kennedy re-emphasized a concept accepted at Bogotá—that responsibility for progress rested primarily with the Latin-American nations themselves. They and they alone could mobilize their resources, enlist the energies of their people, and modify their social patterns to make them equitable. "If this effort is made," he said, "then outside assistance will give vital impetus to progress—without it, no amount of help will advance the welfare of the people."

Reactions in Latin America to President Kennedy's Alliance for Progress were generally favorable, as they had been to President Eisenhower's proposal to Congress in August 1960 and to the Act of Bogotá. Government leaders and most newspapers praised the President's talk. But Castro declared that the "saintly Kennedy" was trying to "buy" Latin America. Communist newspapers and leaders referred to it as a power play to offset gains being made by Castro Communism. Rio's *Correio da Manha* asked pessimistically: "What part will Brazil get? Nothing that will really help," thus demonstrating that some mistakenly looked upon the proposed alliance as a mere aid program, rather than as a collective action for change.

Secretary Rusk hotly denied that the Alliance was purely a response to Castro Communism. (He was wholly correct, as I have documented.) Our offer, he said, was a generous and willing response of one people to the desperate needs of others.

It was, indeed, the next logical step in an evolutionary process. For years we had been providing help to Latin America in increasing volume at considerable sacrifice and even with some danger to ourselves, as was evident in the precarious imbalances in international payments the United States experienced each year after 1957. Undoubtedly the cold war threat in Latin America hastened the action, but only moderately. It did not shape our attitudes or dictate the substance of programs. "The real issue in the Western Hemisphere is poverty," said Dean Rusk. "It is the gap between the rich and the poor in Latin America."

President Kennedy announced that he would request a meeting of the Inter-American Economic and Social Council on the ministerial level to work out the details of the new Alliance. Before the meeting convened he authorized the first loans under Public Law 86-735. To Panama, through the Agency for International Development, funds were allotted for the construction of two hundred rural schools. Guatemala received loans to help intensify its efforts to diversify agriculture and to reduce its dependence on coffee production. Funds were sent to Argentina to train specialists needed in planning systematic social and economic development.

Reaction in the United States was favorable, but some discordant notes were heard. A few knowledgeable persons contended that the effort was too small to make a dent in the problem; they pointed to the increasing population and declared that economic aid would be useless unless the birth rate was held down. Representative Otto E. Passman, Democratic Congressman from Louisiana, called the proposal "slipshod" and "a blank check." Senator Henry C. Dworshak, Republican from Idaho, protested that there had been inadequate preparation for the program, and Indiana's Republican Senator Homer E. Capehart opposed the plan because, he contended, there were no controls on how the money would be spent and no assurance that the recipient nations would remain "friendly" to the United States.

During June and July of 1961, teams of economists and other specialists worked in Washington to prepare materials for the forthcoming Punta del

Este conference in Uruguay. Their organic guide was the Act of Bogotá, so they planned for the broad initiation of self-help projects, financed in part by the United States. They saw that each of the Latin-American countries would have to devise fairly precise ten-year development programs, with first-year, second-year, and subsequent priorities. Patently, technical assistance would be required by many of the cooperating countries, so there evolved a suggestion that a committee of experts should be established and from this group the participating nations could obtain technical assistance in preparing and periodically reviewing their programs; another important consideration was the desire of the United States to have an independent group comment on development plans from the standpoint of their inclusion of needed reforms. This became the most controversial issue at Punta del Este, primarily because the smaller nations feared their programs would not receive the same attention as those of the larger nations.

The head of the United States delegation to the ministerial conference at Punta del Este was Secretary of the Treasury Douglas Dillon, who by now had become widely recognized as a leading architect of our economic help program to Latin America. His experience during the Eisenhower administration in coordinating the activities of national and international lending agencies, in working with President Eisenhower and Assistant Secretary Rubottom, in establishing the Inter-American Development Bank and the new program for an attack on social inequities, and in heading the United States delegation to Bogotá qualified him superbly for his role of leadership at Punta del Este.

It could be argued, I suppose, that the Punta del Este conference was unnecessary, for the bases of a cooperative attack on traditional institutions and social injustices had been formulated and agreed upon in the Act of Bogotá. Another conference, therefore, may have seemed to be mere frosting on the cake.

But such a revolutionary change as had been evolving for several years could not be fixed either hurriedly or merely by agreeing to principles and objectives. Operational details had to be formulated. Objectives had to be translated into specific targets. Thus, for example, the goal of economic advance proclaimed at Bogotá in 1960 became at Punta del Este in 1961 a specifically defined target of 5 per cent increase each year in the gross national products of the Latin-American countries. In the past ten years, only Mexico, Venezuela, and Brazil had attained this minimum goal. Now, all Latin-American countries established this as the norm. Since population growth would be at least 2.5 per cent a year, annual per capita productivity would also have to increase about 2.5 per cent. This, in turn, would influence the preparation of specific projects in each year of the ten-year plans.

The Act of Bogotá, furthermore, was promulgated by a special committee of the Organization of American States. Punta del Este brought together ministers, who as representatives of their Presidents, were in a position to make for their governments final commitments on the details of a charter of action.

Then, too, a new Administration was in power in Washington. It was well for Latin-American leaders to learn more of its attitudes and purposes, and to discover what level of financing it was prepared to provide for the cooperative effort.

Secretary Dillon, in addressing the opening plenary session of the conference, was as forthright as he had been on previous occasions. Each nation should devote larger proportions of its resources to social progress, he insisted, and privileged groups would have to make larger contributions to this end. Tax systems must be modified. Tax evaders must be severely penalized (Latin-American nations probably lose more than $2 billion a year through tax evasion). Taxes should be assessed on the basis of ability to pay. Land reform should yield new patterns in which farmers owned and tilled their own soil. Interest rates to farmers and small businessmen would have to be lowered. All countries would have to prepare short-term and long-term development plans, based on sound analyses, as a basis for obtaining essential credit. If these things were agreed to, the United States would help in many ways, especially with funds, and some loans might be for as much as fifty years.

Reports of the working committees and the final Charter of Punta del Este fill several hundred pages. Only officials directly concerned with implementing the many provisions need be intimately familiar with these. But every citizen of North, Central, and South America should comprehend the full substance of one document prepared and issued by the ministerial representatives. They called it a *Declaration to the Peoples of America*. In time, it may find a place of dignity and significance in history comparable to that of the constitutions of the American nations. With minor deletions, here is the Declaration—a new charter of hemispheric freedom, progress, and social justice:

Assembled in Punta del Este, inspired by the principles consecrated in the Charter of the Organization of American States . . . and in the Act of Bogotá, the representatives of the American Republics hereby agree to establish an Alliance for Progress: a vast effort to bring a better life to all the peoples of the Continent.

This Alliance is established on the basic principle that free men working through the institution of representative democracy can best satisfy man's aspirations, including those for work, home and land, health and schools. No system can guarantee true progress unless it affirms the dignity of the individual which is the foundation of our civilization.

Therefore the countries signing this declaration in the exercise of their sovereignty have agreed to work toward the following goals during the coming years:

To improve and strengthen democratic institutions . . .

To accelerate economic and social development . . .

To carry out urban and rural housing programs to provide decent homes for all our people.

To encourage . . . programs of comprehensive agrarian reform, leading to the effective transformation, where required, of unjust structures and systems of land tenure and use; with a view to replacing *latifundio* and dwarf holdings by an equitable system of property so that, supplemented by timely and adequate credit, technical assistance and improved marketing arrangements, the land will become for the man who works it the basis of his economic stability, the foundation of his increasing welfare, and the guarantee of his freedom and dignity.

To wipe out illiteracy; to extend, as quickly as possible, the benefits of primary education to all Latin Americans; and to provide broader facilities, on a vast scale, for secondary and technical training and for higher education.

To press forward with programs of health and sanitation . . .

To assure fair wages and satisfactory working conditions to all our workers . . .

To reform tax laws, demanding more from those who have most, to punish tax evasion severely, and to redistribute the national income in order to benefit those who are most in need while, at the same time, promoting savings and investment and reinvestment of capital.

To maintain monetary and fiscal policies which, while avoiding the disastrous effects of inflation or deflation, will protect the purchasing power of the many, guarantee the greatest possible price stability, and form an adequate basis for economic development.

To stimulate private enterprise in order to encourage the development of Latin American countries at a rate which will help them to provide jobs for their growing populations . . .

To find a quick and lasting solution to the grave problem created by excessive price fluctuations in the basic exports of Latin American countries . . .

To accelerate the integration of Latin America so as to stimulate the economic and social development of the Continent . . .

This declaration expresses the conviction of the nations of Latin America that these profound economic, social, and cultural changes can come about only through the self-help efforts of each country. Nonetheless, in order to achieve the goals which have been established with the necessary speed, domestic efforts must be reinforced by essential contributions of external assistance.

The United States, for its part, pledges its efforts to supply financial and technical cooperation in order to achieve the aims of the Alliance for Progress. To this end, the United States will provide a major part of the minimum of 20 billion dollars, *principally in public funds*, which Latin America will require over the next 10 years from all external sources in order to supplement its own efforts.

The United States will provide from public funds, as an immediate contribution to the economic and social progress of Latin America, more than one billion dollars during the twelve months which began on March 13, 1961 . . .

The United States intends to furnish development loans on a long-term basis, where appropriate running up to fifty years and at very low or zero rates of interest.

For their part, the countries of Latin America agree to devote a steadily increasing share of their own resources to economic and social development, and to make the reforms necessary to assure that all share fully in the fruits of the Alliance for Progress.

. . . each of the countries of Latin America will formulate comprehensive and well-conceived national programs for the development of their own economies.

Conscious of the overriding importance of this declaration, the signatory countries declare that the inter-American community is now beginning a new era . . .

It was understood by the ministers that they had committed their governments to a decade of reform and development which would cost about $100 billion, or $10 billion a year. The United States indicated that 20 per cent of this would be provided either by the United States or other countries external to Latin America.

The United States commitment is not as formidable as may appear. In the fiscal year 1960–61, the Export-Import Bank authorized loans and guarantees of $773 million for many Latin-American republics—involving more than 570 separate transactions—and it could be expected to lend an average of $400 million a year. The World Bank made, in the same period, nine development loans to Latin-American countries, totaling nearly $150 million. The International Development Association made two loans amounting to $28 million. The Inter-American Development Bank had not made loans but was geared for action, and its resources were now buttressed with a major portion of the $500 million Social Progress Fund under Public Law 86-735. The Agency for International Development and the Development Loan Fund made a few modest loans. Surplus food under Public Law 48 was shipped to Latin-American countries, and under the Alliance for Progress it was expected that such aid would reach a value of $150 million a year.

Further, machinery has been developed to bring capital to Latin America from nine other industrialized nations. Finally, private capital, whose flow to Latin America had slowed appreciably following the Castro revolution, would, if it renewed its confidence in the stability of Latin-American governments and of investment opportunities there, be a great help. Secretary Dillon estimated that United States private investment in Latin America would average $300 million a year.

The United States Government cannot, of course, control the decisions of the international lending institutions. If it is assumed, however, that they will continue to extend credit at the average of the last five years, then, with the Inter-American Bank quickly achieving a good average of lending, the additional drain on United States resources under the Alliance for Progress, if all goes well, might be about half a billion dollars a year.

The two most important assurances we gave at Punta del Este are, first, to make up any deficiency in the promised $2 billion a year that might result from the operations of numerous international, national, and private agencies, and, second, to see to it that a substantial share of all funds came from public sources. (We did not go so far as to *guarantee* $2 billion in foreign funds each year. However, statements in the Charter of Punta del Este, in the *Declaration to the Peoples of America*, and in speeches by Secretary Dillon and other United States officials, have surely caused Latin-American leaders to expect the inflow of this sum annually; any failure in this regard will be interpreted in Latin America as bad faith on our part.)

Several circumstances, however, prevent outright optimism about the financial aspects of the Alliance.

First, the United States itself is in serious difficulty in the field of international balance of payments. Exports of goods and services from the United States continue to exceed imports by several billion dollars a year, but support of our military forces in many areas of the world, military and economic aid to other countries, including Latin America, and a steady flow outward of private investment capital have given us a deficit situation in international balances each year. Between 1957 and 1962 our gold reserves declined sharply. In the same period, outstanding foreign claims against United States gold increased. Hence, late in 1961, foreign claims exceeded our total gold supply by $2.1 billion. But more than $11 billion in gold must by law be held in reserve as backing for our currency so that the deficiency in our gold supply to settle international accounts had reached about $13.5 billion and threatened to get worse.

How long the United States can tolerate this situation without encountering financial difficulties of both domestic and global import merits careful consideration. Secretary Dillon, in testifying before the Senate Committee on Appropriations shortly after the conclusion of the Punta del Este Conference, attempted to quiet the fears of the Congress about this problem. "I wish to emphasize," he said, "that it is the form in which aid is extended . . . that is most relevant to this question. Under the new program, as at present, we will continue to place primary emphasis on the purchase of United States goods and services by aid recipients. The preponderant bulk of foreign aid expenditures will be made in the United States. Such expenditures, which are accompanied by American exports, have no adverse impact on our balance of payments. . . . Our objective will be to reserve between 75 and 80 per cent of the available funds [for international development] for procurement of United States goods and services."

However, it must be noted that this policy, instituted by President Eisenhower when the balance of payments problem became difficult several years earlier, still left us in a precarious situation. Insisting that 80 per cent of additional expenditures for foreign aid be spent in the United States would obviously not solve the problem.

President Kennedy induced the Congress to pass an Act which reduced the duty-free import privilege of each American tourist from $500 to $100. This helped a little, but not as much as might be supposed, for reduced purchases abroad, such as in Mexico, may result in a decrease of purchases from us. President Eisenhower had taken the drastic action of ordering home families of United States servicemen stationed overseas, but this order was canceled by President Kennedy.

The problem remains a vexing one. The most fortunate solution would be a large increase in the export of United States goods and services, but high prices for United States industrial products and farm commodities must temper any hope we might otherwise have in this regard. The assumption by other industrialized nations of an equitable portion of the burden of aid to underdeveloped nations would help, as would any increase in the military forces of other free nations that enabled us to bring troops home. We must keep our interest rate structure such that private funds are not induced unnecessarily to seek more attractive investment opportunities in other industrialized nations. If all such efforts combined do not suffice to assure financial stability, then we must decide in terms of our own self-interest which areas of the world most need our assistance and there concentrate our aid, risky as such a choice might be. The Western Hemisphere and Western Europe *must* remain free. Otherwise, freedom will fall around the globe like dominoes in a row. Of course we want all nations to enjoy the blessings of liberty, but we must accept the fact that the United States cannot for long be the Atlas of the world without danger of collapse. Britain, Western European nations, and Japan should, in my judgment, assume greater responsibility for aid to Africa, the Middle East, and Southeast Asia.

A second deterrent to overoptimism about the financial phases of the Alliance for Progress involves the budgets of the recipient nations. There can be no doubt that the ministerial representatives of the Latin-American Presidents were in earnest in the promises they made in the Act of Bogotá and the Charter of Punta del Este. They intend to work for tax, industrial, agricultural, and other changes which will enable them to obtain local funds required to finance 80 per cent of project costs. But every nation (including the United States) has strong vested interests which often make short work of good intentions. Far-reaching reforms call for statesmanship of the highest and most persuasive type in winning the support of privileged groups or, if need be, in defeating them in legislative halls in ways that do not precipitate violent action.

In Chapter 1 of this book, I reported a conversation I had three years ago with a genial, intelligent Latin-American finance minister who shied away from my suggestion that his country's tax laws should be changed so that well-to-do families contributed more substantially to the achievement of economic progress and social justice in his own country. This friend, in an address made in the United States shortly before the Punta del Este Conference, spoke persuasively of the need for development capital in Latin America, but he did not suggest that Latin Americans repatriate the three and a half billion dollars its wealthy families have invested in the United States and other industrialized countries, nor did he even touch on the possibility of internal tax revision. Instead, he argued that since recipients of loans, grants, and technical aid feel inferior to the grantor, we should levy a tax on the total national products of advanced countries and use the revenues to finance growth in the underdeveloped nations. As a member of the Latin-American aristocracy, he seemingly has not accepted his government's commitment for tax and other reform; he is still looking to external resources for the answer to his nation's problems.

Perhaps the principal threat to the success of the Alliance for Progress is the difficulty Latin-American leaders face in trying to make rapid social reform a reality. How well they will do obviously depends on their personalities, courage, and determination, and on the outcome in each country of struggles among the forces of reaction, democratic liberalism, and Communist imperialism. In some nations, the political atmosphere is explosive. Reactionary groups want no change, and they will resort to violence to prevent it. Communists do not want peaceful reform—they want violent revolutions that will transfer power to ruthless dictators who will take orders from Moscow.

Between these violent extremes are a multitude of disparate groups which favor peaceful and rapid growth. They vary from non-Communist leftists, to moderate reformists, and to socially conscious conservatives. Each such category is fractionated. But the leaders and members of these democratic center groups are all militantly dedicated to justice in freedom. They are therefore compelled in most countries to battle simultaneously with the historic and the new oligarchists; in shaping the strategy of struggle, dissension arises.

History may record as a spiteful irony the coincidence in timing of the creation of the Alliance and the birth of Castro Communism. For now, as the hemisphere is on the verge of a great social and economic revolution forged in and dedicated to peace, it is also on the brink of a violent and bloody revolution. *Revolution in Latin America is inevitable.* Only the form it takes is uncertain.

The crucial question is whether Latin America will plunge into the future on the heels of Castro or whether it will have the patience and wisdom to follow more slowly the procedures initiated by the Alliance.

Scholars and knowledgeable journalists disagree on the probable outcome of the struggles among the internal political forces in Latin America. Some contend that only in bloodshed will desirable social changes be brought about. The Alliance for Progress, they contend, is pallid fare for a people long starved for justice.

I realize that the hemisphere is late with its new promise, and I recognize that social change by democratic methods is difficult and often frustratingly slow. But I am convinced that blood does not have to flow in the streets. If it does, the Castro-type dictatorships of the left or the Trujillo-type dictatorships of the right will triumph, of course.

Democratic procedures must prevail in Latin America, and we must do all we legitimately can to see that they do. The best hope is that men like Beltrán of Peru, Betancourt of Venezuela, Lopez Mateos and Ruíz Cortines of Mexico, Alessandri of Chile, Galo Plaza of Ecuador, José Figueres of Costa Rica, and Lleras Camargo of Colombia—whether they are in office or exercise influence as private citizens—drive ahead with all possible dispatch in their own countries and also provide dynamic leadership among the center forces in the hemisphere. Only strong leaders can unify the fractionated non-Communist leftists, moderate reformists, and socially conscious conservatives.

These men have chosen peaceful revolution. Will they be able to stay on course?

Here the experience of the brave and brilliant Arturo Frondizi must give us pause. Elected President of Argentina, he was confronted by the herculean task of clearing away the financial and political debris left by dictator Juan Perón. He was elected by obtaining substantial support from both anti- and pro-Perón forces. Once in office, President Frondizi set out to save Argentina, and to do so, he had to alienate some powerful factions which at first had supported him. He instituted an austerity program which brought angry mobs into the streets clamoring for the yesterdays of Perón's lavish and irresponsible giveaways. He wooed foreign private investors and made ultra-nationalists furious. The fact that he managed to turn Argentina's $300 million importation of oil into a slight surplus made him no less secure. President Frondizi wriggled perilously around political pitfalls: He outlawed the Communists, refused temporarily to legalize the Perónistas as a political party, and pressured the Castro supporters. He cultivated the military leaders, then defied them. He faced and survived in his three years in office thirty crises which might have brought a lesser man crashing down. And in doing so, he virtually ended unemployment, halted inflation, strengthened the peso, increased exports, speeded industrialization, and improved social services.

But in 1962, Frondizi was ousted by a right-wing military coup, ostensibly to nullify election gains of the Perónistas.

Will Betancourt of Venezuela, or Alessandri of Chile, or Valencia (the new President) of Colombia, or Paz Estenssoro of Bolivia, travel the same tragic road as Frondizi? Or of Prado of Peru? Or will the disparate central groups bury their lesser differences in support of men whose eyes are fixed on the supreme need of building a new society quickly, solidly, surely? We cannot answer these questions, but we can be positive that the Communists and most of the richly privileged will fight as persistently and viciously as the Ku Klux Klan, the Birchers, and the American Communists to prevent peaceful reform.

A study prepared for the Senate Foreign Relations Committee by the Corporation for Economic and Industrial Research (CEIR) estimated the total number of Communist Party members in Latin America to be about two hundred thousand. But this figure does not reveal the full force of Communist influence, for Communist Parties are organized on the Leninist principle of restricting membership to active, full-time, and well-trained agents, capable of guiding the masses with skill and dedication. Others may be fellow travelers, and there are many.

CEIR estimates that there are between seventy thousand and eighty thousand Communists and fellow travelers in Argentina, fifty thousand in Brazil, and thirty thousand-plus in Venezuela. But there were only twelve thousand Communist Party members in Cuba (one authority believes there were twenty-five thousand) when Castro seized power and they were able to bring the country into the international hierarchy. In 1958, the Chilean Communist Party won nine seats in the Chilean Senate and twenty-one seats in the House, despite a membership of only twenty-five thousand. Even in Guatemala, where the party had only five thousand members, Communist leaders were able to infiltrate key governmental posts and agencies in 1954 under the Arbenz regime.

The typical Communist movement in Latin America is not a parliamentary one. Other than in Chile, only twelve Communists are seated in Latin-American national legislatures. Communists prefer to infiltrate and subvert selected groups. Thus, they diligently try to place their two hundred thousand members in key positions in labor unions and student organizations. Cloaked with a degree of respectability, they work for the time they can dominate the country and crush the very groups with which they now associate.

Their success varies with circumstances. They have used their funds to good advantage among trade unionists. Latin-American unions do not have the financial independence of those in the United States, primarily because members cannot afford to pay dues. In nations where governmental support is not offered, the unions are forced to turn to political parties for help. If there is not a strong democratic party, either of extreme or moderate persuasion, only the Communist Party can furnish funds. Since the Communist Party is invariably well financed (CEIR estimates annual expenditures in Latin America to be in excess of $100 million), the unions can receive operating funds, provided they place Communists in key positions. At present, unions with about one million members have open Communist leadership.

Communist organizational skill, discipline, and financial strength have yielded sporadic successes in university elections. According to CEIR, the national organization of Colombian students fell under Communist control in 1957, and Communist influence among students and professors is strong in the leading universities of half the nations of Latin America, especially in Argentina, Brazil, Chile, Ecuador, Peru, Uruguay, and Venezuela. Communists are making a special effort to convert future Latin-American leaders at an impressionable age or at least to instill in them strong anti-North Americanism. Communist "students" usually linger in universities until they are middle-aged.

Recently, infiltrationary methods have been buttressed by propaganda programs fostered by cultural "societies." A long-time student of inter-American affairs, Arthur P. Whitaker, reports that the Soviet Bloc has established about ninety such "societies" throughout Latin America. They seek to polish the image of Soviet Russia as a friend and benefactor whose greatest desire in life is to help the underprivileged in Latin America. To do this, of course, the societies bend their efforts to helping Latin America disentangle itself from "Yankee imperialism." In these attempts to alter the unfavorable impression of the Soviet Union that exists in many Latin-American minds, the "societies" often obtain the support of a national leftist or anti-American figure, such as former President Lázaro Cárdenas of Mexico.

Communists regularly issue more than three hundred newspapers and magazines and many pamphlets. They purchase radio time in spreading the Party line. Short-wave radio broadcasts from Russia are easily heard in Latin America. And, of course, propaganda from Radio Havana is quite easily heard over standard (and hence more common) radios.

Late one night in the United States Embassy in Managua, Nicaragua, I tried to bring in a newscast from the United States. I could not pick up a single home station, but I had no difficulty in obtaining clear signals from eleven Soviet stations. All but one of these programs were in Spanish; the exception was in English. I listened with care, for I found that I was being mentioned in several of the broadcasts. During the afternoon, I had been sent a "manifesto" by university students. It was a typical Communist declaration, ascribing to my visit nearly every possible sinister purpose. A quick investigation revealed that the manifesto had been printed and distributed by about a dozen "students," none of whom actually attended classes at the university. The broadcasts from Russia that same night quoted the manifesto in full, giving the impression, of course, that it was a straight newscast and that the manifesto represented the views of all university students. I have always suspected that the manifesto was drafted in Moscow.

Communist propaganda is most effectively spread from person to person. With the rise of Fidel Castro, this personal method has been intensified. Communist agents carry a fabricated and glowing account of the Cuban revolution to every isolated region in Latin America; omitted is any mention of brutalities and the suppression of freedom; emphasized is the very type of social change which the listeners wish to achieve in their own countries.

With the help of local Party members, the Soviet Union is attempting to develop trade relations which appear to be and sometimes are beneficial to Latin-American nations. Some authorities have warned that the preoccupation of Western Europe with emerging African nations could reduce their purchases from Latin America, and this, combined with even moderate protectionism in the United States (as with oil, copper, lead, zinc), could lead to a substantial increase of Latin-American trade with the Sino-Soviet Bloc. At present, such trade accounts for only 2 per cent of the total, but it is rising about 12 per cent a year.

Thus, the Communists are using tried techniques of subversion and economic influence in an atmosphere of poverty, misery, and social turbulence that is ideal for the breeding of violent revolutions. It is perhaps surprising that the Communists have not achieved more outward signs of success, but they, too, have obstacles to surmount.

The Latin-American concern for spiritual matters and for individualism are opposed to the disciplined, communal, and material aspects of Marxism. Although traditional beliefs and allegiances can be distorted by poverty and lack of opportunity, they remain potent factors with most Latin Americans who enjoy even the bare essentials of life. Since true Communist dogma has limited appeal among religiously oriented peoples, Party members resort to more persuasive arguments: nationalism and anti-Yankeeism. These emotionally charged smoke screens obscure the ultimate purpose of the Party—to come to power in one of two ways: They could seize control in the anarchical conditions caused by a general uprising which lacked the leadership of a strong democratic party, or they could disguise their own organization as a democratic party until they entrenched themselves in power.

Two students of Communism in Latin America, Robert Alexander of the United States and Victor Alba of Mexico, agree that democratic parties of the radical left present the Communists with the greatest obstacles in their struggle for power. The extreme left dissipates the Communist influence to some extent by promising the same radical reforms, fighting the oligarchists, championing the underprivileged—and it does all of this within the democratic framework. The Communists patently recognize this. Hence they wear the shoe on either foot, frequently forming coalitions with right-wing reactionaries against reform movements. In Peru, the Communists have long opposed the radical democratic *Apristas*. In Argentina, they were aligned against the anti-Perónistas. In Cuba, they opposed Castro until he won his revolution, in one instance humiliating him by thwarting the general strike he called in Cuba against Batista. Popular democratic parties favoring peaceful reform do not attract all discontented Latin Americans, but in countries where they thrive, Communists scratch a little harder for supporters.

It is difficult to categorize, in terms comprehensible to us, the democratic or center parties of Latin America—that is, those parties which stand between the Communists, on the one hand, and the entrenched oligarchists, on the other. Each party is conditioned by the social, cultural, and economic environment, by the nature of the opposition in the nation, and most of all by the personalities and attitudes of the party leadership. For convenience, I have labeled these parties as "non-Communist leftists (or radicals)," "moderate reformists," and "socially conscious conservatives." In the context of Latin-American politics, I believe these terms are adequately descriptive, but to the people of the United States they are no doubt misleading. The political spectrum in Latin America differs as between countries, and even more as compared to the United States. All democratic or central parties in Latin America tend to be considerably to the left from ours.

In Venezuela, for example, the entire political spectrum is to the left. While *Acción Democrática* is in the political center in that country—as contrasted to the violent extremists—it is, in our terms, quite radical in its demands.

There are few "moderates" (in our terms) in Latin America; that is, middle-of-the-roaders of the United States variety do not enjoy real strength in most of the Latin-American republics. Latin-American "moderates" are roughly comparable to our most vociferous liberals.

Further, many parties in Latin America consist primarily of personal followers of some magnetic—and perhaps opportunistic—leader, rather than of adherents of a definite program, policy, or philosophy.

These circumstances make it extremely difficult to determine which political groups merit the faith of the United States as we seek to further the programs envisaged in the Alliance for Progress. Our only safe course is to support the efforts of those political sectors which appear genuinely to be seeking to bring about necessary social and economic reforms within a general context of political liberty, as promised in the relevant agreements.

In Mexico, our faith must lie with the dominant political party—the Institutional Revolutionary Party (PRI). In the Latin-American milieu, it may be classified as a moderate reform group. It has provided other popular democratic parties of Latin America with a historic example. In its infancy, it was a typical revolutionary movement—filled with an urge to violence, vengeance, and victory. When it had seized power, it expropriated land, instituted radical reforms, and behaved as revolutionary parties generally do. But gradually, as Mexico achieved a fair degree of social and economic progress, the party became more moderate and fostered democratic institutions.

The reform parties of Costa Rica, Venezuela, Bolivia, Colombia, and Peru are in most respects quite different from one another, but they share with all other such parties in Latin America the desire to achieve far-reaching social and economic changes within a framework of freedom, justice, and democratic institutions.

The most successful of this group has been Costa Rica's National Liberation Party. Its leader, José Figueres, former President of the republic and a wealthy plantation owner, displayed strategic skill and earnestness of purpose in outwitting the Communists in 1948. Since then, Costa Rica has made considerable progress in the realization of political democracy and social and economic development. Figueres became and is today a dominant figure among the moderates of Latin America.

President Romulo Betancourt, Democratic Action Party leader of Venezuela, has more complex and larger problems on his hands than Figueres faced in small, predominantly white Costa Rica. Now a passionate, radical reformer and democratic adherent, Betancourt was a Communist in his younger days. In his career as an enemy of the ruling oligarchy, he was imprisoned in 1928 and narrowly missed being executed, was forced into hiding during the 1930s, was overthrown by the military in 1948 and was hunted by soldiers with orders to shoot him on sight, was exiled in Havana in 1951 where he barely escaped assassination, and was badly burned in 1960 when agents of his enemy, Rafael Trujillo, exploded a car full of dynamite as he passed by. This former Communist is today a leading democratic opponent of Castro and Castro-Soviet imperialism.

President Victor Paz Estenssoro and his radical National Revolutionary Movement Party are attempting far-reaching changes in Bolivia where adverse cultural and economic factors sadly darken the picture. The Liberal Party of Colombia, led by former President Lleras Camargo, considers itself akin to the Popular Democratic parties but by choice its policies are somewhat more moderate.

The *Aprista* Party of Peru is the most active radical party currently not in power. Founded by Victor Raul Haya de la Torre in the 1930s, it almost took control of the government in 1962; it received the largest vote but failed to achieve the constitutionally required third of all votes. By that time a few of the privileged classes of Peru had developed such a consuming fear of Castro Communism and its spread among the Peruvian people that it appeared they might prefer to have power vested in reformers than to risk a triumph of totalitarianism of the left. But the armed forces elite—with the applause if not the open support of many *latifundistas* and wealthy urbanites who had prevented the *Apristas* from coming to power in Peru for twenty-five years—staged a military *coup d'état* on July 18, 1962. Such military coups have been legion in Latin America—and have usually been accepted by the world community. Hence, Peruvian military leaders were astounded when President Kennedy condemned the coup as "a serious setback" for the Alliance for Progress and suspended diplomatic recognition and United States aid to Peru. Venezuela suspended recognition, condemned the military takeover, and pressed for a meeting of the American foreign ministers to consider the Peruvian situation as a danger to the security of the hemisphere. Several other Latin-American countries suspended recognition. These actions did not, however, result in a transfer of power to the *Apristas*, and a month after its initial disapproval the United States recognized the military regime and gradually restored on-going aid programs to Peru.

Radical reform groups, roughly similar to the *Apristas*, but varying greatly in size and influence, exist in most of the five Central-American republics. Many of the Cuban exiles who supported Castro until his dedication to Communism became evident, are of radical democratic persuasion.

Latin-American extremism may sometimes include programs of expropriation and nationalization of certain enterprises, such as mining and public utilities. Invariably it encompasses land and tax reforms and governmental control of economic development. But the basic philosophy remains democratic and it seems reasonably certain that once a radical party is in power and has achieved considerable social progress, radical practices will tend to wane, as they did in Mexico. Further, unlike the Castro Communists, democratic extremists are militantly nationalistic, and would never accept subservience to an extracontinental power.

Another difference is the attitude of the leaders of these movements toward the United States. While Castro vilifies the United States as the hated cause of Cuba's troubles, democratic leaders consider inter-American cooperation to be imperative. It is not possible for them to glorify Uncle Sam too much and retain popular support, however. Thus, when popular democratic leaders offend the nationalistic spirit of the United States, it should be remembered that this may be considered a necessary and even temporary expedient to combat the efforts of Communist propagandists who picture popular democrats as "lackeys of imperialism."

But steering a safe course in maintaining relations with the United States is by no means the greatest problem popular democrats face. As indicated in Peru, Argentina, Ecuador, and Brazil, the crucial difficulty consists of obtaining progressive legislation and essential social change in the face of bitter opposition from the Communist left and the privileged right. The popular democrats are busy with both hands as they are attacked from both sides. Rightists call them Communists. Moscow's and Havana's agents call them reactionaries and tell the people that no meaningful reform will be carried out by these "tools of the privileged classes." Harassed as they are, popular democrats must be certain of their strength before they act. This takes time, and Communists point to delay as proof of their charges. Even if they tried to respond to pressures to transform promises quickly into tangible programs, the popular democrats often would be hampered by a lack of experienced leaders and technicians who could administer agricultural, industrial, and welfare programs. And they cannot count on cooperation from administrative officials who long ruled for the privileged classes. From Communists, they can expect only trouble.

The hope that management, technical, and propaganda skills in behalf of democracy can be developed among many promising younger leaders in Latin America has led to the establishment of the Institute of Political Education in San José, Costa Rica. Founded and maintained by popular democratic parties, this ninety-day school offers training in the psychological and technical skills of political management and reform and in the ideological justification for it. The first class was graduated in December 1960, sending out twenty-three dedicated men prepared to fight for justice in freedom.

The school symbolizes the need to meet the Communists on their own terms with skilled leaders, but falls far short of numerical requirements. But the potential worth of a system of such training institutions is demonstrated by the fervor of Communist attacks on the San José school.

It would be fortunate if nations lacking trained democratic leaders could, in addition to supporting the San José effort, look to Argentina, Brazil, Costa Rica, Chile, Mexico, and Uruguay for training and other assistance, for in these countries the needed skills are possessed by increasing numbers.

In his illuminating book, *Political Change in Latin America*,* John J. Johnson estimates that 35 per cent of all Argentines, 30 per cent of Chileans and Uruguayans, and 15 per cent of Brazilians and Mexicans are members of the middle class. They strongly advocate public education, industrialization, and equitable economic and social progress. These middle segments are composed of skilled workers, technicians, government workers, teachers, and small landowners.

As these groups increase in number and influence, the power strongholds of the extremists are weakened. Even the army officer corps becomes dominated by the middle classes. Increasingly, service academies are opening to young men from other than privileged classes. The Catholic Church carries out extensive welfare programs and supports liberal Christian democratic parties, as in Chile.

Opposition of most oligarchists to the central reform groups and to the Alliance for Progress is as inexorable as that of the Communists. There are few examples in history of privileged groups voluntarily giving up their special blessings in order to promote the general welfare. It is not therefore surprising that twenty fabulously wealthy families in El Salvador stubbornly and persistently oppose every suggestion that the benefits of production reach vaster numbers of the two and a half million who inhabit that tiny nation; or that the wealthy of Brazil, still in control of the legislative branch of government, refuse to permit the enactment of reasonable land laws which might greatly dampen the cry for violence; or that the military cliques of Peru, supported by some of the leading families who long have controlled the nation, should oust an elected President and refuse to permit an *Aprista* to come to power.

* Stanford, California: Stanford University Press, 1958.

But the phalanx of opposing oligarchists has a few absentees. At least some of the elite classes in most of the Latin-American countries realize that they cannot maintain an iron grip much longer. Indeed, Beltrán of Peru and Galo Plaza of Ecuador come from the highly privileged. Figures of Costa Rica, while a representative of the middle class, is a substantial landowner. Such men as these are, unfortunately, still notable exceptions. But in previous chapters of this book, I have discussed the attitudes and practices of the privileged and hence there is no need here for me to analyze their position on social reform, as I have done with respect to the Communists and central democratic groups. Suffice it to say that any modicum of change offered by the privileged classes has little if any mass appeal. Hence, in countries where their control is sternest, violent revolution seems most imminent. Even a miraculous creation of effective popular democratic parties in such nations might not forestall violence, but most likely could prevent leadership from passing automatically to experienced Communists.

(If we become exasperated by the stubborn refusal of many of the privileged of Latin America to support social changes to the extent and with the speed required, we might remind ourselves that at Little Rock and Oxford we gave proof that human attitudes are often not readily changed. The struggle in Latin America pits democratic freedom against totalitarianism, while the struggle in our own Southland pits constitutionalism against anarchy. But in both situations the core of the problem is simple justice, and in both the key to resolution of the problem is intellectual. I do not imply that we should excuse the failure of Latin-American leaders to act correctly. Far from it. I do emphasize that human problems the world over often have a frightful and monotonous uniformity, and that our sins might well enhance our understanding, or patience, and even our compassion.)

We may be friends of the Latin-American privileged (usually they are delightful, socially charming, well-educated, and dynamic persons). But our faith in the future of Latin America, if there is to be one worthy of our trust and help, must be placed with the democratic central groups, and this is why the people of the United States must learn that the Betancourts, Hayas, Figuereses, Beltráns, Paz Estenssoros and all like them, while seeking valiantly and sometimes quite radically to change the established order, are not Communists; instead, they are the best hope Latin America and the United States have of driving the evil force of Communism from the hemisphere and of achieving rising levels of well-being in freedom for the great masses of the people—as has been done in the United States.

The real race is against time. Can the causes of discontent and threatened revolution be removed before they become the banner of organized slaughter?

At Caracas in 1954, the foreign ministers of the Americas declared that Communism is a threat to the peace of the world and should be resisted in this hemisphere. At Santiago, Chile, in August 1959, at a time when Communism was rising in Cuba but had not yet consumed the country, the foreign ministers, including Raul Roa of Cuba, declared that "only under a system founded upon a guarantee of essential freedoms . . . is it possible to attain this goal [safeguarding peace and promoting human advancement] . . . and [we] condemn the methods of every system tending to suppress political and civil rights and liberties, and in particular the action of international Communism or any other totalitarian doctrine."

A year later, in August 1960, the foreign ministers again assembled to consider troubles in the Caribbean. They condemned the Trujillo regime and recommended that all should withdraw recognition; the United States was the first to comply. Then, the ministers turned to Communism and Cuba, and Castro's delegation stalked out of the meeting. The other ministers condemned the intervention by any extracontinental power in the affairs of the American republics; declared that the acceptance of such intervention by an American state jeopardized American solidarity and security; rejected the attempt of the Sino-Soviet powers to make use of any political situation in any American state; and reaffirmed that one American state should not intervene in the internal affairs of another; finally, they again declared themselves supporters of democracy in opposition to all forms of totalitarianism. (It was here that Mexico's Foreign Minister Manuel Tello publicly stated that this resolution should not in his opinion be construed as a repudiation of Cuba—and in so doing caused consternation in the United States and many other American nations.)

The Bogotá Conference of September 1960 was designed to launch an attack on economic backwardness and social injustices, as was the conference at Punta del Este in August 1961. In both cases, the action amounted to a form of collective intervention, and in both cases Cuba dissented.

All of these meetings pointed to the second Punta del Este Conference of January 1962, which was called by Colombia. Secretary of State Dean Rusk headed the United States delegation. During the weeks preceding the meeting, the United States let it be known that its goal was sanctions against Cuba. A group of Central-American nations warned that unless something was done to halt Castro Communism, they would have serious doubts about the effectiveness of the Organization of American States. Mexico and some of the larger countries in South America, however, were clearly against sanctions.

At the conference, Dean Rusk worked day and night to line up support for sanctions against Cuba. With a disregard for subtlety, he pressed harder than any United States official had done for a long time. Some of the Latin Americans became alarmed at the Secretary's warning that failure of the ministers to act against Cuba could hamper the Alliance for Progress by alienating United States Congressmen and the public. It was clear that the United States was tying its promise of aid to Latin America to the actions at Punta del Este.

When the time for decision came, the ministers agreed unanimously (except for Cuba) that Castro Communism is a danger to the unity and freedom of the American republics. They also agreed unanimously (except for Cuba) that the American states are bound together by commitments to human right, social justice, and political democracy, and by their determination to exclude from the hemisphere the intervention of any extra-continental power. Naming names, the ministers unanimously agreed (except for Cuba) that "the present government of Cuba, which has officially identified itself as a Marxist-Leninist government, is incompatible with the principles and objectives of the inter-American system."

Unanimously (except for Cuba), the Ministers ejected Cuba from the Inter-American Defense Board. Unanimously (except for Cuba), they agreed to prohibit all shipments of arms between Cuba and the other American states. They asked the Council of the Organization of American States to explore the possibility of placing an embargo on trade with Cuba, as had been done a year before against the Dominican Republic, and they asserted that the fight against Communism did not involve merely negative reactions to extracontinental intervention and subversion, but that it called for positive acts to promote the social and economic welfare of all the people.

On the key question of excluding Cuba from participation in the inter-American system, the ministers voted 14 to 1 for the measure. Argentina, Bolivia, Brazil, Chile, Mexico, and Ecuador abstained, and Cuba voted no.

This series of actions was a tremendous endorsement of the theory of collective intervention.

But why did six nations abstain from voting for the ouster of Cuba from the Organization of American States when they had joined in condemning

Communism in general and Cuba's acceptance of Communism in particular?

The official explanation given by some of the six, especially Mexico, was that "additional legal and technical steps were necessary before the exclusion of Cuba from participation in the official agencies of the system could be firmly settled." In short, there was nothing in the charter of the Organization of American States to permit the exclusion of a member. I believe Mexico was quite sincere in this. Mexico tends to be legalistic in many international conferences. Further, many Mexican officials have said to me: "If we acted in a good cause without legal authority in this situation when it may seem right, we might do so again when it is not right. We must not set a precedent. You would not violate your own constitution for any reason; we must not do so in international affairs."

But this was not the full explanation for all six of the abstaining countries. I am confident that a few, fearing uprisings in their own countries on the part of the underprivileged who are infatuated with Castro Communism, did not want to go the last mile and be identified with the outright expulsion of Cuba. Some United States newsmen at the conference believed that at least one nation was waiting for large Alliance for Progress commitments as a condition to voting with the United States, but I cannot be so harsh in making a judgment.

It is important to note that at this conference Manuel Tello made a ringing denunciation of Communist incursions into the hemisphere and so redeemed himself for emasculating the anti-Communist declaration a year and a half before at San José. This was the first time a high-ranking Mexican official had ever taken such a stand.

Nine months after the second Punta del Este Conference, representatives of all Latin-American nations, save Cuba which no longer could function in the Organization of American States, met with Secretary Rusk in Washington and unanimously—with unprecedented speed—supported the United States' quarantine against the shipment of offensive Soviet arms to Cuba. They endorsed the proposal of the United States that the Security Council of the United Nations supervise the dismantling of missile bases in Cuba. Several offered the use of their military bases in support of our effort, and others officially stated that their naval vessels or air forces were prepared to cooperate with ours in protecting the Western Hemisphere from the Soviet military threat. The principle of collective security proclaimed at Rio in 1947 was now definitely and dramatically employed against an extracontinental power.

Thus, in a span of less than three years, the reaction of the Latin-

American republics to our initial concern about the Cuban threat turned a full one hundred and eighty degrees. At first, it was both tepid and ambivalent, to say the least. But at Punta del Este early in 1962 the republics demonstrated convincingly that they now recognized with alarm the awful nature of the threat of Castro Communism and its Kremlin masters; their willingness to act collectively (and their willingness to abide by the decision of the majority) at once made the Organization of American States a stronger and more progressive force in the Western Hemisphere. In Washington, in October 1962, early in the crisis caused by Russian offensive missiles in Cuba, they not only supported the United States' policy of readiness to use force in protecting United States and hemispheric security, they actively joined in the effort. They openly, in effect, adopted the view expressed a year earlier by Costa Rica's President Mario Echandi Jiménez: "Non-intervention is an obsolete principle whose revision is becoming increasingly more necessary . . . it is needed to replace this principle with collective action by the Organization of American States."

The new weapon, forged slowly and then hastily sharpened to a razor's edge, can cut several ways. We have seen it brandished in the face of Soviet authorities. It is not impossible that Latin-American military juntas may cringe before it—militarists who overthrow constitutionally elected regimes or refuse to abide by decisions reached through legal processes may also encounter collective intervention by the Organization of American States. And it is not inconceivable that collective intervention will be used against militant Communist uprisings, particularly if a constitutionally elected regime should request assistance. Certainly the new weapon stands today as a warning to oligarchists and Communists alike—a prophecy, perhaps, that the time is rapidly approaching when the democratic forces of the hemisphere will not, under certain conditions, permit either the privileged or the totalitarian conspirators to feed upon or take advantage of the poverty and misery in their countries. To them, the Alliance for Progress and the new policy of collective action represent the end of an era; to their victims, they symbolize the beginning of one.

At this writing the Alliance has had only slightly more than a year in which to operate. It is therefore too early to judge the effectiveness of the Kennedy administration's performance in Latin America, or to predict the outcome of this unique experiment in collective action. Despite a recent crescendo of publicity about all aspects of the Alliance, and a careful review at an Inter-American conference in Mexico City of its progress in each country, some in Latin America still feel that the Alliance is primarily a propaganda move in the cold war; they contend that they have yet to see tangible evidence of its benefits. Too many view it simply as an aid program; they disregard the major role of reform Latin America must play. Some Latin Americans are simply confused: They see the United States make substantial loans for purposes not envisaged by the Act of Bogotá and the Charter of Punta del Este; they see us frown at a military revolt in Argentina and the subsequent suspension of democracy but lend aid to the junta at the same time; and a few months later, in a similar situation in Peru, they witness the United States reacting differently, peremptorily suspending diplomatic recognition and aid.

Washington, meanwhile, frets because the promises at Bogotá and Punta del Este, well-meaning though they were, are slow in coming. State Department and Agency for International Development officials realize the difficulties Latin-American leaders face in instituting the reforms they promised, but that was a crucial part of the bargain, and the United States dares not allow it to be cast aside.

Inter-American relations are, of course, part of the larger issues which today confront the peoples of the world—the issues of totalitarianism versus democratic freedom, socialization versus private enterprise, dialectical materialism versus the Judaic-Christian philosophy.

In my judgment, the only possible salvation for what we loosely call the Western world is for all nations that truly wish to be free and independent—that believe in the free choice of peoples and in the supremacy of human values—to place the common, long-time good above temporary local differences.

One nation cannot truly be the leader of all that wish to be free. It can serve as a focal point. It can give more generously of its substance than others. But it cannot force the free nations to combine their power, or to put aside selfishness. The total strength of the free or Western world is far greater than that of the Communist monolith. The problem is to have this power—intellectual, moral, economic, and military—employed fully and decisively at the crucial times and in the crucial places.

Cooperation implies a willingness to sacrifice and to support the total effort in harmony with individual capacity. Today we have a working alliance in Europe, though even the NATO nations do not equitably share the burden. Furthermore, when difficulty developed in Korea, two nations carried the heavy load. Yet Korea was not essential to the security of the United States—except as it was a matter of principle, the principle that freedom should not be sacrificed to the consuming ambition of a coercive Communist force. If the principle is worthy of defense, it is of equal concern to all free nations.

The greatest task of free world statesmanship is to weld a cooperative society into a dependable, permanent force. This must be done not only by finding a common conviction that the goals of peace with freedom and justice merit the subordination of lesser threats, but also by carrying forward constantly a positive program that promises to make freedom meaningful to all peoples.

This, too, requires constant cooperation, participation, and sacrifice. Again, no one nation can possibly supply the credit, technical knowledge, and leadership involved in a global attack on the ills of men that have beset him since the dawn of civilization. Every nation, no matter how small, must do its part.

In inter-American affairs, we have concentrated too much on the individual relations of twenty nations with the United States, and on the common economic problems which the Latin-American countries have with us. Surely, these matters cannot be neglected, but the time has come when all nations of Latin America must begin to give positive expression to the concept that the peoples of this hemisphere have an inescapable interdependence and a common destiny—not just with us, but with each other, too. We are going to remain free together, or together we shall be enslaved. There is not a nation in this hemisphere—even Bolivia and Haiti with their average incomes of $75 per person per year—that cannot contribute to the common good, the common purpose of the larger community.

I have seen little evidence to indicate that the richest of Latin-American countries feels any real obligation to help the poorest among them. Yet the richest appeals to the United States on the assumption that the more fortunate should help the less fortunate.

The history of relationships among the Americas is replete with shocking mistakes by the United States, and with equally reprehensible actions by Latin-American nations against each other and against us. United States intervention in one country after another; Castro's betrayal of humanity; Panama's offensive attack on United States property and desecration of the United States flag in 1959; indignities heaped upon Vice President and Mrs. Nixon in Venezuela in 1958; the unanswered cries of the suppressed people of Latin America for food, health, and opportunity; the failure of most Latin-American republics to realize their potential—in all of these, all American republics must find reason for shame. But the imperative of our time is to cast aside the lingering effects of history, to cease fruitless indulgence in self-pity and scapegoating. The time has come—indeed, it has already passed—when the American nations must unite in one of history's rare adventures in unity and unselfishness.

Anyone who spent many casual years and eight intensive years traveling and studying in Latin America, as I have done, would find a spiritual satisfaction in the new cooperative opportunity that is now ours. Despite all the shortcomings in attitudes, institutions, and laws which I have discussed, I find, as others must, too, that peoples of all classes in Latin America have an intelligence that is challenging, a vitality and personality that command affection, and a potentiality that is unexcelled. History has held these people in bondage—to some extent self-imposed, to be sure—but now that escape from history is at hand, we may witness a miracle of growth and development which will repay us in abundance for all the understanding and resource we ourselves may put into the effort.

Anyone who thinks on these things, as I have done, is likely to become depressed and discouraged. At such times my thoughts go back to my home town: I see a cozy white house, surrounded by a flourishing orchard, fields of vegetables, and colorful hollyhocks. I sit on the front porch with a brother and we are too content to speak. From the porch we can view the passing of seasons and the tiny segment of the world we know. Interdependence is a word in the dictionary, but its implications escape us and of this we are utterly unconcerned. In remembrance, it is a happy, uncomplicated, simple time, one to be preserved.

But the essence of nostalgia is an awareness that what has been will never be again. We can dream of the isolation of our youth, so few short years ago, but we must live in the reality of complex inter-relationships with others who are unlike us in many ways, and who often dislike us for reasons that to us seem unjustified. Somehow we must break down the barriers of misunderstanding and erect in their place a temple of goodwill.

The undertaking will be arduous and perilous and we must be on guard. Pedro Beltrán has sounded the critical warning: "There is a false notion that we must choose between liberty and welfare. No! Liberty is not sufficient nor authentic without welfare, and welfare is not possible and would be humiliating without liberty."

The real alternatives are between justice and injustice, freedom and enslavement, poverty and plenty—between peaceful revolution leading to progress and violent revolution leading to tyranny. And I might add that now the choice is up to all the Americas. Tomorrow it might not be.

Index

Act of Bogotá, xii, 93, 125, 168, 231, 304, 306, 307, 312, 328; housing, 37; significance, 251

Act of Chapultepec (1945), 49, 184, 185

Adams, John Quincy, 171

Africa, 312; coffee problem, 103, 104

Agency for International Development, 124, 155, 156, 305, 310, 328

Agriculture: reform, 243–44; Latin America, 111–26; U.S. private investments, 114

AID, 29. *See* International Cooperation Administration

Alba, Victor, 318

Alberdi, Juan Bautista, 19

Albizn Campos, Pedro, 278

Alemán, Miguel, 5, 21, 236

Alessandri, Jorge, 132, 242, 314

Alexander, Robert, 318

Alliance for Progress, xii, 8, 12, 59, 94, 302 ff, 319, 320; agricultural reform, 123; aid, conditions of, 325; collective action policy, 327; creation, 166, 313; financial aspects, 310–13; foundation, 230, 251; national commissions, 86; opposition to, 322; principal threat to, 313; purposes, 166, 295–96; reactions to, 304, 327–28; success of failure, 12–13; SUDENE, 25

Almond, Gabriel, 268

American Assembly, 57

"American family of nations," 45

American Institute for Free Labor Development, 92

American Society of Newspaper Editors, 259, 265

Anderson, Samuel W., 8, 65, 195

Arbenz, Jacobo, 315

Arévalo, Juan José, 6

Argentina, 50, 58, 197, 241–42; agriculture, 117; communism, 314, 315, 316, 318; Cuba, 325; economy, 132; education, 26, 28; Eisenhower, Dwight D., 241–42; Eisenhower, Milton, 63, 64–66; income, 15, 22; Indians, 20; industrialization, 141; land reform, 122; leaders, 19, 314; literacy, 23; natural resources, 134; nutrition, 35; progress, 22–23; Tractors for Freedom, 282, 283; U.S.: aid to, 305, intervention, 184, 186, recognition, 171

"Atlantic Community," 45

Avila Camacho, Manuel, 236

Barrett, Edward W., 58

Bartolome de las Casas, Friar, 16

Barton, Carlyle, 203, 204

Batista, Fulgencio, 48, 54, 55, 166, 174, 180, 230, 255–58, 259, 260, 261, 264, 268, 318; dictatorship, 299–300, 301; U.S. and, 246, arms to, 258

Bay of Pigs, 270, 271, 295

Beltrán, Pedro, 11, 205–6, 314, 323, 330

Bennett, W. Tapley, Jr., 9, 65

Benson, Ezra Taft, 202

Benton, William, 85, 108

Betancourt, Romulo, 23, 31, 132, 314, 319–20, 323

Bi-national institutes, 90–91

333

Binder, Dr. Theodor, 83, 93
Birth control, 36
Bissell, Richard M., Jr., 269, 270, 271
Black, Eugene R., 8, 207
Blaine, James G., 172–73
Bogotá, Act of. *See* Act of Bogotá; Conference (1960), 324
Bolívar, Simón, 168, 169, 170–71, 303
Bolivia, 194–95; agriculture, 114, 116–17, 119, 124, 133; Cuba, 325; education, 29; expropriation of foreign-owned properties, 146; income, 15, 21, 74, 329; Indians, 17; leadership, 314; liberation, 168; National Revolutionary Movement, 17, 320; natural resources, 134; nutrition, 35; politics, 319; progress, 21; reforms, 21, 67–68; tin crisis, 75–76; Tractors for Freedom, 282, 283; U.S. aid, 252
Braden, Spruille, 184
Brazil, 198–99, 202; agriculture, 112–13, 114; bi-national institutes, 91; Brasilia, 120; coffee, 103, 106; communism, 315, 316; Cuba, 325; ETA, 119–20; illiteracy, 24; income, 15; industrialization, 127, 141, 142–43; inflation, 131; land reform, 25, 121–22; life expectancy, 112; natural resources, 134; Peasant League, 24, 25, 122; potentiality, 131; progress, 23–25, 306; public health program, 36; society, 23–24; SUDENE, 24–25; taxation, 24; Tractors for Freedom, 282, 283; U.S.: criticism, 206, loan to, 188, recognition, 171, relations, 50, 58, 152, 153; the wealthy, 322; World War II, 183
Britain, 312
Brucker, Secretary of the Army, 223–24
Byrd, Harry F., 282

Cabell, Charles P., 271
Cabot, Jack, 65, 190, 195, 201
Cabot, John Moors, 8
Cabrera, Luis, 20
Calles, Plutarco Elías, 179
Canada: U.S. investments in, 47; wheat production, 106
Canal Zone. *See* Panama Canal
Cantillo, Eulogio, 256–57
Capehart, Homer E., 279, 280, 305
Caplin, Mortimer M., 281
Caracas Declaration (1954), 263, 264
Carbo, Ulises, 277
Cárdenas, Lázero, 20–21, 181, 236, 263, 267, 316
Carías Andino, Tiburcio, 6
Carnegie Foundation scholarships, 34
Carranza, Venustiano, 20, 176, 235

Carrillo Flores, Antonio, 232, 238
Carrillo Flores, Nabor, 237
Castro, Fidel, 48, 50, 83, 146, 158, 174, 231, 238, 255–73, 304, 316, 329; Batista, 230; communism, xii, 4, 11, 166, 167, 230, 246, 247, 259, 261, 264, 268, 272, 273, 295, 301, 313, 315, 318, 320, purposes, 166; confiscation of foreign-owned properties, 114, 146, 149; criticism, 273; on Kennedy, 304; military support, 258; personality, 259; popularity, 255–56; the press, 259; prisoner-tractor exchange, 272, 273 (*see also* Tractors for Freedom Committee); promises, 244; propaganda in Latin America, 80; purposes, 162; rise, 54, 58; Soviet Union, 58; U.S., 246–47, 259, 264, 265–67, 296, 321, recognition of, 274–75. *See also* Tractors for Freedom Committee
Castro, Raul, 256, 261, 268
CEIR. *See* Corporation for Economic and Industrial Research
Central America, politics, 320
Central American Organization, 220
Central Intelligence Agency, 269, 292; Cuban invasion, 269–71
Central University (Venezuela), 32–34
Céspedes, Carlos Manuel de, 299
Chamizal issue, 232–33, 237, 238
Charter of Punta del Este, xii, 37, 109, 168, 307, 310, 312, 328
Chiari, Roberto F., 225, 226
Chile, 196–97, 314; Balmaceda regime, 19; bi-national institutes, 91; birth control, 36; church, 322; communism, 315, 316; copper, 105; Cuba, 325; doctor-patient ratio, 35; economy, 131, 132; education, 23, 28; Eisenhower, Dwight D., 242–46; feudalism, 19; income, 22; Indians, 20; industrialization, 141; land reform, 23, 121, 122; liberation, 170; natural resources, 134; progress, 23; Student Federation, 242–46, 247; Tractors for Freedom, 284; U.S. aid, 123, 252
CIA. *See* Central Intelligence Agency
Clark, J. Reuben, 179
Clay, Henry, 171
Cleveland, Grover, 173
Coffee problem, 102–5
Collective action, 301, 304, 327
Collective security, 185, 186, 263, 326, 327
Colombia, 194, 314; agriculture, 116, 119, 123–24; bi-national institutes, 91; coffee crisis, 75; industrialization, 141; economy, 131; land reform, 122; Liberal

vasion, 269; economic policy, 107; goodwill trip (1946), 187; health, 201–2; international balance of payments, 311; Latin America: interest in, 187, policy, 244–45, 249–50, 251–54, 303, relations, 187–88, trip (1960), 11–12, 163, 239–49; Mexico, 236, 237; National Advisory Committee on Inter-American Affairs, 108, 239; Panama, 202–3; trade policies, 61, 62

Eisenhower, Milton: Argentina visit (1953), 63, 64–66; Brazil, 119; career, 43–44; Central-American trip (1958), 211–29; government salary, 212, 213; Inter-American Bank, 229–30; Johns Hopkins University, 203–4; Kennedy, 274–75, 276, 277, 280, 281, 282, 287, 294; Latin America trip (1953), 32, 46, 84, 140; Mexico, 207–8, 232, 238–39; Nixon, 283; OWI, 56; Project Mercury, 237–38; recommendations, 200, 201, 229, 312; sobriquet, 192; study trips, 187–89 ff, 195; Tractors for Freedom Committee, 274–95; U. S. Department of Agriculture, 99; vice consul, 44, 56

Eisenhower, Mrs. Milton, 189, 190, 203
Eisenhower, Ruth, 203, 208, 211, 212, 289
El Salvador, 219–20; economy, 97–98; illiteracy, 22; progress, 22; Tractors for Freedom, 284; the wealthy, 322
Escritório Técnio de Agricultura Brasil-Estados Unidos, 119. *See* ETA
Estrada Palma, Tomás, 298
ETA, 119–20
Europe, 103; common market, 137; -Latin America: difference in problem, 73, reaction against, 172; post-war, 72, 73; Recovery Program, 72; Tractors for Freedom, 286; Western, freedom of, 312. *See also* Marshall Plan
Ever-normal granary, 99, 106
Export-Import Bank, 8, 9, 80, 136, 149, 153, 154, 155, 156, 157, 182, 207, 252, 309

Fannin, Paul, 283
Farrell, Edelmiro J., 184
Figueres, José, 218, 314, 319, 323
Finney, John W., 278
Fitzgibbon, Russell, *Uruguay: Portrait of a Democracy,* 23
Food for Peace Program, 302
Ford Foundation scholarships, 34
Frelinghuysen, Peter, Jr., 283
Frondizi, Arturo, 23, 50, 132, 134, 241,

242, 282, 314, 315; fall of, 58; inauguration, 210
Fulbright, J. William, 270, 279, 281

Gadsden Purchase, 235
Gardner, Arthur, 54
Germany, 103
Glennan, Dr. Keith, 238
Goldwater, Barry, 279, 281, 284, 288–89, 291
Gómez, José Miguel, 298
Good Neighbor policy, 5, 6, 59, 178, 180–86, 249, 251
"Good Partnership" policy, 188, 189
Goodwin, Richard, 276, 277, 281, 285, 287, 292, 293, 294
Grace, Peter, 146
Guantánamo Bay, 258
Guardia, Ernesto de la, 216
Guatemala, 6, 220–21; agriculture, 123; Catholic Action students, 31; communism, 48, 58, 315; illiteracy, 21; income, 21; Indians, 17; progress, 21; undernationalism, 221; U.S. aid, 252, 305
Guevara, Ernesto "Che," 256, 261, 268

Haiti, 182; income, 22, 329; progress, 22; taxation, 22; U.S.: aid, 252, policy toward, 176
Harrington, Julian F., 216, 221
Hatcher, Andrew T., 282
Haya de la Torre, Victor Raul, 320, 323
Health, 15, 35–37, 112, 253
Hemispheric solidarity, 8
Herring, Hubert, 169; *History of Latin America,* 169 n
Herter, Christian A., 60, 162, 163, 230, 231, 241; National Advisory Committee on Inter-American Affairs, 239, 249
Hickenlooper, Bourke B., 281
Hidalgo, Father, 19
Hill, Bob, 231
Hitler, Adolf, 297, 300
Hoffman, Paul, 74
Holland, Henry F., 158, 201, 204
Holland, Kenneth, 163
Hollywood, 56
Honduras, 6, 217; American library, 91; customs receiverships, 175; education, 29; illiteracy, 217; income, 217; progress, 22; Tractors for Freedom, 283; the wealthy, 22
Hooker, John J., Jr., 285, 286, 287, 293, 294, 295
Hoover, Herbert, 99, 100, 106, 178, 179;

336

Eisenhower, Milton, 274; Latin American policy, 179
Hopkins, Harry, 9
Housing, 15, 37, 129; self-help projects, 209, 248, 250; low-cost, 231; social problem, 222–23. See also Panama
Houston, Sam, 171
Howe, Walter, 245, 246
Huerta, Victoriano, 20, 176, 235
Hughes, Charles Evans, 44, 77, 177; Latin American policy, 178–79
Hull, Cordell, 59, 178, 180, 181, 184, 186
Human resources, 37–40
Humphrey, Hubert H., 284

Ibáñez del Campo, Carlos, 196
Ibarra, Velasco, 29, 194
Illiteracy, 15, 21–23. See Education and under name of country
Imperialism, 167, 173–74, 176–77
Indians, 16–17, 19–21, 26
Industrialization, 122, 127–47, 188; Cuba, 266; political geography and, 135–40; U.S., 128
Infant mortality, 35, 112
Inflation, 130–32
Institute of Political Education, 321–22
Inter-American Bank, 10, 58, 155–56, 162, 163, 205, 206, 207, 209, 219, 227, 250–51, 310; establishment, 11
Inter-American Conference (Caracas), 201
Inter-American Congress, 173
Inter-American Customs Union, 172
Inter-American Defense Board, 325
Inter-American Development Bank, 232, 306, 310; reasons for, 229–30
Inter-American Economic Conference (Buenos Aires, 1957), 207
Inter-American Economic and Social Council, 229, 305
Inter-American Institute of Agricultural Science (Costa Rica), 124
Inter-American Press Association, 89, 90
Inter-American relations, 52, 302 ff, 325, 329–30; Castro philosophy and, 272–73; history, 167–68; improvement, 92–94; intellectual problems, 84–85; low point, 264. See also Interdependence
Inter-American Treaty of Reciprocal Assistance (1947), 185
Interdependence, hemispheric, 40, 45–53, 107, 195, 232, 329–30
International affairs: education program, 85; complexity, 82
International Bank for Rehabilitation and Development, 8, 136, 155, 207, 252; loans, 230; technical assistance, 153

International Cooperation Administration, 33, 116, 117, 123, 189; educational assistance, 34. See AID
International Development Association, 252, 310
International Finance Corporation, 155, 252
Intervention, 162, 168, 174, 184, 272, 300; collective, xii, 166, 168; forceful, 177; Mexico, 20; unilateral, 166, 239, 245; U.S., 50, 59; Wilsonian, 176
Iturbide, Agustín de, 14

Jackson, Andrew, 38
Japan, 312
Jardine, Dr. William M., 44
Javits, Jacob K., 281
Jefferson, Thomas, 38, 77, 303
Johns Hopkins University, xiii, xiv, 10, 37, 203–4, 205, 279, 286
Johnson, John J., Political Change in Latin America, 322
Juliao, Francisco, 24, 25, 122

Kellogg, Frank B., 177
Kennedy, John F., 8, 12, 109, 159, 168, 186; Advisory Committee on Panama, 225; campaign (1960), 54–55; Chamizal issue, 234; Cuban invasion, 269, 270, 271 n; Eisenhower, Milton, 274; international balance of payments, 311; Latin America: legacy, 254, policy, 301, 302–15, 320, 327; Mexico policy, 236; Tractors for Freedom Committee, 274 ff, 287, 289, 294. See also Alliance for Progress
Kennedy, Robert F., 271 n, 285, 293
Kimball, Penn T., 58
Knight, O. A. (Jack), 162–63
Korean War, 328
Khrushchev, Nikita, 48, 159, 261, 262; criticism, 273; Eisenhower challenge, 188
Kubitschek, Juscelino, 120, 131, 202; Operation Pan America, 241

Land Grant Act, 115, 128
Land reform, 23, 121–22, 265, 267, 302, 307. See also under name of country
Latin America: agriculture, 111–26, experiment stations, 116–19; American knowledge of 57–59; attitudes, contradictions in, 80–81; Castro, condemnation of, 272–73, 275, 283–84, 292; common man, 80; conditions, 14–15; Cuba, 326–27; Cuban invasion, 272; cultural orientation, 51; democratic trend, 257; development, early, 15–19; dictators (see

337

Morales, Ramon Villeda, 217
Morales-Carrion, Arturo, 30
Morelos, Father, 19
Morrow, Dwight W., 178, 238; Latin American policy, 179
Morse, Wayne, 279
Munro, Dana G., 163
Murrow, Edward R., 283, 284, 285, 288
Mutual Security program, 72

Nariño, Antonio, 168
National Advisory Committee on Inter-American Affairs, 231, 239, 241, 248, 249
National Aeronautics and Space Administration, 237–38
National commissions, 93, 229. See also under Organization of American States
National Education Act, 91
Nationalism, 45
National Planning Association, 145–46
National Security Council, 200
NATO, 328; Treaty of 1949, 49
New Mexico College of Agriculture and Mechanic Arts, 117
New York Herald Tribune, 282, 283
New York Times, 255, 278, 280
Nicaragua, 179, 218–19; customs receiverships, 175; education, 26, 29; income, 218; progress, 22; self-help housing, 37; Somoza family, 22; U.S.: economic relations, 60, intervention, 177; the wealthy, 22
Nixon, Richard M., 55, 59, 77, 86, 329; Castro conference, 259; Central America trip, 218; Eisenhower, Milton, 283; Latin America trip, 76, 209–11, 212; Tractors for Freedom, 283, 284
Non-intervention, 76–79, 199, 246, 249, 251, 327. See also Good Neighbor policy
Nufer, Albert F., 64
Nutrition, 35, 36. See also under name of country

OAS. See Organization of American States
Odría, Manuel, 78, 195
Office of War Information. See OWI
Olney, Richard, 173
"Operation Pan-America," 202, 241
Organization of American States, xiv, 10, 173, 203, 204, 227, 284, 307; activities, 87–88; agricultural research program, 124; Bogotá center, 37, meeting (1960), 250; Castro, 262; Charter, 50, 185–86; collective action, 327; Council, 86, 325; Cuba, 325; Economic and Social Council, 138; fellowships, 34; information

media, 94; land ownership problem, 249; market stabilization program, 109; national commissions, 85, 86–87, 90; role, 252; San José conference (1960), 262, 263; technical experts, 153; U.S. proposals for social development, 231; Washington meeting (1956–1957), 205
Overby, Andrew N., 8, 65, 195
OWI, 56. See also U. S. Information Agency

Panama, 182, 221–28, 330; education, 26, 28; Eisenhower, Milton, recommendations, 221–23, 225–27; housing, 229; income, 22, 214; Inter-American conference, 10; progress, 22; sovereignty, 216, 221, 227, 228; U.S.: aid to, 305, relations, 50, 81, 213–17, 225–26
Panama Canal, 49, 81, 174–75, 213–17, 221–22, 225–27; internationalization, 227–28
Pan American Sanitary Bureau, 35
Pan American Union, 86, 206, 249
Paraguay, 197; education, 29; income, 22; land reform, 122; progress, 22
Passman, Otto E., 305
Paz Estenssoro, Victor, 21, 67–68, 194–95, 314, 320, 323
Pemex, 158, 159
Penn State University, 8, 33, 197, 203
Pérez Jiménez, Marcos, 33, 34, 78, 132, 190–93, 195, 218, 299; criticism, 273; overthrow, 210–11
Perón, Evita, 65
Perón, Juan, 23, 63, 64–66, 132, 184, 195, 197, 218, 241, 255, 314; Catholic students opposition, 31; criticism, 273; overthrow, 257
Perónistas, 210, 314
Peru, 78, 195, 314, 315; agriculture, 114; Aprista party, 17, 320, 322; communism, 316, 318; economy, 131; income, 21; Indians, 17, 83–84; liberation, 168, 169, 170–71; natural resources, 134; politics, 319, 320; progress, 21; U.S.: economic relations, 60, 188, recognition, 320; the wealthy, 322
Platt Amendment, 174, 297, 298; abrogation, 182
Plaza Lasso, Galo, 29, 314, 323
Point IV Program, 79
Poland, 159; Cuba, 266
Political Change in Latin America, 322
Population, 33–34, 36, 113, 141, 305, 306
Poverty, 111, 114, 126, 130, 162, 230, 246, 303, 305, 317
Prado, Manuel, 195, 315

E33